# Stage and Screen Lives

# Stage and Screen Lives

Selected by **Michael Billington**

OXFORD
UNIVERSITY PRESS

OXFORD
UNIVERSITY PRESS

Great Clarendon Street, Oxford OX2 6DP

Oxford University Press is a department of the University of Oxford.
It furthers the University's objective of excellence in research, scholarship, and education by publishing worldwide in

Oxford New York

Athens Auckland Bangkok Bogotá Buenos Aires Cape Town Chennai Dar es Salaam Delhi Florence Hong Kong Istanbul Karachi Kolkata Kuala Lumpur Madrid Melbourne Mexico City Mumbai Nairobi Paris São Paulo Shanghai Singapore Taipei Tokyo Toronto Warsaw

with associated companies in Berlin Ibadan

Oxford is a registered trade mark of Oxford University Press in the UK and in certain other countries

Published in the United States
by Oxford University Press Inc., New York



First published 2001



British Library Cataloguing in Publication Data
Data available

Library of Congress Cataloging in Publication Data
Data available

ISBN 0-19-860407-6

10 9 8 7 6 5 4 3 2 1

Typeset in DanteMT
by Alliance Phototypesetters, Pondicherry, India
Printed in Great Britain
by T. J. International, Padstow, Cornwall

# Preface

'The best record of a nation's past that any civilization has produced': G. M. Trevelyan's view in 1944 of the *Dictionary of National Biography* highlights the achievement of its first editor Leslie Stephen. Between 1885 and 1900 quarterly volumes rolled out from the presses in alphabetical order by subject. A national institution had come into existence, making its distinctive contribution to the national aptitude for the art of biography.

In his initial prospectus for the *DNB*, Stephen emphasized the need to express 'the greatest possible amount of information in a thoroughly business-like form'. Dates and facts, he said, 'should be given abundantly and precisely', and he had no patience with the sort of 'style' that meant 'superfluous ornament'. But he knew well enough that for 'lucid and condensed narrative', style in the best sense is essential. Nor did he content himself, in the many longer memoirs he himself contributed to the *DNB*, with mere dates and facts: a pioneer in the sociology of literature, he was not at all prone to exaggerate the individual's impact on events, and skilfully 'placed' people in context.

Stephen's powerful machine was carried on by his work-horse of a successor Sidney Lee, who edited the first of the ten supplements (usually decennial) which added people who died between 1901 and 1990. It was in these supplements that all of the memoirs published in this series first appeared, so they were often written soon after the subject died; their authors were frequently able to cite 'personal knowledge' and 'private information'. In such cases there is always a balance to be struck between waiting for written sources to appear and drawing upon living memory while still abundant and fresh. Stephen had no doubts where he stood: he published book-length biographies of his Cambridge friend Henry Fawcett and of his brother Fitzjames within a year of their deaths, and cited Boswell's *Johnson* and Lockhart's *Scott* as proof that the earliest biographies are often the best. Furthermore, memoirs of the recently dead were included in the *DNB* right up to the last possible moment, the press often being stopped for the purpose. Roundell Palmer, for example, died on 4 May 1895 and got into the 43rd volume published at the end of June.

## Preface

So the memoirs published in this series are fully in line with what was *DNB* policy from the outset. Furthermore, all have the virtue of reflecting the attitudes to their subjects that were taken up during their lifetimes. They may not always reflect what is now the latest scholarship, but as G. M. Young insisted, 'the real, central theme of history is not what happened, but what people felt about it when it was happening'. So they will never be superseded, and many are classics of their kind—essential raw material for the most up-to-date of historians. They have been selected by acknowledged experts, some of them prominent in helping to produce the *New Dictionary of National Biography*, which will appear in 2004. All are rightly keen that this ambitious revision will not cause these gems of the *DNB* to be lost. So here they are, still sparkling for posterity.

Brian Harrison
Editor, *New Dictionary of National Biography*

## Stage and Screen Lives—selections from the twentieth-century DNB

# Introduction

How does one select a hundred lives from stage and screen spanning the twentieth century? Some names instantly suggest themselves. How could you imagine the last century without Olivier, Coward, Chaplin, Hitchcock, Shaw, O'Casey, Marie Lloyd, or Eric Morecambe? They not merely adorn British culture: they themselves helped to define and shape it. One measure of greatness is that it becomes either a yardstick against which succeeding generations are measured or an unyielding force against which they rebel. 'Hitchcockian' and 'Shavian' are, for instance, terms constantly applied to any modern suspense-movie or any play of dialectical debate. But past greatness also breeds its own counter-revolution: young actors, who never saw him on stage, now express doubts about Olivier's heroic versatility as compared to Gielgud's stylish grace, and it is commonplace among cineastes to prefer Keaton's deadpan gravity to Chaplin's balletic skill. I hope, however, the chosen entries go a long way towards explaining why certain figures both spawn their own adjectives and continue to dominate our cultural life.

Some figures automatically select themselves. But in editing this anthology I have also looked for pioneers who have radically changed the nature of their chosen art-form. It is hard to imagine modern theatre, for instance, without the directorial clarity of Harley Granville-Barker, the visual imagination of Gordon Craig, the emphasis on meaning of William Poel. British national drama, opera, and ballet companies would hardly exist without a visionary eccentric like Lilian Baylis, who lured the best actors to the Old Vic and then fried sausages in her prompt-corner box during their performances. And the regional repertory movement, which has obstinately survived the short-rations subsidy of successive post-war governments, was nurtured in its early days by wealthy individuals such as Annie Horniman, whose private fortune came from tea, and Barry

Jackson, whose family owned Maypole Dairies. Their achievements are here recorded even though posterity has sometimes altered our perspective. Lewis Casson, midway through the century, writes of Granville-Barker that 'his influence on the theatre of this country fell far short of the hopes inspired by his brilliant start.' Maybe so. Yet a contemporary director such as Richard Eyre sees Granville-Barker as an exemplary figure who not only changed the style of Shakespearian production but revised the form and content of modern theatre.

What I hope this anthology shows, in fact, is the way various art-forms have changed over the course of the past hundred years: in that sense, the volume has its own hidden narrative. In drama, as the century begins, actor-managers like Henry Irving and Herbert Beerbohm Tree cast a giant shadow. With the emergence of Shaw, Granville-Barker, and William Archer, the emphasis shifts away from theatre as a place of heroic individualism towards the exploration of moral dilemmas and social issues. In the inter-war years there is a fascinating contrast between the West End theatre of spectacle and escape, embodied by C. B. Cochran and Coward, and pioneering attempts to explore the world repertory. And, through these pages, you can trace the post-war movement of power away from the commercial empire of H. M. Tennent, run by 'Binkie' Beaumont, towards the Royal Court and its legion of new writers. As Irving Wardle writes, 'Beaumont's West End flourished like a traditional grocery shop, selling reliable brands to regular customers. The fashions of 1956 consigned these brands to the dustbin.'

If theatre radically changed during the twentieth century, cinema grew from laboratory experiment to mass-medium in the course of it. That too is reflected in these pages. What is particularly fascinating is how much Hollywood owed both to East Enders and to the English music-hall tradition. Alfred Hitchcock was the son of a Leystonstone greengrocer and poulterer while Charlie Chaplin was born in Walworth to an Irish mother and a Cockney comedian father. Chaplin and the Lancashire-born Stan Laurel were also both juvenile members of the Fred Karno Company, while Bristol's Archie Leach joined Bob Pender's Knockabout Comedians before transmogrifying into Hollywood's Cary Grant. What emerges from their respective entries is how much their later careers were determined by their early experiences. Philip French records Hitchcock's own admission that his attitude towards authority, fear, and guilt was shaped by 'being sent by his father at the age of five with a note addressed to the superintendent of the local police station where he was locked in a cell for ten minutes and then released with the words "That is what we do to naughty boys."' Chaplin's Dickensian upbringing also clearly led to the creation of his resilient tramp, and it is not hard to see echoes of the young

Cary Grant's acrobatic origins in the sinuous grace and effortless line he brings to his lounge-suited heroes in Hollywood movies, many of them directed, of course, by Hitchcock.

What emerges from these entries is the growth of theatre and cinema over the twentieth century; and, of course, the momentous advent of television, which has created its own icons and folk-heroes. But, sifting through the *DNB*, it is impossible not to be struck by the greater degree of sexual candour that affects the entries as the century progresses. In the earlier years veils are discreetly drawn over the subject's private inclinations. You can read H. H. Child's admirable entries on Henry Irving and Ellen Terry, for instance, without fully grasping that they were lovers; though delicate hints are dropped such as 'certain plays he chose rather for her sake than for his own.' The bisexual nature of another famous actor-manager is also carefully overlooked. But, without lapsing into prurience, later entries are much more honest about the sexual nature of their subject. Indeed the impact of the private life upon the public career is openly acknowledged. Moira Shearer, for instance, tells us that Robert Helpmann, 'a flamboyant homosexual, made a lifelong companion of [Michael] Benthall, who became a leading stage director and a major contributor to their partnership.' What is fascinating about that revelation is the extent to which Benthall's gift for colour, shape, and adeptness in crowd movement fed into Helpmann's balletic work. Equally Benthall's ornate Old Vic Shakespeare productions owed a considerable debt to Helpmann. And in a later era it would be impossible to discuss the work of a playwright like Joe Orton without acknowledging his sexuality. Not only did he gruesomely die at the hands of his partner, Kenneth Halliwell, but, as John Lahr shrewdly observes: 'He was the first contemporary English playwright to transfer into art the clown's rambunctious sexual rapacity from the stage to the page. He aspired to corrupt an audience with pleasure.' These entries accurately reflect the changing nature of the century: not only the banishment of secrecy but the extent to which an artist's sexuality is a formative influence upon his or her work.

But while these entries record artistic progress and social change they also in some areas show continuity; and nowhere is this more visible than in the field of comedy. Of course, comedy has altered with the death of the music-hall and the advent of television. But some things remain constant. And one is the extent to which the genuine comedian makes you laugh even before he or she has uttered a word. Ivor Brown, for instance, points out how George Robey added, to the traditional red nose, 'strongly blackened eyebrows and he chose, as a contrast to the bibulous colour scheme, a long black frock-coat and top hat.' Later he writes of Robey's 'beetling brows, the abrupt and shattering defiance of any unruly laughter, the swift plunge into song and patter.' In a different age Dick Hills paints an equally graphic picture of Eric Morecambe: 'Morecambe's eyebrows arched over the upper rims of his spectacles like twin circumflexes of bewilderment and surprise; his chirpy head movements, like a sparrow's, showed him as always qui vive, while his baggy underlids hinted at the world-weariness and sadness of the clown.' In making an instant comic impact, the eyes clearly have it. And, if there are ocular links between male comedians, you often find strange parallels in the careers of popular female entertainers. A good deal may separate Marie Lloyd (Matilda Wood) and Diana Dors. But both died at an early age (Lloyd at 52, Dors at 53), both were married three times, and both attracted the term 'vulgar', which in this case implies popular approbation. Lloyd's career was on the halls, Dors's mainly in film and television. Yet there was also an odd parallel in the way girlish vitality was subsumed in life-experience. H. H. Child's description of Lloyd's final years could equally well apply to Dors: 'Last came certain studies of shabby and broken-down women, in which she mingled sadness and humour, and showed considerable skill in the impersonation of character.'

In this anthology you will find a mixture of the self-selecting titans, of artistic pioneers, and of popular entertainers. I have also chosen a number of more marginal eccentrics. Hermione Gingold and Beatrice Lillie stake their claim for inclusion by sheer force of personality and by their ability to represent the now-vanished form of intimate revue; though Sheridan Morley, having noted her use of the arched eyebrow and curling lip, says of Lillie that 'her entire career was a sustained monument to anarchic alternative comedy before those terms had ever been invented.' Intriguingly Frank Muir makes a similar claim for another favoured eccentric: 'In the world of broadcast humour in the 1980s it was Arthur Marshall who was the alternative comedian.' His point is that Marshall's intelligent, affectionate humour was a genuine alternative to the kind of political and sexual aggression that passed for comedy at that time. But, although most of us remember Marshall for his hilariously shrill impersonations of hockey mistresses, he links up with commercial theatre in that he was, for a time, a script-reader for 'Binkie' Beaumont. Like Arthur Marshall, Russell Harty was also a former schoolmaster who turned into a broadcasting celebrity and companion to the famous: he earns his place not least because of the brilliance of Alan Bennett's entry, which combines total honesty with a contained vitriol directed towards the tabloid journalists who harassed Harty during his last hospitalized years.

And this, of course, is another criterion—and possibly the most vital—for inclusion in this anthology: the sheer quality of the writing. One of the signal virtues of the *DNB* is that it places a premium not only on style but on the writer's personal knowledge of the subject. This has resulted down the century in some fascinating pairings. Here you will find Eric Ambler writing about James Mason and tracing the fluctuating fortunes of his career almost as if he were the protagonist of one of Ambler's pleasingly labyrinthine novels. John Gielgud provides a vivid portrait of Margaret Rutherford that shows her to be infinitely more than a lugubrious cinematic eccentric: he not only describes her theatrical skill but offers a charming image of her dancing joyously with the stage carpenter after her final performance in *The School for Scandal*. Spike Milligan, from the vantage point of knowledge, claims that the multi-talented Peter Sellers was never happier than when performing in the *Goon Show*. And Margot Fonteyn and Moira Shearer prove themselves to be elegant stylists in writing about, respectively, Lydia Lopokova and Frederick Ashton. The value of personal knowledge is also apparent in Shearer's description of Ashton's working methods: 'He seemed to plan little in advance, to arrive for first rehearsals without original ideas and to use music suggested, even occasionally chosen, by friends.' In this way the dancers themselves became active collaborators in an Ashton creation.

Many of the best entries, from Ralph Richardson on Alexander Korda to Barry Took on Kenneth Williams, are based on first hand knowledge. But that does not mean that the entries should be read uncritically. Indeed I rather hope that some of them will provoke the reader into disagreement. No one, for instance, was better qualified than St John Ervine to write the monumental entry on Bernard Shaw. He was a friend, a fellow playwright and eventually Shaw's biographer. Yet it is hard to agree with him that *The Philanderer* ranks among Shaw's worst plays, that the Epilogue to *Saint Joan* is unnecessary, or that *Saint Joan* is Shaw's equivalent of *The Tempest* and marks the virtual end of his work as a great playwright. In recent years, *Too True to be Good* has emerged as an amazingly prophetic work that anticipates the development of theatrical Absurdism and in both *The Apple Cart* and *On the Rocks* one finds what Eric Bentley has called 'a rounded picture of the political madhouse which directs our destinies.' One can read St John Ervine with pleasure without subscribing to everything he says.

I not only recommend that some entries be read critically; I have also included a number of critics in my selection: partly because they have helped to shape the theatre of their times, partly because their defiant individualism provokes extraordinarily good prose. Thus Ivor Brown writes of James Agate that 'beneath his airy mixture of the country sportsman and the *petit maître* of letters, beneath his exhibitionism and his extravagance, was a random scholarship and a burning devotion to the arts.' Paul Johnson pays just tribute to Philip Hope-Wallace and his delight in skilled performance, while Philip Purser offers a stunningly accurate image of Kenneth Tynan: 'In youth his habit of baring his teeth as he strove to overcome the stammer, coupled with flaring nostrils and a rather skull-like head, gave him the look of a startled rocking-horse.' That, you feel, is rather how Tynan might have described himself.

Anthologies themselves, of course, are always open to criticism; and I am well aware that there are a number of eminent figures, particularly from the first half of the century, whom I have omitted. The people I have included are those who have shaped theatre, ballet, cinema, and television over the twentieth century, those who have enjoyed popular acclaim, and those who have either written rich and stimulating prose or been the cause of it in others. Riffling through past volumes of the *DNB*, I am pleasurably surprised by its enormous human and stylistic variety. I hope that variety is well represented in this selection and that it communicates something of the restless kaleidoscopic vigour that characterized both stage and screen in the twentieth century.

Michael Billington

*December 2000*

# Contents

## Contents

## Contents

# Contents

## Contents

## Contents

## AGATE James Evershed

(1877–1947)

Dramatic critic, was born at Pendleton, Lancashire, 9 September 1877, the eldest of the six children of Charles James Agate, cotton manufacturer's agent, and his wife, Eulalie Julia Young. Although generally regarded during his lifetime as the writer from Manchester who had conquered London in the 'man from the provinces' manner of Arnold Bennett and Mr. J. B. Priestley, Agate was not of Lancashire ancestry. His father came originally from Horsham, Sussex, and his mother was a Yorkshirewoman who had been educated in France and Germany and had studied the piano under a pupil of Chopin. The young Agates were taught to speak French fluently and to appreciate the fine points of music and the arts. Their father was chairman of the committee of the Unitarian chapel which the family attended; James in his teens was its secretary. Charles Agate was also a keen theatregoer who had once run away from home to see Macready. He encouraged his children to visit good plays and took James to see Sarah Bernhardt perform; she became for the child the model of theatrical performance ever after; his only sister May later studied under her in Paris.

Agate was educated at Giggleswick and at Manchester Grammar School and there is no record of exceptional precocity. Oxford or Cambridge would have suited him perfectly but he went into his father's business, learned to weave, and sold grey cloth for seventeen years. Although his mind was more concerned with the arts than with the cotton trade, he was no urban aesthete in a city which then had the best of plays and music continually available: he liked to live in Derbyshire, to dress like a sporting farmer, and to own and to exhibit show hackneys.

At the same time he began dramatic criticism with the *Daily Dispatch* in Manchester; after a year, in 1907, he joined the *Manchester Guardian* team of critics which included C. E. Montague and Allan Monkhouse. With them he concluded his 'further education' in letters.

During the war of 1914–18, with his experience of horses, Agate was sent as a captain in the Army Service Corps to buy hay in the south of France. This duty gave some leisure for writing. His first book, in the form of letters, *L. of C. (Lines of Communication)*, came out in 1917 and was followed by a book of essays of the theatre, *Buzz, Buzz!* (1918). His wartime marriage to a Frenchwoman was soon dissolved.

Back in London Agate bought, with characteristic caprice, a general store in south London. He was also able to write a 'personal novel' called *Responsibility* (1919) which had his abundant vivacity to cover up the absence of a narrative technique. Rapidly failing as a shopkeeper, he no less rapidly succeeded as a critic. In 1921 Filson Young appointed him to the chair of dramatic criticism on the *Saturday Review*, a covetable post once held by G. B. Shaw whose contributions had fired Agate with the ambition to become a dramatic critic. Here he was in his element and on his toes; the brilliance that he displayed won him, in 1923, the theatre critic's post on the *Sunday Times* which he held until his death. He was also dramatic critic for the British Broadcasting Corporation from 1925 to 1932.

Agate published, as well as many volumes of reprinted essays and notices, two more novels, *Blessed are the Rich* (1924) and *Gemel in London* (1928). But fiction about others was less his line than fact about himself. He set out accordingly to be the diarist of his epoch and in twelve years from 1935 wrote nine volumes under the title of *Ego*, the last appearing posthumously. They record chiefly the books, plays, personalities, club talk, and Bohemian life of the time: Agate had no interest in politics or social problems and this limited what might have been a wonderful landscape of London life. Yet, within its limits, the *Ego* series is remarkable for its constancy of wit in causerie and comment, ranging from the pert to the profound.

Agate never lost his sense of himself as a character bestriding his own stage. Unashamedly the egoist, he played the part with a nice mixture of humour and panache. Also he performed with rare energy, for he worked interminably to shape a paragraph to his taste. Beneath his airy mixture of the country sportsman and the *petit maître* of letters, beneath his exhibitionism and his extravagance, was a random scholarship and a burning devotion to the arts, or what he thought best in the arts; he was as much excited by music and painting as by writing for reader or playgoer. When the best was on the table he was omnivorous and insatiable. Because of this he took his place in the great line of English critics. He was a lover of the French classical drama, of Shakespeare, of emotional splendour, of the rattle of wit, and of all that had the flow of soul. For the later feast of reason as set by Shaw and his disciples he had less appetite. Deemed capricious of judgement by authors and actors, he was none the less credited with complete integrity. What he disliked he damned with wit and no mercy: what he liked he fought for with wit and no hesitation. He enjoyed a battle of argument as he enjoyed the beauty of a horse in movement. He was a hedonist in the best sense, seeking pleasure of the senses to the end; but his hedonism was mitigated by discernment. His model was Hazlitt and it may fairly be assumed that Hazlitt would have approved his devotee. He died in London 6 June 1947.

[Personal knowledge.]

Ivor Brown

*published 1959*

## ALBERY Sir Bronson James

(1881–1971)

Theatre director, was born at Greenhithe, Kent, 6 March 1881, the second in the family of three sons of James Albery, dramatist, and his wife, Mary Moore, actress, afterwards Lady Wyndham. He was called after the American dramatist, Bronson Howard. His father died when he was eight and he and his two brothers were brought up by their mother, who returned to the stage when James Albery was no longer able to write. He was educated at Uppingham and Balliol College, Oxford, where he obtained a second class in modern history in 1903. He was called to the bar at the Inner Temple in 1904 but his legal career was brief (though the intricacies of theatrical contracts would never defeat him).

His first theatrical venture, with Allan Aynesworth at the Criterion in 1914, was Cyril Harcourt's comedy, *A Pair of Silk Stockings*; they put on two other plays that year. The war, in which he served in the Royal Naval Volunteer Reserve from 1917 to 1919, ended, for the time being, his connection with the theatre which he resumed in 1920 with a revival, at the Kingsway, of *The Knight of the Burning Pestle* by Francis Beaumont and John Fletcher. In this production by (Sir) Nigel Playfair (which originated at the Birmingham Repertory Theatre) and ran for ninety-seven performances, the very young (Sir) Noël Coward surprisingly played the grocer's apprentice.

From his mother Bronson Albery inherited his business sense; for, although primarily a *comédienne*, it was her drive that led Sir Charles Wyndham to enlarge his theatrical empire—which began at the Criterion—and to build Wyndham's in 1899 and the New in 1903 (renamed the Albery in 1973). Mary Moore had played in *David Garrick* with Charles Wyndham in many revivals, so it was understandable that Bronson Albery's next choice of production should be a musical version of the play at the Queen's in 1922. He would now be of great help to his mother in the running of the three family theatres, and in 1922 (Sir) Lewis Casson and

(Dame) Sybil Thorndike began their association with him. Sybil Thorndike's performance in *The Cenci* at a special matinée at the New convinced G. B. Shaw that she would be perfect for Saint Joan. With some misgivings, as it had a long cast and was, unfashionably, a costume play, in 1924 Albery agreed to do *Saint Joan* which presently broke all existing records at the theatre.

When he found the family theatres' atmosphere restricting, he was glad to help to establish the Arts Theatre Club in 1927. Nor was he obsessively commercial; when he saw the Compagnie des Quinze at the Vieux-Colombier in Paris, he decided that discerning London audiences should be given a chance to see these actors. In 1931 he brought them, in *Noë*, to the Arts and then to the Ambassador's realizing, as he told W. A. Darlington that 'the venture must lose'. After his mother's death in that year, he and Wyndham's son, Howard, were in joint command of the three theatres. From the Arts he transferred to the Criterion in 1932 Ronald Mackenzie's *Musical Chairs*, with (Sir) John Gielgud. This was the beginning of an association that would do much for both actor and manager. During his years at the New—in *Richard of Bordeaux, Hamlet, Romeo and Juliet, Noah*, and *The Seagull*—Gielgud built his unchallenged position, and Albery would be regarded as a manager of distinction and taste. Though after 1935 they no longer worked together, they remained friends; Gielgud had always found 'Bronnie' encouraging and never unduly interfering, but he was also shrewd enough to withdraw from the production of a play (by Emlyn Williams) in which Gielgud appeared and which ran a week.

During World War II while the New Theatre housed the Old Vic Company in seasons of classical acting at its best, Albery was joint administrator from 1942 to 1944 with (Sir) Tyrone Guthrie. Thenceforward he would be increasingly a theatre committee man, serving on such bodies as the Arts Council from 1948, the British Council drama advisory committee (1952–61), and the Society of West End Theatre Managers, of which he was president from 1941 to 1945 and 1952 to 1953. As a reader of plays his wife was of great help; perhaps through her influence he presented in 1946 the semi-autobiographical *Red Roses for Me* by Sean O'Casey. His manner was quiet; he gave an impression of shyness, though at the Garrick Club he was a popular member and a particularly keen bridge player. He was knighted in 1949 and was a chevalier of the Legion of Honour. His son Donald succeeded him in management.

He married in 1912 Una Gwynn (died 1981), daughter of Thomas William Rolleston, of Glasshouse, Shinrone, the Irish scholar, poet, and friend of W. B. Yeats. They had two sons and two daughters. Albery died in London, 21 July 1971.

[*The Times*, 22 July 1971; family papers; Wendy Trewin, *All on Stage, Charles Wyndham and the Alberys*, 1980; personal knowledge.]

WENDY TREWIN

*published 1986*

## ALBERY Sir Donald Rolleston

(1914–1988)

Theatrical manager, was born 19 June 1914 at 33 Cumberland Terrace, London, the elder son and second of four children of (Sir) Bronson James Albery, theatrical manager, and his wife Una Gwynn, daughter of Thomas William Rolleston, Irish scholar and poet. Educated at Alpine College, Switzerland, he joined the family firm of Wyndham & Albery, the owners and managers of three London theatres: the Criterion in Piccadilly Circus, and Wyndham's and the New (after 1972 the Albery), both built by his grandmother, the actress Mary Moore, and Sir Charles Wyndham, her partner and second husband. His first position of importance, as general manager of the Sadler's Wells Ballet (1941–5), was complicated by wartime emergencies. On one occasion he arrived in Bath to find that the trucks containing scenery and costumes were immobilized in a siding close to unexploded bombs.

On first nights at his theatres Donald Albery, a tall lean figure, would be seen walking about the auditorium with a slight limp. He was prematurely bald, with a long narrow face, and in later years his resemblance to his father became more marked. He inherited the family business sense, though his taste in plays was modern whereas Sir Bronson was known for his classical productions. In 1953 he formed his own company, Donmar, and his choice of dramatists included Graham Greene, Tennessee Williams, Edward Albee, Jean Anouilh, and (Dame) Iris Murdoch (adapted by J. B. Priestley). Greene's *The Living Room*, with Dorothy Tutin, was his favourite production, and *I am a Camera*, John van Druten's adaptation from Christopher Isherwood, gave him 'enormous pleasure'.

Although he ran his theatres with an eye to commercial success he could spring surprises, and on occasions was prepared to take risks. He had youthful memories of going to Paris with his parents to see the Compagnie des Quinze, which Bronson admired and brought to London knowing that their appeal would be limited. On hearing about Samuel Beckett's *Waiting for Godot*, Albery went to Paris and decided to put it on in London. He hoped to cast the play with star names for the tramps, but after two years of failing to persuade any of them—including Sir Laurence (later Baron) Olivier and Sir Ralph Richardson—the play went on at the Arts Theatre Club directed by the young (Sir) Peter Hall and without stars (1955). Greatly daring, he transferred it to the Criterion in the heart of the West End, where it survived for nearly 300 performances though the audiences were frankly puzzled. Many left at the interval; the performances were disturbed by shouts of 'Take it off!', 'Rubbish!', and 'It's a disgrace!' The run was dogged by illness in the cast and inadequate understudies. In these unhappy circumstances the high teas provided by the management between the Saturday performances were greatly appreciated.

During the late 1950s and 1960s the idiosyncratic productions of Joan Littlewood at the Theatre Royal, Stratford East, appealed to Albery. Under his management they came to the West End and some went to New York—another example of his adventurous spirit. These included *A Taste of Honey* and Brendan Behan's *The Hostage* (both 1959) and *Fings Ain't What They Used T'Be* (1960). Out of gratitude to Joan Littlewood he presented a crystal chandelier to the Theatre Royal. This connection brought him his greatest success, the musical *Oliver!* (1960) by Lionel Bart (who also wrote the score of *Fings Ain't*). *Oliver!* had been turned down by three managements and opened so disastrously at Wimbledon that doubts were expressed at the wisdom of bringing it into the West End, where advance bookings (at the New) amounted to just £145. A new musical director had to be found at the last moment, but the first night changed these gloomy expectations, and the Sean Kenny revolving set on which everything in Dickens's novel happened was rapturously received. *Oliver!* ran for 2,618 performances and has since been revived.

In 1960, against strong competition from Bernard (later Baron) Delfont, Albery added the Piccadilly to the Wyndham–Albery empire. Thus 3,360 seats were offered to the public at every performance in these four theatres. At one point, when it looked as if the Criterion, the oldest of them, would be endangered by a Piccadilly Circus development scheme, Albery leaped eagerly into the fray and fought hard—enjoying the battle—and finally won. After *Oliver!* he produced several other musicals: in 1966, a failure, *Jorrocks*, which lost £70,000; and in 1968 a success, *Man of La Mancha*, which called for extensive structural alterations to the Piccadilly stage, and so, by special permission of the lord chamberlain, the safety curtain was never lowered during the run. Albery was the first manager to investigate the tourist trade in relation to the theatre. This pioneering survey proved beyond doubt that without overseas visitors the theatres would suffer irreparably (though this situation had been suspected for years).

When Sir Bronson Albery died in 1971 Donald Albery took control. In 1977 he became the third member of his family to receive a knighthood; in the following year he sold the theatres and retired to Monte Carlo. Ian Albery, his son by his first wife, carried on for a time. During the Albery regime their theatres were regarded as being among the best run in London, and the two back-to-back theatres, Wyndham's in Charing Cross Road and the Albery in St Martin's Lane, housed some of the most interesting productions of the period. From 1958 to 1978 Albery was also a director of Anglia Television.

Albery was married three times. In 1935 he married Rubina ('Ruby'), daughter of Archibald Curie Macgilchrist, medical officer in India; she died in 1956 as a result of injuries incurred in a World War II air raid. They had one son. In 1946, the year of his divorce from Ruby, he married (Cicely Margaret) Heather, daughter of Brigadier-General Reginald Harvey Henderson Boys. They had two sons and one daughter. The marriage was dissolved in 1974 and in 1978 he married Nobuko, daughter of Keiji Uenishi, businessman, and former wife of Professor Ivan Morris. Albery died in Monte Carlo 14 September 1988.

[Wendy Trewin, *All on Stage, Charles Wyndham and the Alberys*, 1980; Peter Bull, *I Know the Face, But...*, 1959; family papers; personal knowledge.]

Wendy Trewin

*published 1996*

## ALEXANDER Sir George

(1858–1918)

Actor-manager, whose original name was George Samson, the only son of William Murray Samson, a Scotch commercial traveller, by his wife, Mary Ann Hine Longman, was born at Reading 19 June 1858. He was educated at private schools at Clifton and Ealing, and at the High School, Stirling, and had some thought of studying medicine. His father, however, placed him with a London firm, Leaf & Co., drapers' warehousemen, and in 1875 he entered on a commercial career. He almost immediately became interested in theatres, and in the same year joined an amateur dramatic club. He first appeared on the stage, as an amateur, in 1875 at the old Cabinet Theatre, King's Cross, as Henri de Neuville in *Plot and Passion*. After four years of commercial life he finally made up his mind to become a professional actor. He obtained an engagement with Miss Ada

Swanborough, and made his first professional appearance at the Theatre Royal, Nottingham, 8 September 1879, as Charles in *His Last Legs* and Harry Prendergast in *Snowball*. The same year he joined the *Caste* comedy company on tour, playing leading juvenile parts. He made his first professional appearance in London at the Standard Theatre, Bishopsgate, 4 April 1881, as Freddy Butterscotch in *The Guv'nor*. At the end of the same year he was engaged by (Sir) Henry Irving for the Lyceum Theatre, and appeared there 26 December 1881 as Caleb Deecie in a revival of *Two Roses*. He also appeared there as Paris in Irving's revival of *Romeo and Juliet*. He was next engaged for the Court Theatre, where he played in *The Parvenu*. He then joined Miss (Ellen) Wallis's company on tour, playing such parts as Orlando, Romeo, Benedick, Posthumus Leonatus. At a series of matinées in London at the Gaiety Theatre, February–April 1883, he played most of these parts. In June 1883 he appeared at the Adelphi Theatre in *Ranks and Riches*, and was next engaged by (Sir) John Hare and William Hunter Kendal for the St. James's Theatre, appearing there in *Impulse*, *Young Folks' Ways*, and other pieces. When Mary Anderson (Madame de Navarro) produced W. S. Gilbert's *Comedy and Tragedy* at the Lyceum, 26 January 1884, he played the part of D'Aulnay. He rejoined the St. James's company, and on 17 April 1884 appeared there as Octave in *The Ironmaster*. He was then re-engaged by Irving for the Lyceum, and after playing De Mauprat in *Richelieu* (August 1884) he accompanied Irving on his second American tour, playing the leading juvenile parts in the Lyceum repertory. Returning to London in 1885, he played several of the same parts. In *Faust*, produced at the Lyceum on 19 December 1885, he appeared as Valentine, and shortly afterwards succeeded H. B. Conway (Henry Blenkinsopp Coulson) in the title-rôle, which he continued to play throughout the run of the play. He remained with the Lyceum company for four years as leading man, appearing as Ulric (in *Werner*), Claudio (in *Much Ado About Nothing*), Thornhill (in *Olivia*) and, after a further American tour, Silvio (in *The Amber Heart*), Macduff (in *Macbeth*). In September 1889 he appeared at the Adelphi Theatre in *London Day by Day*; and while still engaged there he entered on his career as manager. His first production was at the Avenue Theatre (1 February 1890) when he presented *Dr. Bill*. Six weeks later he played the leading part in this piece, and after having produced *The Struggle for Life* (25 September 1890) and *Sunlight and Shadow* (1 November 1890), in both of which he played the leading parts, he entered on his management of the St. James's Theatre (31 January 1891) which continued until the time of his death. During these twenty-seven years he produced notable plays, some of which were great artistic and financial successes. Among the more important may be mentioned *The Idler* by Haddon Chambers (26 February 1891) in which he played Mark Cross; *Lady*

*Windermere's Fan* by Oscar Wilde (20 February 1892) in which he appeared as Lord Windermere; and *Liberty Hall* by R. C. Carton (3 December 1892) in which he played Mr. Owen. On 27 May 1893 he produced *The Second Mrs. Tanqueray* by (Sir) A. W. Pinero, which proved one of his greatest triumphs and established Mrs. Patrick Campbell as an actress of the first rank. In this play he took the comparatively unimportant part of Aubrey Tanqueray, but the production was a noteworthy achievement. Other productions were *The Masqueraders* by Henry Arthur Jones (April 1894); *The Importance of Being Earnest* by Oscar Wilde (February 1895); *The Prisoner of Zenda* by 'Anthony Hope' (January 1896); *The Princess and the Butterfly* by Pinero (March 1897); *The Ambassador* by 'John Oliver Hobbes' (June 1898); *Paolo and Francesca* by Stephen Phillips (March 1902); *If I were King* by Justin Huntly M'Carthy (August 1902); *Old Heidelberg* (March 1903); *His House in Order* by Pinero (February 1906); *The Thief* (November 1907); *The Thunderbolt* by Pinero (May 1908); *Mid-Channel* by Pinero (September 1909); and *Bella Donna* by J. B. Fagan, from Robert Hichens's novel (December 1911). Most of these were highly successful, and the St. James's was accounted one of the foremost theatres in London. In addition Alexander staged successful revivals of *As You Like It* (1896) and *Much Ado About Nothing* (1898). In September 1905 he accepted a special engagement at Drury Lane Theatre, where he appeared in (Sir) Hall Caine's play, *The Prodigal Son*. He twice gave private performances by royal command—at Balmoral (16 September 1895) before Queen Victoria, when *Liberty Hall* was performed, and at Sandringham (4 December 1908) before King Edward VII, when *The Builder of Bridges* by Alfred Sutro was the play selected. He also played the leading part of Alfred Evelyn in *Money* before the German Emperor at Drury Lane (17 May 1911). He made his last appearance at the St. James's Theatre in July 1917 in *The Aristocrat* by Louis N. Parker, and died after a long illness, at his home, Little Court, Chorley Wood, Hertfordshire, 16 March 1918. He was knighted in 1911, and was, in addition, a liveryman of the Turners' Company, president of the Royal General Theatrical fund, and a vice-president of several theatrical benevolent funds; he represented South St. Pancras on the London County Council from 1907 to 1913.

Alexander had a fine stage presence; he was tall, dignified, and refined. If he was never a brilliant actor, his work had always a certain distinction; and his charm of manner evoked sympathy and attention. His voice was good, though certain mannerisms made him an easy prey for the mimic. His taste in dress was regarded as above reproach. As a manager, he endeavoured to obtain the best which offered in the way of native drama, and to surround himself with the best artists available. His management of the St. James's Theatre was throughout a notable achievement. He left a fortune of over £90,000. In 1882 he married Florence Jane, daughter of Edward Théleur, but died without issue.

[*The Times*, 16 March 1918; *Who's Who in the Theatre*; correspondence; personal knowledge. Portraits, *Royal Academy Pictures*, 1910 and 1916.]

JOHN PARKER

*published 1927*

## ARCHER William

(1856–1924)

Critic and journalist, was born at Perth 23 September 1856, the eldest son of Thomas Archer, formerly of Gracemere, Queensland, by his wife, Grace Lindsay, daughter of James Morison, of Muirton, Perth. Thomas Archer and his wife led a wandering life, but when in Scotland regularly attended the meetings of two small separatist religious sects, the Walkerites and the Glassites. Members of the Archer family were to be found in Norway and in Australia. To these family connexions may be traced William Archer's later love of Norwegian literature and of travel, the strength of his moral principles, his anticlericalism, and, through mental reaction, his vehement rationalism. He was educated at Perth Academy, George Watson's College, Edinburgh, and Edinburgh University. He was trained as a lawyer and called to the bar by the Middle Temple in 1883, but never practised. In 1875 Archer sent an article to the *Edinburgh Evening News* and, while still at college, became a leader-writer for that paper at a salary of £80 a year. After leaving the university he made a tour of the world in visiting his parents in Australia (1876–1877)—he had already travelled in Scandinavia—and after another short spell on the staff of the *Edinburgh Evening News*, he settled in London in 1878.

Archer began his career in London as dramatic critic on the *London Figaro* (1879–1881): he also contributed articles to the rationalist press under a pseudonym. Despite the protests of some of his friends, he devoted himself mainly to a study of the theatre, and subsequently became a critic for the *World*, the *Nation*, the *Tribune*, the *Morning Leader*, and the *Manchester Guardian*.

When Archer first began this work in London, the English stage, occupied for the most part with mechanical French farce and puerile melodrama, was passing through a poor period. But by the 'nineties, when Archer's reputation and influence as a critic had become established, especially through his *Study and Stage* articles in the *World* (reprinted as *The Theatrical World*, 5 volumes, 1893–1897), a definite change was taking place: mingled with plays like *Trilby* and *Diplomacy* the dramas of Pinero, Wilde, Barrie, and Ibsen were beginning to be played and a higher standard of theatrical performances created. This change was largely due to Archer. Although he was not the first translator of Ibsen, his translation of *The Pillars of Society* was the first of Ibsen's plays to be produced in London (at the Gaiety Theatre in 1880); and although his translations were open to certain criticisms they became the most popular, and materially helped the growth of the appreciation of Ibsen by the English public. Archer also edited the prose dramas of Ibsen (5 volumes, 1890–1891) and the collected works of Ibsen (11 volumes, 1906–1907).

Archer wrote several books about the theatre, the best of which are *Masks or Faces?* (1888) and *Play-making* (1912). He also published *Poets of the Younger Generation* (1901) besides much miscellaneous journalistic work. In 1908 he paid a visit to the United States in order to study the race problem; in 1910 he went to Spain to investigate the case of Francisco Ferrer, who had been executed for what Archer considered unjust and obscurantist reasons; and in 1912 he travelled through India and the East. As results of these visits he published *Through Afro-America* (1910), *The Life, Trial, and Death of Francisco Ferrer* (1911), and *India and the Future* (1917). He also edited the works of Congreve (1912) and a selection of the plays of Farquhar (1906).

On the outbreak of war in 1914 Archer devoted himself energetically to propaganda work for the British government. Long before the War he had joined the Inns of Court Volunteers—and in this corps his only son now received a commission. In 1918 his son was killed, and the shock induced him to make some experiments with spiritualism—not, indeed, for the first time. But his enthusiastic rationalism did not desert him, and for the last seven years of his life he used his pen powerfully, if a little crudely, in regular religious controversy. Archer's last book on the drama, *The Old Drama and the New*, was published in 1923; and in the same year his one successful play, *The Green Goddess*, into which he put his great knowledge of stagecraft and the plot of which he obtained in a dream, was produced at the St. James's Theatre, London: it had been performed in New York two years previously. His other plays are *War is War* (1919), *Martha Washington*, *Beatriz Juana*, and *Lidia* (all published posthumously, 1927): the last two are in black verse. He died in London 27 December 1924 after an unsuccessful operation.

Archer is described as 'physically a tall upstanding well-built Scot' [G. B. Shaw, introduction to Archer's *Three Plays*, 1927]. He was a man of wide culture and varied interests, who spoke many languages, and had travelled widely. He was lamented in Norway as her 'unselfish and self-sacrificing friend'. He worked for the abolition of the theatrical censorship, for the formation of a national theatre [see *A National Theatre Scheme and Estimates* by William Archer and H. Granville Barker, 1907], and for a time he was actively connected with the League of Nations Union. As a critic he may have been somewhat harsh in his principles, too rigid in his logic, and lacking in the elasticity of mind of his contemporary, Arthur Bingham Walkley; but his emphasis on good dramatic structure and his hatred of slovenliness in any form were a necessary and vital help to all young dramatists. It is perhaps significant that when Bernard Shaw, a close friend of his, read him his first play, Archer went to sleep. That he was a man of deep and genuine humour is proved both by the testimony of his friends and by a study of his writings. His incorruptible honesty made a real impression on the English stage, and his translations and teaching contributed to the knitting together of European culture.

Archer married in 1884 Frances Elizabeth, daughter of John Trickett, a retired civil engineer, and had one son.

[*The Times*, 29 December 1924; *Manchester Guardian*, 29 December 1924; *Observer*, 4 January 1925; L. Aas, *William Archer*, 1920; Charles Archer, *William Archer—Life, Work, and Friendships* (in MS.); J. M. Robertson, biographical Introduction to *William Archer as Rationalist*, 1925; 'Personal Note' by G. Bernard Shaw prefixed to Archer's *Three Plays*, 1927.]

M. P. Ashley

*published 1937*

## ARMSTRONG William

(1882–1952)

Actor and producer, eldest son of John Armstrong and his wife, Annie Tait, was born in Edinburgh 30 November 1882. His father, a grocer who forgave too many debts to be prosperous, brought William up to be proud of an ancestry which included many schoolmasters and ministers, to be a devout Baptist and a crusading teetotaller, singing

When the wine around you is passing,
Have courage, my boy, to say 'No',

at Band of Hope concerts. He never forgot his Edinburgh background and, since he was a brilliant raconteur, his stories of Edinburgh life; of his experiences as a conductor of Polytechnic tours; and of theatrical personalities—notably Mrs. Patrick Campbell—were a delight to his friends and, when broadcast, to wider audiences.

He was educated at Heriot's School but left at fourteen. His main interest was music and he wanted to be a schoolmaster. Helped by the Carnegie Trust, he was enrolled as a student in the faculty of music at Edinburgh University; but, as always, his interest was in performance not theory and, although he passed his first professional examination for the degree of Mus.B., the purely theoretical study of music chilled him and he turned to the theatre. He joined an amateur dramatic society; frequented the sixpenny gallery at the Lyceum to see Sir Henry Irving and (Sir) Herbert Beerbohm Tree, and (Dame) Ellen Terry; and founded the Edinburgh University Dramatic Club with (Sir) J. M. Barrie as president. By the time he was twenty-six he had started his career as a professional actor with (Sir) Frank Benson, playing Jamy in *Henry V* at the Stratford Memorial Theatre. He was tall, willowy, with reddish fair hair and a Scottish accent; shy but with a gift of humour which won him friends. He interested G. B. Shaw, who wrote the one-act play *The Music Cure* for him and Madge McIntosh. He acted innumerable parts with reasonable success, and was for two years a member of the Glasgow Repertory Theatre.

His connection with Liverpool began in 1914 when he became a member of the 'Commonwealth', an experiment which kept the Repertory Theatre alive during the early war years. He was remembered; and when, in 1922, a permanent producer was needed, he was offered the post. From 1922 as producer, and from 1923 to 1944 as a director as well as producer, he ran what was undoubtedly the most successful repertory theatre in the country. From his Liverpool base he had a great influence upon the English theatre. Under him, the Liverpool Repertory Theatre certainly did not become, as had been hoped, the centre of a new school of dramatic writing; but, at a time when English playwrights had ceased to be inspired by the energies of Shaw, Galsworthy, and Granville-Barker and were seeking new forms amid the drawing-room dramas of (Sir) Noël Coward, Somerset Maugham, and Frederick Lonsdale, Liverpool became a great school of acting. Players, later well known and even famous, grew up under him, (Sir) Michael Redgrave, Rex Harrison, Diana Wynyard, Marjorie Fielding, Robert Donat, Wyndham Goldie, Cecil Parker, Harry Andrews, and Alan Webb among them. He was not intellectual in his approach and never forced his own interpretation of a play upon his company; he rather seemed to feel for the tone, the pace, and the style which was developing. Generous, emotional, easily moved by pathos and by beauty, he demanded, and recognized, sensibility in his actors; but his irrepressible humour made him detect instantly, with destroying laughter, a false note. His musical background affected his work; he listened for the harmonies in a play, rather than analysed it, and changed moves and intonations because they were discordant rather than because they did not fit into a preconceived pattern. His informality, his wit, his appreciation of youth, made young actors and actresses flock to Liverpool where they flowered under his willingness to develop their talents rather than force them into a mould. They left with an unforgettable training in a flexible, sensitive style of acting which could never be forced or heavy-handed.

He made the Repertory Theatre a powerful influence in Liverpool life and, although the laddie from Edinburgh had become a sophisticated and even flamboyant man of the theatre, he never lost his shrewd hold on those financial realities which reassured his fellow directors, many of them Liverpool business men. He gave the Shute lectures on 'The Art of the Theatre' at the university of Liverpool in 1928: was made an honorary M.A. by the university in 1930, and was appointed C.B.E. in 1951 for services to the Liverpool and Birmingham repertory theatres. He left Liverpool in 1944; directed many plays in London and was assistant director to Sir Barry Jackson at the Birmingham Repertory Theatre in 1945–7. He died, unmarried, at his home near Birmingham 5 October 1952. A portrait of him by Wilhem Kaufman hangs in the Walker Art Gallery, Liverpool.

[Grace Wyndham Goldie, *The Liverpool Repertory Theatre*, 1935; *Who's Who in the Theatre*; private information; personal knowledge.]

GRACE WYNDHAM GOLDIE

*published 1971*

## ASHTON Sir Frederick William Mallandaine (1904–1988)

Dancer, and founder and choreographer, with (Dame) Ninette de Valois, of the Royal Ballet, was born 17 September 1904 in Guayaquil, Ecuador, the youngest of four sons of George Ashton, a minor diplomat working for a cable company, and his wife, Georgiana Fulcher, who came from a Suffolk family. Later there was a much-loved younger sister, Edith. The family moved to Peru, where Ashton attended the Dominican School in Lima. In 1917 he was taken to see a performance by Anna Pavlova—'she injected me with her poison'—and resolved to make dancing his life. In 1919 he was sent to England, to Dover College, which he hated, and to spend holidays in London with family friends. With them he saw Isadora Duncan and many dance companies, including that of Sergei Diaghilev in his disastrous production of *The Sleeping Princess* in 1921.

In 1922, aged eighteen, he began dance lessons with Léonide Massine and, later, with (Dame) Marie Rambert. Lacking height, he was nevertheless slim and elegant with a long, large-featured face and melancholy eyes, which would be effective in his future stage career. His dancing talent was not great, and his 'passionate laziness' was noted by Rambert, but this perceptive woman already sensed choreographic talent in the young man. The suicide of Ashton's father in South America brought his impoverished mother to England to join her son. They shared a series of inadequate lodgings while Ashton attended Pavlova's London performances and the last seasons of Diaghilev's Ballets Russes. At one of these he met the Russian designer, Sophie Fedorovitch, who would become his lifelong friend and collaborator.

Rambert, with her group of pupils, gave Ashton an enviable springboard as a budding choreographer; her generous encouragement launched his future career. He composed solos, *pas de deux*, and short ballets for revues, musical shows, the Camargo Society, and the Ballet Club, which later became the Ballet Rambert. His first work of importance was *A Tragedy of Fashion* in 1926 for the revue, *Riverside Nights*. In the thirty years which followed, Ashton choreographed many of his best ballets: *Façade* for the Camargo Society (1931); *Les Rendezvous*, Vic-Wells Ballet for Ninette de Valois (1933); an American interlude to arrange dances for the Virgil Thomson/Gertrude Stein opera, *Four Saints in Three Acts* (1934); and *Le Baiser de la Fée* at Sadler's Wells in 1935, which inaugurated his long partnership with (Dame) Margot Fonteyn. Leaving Rambert for the larger stage of de Valois' company, his most successful works were *Apparitions* and *Nocturne* (1936), *Les Patineurs* and *A Wedding Bouquet* (1937), *Horoscope* (1938), and *Dante Sonata* and *The Wise Virgins* (1940–1).

Ashton served with RAF intelligence during World War II, but was given leave in 1943 to choreograph a new ballet, *The Quest*, with a score by (Sir) William Walton. After the war, with the Sadler's Wells company resident at the reopened Royal Opera House, Covent Garden, Ashton choreographed the ballet considered by many his most perfect—César Franck's *Symphonic Variations* (1946). He ventured into opera production in 1947, at Covent Garden and Glyndebourne, and in 1948 choreographed two short works, *Scènes de Ballet* and *Don Juan*, and Sergei Prokofiev's *Cinderella*, the first three-act British ballet. In 1949 and 1950 ballets in Paris and New York were less successful. In 1951 Ashton also choreographed his first film, *The Tales of Hoffmann*, and this was followed in 1952 by *The Story of Three Loves*. At Covent Garden his highly successful ballet *Daphnis and Chloë* was performed in 1951, to be followed in 1952 by Léo Delibes' three-act *Sylvia*.

Ashton's entire life was lived in the ballet world. From 1953 until the late 1970s he continued to invent and produce work of varying shades and character. Among his notable achievements were *Homage to the Queen* (1953); *Romeo and Juliet* for the Royal Danish Ballet (1955); *Ondine* (1958); *La Fille Mal Gardée* (1960); *Marguerite and Armand* (1963); *The Dream* (1964); *Enigma Variations* (1968); and *A Month in the Country* (1976). He may have reached his largest public with the charming dances for the 1970 film, *Tales of Beatrix Potter*, in which he appeared as Mrs Tiggywinkle. He was both principal choreographer (1933–70) and director (1963–70) of the Royal Ballet.

Ashton was a lyrical choreographer, considered by many to be peerless in this field, though his approach to choreography was idiosyncratic. He seemed to plan little in advance, to arrive for first rehearsals without original ideas, and to use music suggested, occasionally even chosen, by friends. He would ask dancers to invent steps to musical phrases, sometimes selecting ones he liked and discarding others, sometimes discarding everything and commanding new inventions. In this unorthodox manner many of his best-known ballets were built; the original cast of dancers in each production took a considerable part in its creation, the resulting choreography reflecting their particular talents and style. Margot Fonteyn, for whom he made the majority of his ballets, brought into every Ashton role her love of floating, aerial movements while carried by her partner.

Ashton was homosexual and had several enduring relationships during his long life. Over the years he lived in charming, comfortable apartments and small houses in London and in a large country house at Eye in Suffolk, with ten acres, a lake, and a terraced room filled with his collection of Wemyss pottery, vividly displayed in well-lit glass cabinets. He was a supreme socialite, loving gossip and good living, which caused a certain florid portliness in his later years. His sense of humour was delightful and he was an amusing, often witty, companion. He adored everything connected with royalty and became a particular friend of his near contemporary, the queen mother. He was much honoured, receiving the CBE (1950), a knighthood (1962), CH (1970), and the OM (1977). He was given the freedom of the City of London (1981) and the Legion of Honour (1960). He had honorary degrees from Durham (1962), East Anglia (1967), London (1970), Hull (1971), and Oxford (1976). He died 18 August 1988 at his house in Eye.

[Z. Dominic and J. S. Gilbert, *Frederick Ashton, a Choreographer and his Ballets*, 1977; David Vaughan, *Frederick Ashton*, 1977; personal knowledge.]

MOIRA SHEARER

*published 1996*

## ASKEY Arthur Bowden

(1900–1982)

Actor and entertainer, was born 6 June 1900 at 19 Moses Street, Liverpool, the elder child and only son of Samuel Askey, secretary of the firm Sugar Products, of Liverpool, and his wife, Betsy Bowden, of Knutsford, Cheshire. Six months after his birth the family moved to 90 Rosslyn Street. He was educated at St Michael's Council School and the Liverpool Institute. His social life was mostly centred round the church. Apart from Sunday services there were Sunday school, the Band of Hope, Scripture Union, and choir practice. He started in the choir as a probationer and was paid three pence a month. Eventually he became head boy. His most memorable singing performance was when the Lady chapel of Liverpool Cathedral was consecrated. He sang solo in the presence of the archbishops of Canterbury and York.

As a schoolboy his summer holidays were spent at Rhyl in north Wales. It was there that he first became addicted to the light entertainment business. A pierrot troupe called 'The Jovial Sisters' performed three times a day on a small wooden stage on the sands. Askey would arrive well before each performance and sit on the sands as near to the stage as he could get. He saw every performance and at the end of the holiday he knew all the words and music of every item. All this remained in his memory and was to be of great use later in his career.

At the age of sixteen Askey went to work at the Liverpool education offices at a salary of £10 a month. After the outbreak of war in 1914 he was often asked to sing to wounded soldiers and apart from solos would sometimes sing duets with Tommy Handley, another Liverpudlian destined for show business stardom. In June 1918 he became a private in the Welch Regiment. His army career was short-lived because when peace came in November he was demobilized and returned to the education office.

He soon became fascinated with concert parties. As often as possible he would cross the Mersey to the Olympian Gardens at Rock Ferry where touring shows appeared each week. He memorized his favourite items, especially the jokes, and was secretly determined one day to join a concert party. Later he spent his summer holidays at Douglas in the Isle of Man where there were no less than four concert parties and again he was able to add to his repertoire of jokes and comic songs. He also entered and won prizes at talent competitions. He started his own amateur concert party called 'The Filberts' and joined another as the pianist.

His yearning to become a professional entertainer caused him to write for interviews with theatrical agents in London. When these met with no success he resigned himself to a settled career at the Liverpool education office. In 1924 Askey landed his first professional job as a comedian in a concert party called 'Song Salad'. He was offered a thirty-week tour at £6. 10s. a week. As his salary at work was £3 a week he decided to accept the offer and leave the education office, even though this entailed the extra expense of living accommodation. The concert party was a natural stepping-stone to pantomimes, in several of which Askey appeared with considerable success.

Askey now felt he could afford a wife and in March 1925 he married (Elizabeth) May (died 1974), daughter of Walter Swash, publican. They had one daughter, Anthea. Askey was soon to be introduced to a branch of the entertainment business which was to be his main source of income for the next twelve years—after-dinner entertaining. There were Masonic lodges, city companies, staff dinners, Central Hall concerts, and Sunday League shows. The fee was anything from two to five guineas and sometimes he would appear at as many as three in one night. After several such engagements he was offered occasional weeks touring the music halls but as the salary would have been much less than he could earn with his Masonics, he turned down the offers.

He and his wife then moved to a flat in Golders Green. In 1938 Askey joined Powis Pinder's 'Sunshine' concert party at Shanklin, Isle of Wight, where he was a resounding success for the next eight years. There he was discovered by the BBC who engaged him for a new radio show called 'Band Waggon', in which his partner was Richard Murdoch. The show, first broadcast in January 1938, was an enormous success. The broadcasts were followed by a tour of music halls and performances in the London Palladium in 1939. Richard Murdoch then joined the Royal Air Force, bringing 'Band Waggon' to an end. He was, however, given leave to appear with Askey in four films, *Band Waggon, Charlie's Big-hearted Aunt, The Ghost Train*, and *I Thank You*.

After 'Band Waggon' Askey appeared in a number of successful musical shows in London's West End: *The Love Racket* (1943), *Follow The Girls* (1945), *The Kid from Stratford* (1948), *Bet Your Life* (1952), and *The Love Match* (1953). He also appeared in many more films and was now an established star in most forms of entertainment. His later films included *Back Room Boy, King Arthur was a Gentleman, Miss London Limited*, and *Bees in Paradise*. Amongst these engagements Askey managed to fit in a very successful tour of Australia (1949–50). In 1969 he was appointed OBE and in 1981 CBE.

Later in his life he slowed down a little but was never short of offers for films, concerts, television, and radio programmes. His popularity was such that he appeared in no less than ten Royal Command Performances—in 1946, 1948, 1952, 1954, 1955, 1957, 1968, 1972, 1978, and 1980. He is also the only celebrity to have been twice the subject of television's *This is Your Life*.

Arthur Askey stood just five feet three and was able to use his lack of inches for much humour. He always wore glasses and in his earlier and prime professional days had red hair which his daughter inherited. He was always smartly dressed except when portraying a character. He was not a dancer though one critic wrote 'He didn't dance but looked as if he could.' He was a 'busy' little comedian given to extravagant gestures and darting movements, sometimes carried to excess. This exuberance prevented him from coming to immediate terms with television but he later conquered this shortcoming. He was at his best in a large theatre production such as pantomime and musical comedy. He later learned what many comedians lack—repose. His rapport with the public was such that few comic performers can have achieved greater popularity.

After his eightieth birthday his health began to fail but he remained cheerful and full of humour. His last public appearance was in pantomime at the Richmond Theatre in 1981. He died in St Thomas's Hospital 16 November 1982. His autobiography, *Before Your Very Eyes*, was published in 1975.

[Arthur Askey, *Before Your Very Eyes*, 1975 (autobiography); personal knowledge.]

RICHARD MURDOCH

*published 1990*

## AYLMER Sir Felix Edward

(1889–1979)

Actor, was born 21 February 1889 at Corsham, Wiltshire, the second child in the family of five sons (one of whom died as a child) and one daughter of Lieutenant-Colonel Thomas Edward Aylmer-Jones, Royal Engineers, and his wife, Lilian Cookworthy. He was educated at Magdalen College School and Exeter College, Oxford, where he took second classes in both mathematical moderations (1909) and physics (1911). After an undergraduate attachment to OUDS, he decided to join the stage, to his parents' displeasure.

He commenced a course of stage training under the celebrated teacher Rosina Filippi. His first professional appearance was as a two-line Italian stooge with (Sir) E. Seymour Hicks at the Coliseum in 1911, just after his twenty-second birthday. He then appeared in *Romeo and Juliet* at the New Theatre and in two memorable Shakespearian productions (1912) at the Savoy by Harley Granville-Barker. In 1913 he joined the company of (Sir) Barry Jackson at the Birmingham Repertory Theatre. This splendid training was interrupted by the war of 1914–18, in which Aylmer served in the Royal Naval Volunteer Reserve, hurrying back to the Birmingham stage and his wife as soon as hostilities had ceased. During the war he had married Barry Jackson's niece Cecily (died 1975), daughter of Robert Taaffe Byrne, managing director of the Leyland of Birmingham Rubber Company. They met when he played Prospero to her Miranda and on his return after the war they appeared together again as Sir Peter and Lady Teazle. They had one daughter and two sons, who both died young.

During the following years Aylmer was seen in many West End plays, including *The Doctor's Dilemma* (Kingsway, 1926) and *The Flashing Stream* (Lyric, 1938). He also appeared in plays in New York, such as *Loyalties* (Gaiety, 1922), produced by Basil Dean, and *The Last of Mrs Cheyney* (Fulton, 1925). Some of his greatest successes were acting the parts of members of the professions of law and diplomacy. For John Drinkwater in 1928, he played at the Royalty a KC in the long-running comedy *Bird in Hand*. This was followed by the role of a councillor of state in *Jew Süss* (Duke of York's, 1929) and then that of a crooked solicitor in the 1934 revival at the Sadler's Wells and the Shaftesbury of *The Voysey Inheritance* by Harley Granville-Barker. He was also the judge in Enid Bagnold's *The Chalk Garden* (Haymarket, 1956). Diplomats which he played included the Foreign Office official in the 1954 production of *The Spider's Web* by (Dame) Agatha Christie.

Aylmer was not fond of Shakespeare. He once confided: 'I am a bit of an anti-Shakespearian. I acknowledge his greatness, of course—but, you know, Shakespeare has done so much harm to actors. He has been responsible for so much work that is artificial and unreal that in my time he has seemed a machine for manufacturing ham actors who do not understand the psychological contents of the parts and the poetry. Everyone has to do Shakespeare if they want to make a reputation but it seems to me that they seldom do their best work in his plays. He stretches an actor's emotional range, of course—but then so do Ibsen and Strindberg.' Aylmer preferred G. B. Shaw, whom he first met very early in his career. He played Shaw repeatedly and indeed appeared in three different parts in *St. Joan* alone.

Not one to enthuse about the rapport normally enjoyed by stage actors with a live audience, he preferred the medium of the film. He claimed that the work the film actor had to do, under the close-up of the camera's pitiless eye, called for a greater skill than anything required on stage. He appeared in a number of supporting parts in large-scale films for American directors: Plautius, a Roman converted to Christianity, in *Quo Vadis?* (1951), Isaak of York, the Jewish father of Elizabeth Taylor's Rebecca in *Ivanhoe* (1953), Merlin to Mel Ferrer's King Arthur in *Knights of the Round Table* (1953), and, in spite of his antipathy towards Shakespeare, two memorable performances in productions by Laurence (later Lord) Olivier, namely Polonius in *Hamlet* (1948) and the Archbishop in *Henry V* (1944). Television too brought him fame: he appeared with Hugh Griffith in the popular comedy series entitled *The Walrus and the Carpenter* and as Father Anselm with Derek Nimmo in *Oh Brother!* a successful series about life in a monastery.

In 1959 he published a book *Dickens Incognito*, as a result of research which had led him to some startling conclusions about that author's private life. The book created a sensation. However, the bubble burst within a week as other Dickens lovers pounced on a flaw in his argument and found gaps in his research. This upset could have humiliated a lesser man but was met by Aylmer with rueful amusement and perfect sang-froid. He was not deterred from writing a second book entitled *The Drood Case*, which was published in 1964.

He gave great service to his profession as an outstanding president of the British Actors' Equity Association from 1949 to 1969. In his official capacity, in 1963 he criticized the dirty and insanitary conditions still obtaining even in some West End theatres. He was also vice-president of the Royal Academy of Dramatic Art when the principal, John Fernald, resigned in 1965 after a disagreement on policy with the council. In 1950 Aylmer was appointed OBE for his services to the stage and in 1965 he was knighted.

Having spent some time in Germany when he was a student, Aylmer later translated a number of plays from German. One of his favourite hobbies was composing limericks, clerihews, and verse for newspaper competitions. In this he vied with his son Ian, and together they won a number of prizes. His daughter Jennifer was for several years connected with the British Theatre Museum in London. A stroke precipitated Aylmer's retirement to his country house near Cobham where he continued to live until shortly before he died, at a nursing home in Sussex, 2 September 1979.

[Personal knowledge.]

Derek Nimmo

*published 1986*

## BADDELEY Hermione Youlanda Ruby Clinton (1906–1986)

Actress, was born 13 November 1906 in Broseley, Shropshire, the youngest of four daughters (there were no sons) of William Herman Clinton-Baddeley, composer, and his wife, Louise Bourdin. A descendant both of Sir Henry Clinton, a British general in the American War of Independence, and Robert Baddeley, the actor and pastry-cook who bequeathed the annual fruit cake to the cast playing at Drury Lane, she combined aspects of both these ancestors in her long and eventful career. Her immediate senior sister, Angela Baddeley, was also a successful actress. Their theatrical education was at the Margaret Morris School of Dancing in Chelsea, where the pupils considered themselves vastly superior to the more competitive Italia Conti children.

Hermione's first great success was under Basil Dean's management, playing a badly behaved waif from the slums with a famous plate-smashing scene in Charles McEvoy's *The Likes of Her* at the St Martin's theatre (1923). The next year Dean cast her as a murderous Arab urchin in *The Forest*, by John Galsworthy. Having established a career as a dramatic actress she switched to comedy in *The Punch Bowl* (1924), a revue at the Duke of York's, where she danced with Sonny Hale and credited her formidable comic technique to lessons learned from the comedian Alfred Lester. She joined *The Co-optimists*, at the Palace theatre, in the same year. In *On with the Dance* (1925), (Sir) Noël Coward's revue for (Sir) Charles Cochran, she created (with Alice Delysia) Coward's topically satirical 'poor little rich girl'. This was the first of four productions for Cochran and then, among a number of undistinguished comedies, farces, and musicals, she also played Sara in *Tobias and the Angel* by James Bridie (Westminster, 1932). She had a long run in *The Greeks Had a Word for It*, which transferred from Robert Newton's Shilling theatre in Fulham to the Duke of York's in 1934.

With *Floodlight* by Beverley Nichols (Saville, 1937) she began a long period as a queen of revue, having also plunged into an increasing social whirl with her husband, David Tennant, for whom she often performed in cabaret at his club, the Gargoyle. Herbert Farjeon's wit in *Nine Sharp* (subsequently *The Little Revue*, 1940) provided the perfect launching-pad for her inspired clowning, bravura characterization, and skill at quick costume and make-up changes. Her most popular characters included an old girl at Torquay, a Windmill girl in 'Voilà les Non-Stop Nudes', and her prototype funny ballerina, Madame Allover. When she was ill, five understudies barely kept the curtain up.

In her autobiography she suggests that she recruited Hermione Gingold to *Rise Above It* at the Comedy (1941). It was a legendary, explosive partnership, with Gingold's daunting control of laughter and Baddeley's penchant for wild improvisation. They were reunited less successfully in *Sky High* at the Phoenix the next year. Their final joint venture, Noël Coward's *Fallen Angels* at the Ambassador's in 1949, inspired the fury of the author at the liberties they took. He was mollified when the show became a fashionable success. Meanwhile, as a dramatic actress Hermione Baddeley's two outstanding successes were as Ida in Graham Greene's *Brighton Rock* (Garrick, 1943), which she repeated in the Boulting Brothers' film (1947), and in *Grand National Night* (Apollo, 1946), by Dorothy and Campbell Christie. Her American début in *A Taste of Honey* (1961) led to an invitation from Tennessee Williams to create the role of Flora Goforth in *The Milk Train Doesn't Stop Here Anymore* at the Spoleto festival (1962) and on Broadway a year later. A newspaper strike killed the play but Williams greatly admired her performance.

In England she played in many films from 1926 (*A Daughter in Revolt*)—most notably in *Kipps* (1941), *It Always Rains On Sunday* (1947), *Quartet* (1948), *Passport to Pimlico* (1949), and *The Pickwick Papers* (1952). She was nominated for an Oscar in 1959 for *Room at the Top* (1958) and had a Hollywood success as the housekeeper, Ellen, in *Mary Poppins* (1964). For the last twenty years she lived mainly in Los Angeles and became a familiar face on television in situation comedies, especially *Bewitched* and *Maude*.

Always known as 'Totie', and originally a petite and delicate gamine, Hermione Baddeley grew into a still small, but fuller figured beauty and this lent authority to her later blowsier characterizations. In 1928 she married David Pax Tennant, son of Edward Priaulx Tennant, first Baron Glenconner, MP for Salisbury. They had a son and a daughter. The marriage was dissolved in 1937 and in 1941 she married Captain J. H. ('Dozey') Willis, MC, of the 12th Lancers, the son of Major-General Edward Henry Willis, of the Royal Artillery. This marriage was later dissolved. She enjoyed a stormy romance with the actor Laurence Harvey, but they did not marry. She died in Los Angeles, at the Cedars Sinai Hospital, 19 August 1986.

[Hermione Baddeley, *The Unsinkable Hermione Baddeley* (autobiography), 1984; *The Times*, 22 and 27 August 1986; *Contemporary Theatre, Film and Television*, vol. iv, 1987; Phyllis Hartnoll (ed.), *The Oxford Companion to the Theatre*, 1983; Ephraim Katz, *The International Film Encyclopaedia*, 1980; David Quinlan, *The Illustrated Directory of Film Character Actors*, 1985; personal knowledge.]

NED SHERRIN

*published 1996*

## BANCROFT Sir Squire Bancroft

**(1841–1926)**

Actor and theatrical manager, the elder son of Secundus Bancroft White Butterfield, oil merchant, of Rotherhithe, by his wife, Julia, daughter of Thomas Anthony Wright, was born at Cristall's Cottage, Rotherhithe, 14 May 1841. In December 1867 he took the surname of Bancroft, and as Squire Bancroft married in that month Marie Effie Wilton [see below]. One son was born of the marriage.

Fatherless before he was seven, Bancroft was educated at private schools in England and in France, and in January 1861 went on the stage under the name of Bancroft at the Theatre Royal, Birmingham. Till the spring of 1865 he played in provincial stock companies; and at Liverpool early in 1865 he first acted with his future wife, Marie Wilton, who then engaged him for the Prince of Wales's Theatre, London. There, on 15 April 1865, he appeared for the first time in London in the comedietta *A Winning Hazard*, by J. P. Wooler. In 1867 he succeeded Henry James Byron as joint manager with his wife of the Prince of Wales's. In that partnership Bancroft, who was prudent, pertinacious, and laborious, soon came to be predominant, always keenly criticized but loyally supported by his brilliant wife.

Their mainstay at first were the comedies of Thomas William Robertson. *Society* and *Ours* were followed by *Caste*, *Play*, *School* (the most remunerative of all), and *M.P.* Carefully nursed and opportunely revived, they won nearly half the profits made at that theatre. Other successful plays produced there were: *Man and Wife* by Wilkie Collins, *Sweethearts* by (Sir) W. S. Gilbert, and two adaptations from Sardou, *Peril* (*Nos Intimes*) and *Diplomacy* (*Dora*). In April 1875 an elaborate production of *The Merchant of Venice* was quickly withdrawn, owing to Charles Coghlan's failure as Shylock. Revivals of *The School for Scandal*, Bulwer Lytton's *Money*, Dion Boucicault's *London Assurance*, J. B. Buckstone's *Good for Nothing*, and *Masks and Faces* by Charles Reade and Tom Taylor, were all successful. The theatre became too small for the Bancrofts' public; and in 1879 they took the Haymarket Theatre, rebuilt it, and opened it on 31 January 1880. On that night a disturbance was created by spectators who resented the abolition of the pit in order to make room for more stalls. The financial success of the management continued almost unbroken with revivals of *School*, *Ours*, and *Caste*, two new adaptations from Sardou, *Odette* and *Fedora*, new presentations of *The Rivals*, and of Tom Taylor's *Plot and Passion* (1881) and *The Overland Route* (1882) and a new comedy, *Lords and*

*Commons* (1883), by (Sir) A. W. Pinero. On 20 July 1885 Mr. and Mrs. Bancroft retired from management, with a profit on the twenty years of £180,000.

The Bancrofts effected great reforms both in theatrical art and in theatrical business, and their management at the Prince of Wales's Theatre inaugurated a new era in the development of modern dramatic art. In casting plays they thought first of the general effect, and so often themselves took small parts that public and critics complained of their self-suppression. In rehearsing they introduced (with the help of T. W. Robertson) the subtle interaction of characters and situation which is the basis of subsequent dramatic art. In staging they sought for naturalism, reflecting the choicer taste of their own time. They greatly increased the pay and improved the conditions of their players, a reform in which they were soon to be followed by (Sir) Henry Irving. Their heavy expenses were met by raising the price of seats; they were the first to charge (in 1874) half-a-guinea for a stall. This general refinement, before and behind the curtain, together with the social success of Mr. and Mrs. Bancroft themselves, brought 'Society' back to the theatre and attracted to the stage young people of gentle birth.

Bancroft was a good actor. His special part was the 'swell' (such as Captain Hawtree in *Caste*), a type which he rescued from convention and turned into a reflection of real life. But his Triplet (his favourite part) in *Masks and Faces*, his Faulkland in *The Rivals*, and his Orloff in *Diplomacy* showed his power in pathos, high comedy, and tense drama. It was Henry Irving's opinion that Bancroft had 'left his best work as an actor undone' through paying too much attention to management. His choice of plays and players was sagacious; and as producer he knew his limitations well enough to seek help from Robertson, Coghlan, and Pinero.

During his forty-one years of life after retirement, Bancroft returned to the stage twice; to play the Abbé to Henry Irving's Landry in *The Dead Heart* at the Lyceum in 1889, and in 1893 to play Orloff for (Sir) John Hare at the Garrick. For the rest, he was content to watch, and generously to relieve with money or advice, the struggles of his successors in the theatre, and to enjoy, at his house, 18 Berkeley Square, or later at his flat, A1, The Albany, his social success and his many friendships. Tall, erect, and handsome to the last, he was a well-known figure in the West End of London. About the early 'nineties he began a series of public readings of Dickens's *A Christmas Carol*, by which, in the United Kingdom and in Canada, he raised more than £20,000 for the hospitals. He was president of the Royal Academy of Dramatic Art, and a member of the lord chamberlain's advisory board for licensing of plays. He was knighted in the jubilee honours of 1897, and died at his flat in London 19 April 1926.

Portraits and caricatures of Bancroft are many. The chief is a three-quarter length in oils by H. G. Riviere in the National Portrait Gallery; a replica of this is in the Garrick Club, which also possesses a bust by Count Gleichen and the original cartoon by 'Spy' which appeared in *Vanity Fair* 13 June 1891.

Marie Effie Wilton, Lady Bancroft 1839–1921, actress and theatrical manager, the eldest of the six daughters of Robert Pleydell Wilton, provincial actor, by his wife, Georgiana Jane Faulkner, was born 12 January 1839 at (as she believed) Doncaster. She went on the stage in childhood, and won praise from Charles Macready, with whom she acted Fleance; from Charles Kemble, who saw her play Arthur in *King John*; and from Charles Dillon, manager of the Lyceum Theatre, London, who in September 1856 brought her to London to act Henri in *Belphegor* by Charles Webb, at the Lyceum. In that programme she also appeared as Perdita in William Brough's extravaganza of that name. Thus began her brilliant career in burlesque: at the Haymarket Theatre under John Baldwin Buckstone, at the Adelphi Theatre under Benjamin Nottingham Webster, and at the old Strand Theatre under Mrs. Ada Swanborough. As Pippo (one of her many boy-parts) in H. J. Byron's *The Maid and the Magpie* she won high praise from Charles Dickens; and there is much contemporary evidence of her great ability and charm.

Marie Wilton's ambition, however, was to play comedy; and in order to be free to do so she borrowed in January 1865 £1,000 from her sister Emma's husband, Francis Drake, took the rather disreputable little Queen's Theatre in Tottenham Street, did it up very prettily, obtained permission to name it the Prince of Wales's Theatre, and on 15 April 1865 opened it in partnership with H. J. Byron. The first programme consisted chiefly of burlesque. In June they produced a new comedy by Byron, *War to the Knife*, and in November Marie Wilton took a bold step in staging *Society* by T. W. Robertson. The acceptance of this comedy and the realism and daintiness of its mounting began a new era in English theatrical art, the chief credit for which belongs to Marie Wilton. *Ours* was produced on 15 September 1866; and after the Christmas programme of that year burlesque was seen no more at the Prince of Wales's.

To the Robertson comedies Marie Wilton's roguish humour and fine technique were invaluable; she was equally good as a well-bred girl, like her favourite Naomi Tighe in *School*, and as a girl of the people, such as Polly Eccles in *Caste* or Nan in Buckstone's *Good for Nothing*; while as Lady Teazle, as Jenny Northcott, first young and then middle-aged, in *Sweethearts*, and as Peg Woffington in *Masks and Faces*, she proved herself an actress of genius in more than one type of comedy. The descriptions of her acting contributed by Sir A. W. Pinero and Sir J. Forbes-Robertson to Sir

Squire Bancroft's book, *Empty Chairs*, show wherein her talent consisted. But, as the theatre prospered her acting was more and more sacrificed to its success and to the claims of social life. Her appearances became fewer, and her parts such as she was obliged to 'write up' in order to make them effective.

In private life Lady Bancroft was scarcely less amusing than on the stage, and her warm heart and merry nature won her a host of friends in all classes of society. Soon after her retirement in 1885 she was received into the Roman Catholic Church; and she occupied some of her long leisure in writing three plays and a novel. She died at Folkestone 22 May 1921.

A portrait of Lady Bancroft by T. Jones Barker is in the National Portrait Gallery. A bust by Count Gleichen is in the Garrick Club.

[*The Times*, 14 December 1867, 23 May 1921, and 20 April 1926; *Mr. and Mrs. Bancroft on and off the Stage: Written by themselves*, 1888; revised and brought down to 1909 as *The Bancrofts: Recollections of Sixty Years*, 1909; Squire Bancroft, *Empty Chairs*, 1925; W. D. Adams, *Dictionary of the Drama*, 1904; *Who's Who in the Theatre*, 1912; personal knowledge.]

H. H. CHILD

*published 1937*

## BARRIE Sir James Matthew

(1860–1937)

*Baronet*

Playwright and novelist, was born at Kirriemuir, Forfarshire, 9 May 1860, the ninth child and third youngest son of David Barrie, hand-loom weaver, of Kirriemuir, by his wife, Margaret, daughter of Alexander Ogilvy, stonemason. He was educated first at Glasgow Academy, where his brother Alexander was a teacher, and, from 1873, when Alexander was appointed inspector of schools of the district, at Dumfries Academy. He matriculated at Edinburgh University in 1878, and graduated M.A. in 1882. From his boyhood he had determined to write, and in January 1883 he was appointed leader-writer and sub-editor on the *Nottingham Journal*. His articles were thorough and complete within the required length and he had enough spare time for sketches and stories which he dispatched at a venture. Some, in which Kirriemuir was disguised as 'Thrums', were published anonymously in the *St. James's Gazette*, of which Frederick Greenwood was editor.

Against Greenwood's advice Barrie moved to London in March 1885 and again lived without struggling. He wrote for many magazines and now (Sir) W. Robertson Nicoll began his staunch support of his brother Scot by publishing serially (1887–1888) over the signature of 'Gavin Ogilvy' in the *British Weekly* Barrie's 'When A Man's Single, A Tale of Literary Life'. Barrie published his first book, *Better Dead*, in November 1887 at his own expense. It was an immature joke, cost one shilling, but almost paid its expenses. The years 1888 and 1889 were memorable ones in the author's life. In 1888 Messrs. Hodder and Stoughton published *Auld Licht Idylls*, sketches of Thrums, and *When A Man's Single* under Barrie's own signature. 'Gavin Ogilvy' was expiring. He died in December after signing his name to *An Edinburgh Eleven*, a skit on his professors, published by Nicoll in paper covers as a Christmas extra to the *British Weekly*. In 1889 Hodder and Stoughton published *A Window in Thrums*, a companion volume of Scottish episodes, and Donald Macleod accepted 'The Little Minister' for serial publication in *Good Words*. In 1890 *My Lady Nicotine* was published. It aroused comment because of its pleasant humour and a growing curiosity to know what, if any, brand of smoking mixture was disguised as Arcadia.

In 1891 Barrie's bent towards the stage began to unfold. In April a play by himself and Henry Brereton Marriott Watson, *Richard Savage*, was produced at a matinée. In May *Ibsen's Ghost* was put on as a front piece by J. L. Toole at the suggestion of (Sir) Henry Irving, and in July the *British Weekly* brought out a sixteen-page illustrated supplement, *J. M. Barrie, a Literary and Biographical Portrait*. It was early, perhaps, for so recently fledged an author to achieve a recognition from the press so noticeable. At the year's end, Toole paid £200 for a three-act farce, *Walker, London*, which ran for 511 consecutive performances from 25 February 1892. But more profitable was Barrie's first novel, *The Little Minister*. Its publication in book form in October 1891 was secured for Messrs. Cassell by (Sir) T. W. Reid, who, always alert to fresh talent, had attached Barrie to the staff of his new weekly paper the *Speaker* with (Sir) Arthur Thomas Quiller-Couch, H. W. Massingham and Augustine Birrell. *The Little Minister* was an instantaneous success.

But Barrie was looking to the stage as a means of expression. He collaborated with (Sir) A. Conan Doyle in a libretto for Richard D'Oyly Carte's opera company at the Savoy Theatre, *Jane Annie; or, The Good Conduct Prize* (May 1893), without success; and, commissioned by Irving, he completed *The Professor's Love Story* in the autumn of 1892. Irving was not satisfied and the play went the round of West End managers. The American rights were secured by Edward Smith Willard for £50 and he played in it in the United States with marked success. Under new arrangements, for Barrie now had Arthur Addison Bright as his agent, Willard produced *The Professor's Love Story* at the Comedy Theatre, London, in June 1894 and transferred it to the Garrick Theatre. It had a combined run of 144 performances.

In that year (1894) Barrie married Mary, daughter of George Ansell, a licensed victualler in Bayswater. She was a young actress who had played Nanny O'Brien in *Walker, London*. After a honeymoon in Switzerland they settled in 1895 in Gloucester Road, South Kensington, where they remained for seven years. There were no children of the marriage.

Meanwhile Barrie was working upon a tribute to his mother, *Margaret Ogilvy* (1896), written with a frankness of affection from which a good many authors would have shied and which took and held the favour of his more tender admirers; and upon two novels of Scottish life, *Sentimental Tommy* (1896) and its sequel, *Tommy and Grizel* (1900). The two books make an odd story and contain an analysis of a tortured literary mind and the tragical consequences to which it might lead, with a glimpse, by the way, of the Peter Pan who was to be. A fanciful description of a Scottish boy, Tommy, in a slum of south London, his mother's renunciation of Aaron Latta, the coward to whom she had been betrothed, and her flight from Thrums to London with Sandys, her braggart husband, her struggle to bring up her two children, Tommy and Elspeth, Tommy's inventions and stories of a Scottish village which he had never seen, and the rescue of himself and Elspeth by Latta on their mother's death are the bare bones of the first book. But it is in the analysis of the boy dramatizing himself and in his invented stories of the unknown but wonderful small town in which the interest lies. From London the two children are transplanted to Thrums, where Tommy becomes the leader of the village boyhood, always playing a part, now Elspeth's protector, now the champion of Griselda, the Painted Lady's daughter, now Charles Stuart on the run in the heather, now the antagonist of Cathro the schoolmaster, but sometimes with a laugh as he catches a glimpse of what he really is and contrasts it with the heroic figure which he cannot but make himself out to be. *Tommy and Grizel* carries on the account. These were the last novels which Barrie wrote. *The Little White Bird* (1902), *Peter Pan in Kensington Gardens* (1906), and *Peter and Wendy* (1911) are all variations upon the theme of Peter Pan.

At this time Charles Frohman, the American impresario, was seeking a play which would give an opportunity to Maude Adams, a young actress in whom he had great faith. A dramatized version by Barrie of *The Little Minister* followed the book too closely to appeal to Frohman; but Barrie changed the character and origin of the heroine, and *The Little Minister* appeared successfully at Washington in September 1897. Mr. Cyril Maude and Frederick Harrison produced it at the Haymarket Theatre (November 1897) with Maude as the Little Minister and Winifred Emery, his wife, as Lady Babbie. It ran for a year and Barrie acknowledged afterwards that between England and America this play brought him £80,000.

A cricket-match arranged by Barrie at Shere in 1887 with players who mostly had played little cricket before included Joseph Thomson, the explorer of Morocco. He invented for the team the name of Allahakbarrie. For four or five summers the Allahakbarries played not too strenuous cricket at Broadway, Shere, and other places. Later, county cricketers and really fast bowlers were admitted, two-day matches were played, and the team foundered. The summer months were spent at Black Lake Cottage, a small house opposite to Moor Park by Farnham which Barrie, in 1900, had given to his wife, and, cricketing being over, Barrie gave himself to the writing of plays and the building up, among the pine-trees above the garden in company with the five little boys of Arthur Llewelyn Davies, of the story of *Peter Pan*. But other work was completed first. *The Wedding Guest*, produced by Arthur Bourchier at the Garrick Theatre in September 1900, was hardly a success and certainly not a failure. It ran for 100 performances—a play in the fashionable mould, a problem play, as the saying went. An artist marries the daughter of the great house in the great house and a witness is brought in from outside according to Scottish custom, a woman who a year ago was the mistress of the artist. She now carries a baby. The disclosure, the intolerant ignorance of the girl-wife, the gradual compromise by which the crisis is smoothed over are all in the fashion of the day. The wise old spinster is the kindly Felice of *The Little Minister* and a family relationship exists between the Earl of Rintoul and Mr. Fairbairn, but there is more of Barrie in *Sentimental Tommy* than in either of these plays.

*Quality Street* was first performed at Toledo, Ohio, in October 1901 and was transferred to the Knickerbocker Theater, New York, with Maude Adams as Phoebe Throssel. Barrie was now established as a successful dramatist in both England and America, and *Quality Street*, a sentimental comedy set in a small English town during Napoleonic days, had an equal success in both countries. In London at the Vaudeville Theatre (September 1902) Phoebe Throssel was played by Miss Ellaline Terriss and Valentine Brown, the dashing young doctor, by her husband, (Sir) Seymour Hicks. The comedy was not for everyone. There were playgoers who felt moments of embarrassment at the more cloying passages, but the play with its twists of plot and humour kept the stage for 459 performances, was revived at the Haymarket Theatre in August 1921, and, translated into German as *Qualität Strasse*, ran for months in Berlin during the war of 1914–1918.

Three months before *Quality Street* was produced in London, Barrie moved to a small regency house, Leinster Corner, facing the Bayswater Road, with a stable behind which he turned into a study. Across the road were Kensington Gardens to which Barrie obtained a much-treasured private key from the first commissioner of Works. There, with Luath, his Newfoundland, almost as big as himself, he might be seen on any day dreaming over *Peter Pan.*

A more ambitious play, *The Admirable Crichton,* was presented by Frohman in November 1902 at the Duke of York's Theatre. Here was that valuable touch of acidity which keeps plays alive. It is the story of a radical peer with a tory soul, the Earl of Loam, who believes at 5 o'clock once a month in the equality of the classes, and a butler, Crichton, who believes that rank is the order of nature. The first act shows Lord Loam and his daughters having tea in the drawing-room with their servants. In the second act they have been wrecked upon a deserted Pacific island and nature begins to put Crichton, the ingenious butler, in his rightful place. In the third act he is king of the island. The house which he has built is lit with electricity, a chain of bonfires round the coast awaits only the movement of a switch to burst into flames, and the daughters, great hunters and good cooks, with the invaluable Cockney Tweeny, all aspire to Crichton's hand. Crichton's choice is Lady Mary, the eldest daughter, but as he is on the point of announcing his choice a ship is seen on the horizon and its hooter is heard. Crichton is faced with a problem: do nothing, and the ship will go: reply, and once more he is a butler. With a pull of the lever he sets the bonfires burning, and as the officers of the rescue ship enter the house he replies to a timid word from Lady Mary, 'Milady'. In the fourth act the old order has uncomfortably returned. A book has been written about the family experiences in which Crichton is hardly mentioned. He gives notice of his intention to marry Tweeny and take a public-house, 'The Case Is Altered'. After the war of 1914–1918, Barrie changed the last act to the play's disadvantage by leaving Crichton's fate uncertain. A pity, for the reader may be quite sure that within two years 'The Case Is Altered' would have become a Grand Hotel. No doubt both Lord Loam and Crichton are larger than life, just as are so many of the characters of Dickens, but it does not follow, any more than in the case of Dickens's characters, that they are untrue. This play, with an admirable cast—(Dame) Irene Vanbrugh, (Sir) Gerald du Maurier, Henry Brodribb Irving, and Henry Kemble—ran for 328 performances and was followed, in September 1903, by an odd comedy, *Little Mary.* The crêche boxes of children (to reappear, children and all, in *A Kiss For Cinderella*) at the back of the parlour of a chemist's shop, and the dialogue between the twelve-year-old granddaughter of the chemist and the Earl of Carlton open the play in the true Barrie fashion. It owed its success to some excellent scenes between the Earl of Carlton and his son Cecil and the alacrity with which the public took up the phrase 'Little Mary' as a euphemism for 'stomach'.

*Peter Pan* had grown to full stature in the pinewoods behind Black Lake Cottage and now sought for his shadow in the nursery of the Darlings at the Duke of York's Theatre on 27 December 1904. Nana, the dog-nurse, Tinker Bell, Wendy, the Never Never Land, the kindly Red Indians, the furious pirates, Smee, Starkey, with Captain Hook at their head, and, above all, the crocodile with the eight-day clock ticking away inside of him are household words to-day, but in 1904 no one but Barrie had any faith in them. (Sir) H. Beerbohm Tree thought that Barrie had gone mad. Frohman wanted to defer the production. Barrie himself from the beginning was confident that *Peter Pan* would not only attract but would be produced at Christmas-time year after year. For a fortnight it looked as if Tree and Frohman were going to be justified. Then children of all ages flocked to the play until it closed on 1 April 1905, to be revived at nearly every Christmas season afterwards. The lagoon scene was added for the first revival. It explains why the Red Indians protected the children from the pirates. Was not Tiger Lily rescued by Peter Pan at the risk of his life? 'To die', he said with a shaking voice, 'will be an awfully big adventure.' The line is to be remembered if only because it was quoted by Barrie's great friend Frohman as he plunged to his death in the *Lusitania*.

Four days after *Peter Pan* was shelved for the summer *Alice-Sit-by-the-Fire* was produced at the same theatre. It was written for Ellen Terry, but the theme had little life in it and she never felt easy in her part. Nevertheless, it ran for 115 performances, a satire upon the social play of the times which has not been revived. The year 1906 was the cause of another satire still less successful. A friend of Barrie was standing for the liberal party in the heart of the tariff reform area and won the seat. Barrie was present at the final meetings and on his return to London wrote with considerable enjoyment *Josephine*. It is a political burlesque and Barrie admitted that he had been so careful to baffle the censor, who banned political plays, that he had made it quite unintelligible to any audience. Frederick Harrison of the Haymarket Theatre nibbled at it and refrained. Gerald du Maurier, cast for Josephine, refused to act the part. Frohman the faithful came to the rescue and with two one-act plays put on the first triple bill at the Comedy Theatre in April. It failed completely and all three plays have ceased to exist in any form.

None the less, the idea of a play with a political environment clung, and two words spoken by his friend from a balcony out of an expiring throat after his election were an inspiration. *What Every Woman Knows* opens with a flawless first act. John Shand, the young ticket-collector-student, enters into a contract with the father, Alick Wylie, to marry Maggie, sister of David and James Wylie, the girl without charm, in five years if called upon to do so, in return for £300. In the second act Shand is returned to parliament. He has the support of two aristocratic friends, the Comtesse de la Brière and her niece, Lady Sybil Tenterden (originally Lazenby). Maggie proposes to cancel their contract. This he declines to do. In the third act he is married but is caught by Maggie in an avowal of passion to Lady Sybil. Maggie determines to fight for her man. Her method is to send him for a holiday to the country house of the Comtesse de la Brière where Lady Sybil is staying. In the fourth act the cards have been stacked in favour of Maggie. Lady Sybil and John Shand thrown together are unutterably bored. The Cabinet minister, responsible for a speech to be made by Shand at a big political rally, finds the draft shown to him unworthy of the occasion: and then 'all's well' is reached by the emergence of Maggie with a new draft containing the quips which had made Shand famous, the delight of the Cabinet minister, and the reconciliation of husband and wife. The play was one of Barrie's greatest successes in London. It opened in September 1908 at the Duke of York's Theatre.

Barrie's enthusiasm for the stage then dwindled for a time. In October 1909 he obtained a divorce from his wife and in November moved to a flat in Adelphi Terrace overlooking the river. In March 1910 he was responsible for a triple bill at the Duke of York's Theatre consisting of his own *Old Friends* and *The Twelve-Pound Look*, and *The Sentimentalists* by George Meredith. Meredith's one-act play failed and was replaced by Barrie's *A Slice of Life*. Repertory seasons were in the air and with this triple bill *Justice* by John Galsworthy, *The Madras House* by Harley G. Granville-Barker, and *Misalliance* by Mr. Bernard Shaw were alternatively staged. The season was unsuccessful. Again there was an interval.

In May 1912 occurred something which, on account of its astuteness, no survey of Barrie's life can disregard. There appeared by the water in Kensington Gardens a bronze statue of Peter Pan blowing his pipes. There was no unveiling ceremony. Barrie had thought of it, had commissioned Sir George Frampton to make it, had paid for it, and had arranged with the first commissioner of Works to have it privately erected. A question was asked about it in parliament when it was discovered; but the statue was so appropriate and so clearly an embellishment that authority did not disturb it.

In the autumn of 1912 came another triple bill at the Duke of York's Theatre of which Barrie's play *Rosalind* alone found favour. Next year (1913) the King created him a baronet, and in the autumn he finished at last a play in three acts, *The Adored One, A Legend of the Old Bailey*. It treated a trial for murder as a lark. Some, like Sir John Hare who played the judge, had doubts of its success, but if Barrie could get away with *Little Mary*, why not with *The Adored One*? Mrs. Patrick Campbell, a tower of strength, was the murderess, but even during the first act the author felt the temperature of the house falling and knew that the play had failed. It was altered in vain and languished for ten weeks from 4 September 1913, before it died. All that remains of it now is a one-act play, *Seven Women*. On the outbreak of war in 1914, Barrie's help was called upon and given. For special charity performances he wrote one-act plays of which many have disappeared for ever. In 1915 soldiers returning for forty-eight hours' leave from the squalor of the trenches wanted music, gaiety, bright lights, faces, and frocks—revues, not Ibsen. Barrie wrote *Rosy Rapture, The Pride of the Beauty Chorus*. Gaby Deslys, a French actress, famous for her acrobatic dancing, played Rosy, but the revue, which included some cinematography, wobbled. Frohman in New York was sent for to pull it together, but he went down in the *Lusitania* and once more a Barrie play had a short run.

In 1916, however, he took new life with Gerald du Maurier. *A Kiss For Cinderella*, produced at Wyndham's Theatre in March, ran to full houses for 156 performances and was revived that Christmas at the Kingsway Theatre. The babies in boxes had crept in from *Little Mary* and the 'slavey' from *Alice-Sit-by-the-Fire*, but du Maurier, as Robert the policeman one moment and Prince Charming of the pantomime the next, was new, and Cinderella's dream of a state ball at Buckingham Palace was as brilliantly funny a scene as its author ever wrote.

For a good many years Barrie had had in his mind the theme that if people had a second chance they would in their new environment make the same mistakes which they had made before. The idea was taken out and dusted, as it were, and put back again. But in the spring of 1917 he set to work upon it and in October *Dear Brutus* was produced—again by du Maurier—at Wyndham's Theatre. Barrie had added the poetry of a midsummer night, the mystery of a magic wood, and Lob from old English folk-lore as a host. In the first act the drawing-room curtains are torn aside to reveal the magic wood and one by one the ill-assorted guests wander out through the French windows into their other life. In the third act they gradually come to themselves, except in the case of Dearth, the artist, to whom must be attributed the triumph of the play. In the first act his wife, Alice, who was his model, and Dearth, who drinks, are estranged. During the imaginary other life he is shown painting with a daughter to keep him company and the long scene between these two charmed everyone who saw it. In the last act Dearth and his wife are reconciled and, in a subtle piece of theatre, are seen crossing the window arm in arm with the dream child following them. The play ran for 365 performances.

*Mary Rose*, with a fantastic sub-title, *The Island That Wants To Be Visited*, followed at the Haymarket Theatre in April 1920. It is a romantic theme with embarrassing moments for those too fastidious for the emotional frankness with which Barrie could always write but never speak, some admirably drawn characters, and one or two vital scenes which brought people again and again to the theatre: that scene, for instance, where the elderly husband and wife admit to each other that, although they had believed themselves heart-broken, happiness would keep breaking through.

During the past ten years Barrie had written a great number of one-act plays, many of which, like *The Twelve-Pound Look* (1910), *The Old Lady Shows Her Medals* (1917), and *Shall We Join the Ladies?*, were masterpieces of construction. *Shall We Join the Ladies?* was first performed with a star cast at the opening of the new theatre of the Dramatic Academy (May 1921). A simpleton, as his twelve guests think, announces that his brother has been murdered and that the murderer is among his guests. One after another they fall into traps which the simpleton has laid for them, and at the end it seems that any one of them might be guilty. Possibly the author himself was no more aware which one than the audience.

There remains of his plays *The Boy David*, a dramatization of the biblical story. It opened in London in December 1936 in a theatre probably too large (His Majesty's), was long enough delayed to outlive expectation, and was too thin in characterization. It ran for only 55 performances, a pity, since it was the last work which Barrie did.

In this tale of rare failure and much achievement, Barrie only thrice owed his inspiration to the circumstances of the day: *Josephine*, the political skit, *The Wedding Guest*, the problem play, and *The Well-Remembered Voice* (1918), the war hunger for lost sons. In two other one-act plays, *The Old Lady Shows Her Medals* and *The New Word* (1915), he was merely using the war as a background for his own ideas. Few authors have been more individual.

Barrie died in London 19 June 1937. He received honorary degrees from the universities of St. Andrews (1898), Edinburgh (1909), Oxford (1926), and Cambridge (1930); was elected lord rector of St. Andrews University in 1919 and chancellor of Edinburgh University in 1930; and was appointed to the Order of Merit in 1922.

There is a drawing of Barrie, by W. T. Monnington, which has been placed in the National Portrait Gallery.

[Denis Mackail, *The Story of J.M.B.*, 1941; *The Plays of J. M. Barrie*, edited by A. E. Wilson, 1942; personal knowledge.]

A. E. W. Mason

*published 1949*

## BAYLIS Lilian Mary

(1874–1937)

Theatrical manager, was born in London 9 May 1874, the eldest daughter of Edward William Baylis, singer, by his wife, Elizabeth Cons, singer and pianist. She was educated at home and trained at an early age as a violinist under J. T. Carrodus, appearing in public when only seven years old at the entertainments organized by her aunt Emma Cons in the 'Royal Victoria Coffee Music Hall', as it was then called. Miss Cons had secured a lease of the theatre in Lambeth originally (1818) called the Royal Cobourg Theatre and renamed (1833) the Victoria Theatre, familiarly known as the 'Old Vic': she reopened it as the Royal Victoria Coffee Music Hall on 27 December 1880. Miss Cons, a social worker closely associated with Charles Kingsley, John Ruskin, and Octavia Hill, seems to have been led to take this step by John Hollingshead, the famous manager of the Gaiety Theatre: their idea was to open a popular music-hall for the working classes in which no alcoholic liquor should be obtainable. In 1890 the Baylis family emigrated to South Africa, where they toured the country giving musical entertainments under great difficulties of transport. Lilian Baylis eventually settled in Johannesburg, where she taught music and trained a ladies' orchestra; but in 1898 Miss Cons persuaded her niece to return to England to assist her in the management of the Royal Victoria Hall. Hitherto the entertainments had consisted of oratorio and ballad concerts interspersed with variety and scientific lectures, as well as temperance meetings. Plays and operas could not be given under the lord chamberlain's regulations, but in the case of opera these were evaded by presenting selections from operas with *tableaux vivants* in costume. Lilian Baylis became acting manager in 1898 and in 1899 engaged Charles Corri as musical director. This partnership lasted for over thirty years, during which time the musical activities of the hall were considerably developed, although symphony concerts were financially unsuccessful. Miss Baylis was one of the first to seize on the cinematograph as a popular entertainment, especially for children, but dropped it after a few years when it became a general commercial enterprise which presented films which she considered unsuitable for the young.

Miss Cons died in 1912 and Lilian Baylis became sole manager of the hall. Miss Cons's interests had been primarily social and religious; her niece shared these interests but was now free to raise the whole artistic standard of her theatre, which she advertised as 'The People's Opera House'. William Poel, who had been manager from 1881 to 1883, had offered to bring his own dramatic company in 1906, but this offer had had to be refused owing to the lord chamberlain's regulations; an offer of Shakespeare recitals in costume made by Mr. George Owen and Mr. William Bridges-Adams in 1911 came to nothing. After 1912 the restrictions seem to have been lifted; a few plays of a popular type were performed, but with little success. In April 1914 Miss Rosina Filippi presented Shakespeare for the first time, and also *The School for Scandal*. She had wished to perform Mr. Bernard Shaw's *Candida*, but this play was abandoned, probably because no suitable actress was available for the name part.

The development of the Old Vic as the 'home of Shakespeare' was first made possible by the war of 1914–1918, which rendered all theatrical enterprise so precarious that actors of distinction were glad to join a Shakespeare company at the Old Vic at very modest salaries for the sake of a secure engagement. Between 1914 and 1923 all the plays of Shakespeare were performed there under various producers; Miss Baylis took no part in production but limited herself to general management. By the end of the war the Old Vic had become one of London's leading theatres, drawing audiences from all parts of the capital, and Miss Baylis began to be aware that she was now doing what should have been the work of a national theatre. Sadler's Wells Theatre in Islington was acquired and rebuilt, mainly through the energy of (Sir) Reginald Rowe, and reopened in 1931 as an 'Old Vic' for north London; after a short time it was found more practicable to confine performances there to opera and ballet, drama being given at the Old Vic. Miss Baylis found herself obliged to delegate much of the management to others, but controlled the two theatres to the end of her life. She died at Stockwell 25 November 1937.

Lilian Baylis's achievement was the creation of a true people's theatre and opera-house out of what had begun as a philanthropic temperance institution. She had the reputation of being a hard woman, because she was always struggling with inadequate resources: she herself admitted that she was ill-educated, but she had a sure instinct for finding the right collaborators. She was devoutly religious, full of broad-minded humanity, and she kept her theatres going mainly by the intense personal affection and idealism which she inspired in all who worked with her.

Miss Baylis was appointed C.H. in 1929 and received honorary degrees from the universities of Oxford (1924) and Birmingham (1934).

A chalk drawing of Miss Baylis, by (Sir) William Rothenstein (1922), and an oil painting, by Ethel Gabain, are at Sadler's Wells Theatre. A third portrait by Charles E. Butler, hangs in the Old Vic Theatre.

[*The Times*, 26, 29, and 30 November 1937; Sybil and Russell Thorndike, *Lilian Baylis*, 1938; Lilian Baylis and Cicely Hamilton, *The Old Vic*, 1926; E. C. Harcourt

Williams, *Four Years at the Old Vic, 1929–1933*, 1935; *Vic-Wells. The Work of Lilian Baylis*, edited by E. G. Harcourt Williams, 1938; E. J. Dent, *A Theatre for Everybody*, 1945; Norman Marshall, *The Other Theatre*, 1947; *Who's Who in the Theatre*, 1936.]

EDWARD J. DENT

*published 1949*

## BEAUMONT Hughes Griffiths

(1908–1973)

Theatrical manager, was born 27 March 1908 in Hampstead, London, the only son of Mary Frances Morgan (née Brewer) and a Mr Beaumont with whom she departed from London to Cardiff after separating from her first husband, Morgan Morgan, barrister-at-law.

Throughout his life, 'Hugh' Beaumont preserved a passion for anonymity, and little is known of his childhood apart from an early friendship with Ivor Novello (a close neighbour) and his precocious appointment, at the age of sixteen, as assistant manager of the Prince of Wales Theatre, Cardiff. Still in his adolescence, he moved on to a series of other minor managerial jobs before joining the firm of Moss Empires as assistant to H. M. (Harry) Tennent, administrator of Drury Lane, with whom, in 1936, he founded the producing management of H. M. Tennent Ltd. Neither at that time, nor after Tennent's death in 1941, was anything done to publicize the name of Beaumont, but it was at his persuasion that the firm came into existence and through his gifts that it sustained its long supremacy in the West End.

Beaumont and Tennent went into business with a £10,000 float from a stockbroking member of the Cripps family. That was a reasonable sum in the days when a West End play could be presented at the average cost of £1,000. However, the partners lost much of their starting capital on a series of flops before they struck lucky with the 1937 production of Gerald Savory's *George and Margaret* which ran for 799 performances at Wyndham's. This was followed by Dodie Smith's *Dear Octopus* and other long-running shows which established Tennents as a highly profitable concern that magnetized backers like a triple-crown Derby winner.

It was during these first years that Beaumont struck up a lifelong and professionally fertile friendship with (Sir) John Gielgud. All Beaumont's early experience had been on the business side. He was, Gielgud said, 'a modern man with no pretensions to education at all and no knowledge except what he had learnt as he became successful'. Throughout his career, his main objective was to have as many productions as possible playing in London. What those productions were, however, reflected a taste acquired partly from Gielgud, with whom he broke into classical territory with a 1939 *Hamlet*, and continued with the famous wartime seasons at the Phoenix and the Haymarket, and again at the Phoenix and the Lyric, Hammersmith, during the 1950s. He also developed a love for superbly dressed, resplendently cast high comedy for which the name of Tennents became a byword.

What won Beaumont such allies as Gielgud and (Sir) Noël Coward in the first place was an array of personal and managerial skills which he put unreservedly at their disposal. He saw it as his mission to produce the best artists under the best possible conditions: and, having decided who the best were, he looked faithfully after their interests with an invincible blend of paternal care, oriental business acumen, and courteously absolute authority. 'The iron fist', (Sir) Tyrone Guthrie said of him, 'was wrapped in fifteen pastel-shaded velvet gloves.' Those who worked with him, actors and playwrights alike, had total faith in his artistic judgement. His theatre followed the West End star system, but whereas the usual practice was for a star to appear with a supporting company, stars appeared in constellations on the Tennents stage, persuaded by Beaumont to exchange solitary glory for the satisfaction of working with their equals.

Tennents never owned theatres. They had a long-standing tenancy at the Queen's and the Globe, and periodically occupied the Haymarket and theatres of the Albery group. During the war their profits were subject to the 40 per cent entertainments tax from which Beaumont sought exemption by forming a non-profit-making subsidiary—Tennent Productions—for the presentation of classical work. By the end of the war he had thus amassed a surplus of £70,000 with which, in 1946, he also took over the Lyric, Hammersmith, for classical seasons and West End try-outs by the newly created Company of Four.

The immediate post-war years marked the zenith of Tennents' prestige: a gathering of major stars and new names (including Christopher Fry and Peter Brook) mobilized in a lavish firework display exactly matching the anti-austerity mood of the time. However, there were also growing murmurs against Tennents' non-profit-making status, which reached a head with the officially 'educational' première of *A Streetcar Named Desire* (1949), at which the Arts Council withdrew its support and the Inland Revenue promptly converted the charitable surplus into unpaid tax, and put in a large demand which Beaumont unsuccessfully contested in the House of Lords.

This defeat did nothing to shake the firm's theatrical fortunes or diminish Beaumont's power (in Guthrie's words) as the man, more than any other, who could 'make or break the career of almost any worker in the British professional theatre'.

What did bring the firm into decline was the explosion of new writing that began from the Royal Court theatre in 1956, and the growth of subsidized theatre at the expense of the commercial sector. Beaumont's West End flourished like a traditional grocery shop, selling reliable brands to regular customers. The fashions of 1956 consigned these brands to the dustbin; though Beaumont struggled to replace them with such newcomers as Robert Bolt and Peter Shaffer. Nor was there any effective way of fighting subsidized competition by a manager who lived by the ethic that the theatre should stand on its own feet.

During his twenty years of supremacy, Beaumont did more to raise the standard of the London theatre than any other manager, past or present. The new stage that overwhelmed him was one that he had done much to create. A homosexual, he had no family outside the theatre which was his business, his pleasure, and his life. He died in London 22 March 1973.

[*The Times*, 23, 28, and 29 March 1973; *Spectator*, 31 March 1973; private information.]

IRVING WARDLE

*published 1986*

## BENSON Sir Francis Robert ('Frank') (1858–1939)

Actor-manager, was born at Tunbridge Wells 4 November 1858, the third son and fourth child of William Benson, barrister, of Alresford, Hampshire, by his wife, Elizabeth Soulsby, daughter of Thomas Smith, of Colebrooke Park, Tonbridge. He was educated at Winchester and New College, Oxford, but gained no academic honours. He became famous at the university as an all-round athlete, devoting himself to football, cricket, rowing, and running, his greatest achievement being the winning of the three-mile race against Cambridge.

Always attracted to the theatre, Benson became one of the leaders of the movement which led in 1884 to the foundation of the Oxford University Dramatic Society. In the hall of Balliol College, in June 1880, he took part in a performance of the *Agamemnon* of Aeschylus, in which he played the part of Clytemnestra with considerable success. This performance was repeated at the St. George's Hall, London, in September of the same year, and his success turned Benson's thoughts to the adoption of the stage as his profession. In July 1881 he took the Imperial Theatre, London, for a single performance of *Romeo and Juliet*, and appeared as Romeo. He then studied voice production under Emil Bencke and Hermann Vezin, and at the invitation of Ellen Terry, who had witnessed his performance of Clytemnestra, he was invited in July 1882 to take part in a private Shakespearian reading of *Much Ado About Nothing*, at the house of Sir Theodore Martin, appearing as Don Pedro, with (Sir) Henry Irving as Benedick and Lady Martin (Helen Faucit) as Beatrice.

Benson made his first appearance on the professional stage at the Lyceum Theatre in September 1882, when he played Paris in Irving's production of *Romeo and Juliet*, with Ellen Terry as Juliet. On her advice, he then joined the Shakespearian company of Miss Alleyn and Charles Bernard, in order to gain experience, and a few months later he was a member of a company under the management of Walter Bentley, a well-known Shakespearian actor. This manager became involved in financial difficulties, and Benson, with monetary aid from his father, promptly acquired the company. He opened under his own management in a hall at Airdrie, Lanarkshire, in May 1883, with *The Corsican Brothers* and *Cramond Brig*, and in this modest way the famous Benson repertory company came into being.

It was not long before Benson had established a sound reputation and the Benson company became an important factor in the provincial theatre. He gathered together a very capable band of actors, and by 1886 his company was of sufficient importance to be invited to provide the Shakespearian festival at the Memorial Theatre, Stratford-on-Avon, where he appeared for the first time, in April of that year, playing Richard III. During the next thirty-three years he provided the plays for twenty-eight spring festivals and some half-dozen summer festivals at the theatre, in the course of which period he presented all Shakespeare's plays except *Titus Andronicus* and *Troilus and Cressida*. In addition he presented many old comedies and one or two modern plays. In recognition of his services to Stratford-on-Avon, Benson received the freedom of the borough in 1910, an honour only once previously conferred on an actor, namely, David Garrick, in 1769. He appeared as director of the Stratford festival for the last time in 1919, and at the birthday celebrations that year he was presented with a handsome gift by Stratfordonians and festival patrons.

Benson's first London season was given at the Globe Theatre, where, in December 1889, he opened with a revival of *A Midsummer Night's Dream*, which was performed 110 times, a record at that date. Revivals of *The*

*Taming of the Shrew, Hamlet,* and *Othello* were also presented. His next London season, the most important of his eight London ventures, began at the Lyceum Theatre in February 1900, with a revival of *Henry the Fifth*. Subsequent seasons were given at the Comedy (1901), Adelphi (1905), St. James's (1910), Shaftesbury (1914), Court (1915), and St. Martin's (1920) theatres. At the height of his success there were no fewer than three of his companies touring the country. In addition, he toured in Canada and the United States of America, in 1913–1914, and in South Africa, in 1921. During his Canadian tour Montreal University conferred upon him the honorary degree of LL.D.

At the Shakespeare tercentenary performance, given at Drury Lane Theatre on 2 May 1916, Benson appeared in the title-role of *Julius Caesar*, and at the conclusion of the performance was knighted by King George V, in the stage-box, the only occasion on which an actor had been knighted in a theatre. The ceremony was performed with a 'property' sword, no other being available.

Although he was nearing the age of sixty, from 1916 to 1918 Benson served in France as an ambulance-driver, and received the French croix de guerre. In June 1925, in the picture-gallery of the Stratford Memorial Theatre, Dame Ellen Terry unveiled the stained-glass windows to Old Bensonians, including one in memory of the ten players of the company who had fallen in the war.

Benson was never a great actor, and he was handicapped somewhat by defects of voice and gait. Richard II and Petruchio in *The Taming of the Shrew* were among his best performances. His Richard had much grace and dignity and his Petruchio was full of excellent touches. He also gave a notable performance as Caliban in *The Tempest*. Many of the numerous parts which he undertook, including Hamlet, Othello, Shylock, and Henry V, were quite uninspired. It was not his acting which made Benson great, nor his teaching. His genius lay in the opportunities which he afforded to the many capable young artists whom he gathered round him, many of whom achieved greater fame than Benson himself. His company became the nursery for the English stage. It is truly said of him that he gave the best years of his life to spreading the love of Shakespeare throughout the world. In his efforts he exhausted the whole of his considerable personal fortune, and in July 1933 he was granted a civil list pension of £100.

Benson made his last appearance in London in 1933; this was at the Winter Garden Theatre, as Dr. Caius in *The Merry Wives of Windsor*. He published his reminiscences, *My Memoirs* (1930), and a short work entitled *I Want to Go on the Stage* (1931). In July 1886 he married Gertrude Constance, daughter of Captain Morshead Fetherstonhaugh Samwell, of the Indian army, and had a son and a daughter. Lady Benson was a capable actress, and played leading parts in his company for many years. Their son was killed in action in France in 1916. Benson died in London 31 December 1939.

An early portrait of Benson, by Hugh Riviere, hangs in the picture gallery of the Shakespeare Memorial Theatre. Of a drawing of him as Mark Antony, by Will Ledbury, and of another by R. G. Eves (1927), the whereabouts are uncertain.

[*The Times*, 1 January 1940; *Who's Who in the Theatre*, 1939; Sir F. Benson, *My Memoirs*, 1930; Lady Benson, *Mainly Players*, 1926; personal knowledge.]

JOHN PARKER

*published 1949*

## BROWN Ivor John Carnegie

(1891–1974)

Journalist, author, theatre critic, and wordsmith, was born 25 April 1891 in Penang, Malaya, the younger of two sons of Dr William Carnegie Brown, of Aberdeen, and his first wife, Jean Carnegie. His father, a graduate of Aberdeen University and an expert in tropical diseases, had a practice in the Federated Malay States.

Ivor Brown was sent to England to be educated at Suffolk Hall preparatory school and then Cheltenham College. After a year's private tuition by a crammer, he headed the Balliol scholarship list, and took a double first in classical honour moderations (1911) and *literae humaniores* (1913). He passed sixth into the Civil Service, and was sent to the Home Office. His career lasted two days, still something of a Whitehall record. For his first job he was instructed to minute an application by Staffordshire policemen for an increased provision of water-closets. He wrote his comments and walked out, to earn his living as a free lance by writing about more interesting matters.

During the war he was a conscientious objector, and hotly engaged in progressive politics. He lectured for the Oxford tutorial classes committee; published two ephemeral books of political theory and three novels; and wrote iconoclastic articles for the *New Age*. His versatile, profuse, and very fast pen fitted him exceptionally for journalism so in 1919 he joined the London office of the *Manchester Guardian*. There he wrote everything from editorials to colour pieces about sport; but particularly he wrote about the theatre, which became the master passion of his life. He was dramatic critic for the *Saturday Review* from 1923 to 1930.

In 1916 he married Irene Gladys, the elder daughter of Bertha (Posener) and Carl Hentschel, a photo-engraver who made blocks for Fleet Street newspapers. She was a professional actress who became a successful director of plays. Her knowledge of the far side of the footlights enriched her husband's criticism. There were no children of the marriage.

In 1926 Brown was appointed Shute lecturer on the art of the theatre at Liverpool University. In 1929 he became theatre critic of the *Observer*, and for the next thirty years, through a period of change, experiment, and brilliance on the London stage, he was the most influential and perceptive voice in British dramatic criticism. In 1939 he was made professor of drama to the Royal Society of Literature. When the Council for the Encouragement of Music and the Arts (CEMA, later to become the Arts Council) was set up during World War II, Ivor Brown was the obvious choice for its director of drama (1940–2).

When J. L. Garvin retired from the editorship of the *Observer* in 1942, Brown was appointed to the post. He carried on as chief dramatic critic, and managed also to make time to write regular leading and feature articles, and, when the muse struck, elegant satiric verses. As editor Brown led the *Observer* with a light and liberal hand through the difficult wartime shortages of staff and newsprint. He put news on the front page; introduced new blood; broadened the paper's interests and changed its typography; and made it exceptionally well written.

But writing was the element in which he lived; so in 1948 he resigned to have less administrative work and more time for writing. He continued as dramatic critic until 1954, and carried on writing as naturally as breathing for the rest of his life.

Brown published more than seventy-five books, including novels, essays, biography, autobiography, criticism, coffee-table books, and even a light and not very good play. He was among the most prolific and versatile writers of his generation. As well as using the English language expertly, he was one of those logophiles, like F. G. and H. W. Fowler and Eric Partridge, thrown up regularly by the English, who are fascinated by the language itself. He became famous for his word books, agreeable rambles around correct usage and philology, enlivened by literary allusion, quotation, wit, and personal anecdote. He wrote thirteen in all, collecting words as other men collect porcelain. In the first, *A Word in Your Ear* (1942), he was observing how gargantuan journalese was ruining such good old words as 'epic', 'odyssey', and 'tragedy'. In *A Charm of Names* (1972) he explored the history of Christian or given names from Abigail to Zuleika, not forgetting Ivor. He was the most good-humoured of prescriptivists, but incorrigibly convinced that there exists such a thing as correct English, and that it is to be preferred to the other kind.

Shakespeare was another lifelong enthusiasm. Brown wrote a number of books about him full of amateur common sense and expert theatrical and linguistic wisdom. He was a very professional master of the English language and literature, happiest when writing, which he did very fast, chewing the end of his handkerchief on the rare occasions when he was stuck for a word or an idea.

He was a big, burly, shy man, with Aberdonian *gravitas*, who could suddenly spark with a flash of frivolity or frolic.

He was chairman of the British Drama League from 1954 to 1965, a fellow of the Royal Society of Literature, and an honorary LL D of St. Andrews and Aberdeen universities (1950). After the war he lectured much in Denmark, which conferred on him a knighthood of the Order of Dannebrog. In 1957 he was appointed CBE.

He died in London 22 April 1974.

[*The Times*, 23 April 1974; J. B. Priestley in *Observer*, 28 April 1974; Ivor Brown, *The Way of My World*, 1954.]

PHILIP HOWARD

*published* 1986

## BUCHANAN Walter John (Jack)

(1890–1957)

Actor and theatre manager, was born 2 April 1890 at Helensburgh, near Glasgow, the son of Walter John Buchanan, auctioneer, and his wife, Patricia Purves McWatt. Educated at Glasgow Academy, he spoke of becoming a barrister, but his heart was set on the stage from the first, and particularly he saw himself as a comedian, although he feared his height might militate against this ambition.

After a brief spell in the family business, Buchanan appeared first on the professional stage at the Edinburgh Empire in 1911, billed as 'Chump Buchanan, patter comedian', 'Chump' being a sobriquet from his schooldays. Northern provincial music-halls at this period were a tough training-ground for the stage aspirant, and in his later years of prosperity Buchanan would relate his hard experiences 'on the halls' when his efforts to entertain were vociferously rejected. But, in his own words, something personal came through at last when he obtained material which suited him.

On 7 September 1912 he made his first appearance in London, at the Apollo Theatre, in a comic opera called *The Grass Widows*, and during 1913 and 1914 he appeared and understudied in revues at the Empire Theatre, Leicester Square. Rejected by the army—at no time in his life was his health robust—during 1915 and 1916 he came into prominence playing the George Grossmith part on tour in *To-night's the Night*; and in 1917 he succeeded Jack Hulbert, acting, singing, and dancing in the revue *Bubbly* presented by André Charlot at the Comedy Theatre. Other wartime revues followed and Jack Buchanan soon established himself on the west-end light musical stage as a comedian of talent and promise.

In October 1921 he enhanced his reputation in another Charlot revue, *A to Z*, in which he played the lead, produced the sketches, and staged the musical numbers. In December 1922 he appeared for the first time under his own management in *Battling Butler* at the New Oxford Theatre, and at the end of the following year went to America, opening in New York at the Times Square Theatre (with Gertrude Lawrence and Beatrice Lillie) in *André Charlot's Revue of* 1924 in which he scored a great personal success. This was the first of many visits to New York, and he remained throughout his subsequent career as acceptable to audiences there as in Great Britain.

In May 1924 came *Toni* at the Shaftesbury Theatre, London, and thenceforth at regularly long intervals until 1943 he was to present, produce, and play the leading part in a succession of musical comedies, through all of which he sang and danced and joked his nonchalant way with a seemingly lazy but most accomplished grace. Everything he did on the stage bore the stamp of his personality and was done with an effect of consummate ease, yet without casualness. The hunched shoulders, the sidelong smile, the husky audible diseur's voice, the quick light step across the stage on the balls of his feet, and the loose lithe limbs weaving themselves into easy rhythmical patterns in his step-dances, all were characteristic. Of the long series mention may be made of *Sunny* (1926), *That's a Good Girl* (1928), and *Stand up and Sing* (of which he was part-author, 1931), all at the Hippodrome.

There was some truth in the statement made after his death that Buchanan was the last of the 'Knuts'. With dark wavy hair, fine eyes, and a tip-tilted nose, he was attractive rather than good-looking, but his very tall slim figure well set off the faultless cut of his clothes, and he was regarded as something of an *arbiter elegantiarum* by a generation which admired, if it could not emulate, the sartorial perfection of the white tie, white waistcoat, and tails which were his stage emblem. (He was the first to adopt, *circa* 1924, the later prevailing fashion of a double-breasted dinner jacket.) But if he remained the dandy, his innate modesty and humour steadfastly resisted his becoming at any time a matinée idol, a role which some of his more fervent admirers would have assigned him. He was first billed as a comedian, and as a comedian he himself would have preferred to remain and be remembered. He used to say that nature gave him long legs and a croak, but the long legs enhanced the pleasure of watching the timing and gymnastic of his tap-dancing, and the croak was curiously tuneful. With his quiet unforced technique, no one knew better how to put across the words and music of a song with charm and effect.

In June 1944 at the Savoy Theatre Buchanan broke new ground when he appeared in a straight part, that of Lord Dilling in an Edwardian version of *The Last of Mrs. Cheyney* by Frederick Lonsdale. The light charm of Buchanan's Dilling bore little relation to the amoral character which Lonsdale drew and Sir Gerald du Maurier had portrayed in 1925, but the performance confirmed what many had long suspected, that Buchanan was a comedy actor of the first rank, with a split-second sense in the handling of lines, and an unaffected ease of manner. These qualities were borne out in subsequent straight parts which he played during the last years of his career.

In 1951 on the sudden death of Ivor Novello Buchanan succeeded to the part of Nikki, written by Novello for his own production of *King's Rhapsody* at the Palace Theatre. This was a courageous and as it proved fully justified venture, but the role of romantic hero was not perhaps entirely congenial to his personality.

Buchanan acted fairly regularly in films after 1925, many of them rather makeshift versions of his musical comedy successes. Special mention should be made of *Monte Carlo* (1931) directed by Ernst Lubitsch; *Good Night, Vienna* (1932); *Break the News* (1938), directed by René Clair, in which he appeared with Maurice Chevalier; *The Band Waggon* (1954), in which, besides singing and dancing with Fred Astaire, he caricatured the actor-manager-producer in the grand manner of a former day; and finally, *The Diary of Major Thompson*, released after his death, a film adaptation of Pierre Daninos's best-seller, in which he acceptably portrayed the French conception of the conventional Englishman.

Among his fellow players Buchanan's encouragement of talent, his quixotic generosity, and his loyalty became something of a theatrical legend. Throughout most of his career he had extensive theatre business interests. He financed the building of the Leicester Square Theatre, and at the time of his death had control of the Garrick Theatre and the King's Theatre, Hammersmith. He was also an early speculator in television.

In 1915 Buchanan married an actress vocalist, Drageva, daughter of the late Drago Dragev Sava, merchant. The marriage was dissolved. In 1949 he married Susan Bassett, of Maryland and New York. There were no children. He died in London 20 October 1957.

There were drawings of Buchanan in *Punch* by W. K. Haselden (21 May 1924), J. H. Dowd (1 June 1938), and G. L. Stampa (24 October 1945).

[*The Times*, 21 October 1957; private information; personal knowledge.]

D. Pepys Whiteley

*published 1971*

## BURTON Richard

(1925–1984)

Actor, was born Richard Walter Jenkins 10 November 1925 at Pontrhydyfen, a small Welsh village in the Rhondda Valley, four miles from Port Talbot, the son of Richard Jenkins, a miner, and his wife, Edith Maud Thomas, who had worked as a barmaid at the Miners Arms public house in the village. He was their sixth son, the twelfth of their thirteen children. His mother died in October 1927, and he was brought up by his eldest sister, Cecilia, and her husband, Elfed. The family spoke both Welsh and English and Richard was able to speak Welsh for the rest of his life. He was educated at Eastern Primary School, Port Talbot, and Port Talbot Secondary School. At fifteen he left school to work in the men's outfitting department at the local Co-operative store. Bored, he joined a youth club and experienced the exhilaration of amateur dramatics. Wanting to play rugby, he became a cadet in the local Air Training Corps, where one of the officers was Philip H. Burton, the senior English teacher at the Secondary School and a theatre lover. In appearance young Richard Jenkins was of medium height with fine, wide, blue eyes. Sturdily built, he had the body of a rugby half-back, long and solid in the trunk, but with short legs. He was troubled by boils and his skin was pitted by acne. Nevertheless he was considered extremely attractive. Convinced that in education lay escape from his job, he now focused all his charm on Philip Burton and in September 1941 was readmitted to the Secondary School. He moved into the teacher's lodgings and in 1943, after matriculating, legally renounced his own surname and became Richard Burton.

He made his début in London as Glan in Emlyn Williams's play, *The Druids' Rest*, on 26 January 1944. When the play closed he was called up. On a special six-month wartime course at Exeter College, Oxford, he read English, while also undergoing RAF training. His tutor, Nevill Coghill, a gifted amateur director, was captivated by him. Casting Burton as Angelo in his Oxford University Dramatic Society production of *Measure for Measure*, Coghill proclaimed him 'a genius'. Demobilized in 1947, Burton returned to the theatre. In 1948, filming *The Last Days of Dolwyn*, he met the actress Sybil Williams from Ferndale—also a Welsh mining village—where she had been brought up by aunts after the death of her parents. Her father was an under-manager in a coal mine. Sybil and Burton were married in 1949 and had two daughters: Kate (1957) and Jessica (1959).

In 1949, in *The Lady's Not For Burning*, the stillness and simplicity that would become Burton's trademark attracted considerable attention. After his Prince Hal at Stratford-upon-Avon in 1951, his future was assured. His first Hollywood film, *My Cousin Rachel* (1953), also brought him the first of seven unsuccessful Academy award nominations and won him the coveted lead role in *The Robe* (1953). In 1953 at the Old Vic he played his first *Hamlet*. The voice, beautifully modulated, and the physical presence so controlled, created an impression of sensitivity combined with a startling virility. In 1955 his *Henry V* won him the *Evening Standard* Best Actor award. When he alternated the roles of Othello and Iago in 1956 (with John Neville) his reputation as a classical actor seemed unassailable.

Burton was notorious for his romantic exploits behind the scenes. He also had a reputation as both a compelling story-teller in the Welsh tradition and as a fierce drinker. Asked where his ambition lay next—Macbeth perhaps, or Lear?—no one took his reply seriously: 'I want to be a millionaire.' However, when the season finished he settled in Switzerland; he would never appear on the London stage again. In 1960 he played King Arthur in the musical *Camelot* in New York. In 1961 he arrived in Rome to play Mark Antony in the film *Cleopatra* (1963) starring Elizabeth Taylor (the English-born daughter of Francis Taylor, art dealer, who had moved to America on the outbreak of World War II). Burton separated from his wife.

During the next thirteen years he made over twenty films, few of which pleased him or the critics, but as the spy in *The Spy Who Came In From The Cold* (1966) he was superb and *Who's Afraid of Virginia Woolf?* (1966), with Elizabeth Taylor, was justifiably acclaimed. He had married Elizabeth Taylor in Canada in 1964 (his divorce was finalized that year), *en route* to New York with *Hamlet*. He was her fifth husband; she had two sons and a daughter by previous marriages. In 1966 he returned to Oxford to raise money for the OUDS, appearing in the title role of *Dr Faustus* with Elizabeth Taylor as Helen of Troy. They gave their services free but the critics savaged him. When he said he yearned to be an academic, an honorary fellowship at St Peter's College, Oxford, was arranged (1973) but the realities of a don's life made him abandon the experiment.

Burton was appointed CBE in 1970. His drinking was now addictive and in 1974 his marriage to Elizabeth Taylor was dissolved; they remarried a year later in Botswana and divorced again in 1976. He married Susan Hunt, the English daughter of Frederick Miller, lawyer, and ex-wife of racing driver James Hunt, while playing in *Equus* on Broadway (1976). *Equus* impressed the critics and was filmed.

In 1980, recreating his role in *Camelot*, he collapsed in Los Angeles and underwent surgery on his spine. Fighting alcoholism, he filmed *Wagner*. His marriage was dissolved in 1982 and in 1983 he married Sally Hay, an English continuity girl he had met while making *Wagner*. She was the daughter of Jack Hay, motoring correspondent for the *Birmingham Post*. In his last film, *Ellis Island*, Burton played the father of his real-life daughter, actress Kate Burton. He died of a cerebral haemorrhage 5 August 1984 in hospital at Geneva, and was buried at Celigny, Switzerland, where he lived.

Burton had made his début when the London stage was dominated by actors of flamboyant lyricism—(Sir) Michael Redgrave, (Sir) John Gielgud, and Laurence (later Lord) Olivier. His sheer sexuality had confounded and excited critical opinion. Now the obituaries deplored his failure to fulfil expectations, but these were expectations other people had predicted for him. He had done what he wanted with his life: he had achieved fame and riches and experienced passion. Above all he had escaped from the steelworks, the mines, and the Co-op, and a life of stultifying mediocrity that as a young Welsh boy must have once seemed his inevitable destiny.

[Paul Ferris, *Richard Burton*, 1981; Penny Junor, *Burton*, 1985; J. Cottrell and Fergus Cashin, *Richard Burton*, 1971; personal knowledge.]

Keith Baxter

*published 1990*

## BYAM SHAW Glencairn Alexander ('Glen') (1904–1986)

Actor and director of theatre and opera, was born 13 December 1904 in Addison Road, London, the fourth in the family of four sons and one daughter of John Byam Lister Shaw, painter, illustrator, and founder of the Byam Shaw School of Art, and his wife, Evelyn Caroline Pyke-Nott, miniaturist. He went to Westminster School as a day-boy during World War I and his contemporaries included his elder brother, James, who became a distinguished art historian, and (Sir) John Gielgud, who was to be a lifelong friend and colleague.

While James won a scholarship to Christ Church, Oxford, and Gielgud to the Royal Academy of Dramatic Art, Glen next surfaced on 1 August 1923 as an apparently untrained professional actor in *At Mrs Beam's* at the Pavilion theatre, Torquay. In the era of the matinée idol Byam Shaw's dazzling and lifelong good looks, together with the reported encouragement of his cousin May Ward, a close friend of (Dame) Ellen Terry, may have been enough to make him take the plunge into acting. His first London appearance in 1925 was as Yasha in *The Cherry Orchard* (John Gielgud was Trofimov) and in the next four years he had the good fortune to appear in three more Chekhov plays.

In 1929 he married the actress (Madeleine) Angela (Clinton) Baddeley, the elder sister of Hermione Baddeley. Their father, William Herman Clinton-Baddeley, was an unsuccessful composer. The Byam Shaw marriage was a supremely happy one, both domestically and professionally, until Angela's death in 1976. They had a son and a daughter.

After a tour together to South Africa in 1931 Byam Shaw appeared memorably at the Lyceum in 1932 in Max Reinhardt's mime play *The Miracle*, which starred Lady Diana Cooper as the Madonna. In 1933 the long and mutually rewarding association with John Gielgud began when Byam Shaw took over the Gielgud part in the long running *Richard of Bordeaux* by Gordon Daviot (i.e. Elizabeth Mackintosh). In 1934 he was Darnley in Daviot's *Queen of Scots* and later Laertes in Gielgud's longest running *Hamlet*, each time directed by Gielgud. In 1935 he played Benvolio in the famous *Romeo and Juliet* with Laurence (later Baron) Olivier, (Dame) Edith Evans, and (Dame) Peggy Ashcroft. During the play's run there was the beginning of a sea change in Byam Shaw's career. He assisted Gielgud in directing *Richard II* for the Oxford University Dramatic Society—Vivien Leigh was the Queen and Michael Denison played three small parts—and he was as stimulating, firm, and courteous to his undergraduate cast as he was always to be to professional companies. He had now found his true *métier*; he had never enjoyed acting. Until the war, however, he continued to act, mostly in supporting parts in prestigious Gielgud productions, but also, importantly for the future, with (Sir) Michael Redgrave, George Devine, and Peggy Ashcroft in Michel-St Denis's short season at the Phoenix. But he was now directing too, and in 1938 was engaged to direct Gielgud in Dodie Smith's *Dear Octopus*.

He had joined the Emergency Reserve of Officers before the war and with his brother James was commissioned into the Royal Scots in 1940.

They both served in Burma from 1942 and were both wounded. Byam Shaw ended his service in 1945 as a major making training films in India. By 1946 he had joined St Denis and Devine in running the Old Vic Centre, which combined a school of acting, an experimental project, and the Young Vic Company. Byam Shaw also found time to direct *The Winslow Boy* by (Sir) Terence Rattigan (with Angela in a key role)—the start of another rewarding association—and also three Shakespeare plays at the Vic. Despite much success in all fields the three partners fell foul of the Vic governors and of the theatre's top-heavy and largely hostile administration and resigned in 1951.

Fortunately for Byam Shaw and the British theatre there followed his great work at Stratford, first as co-director with (Sir) Anthony Quayle (1952–6) and then on his own, until handing over to his chosen successor (Sir) Peter Hall in 1959. Byam Shaw directed fourteen plays at Stratford, notably *Antony and Cleopatra* (Redgrave and Ashcroft), *Macbeth* (Olivier and Leigh), *As You Like It* (Ashcroft), *Othello* (Harry Andrews and Emlyn Williams), and *King Lear* (Charles Laughton and Albert Finney); and chose companies which were a magnet to directors of the calibre of Hall, Peter Brook, and Gielgud. He helped transform Stratford from a worthy tourist trap into the country's theatrical capital. Ironically the company became 'Royal' only after he left.

As a freelance director in the 1960s he was much in demand. Then suddenly, though self-confessedly tone deaf, he turned to opera; and, unencumbered by musical considerations, brought his special gift for clarifying texts to the service of outrageous operatic story-lines, inculcating in principals and chorus his passion for theatrical truth. From *The Rake's Progress* at Sadler's Wells (1962) to Wagner's *Ring* at the Coliseum (1973) he directed in all fifteen operas, sweeping the stage before first nights 'to calm his nerves'. The decoration of the Coliseum's safety curtain was taken from a painting by his father.

Byam Shaw was slim, neatly and untheatrically dressed, with shoes always highly polished; his white hair, ruddy complexion, and searching brown eyes were those of the archetypal senior officer. Even his quiet voice and beautiful manners cloaked a steely authority. He did not aspire to be a virtuoso director, manipulating the playwright's intentions to conform to a subjective vision. He was content to be an interpreter, but he brought to that characteristically modest role the highest level of research, intuition, and love of the theatre and its workers.

He was appointed CBE in 1954 and was given an honorary D.Litt. by Birmingham University in 1959. He died in a nursing home in Goring on Thames 29 April 1986, not far from his house at Wargrave.

[Michael Billington, *Peggy Ashcroft*, 1988; Michael Denison, *Double Act*, 1985; private information; personal knowledge.]

MICHAEL DENISON

*published 1996*

## CAMPBELL Beatrice Stella

(1865–1940)

Better known as Mrs. Patrick Campbell, actress, was born in Kensington 9 February 1865, the youngest daughter and child of John Tanner, the son of an army contractor to the British East India Company and a descendant of Thomas Tanner, bishop of St. Asaph. Her mother was Maria Luigia Giovanna, daughter of Count Angelo Romanini, an Italian political exile. Beatrice Tanner was educated at Brighton and Hampstead, and in Paris, and studied for a short time at the Guildhall School of Music. In 1884, when she was nineteen, she eloped to marry Patrick Campbell, who had then a small post in the City: his father owned property at Stranraer.

In October 1888 Mrs. Patrick Campbell went upon the professional stage, making her first appearance in a play called *Bachelors* at the Alexandra Theatre, Liverpool. After touring in the company of (Sir) Phillip Ben Greet (Rosalind and Viola were among her parts), she arrived in London in March 1890, playing Helen in *The Hunchback* at the Adelphi Theatre. During the following year the Gattis engaged her for the Adelphi where she acted between August 1891 and the spring of 1893 in such melodramas as *The Trumpet Call* and *The Black Domino*. Shortly after *The Black Domino* opened she received a fortnight's notice from the Gattis (who were paying her £8 a week) on the grounds that her voice and gestures were ineffective and that nothing she said or did 'got over the footlights'. It was at this time that her performance was seen by Mrs. Alexander and Graham Robertson, the artist, who knew that (Sir) George Alexander wanted an actress to play the part of Paula Tanqueray in the new drama, *The Second Mrs. Tanqueray*, by (Sir) A. W. Pinero at the St. James's Theatre. Negotiations followed, made difficult by the attitude of the Gattis who wished to keep Mrs. Campbell when they heard that she was sought for the St. James's. At last she was released, and, thanks to the generosity of Elizabeth Robins, who had been cast meantime for Paula and withdrew in Mrs. Campbell's favour, this almost unknown player—'the fragile creature of Italian origin', as Pinero called her—had her chance. From the moment that she walked upon the stage of the St. James's on the night of 27 May 1893, her success was astonishing. Mrs. Campbell had a dark Italian beauty and a rich and expressive voice: it was soon realized that none of her contemporaries had her gift for portraying passionate, complex women, 'the flash and gloom, the swirl and the eddy, of a soul torn by supposed intellectual emotion', as (Sir) Edmund Gosse put it in a letter to her written in 1895. She might fail in the simplicities, but properly cast she was unexampled. William Archer wrote of her Paula: 'Never was there a more uncompromisingly artistic piece of acting. It was incarnate reality, the haggard truth.' John Davidson in a letter to her written in 1901 said: ' "Paula" is like an opal of many hues and lustres, with stains of life, and wounds of passion through which the disastrous fires glow that shatter it in the end.' Although, as Mr. Hamilton Fyfe has noted, Davidson did not attribute this merit entirely to the actress, no other player of Paula has left the same impression or shown the same temperamental brilliance.

Later during the 'nineties, when her fame was at its height, Mrs. Campbell appeared in such parts as Dulcie Larondie in Henry Arthur Jones's strong, romantic play, *The Masqueraders* (St. James's, April 1894); Agnes Ebbsmith, who threw the Bible into the fire, in Pinero's *The Notorious Mrs. Ebbsmith* (Garrick Theatre, March 1895); Fedora, in the play of that name (Haymarket Theatre, May 1895); Juliet to the Romeo of (Sir) Johnston Forbes-Robertson at the Lyceum Theatre (September 1895), a part to which she was less fitted; and Magda in Sudermann's drama of that name, also at the Lyceum (June 1896), in which she was superb in revolt and indignation. Although the play failed on its first production, she acted in it often during her later career. In November 1896 she appeared at the Avenue Theatre as the Rat Wife in Ibsen's *Little Eyolf*. She was generally considered to have been miscast as Ophelia to Forbes-Robertson's Hamlet at the Lyceum (September 1897), although Mr. Bernard Shaw defended her in the *Saturday Review*. 'Mrs. Patrick Campbell,' he wrote, 'with that complacent audacity of hers which is so exasperating when she is doing the wrong thing, this time does the right thing by making Ophelia really mad. The resentment of the audience at this outrage is hardly to be described. . . . Playgoers naturally murmur when something that has always been pretty becomes painful; but the pain is good for them, good for the theatre, and for the play.' Nine months after this, in June 1898, Mrs. Campbell had one of her most memorable successes as a Mélisande of haunting beauty in Maeterlinck's *Pelléas and Mélisande* (Prince of Wales's Theatre, June 1898), with (Sir) John Martin Harvey as Pelléas. Her Lady Macbeth (Lyceum, September 1898) was played with what A. B. Walkley termed 'a mysterious sensuous charm'.

In September 1899 Mrs. Campbell went into management at the Prince of Wales's, opening with a failure, Chester Bailey Fernald's Japanese play, *The Moonlight Blossom*. The financial loss was heavy. In April of the next year Mrs. Campbell had a deep personal grief when her husband was killed fighting in South Africa. Her management remained unfortunate financially, but she had a run of artistic successes in such parts as Mrs. Daventry (Royalty Theatre, October 1900) in the play *Mr. and Mrs. Daventry*, based by Frank Harris on a scenario of Oscar Wilde; Mariana in a revival of José Echegaray's play of that name (Royalty, May 1901); and Mrs. Clara Sang, the bedridden wife in Björnstjerne Bjørnson's *Beyond Human Power* (Royalty, November 1901). During January 1902 she acted for the first time in New York, as Magda. When she returned to London she appeared in a series of unimportant productions interrupted by one famous revival: that in which she played Mélisande in French to the Pelléas of Sarah Bernhardt (Vaudeville Theatre, July 1904). According to W. L. Courtney in the *Daily Telegraph*, Mrs. Campbell's Mélisande was 'in its French form more gracious and childlike and poetic than we have ever seen it before'. After 'a nightmare', Mrs. Campbell's word for the melodrama *The Bondman* by (Sir) Hall Caine (Drury Lane Theatre, September 1906) in which she appeared as Greeba, there came the triumph of a few Court Theatre matinées of Ibsen's *Hedda Gabler* (March 1907). Mrs. Campbell, physically nothing like Ibsen's description, was a mistress of heat and light and sound; she saw Hedda as 'a proud, intelligent woman, a well-bred woman in the highest sense. A vital creature, suffocated by the commonplace.' Another visit to the United States of America followed, and then an English tour. Next Mrs. Campbell gave matinées at the New Theatre (November 1908) of Arthur Symons's version of Hugo von Hofmannsthal's *Elektra* and of Yeats's *Deirdre*. In January 1909 she played Olive in Rudolf Besier's *Olive Latimer's Husband* (Vaudeville), and in September of that year Mieris in the ill-fated *False Gods* by J. B. Fagan, with Sir H. Beerbohm Tree at His Majesty's Theatre.

Mrs. Campbell spent the year 1910 in America. Back in London she opened at the Haymarket (March 1911) in Besier's *Lady Patricia*. Here it was said of her that she burlesqued with much humour both herself as an actress and the kind of woman she had been impersonating for so long. At the St. James's (December 1911) she appeared with Sir George Alexander for the first time in seventeen years: the part—one she had refused more than once and never liked—was Mrs. Chepstow in the drama *Bella Donna*, by Fagan and Mr. Robert Hichens. After a revival at the St. James's (June 1913) of *The Second Mrs. Tanqueray* and her performance of Leonora in *The Adored One* by Sir J. M. Barrie (Duke of York's Theatre, September 1913), Mrs. Campbell found one of her last major successes, Eliza Doolittle, the flower-girl Galatea of Mr. Bernard Shaw's *Pygmalion*. 'I invented a Cockney accent and created a human Eliza' she wrote later of a part that she played first at His Majesty's (April 1914) and afterwards in the United States. Mr. Shaw was always a firm friend: his letters to her are the crown of the autobiography which she published in 1922.

During the rest of her career Mrs. Campbell's star slowly waned. She had such effective parts as Rosalie la Grange in *The Thirteenth Chair* (Duke of York's, October 1917), George Sand in *Madame Sand* (Duke of York's, June 1920), and Anastasia in *The Matriarch* (Royalty, May 1929). There were also revivals of *Macbeth* (Aldwych Theatre, November 1920, with the American actor James K. Hackett); *Hedda Gabler* (Everyman Theatre, May 1922); and Ibsen's *Ghosts* (in which she played Mrs. Alving, Wyndham's Theatre, March 1928). But much of her time was spent in touring and her new parts were few and unimportant. She never regained her full hold on the West End stage, and during the last years of her life she was engaged chiefly in minor film work in America. To the end she retained her sense of humour and cutting wit. Off the stage she was tempestuous, tactless, and good-hearted; upon it she was an actress in the grand manner. A modern critic, James Agate, said of her at her death: 'In my life I have seen six great actresses, and six only. These are Bernhardt, Réjane, Mrs. Kendal, Ellen Terry, Duse, and Mrs. Patrick Campbell.' She died of pneumonia at Pau 9 April 1940. In 1914 she had married, as his second wife, (Major) George Frederick Myddleton Cornwallis-West. By her first husband she had a son, who was killed in action in France in 1917, and a daughter, Stella Patrick Campbell, an actress who appeared often with her mother.

A portrait of Mrs. Campbell as Paula Tanqueray was painted by Solomon J. Solomon in 1894, and another was painted by Prince Pierre Troubetzkoy.

[*The Times*, 11 April 1940; Mrs. Patrick Campbell, *My Life and Some Letters*, 1922; H. Hamilton Fyfe, *Sir Arthur Pinero's Plays and Players*, 1930; G. Bernard Shaw, *Our Theatres in the Nineties*, vol. iii, 1932; A. E. W. Mason, *Sir George Alexander and the St. James' Theatre*, 1935; James Agate, *Ego 4*, 1940; *Who's Who in the Theatre*, 1939.]

J. C. Trewin

*published 1949*

# CHAPLIN Sir Charles Spencer

(1889–1977)

Film actor and director, was born 15 April 1889 in East Street, Walworth, London, the son of Charles Chaplin, variety comedian, and his wife, Hannah ('Lily Harley'), daughter of Charles Hill, cobbler, of county Cork. The birth appears not to have been registered. His father drank and the parents separated a year after Charles was born; however the mother was successful enough as a vaudeville singer to support herself and her two sons (the elder, Sydney, was the result of an early affair which had taken her to South Africa). But her voice failed, engagements dwindled, and the family was reduced to the workhouse. Mental instability followed, and Chaplin has described how as a child, with his brother at sea in the navy, he struggled alone in London to keep alive, employed as newsboy, printer's boy, doctor's boy, and, for a brief disastrous adventure, glass-blower. He had for a time been a member of a team of clog-dancers, the Eight Lancashire Lads; he continued to dream of the stage, and when Sydney, released from the navy, was back in London and able to help him he found employment in the theatre, first in a short-lived play called *Jim*, then as the page-boy in *Sherlock Holmes*, which with H. A. Saintsbury in the title-role toured for three years. Music hall followed; he joined Sydney in the Fred Karno Company. He quickly learned the vaudeville technique which was to serve him so well. Soon he was in America, touring with the second Karno company. In 1913 he received an invitation from Keystone, a company producing short comic films. Doubtful of his future in the world of the cinema, he hesitated, but the offer of $150 per week persuaded him, and at the end of the year he was in Hollywood, working for Mack Sennett.

The story of his beginnings in the cinema is familiar. There was an inauspicious start: then Sennett told him to go and pick out a costume and make-up of his own choice. He selected baggy trousers, outsize shoes, a tight jacket, a hat too small, a moustache, and a cane. With the outfit the idea of the character grew in his mind. There was, of course, no script; he knew only, he was to say, that Mabel Normand (she was a star of silent comedy) was involved with her husband and a lover. He was not allowed to develop the character he had created. The old hands could not accept what they saw as his stage technique. Used to inventing his own comic business, he chafed.

In May 1914 he was allowed to write and direct a one-reel piece. His creative career had begun; and for the next four years, first with Keystone, then with other companies—Essanay, Mutual, First National—he made the series of short silent comedies which were to establish him as the darling of the public. The figure in the baggy pants became the universal Tramp. The titles are indicative: *The New Janitor* (1914), *The Rink* (1916), *The Floorwalker* (1916). Chaplin appeared as various characters; he was the fireman, the roller-skater, the boxer, the pawn-broker, the immigrant, and the patient in the sanatorium. In the earlier pieces he was the scallywag capable of snatching the coin from the blind man's wallet. But the character softened and absorbed sentiment. Pathos was added to laughter.

By the end of 1918 he was extending not only in emotional scope but in length. His ironic joke about the miseries of trench warfare, *Shoulder Arms* (1918), ran for three reels, and in 1920 there came the first of his feature films, *The Kid*, a story with fully developed action. It was followed in 1923 by the four-reel *The Pilgrim*, and Chaplin, now his own master, took a rest. There was a much fêted visit to London, Paris, and Berlin; then he embarked on an experiment in a mood alien from the works which had made him world-famous. Himself appearing for no more than a few moments, and with Edna Purviance from his short comedies cast as the heroine, he directed *A Woman of Paris* (1923), a melodramatic story of a country girl frustrated in love who becomes a notorious Paris beauty; Adolphe Menjou played the insouciant seducer. The playing had a restraint far ahead of the period. But without the expected Chaplin comedy the film was a failure. Withdrawn, it remained a mere title in film history books until the 1980s, when it was revived to a critical acclaim greater than it deserved. Its chief interest is still historical. Fortunately Chaplin returned to the path of his true genius. In 1925 he made *The Gold Rush* with its enchanting visual jokes such as the hand-dance and the meal off a shoe. In 1928 *The Circus* followed.

In 1931 there was *City Lights*, perhaps the culmination of Chaplin's career. In Europe again, he was hailed by the great and the humble; he was admired by G. Bernard Shaw and royalty received him. Police had to restrain crowds gathered to see him. Nevertheless times were changing in the cinema for the screen had found its voice; now Chaplin was faced with the challenge of the 'talkies'. He compromised: *City Lights* had sound, but it was not a 'talkie'; in one hilarious moment he mimicked the hiccups of a man who has swallowed a toy whistle but he did not speak. Five years later he was still compromising; in *Modern Times* (1936) Chaplin contented himself with a nonsense song. And he was committing himself to political opinions; the film, ridiculing the mechanization of factory work, was taken as a defence of unions and the labour movement. Political unpopularity (Chaplin was openly pro-Russian) in the United States was followed by moral attack when he was involved in a painful paternity case.

His Hitler satire, *The Great Dictator* (1940), failed to win back his popular esteem. He was losing the sureness of his touch in mingling comedy and sentiment—for example, the fervour of his final speech in *The Great Dictator* seemed hollow. The American public turned against its favourite—who had never renounced his British citizenship.

Chaplin was shedding the Tramp character. In *The Great Dictator*, with Chaplin attempting the role of a political leader, the figure of a barber shared the narrative with a satirized Hitler figure. Seven years later, in *Monsieur Verdoux* (1947), he completely abandoned his famous early character; now he was playing a multiple murderer who, comparing his handful of deaths with the massive exterminations of war, becomes the advocate of pacifism. It was a brilliant film; but it was a failure with the public. Chaplin was to make one more film in America, *Limelight* (1952), a sentimental tale of an old music-hall star and the young dancer he befriends. Chaplin's name carried it through, but Buster Keaton, playing a minor role, outshone him. When he left the United States for the European première the American government banned his re-entry and he took up residence in Switzerland. His two last films were made in Britain: *The King in New York* (1957), an attempt, only momentarily successful, to revive his old comedy style, and *A Countess from Hong Kong* (1966), a romantic comedy in which he directed Sophia Loren and Marlon Brando but himself made only brief appearances.

Chaplin was the supreme example of the artist in one sphere of entertainment who was able not only to transfer to a much larger field the talents he had acquired but also to transform the development of the second sphere. Beginning in the British music hall, given a chance in the American cinema, he had insisted that he had something to contribute: insisted against opposition, for his physical comedy—the falls, the run suddenly halted by the limits of the stage—was at first pure vaudeville. But nature had endowed him with a genius for invention. Creator as well as performer, he observed the oddities of human behaviour and enshrined them in a superb gallery of fictions. To the character he had invented in his first days in Hollywood he added social and political satire—and emotional range. He was the born novelist who wrote in visual absurdities. Enormously gifted, he composed music for his films and wrote autobiographical books which stand the test of time. The miseries of his childhood, combined with the triumph of his maturity, gave him the confidence to attack the society which had fostered him, and inevitably he was attacked as a result. His latest work was flawed by sentimentality; and like many comedians he sometimes stretched his gifts beyond their proper limits. But his invention was boundless; and in *Monsieur Verdoux* he showed that his genius went far beyond physical comedy. His finest films were illuminated by passages of a visual brilliance which have never been surpassed. It is possible to argue that his best work is to be found in the short pieces which preceded his feature-length successes: in *Easy Street* (1917), for example, or in the miraculous details of *The Pawnshop* (1916). But however one assesses his genius, he must be recognized as one of the creators of the art of the cinema.

In social encounters Chaplin was an easy and inspiring companion, eager to lavish on chance acquaintance his gifts as raconteur and mimic. In 1962 he received honorary D.Litts. from Oxford and Durham universities and in 1971 he became a commander of the French Legion of Honour. In 1973 he was received back into the American film establishment and given a special Oscar. He was appointed KBE in 1975.

He was married four times: in 1918 to Mildred Harris (died 1944); in 1924 to Lolita McMurry ('Lita Grey'); in 1936 to Marion Levy ('Paulette Goddard'). These three marriages, which were stormy and racked with scandal, ended in divorce (in 1920, 1927, and 1942). Of the first there was a son who lived three days, of the second two sons, and of the third no children. Finally in 1943 he married the daughter of the playwright Eugene O'Neill, Oona, with whom he lived happily for the rest of his life. They had three sons and five daughters, one of whom, Geraldine Chaplin, achieved considerable success as a film actress. Chaplin died 25 December 1977 at his home, Vaud, Vevey, Switzerland. There is a statue by John Doubleday (1981) in Leicester Square.

[Theodore Huff, *Charlie Chaplin*, 1952; Charles Chaplin, *My Autobiography*, 1964, and *My Life in Pictures*, 1974; David Robinson, *Chaplin, his Life and Art*, 1985.]

DILYS POWELL

*published 1986*

## CLEMENTS Sir John Selby

**(1910–1988)**

Actor, manager, and producer, was born 25 April 1910 at 1 Carlton Terrace, Childs Hill, Hendon, Middlesex, the only child of Herbert William Clements, barrister, and his wife, Mary Elizabeth Stephens. He was educated at St Paul's School and spent one term at St John's College, Cambridge. He was forced to withdraw from the college, where he had begun to study history, because sudden financial loss meant his family could no longer afford the fees. His mother's great friend, Marie Löhr, gave him his first job at the age of twenty at the Lyric theatre, Hammersmith. In 1931 he joined the Shakespearian Company run by Sir (P. B.) Ben Greet, and at twenty-five, in 1935, was sufficiently confident to found the Intimate Theatre, Palmers Green, as a weekly repertory company which he managed, directed, and acted in until 1940. In the first year he produced forty-two plays there, playing thirty-six leading parts.

In 1936 he married his first wife, Inga Maria Lillemor Ahlgren. They had no children and the marriage was dissolved ten years later. In 1946 he married the actress Kay Hammond, whose real name was Dorothy Katherine, daughter of Sir Guy Standing, KBE, of the Royal Naval Volunteer Reserve. Kay was formerly the wife of Sir Ronald George Leon, third baronet, and mother of Sir John Leon, fourth baronet, later better known as the actor John Standing. She and Clements had no children.

During the war Clements had produced many plays for ENSA and also organized a revue company to entertain the troops at out-of-the-way places. John Clements and Kay Hammond together became one of the best known theatrical couples of their day. In 1944 they acted at the Apollo in *Private Lives*, by (Sir) Noël Coward, an enchanting production with which Coward was delighted. In 1946 Clements appeared as the Earl of Warwick in *The Kingmaker* at the St James's theatre, which he himself managed. He presented and directed *Man and Superman* in 1951 at the New theatre, playing the role of John Tanner.

In addition to his many productions and performances, Clements was a successful broadcaster on the radio, taking part with Kay Hammond in the weekly discussion programme, *We Beg To Differ*. Their comic rivalry on the air delighted audiences. From 1955 Clements was adviser on drama for Associated Rediffusion, one of the first independent television companies, for which he was contracted to produce a number of television plays. In July 1955 he joined the board of directors of the Saville theatre, the management of which came under his personal control.

In 1960 Kay Hammond became paralysed after a stroke and was confined to a wheelchair for the remaining twenty years of her life. Clements joined the Old Vic Company in 1961, making his first appearance in New York in the title part of *Macbeth* in 1962. In 1966 he took on the challenge of directing the Chichester festival theatre when Sir Laurence (later Baron) Olivier left to found the National Theatre. His boundless enthusiasm and love of the theatre overcame any initial reluctance on the part of the actors he approached for his first season at Chichester to join him 'in the wake of Larry'. He was able to recruit Celia Johnson and Bill Fraser and splendid supporting casts, who were very loyal to him. His seasons were independent and enterprising and he was always encouraging, calm, and resourceful in times of crisis.

As a director he was businesslike, almost prosaic, and very logical, never selfish and always courteous. Six feet tall, with a handsome face and slightly 'jug' ears, he had kind eyes and excellent hands. He was one of the last actor-managers in the country. In Chichester he was not only the director of four plays each summer season, but also played, among other parts, Macbeth, Antony, and Prospero, as well as two of Jean Anouilh's heroes, the general in *The Fighting Cock* and Antoine in *Dear Antoine*. It was his appreciation of the literary tradition of drama that gave him the courage to present *The Fighting Cock*, which had been a great success in its original French version in Paris. *Heartbreak House*, in which he played Shotover, was one of his most memorable productions.

Clements also acted in a number of films, including *Things to Come* (1936), *South Riding* (1937), *The Four Feathers* (1939), *Oh What a Lovely War!* (1969), and *Gandhi* (1982). He was appointed CBE in 1956 and knighted in 1968. A member of the council of Equity in 1948–9 and vice-president in 1950–9, he was also a popular trustee of the Garrick Club.

He left Chichester in 1973 to spend more time with his wife, for they were a devoted couple. She died in 1980. Clements died 6 April 1988 at Pendean Convalescent Home near Midhurst, where he spent the last two years of his life.

[Personal knowledge.]

BESSBOROUGH

*published 1996*

## COCHRAN Sir Charles Blake

**(1872–1951)**

Showman, was born 25 September 1872 in Brighton. It was probably his sense of showmanship which caused him to claim Lindfield, Sussex, where he spent many early holidays with his grandfather, as his birthplace. His father, James Elphinstone Cochran, was a tea merchant and a keen theatre- and race-goer. His mother, Matilda Walton, daughter of a Merchant Navy officer, was the widow of a Mr. Arnold by the time she was twenty-one. She lived to be ninety. By her first marriage she had one son, and by her second nine children, of whom Charles was the fourth.

Cochran was educated at Brighton Grammar School where, on his first day, he met Aubrey Beardsley, with whom he came to share a study. Later, through Aubrey's sister, Mabel, Cochran met the *Yellow Book* circle including Walter Sickert, (Sir) Max Beerbohm, (Sir) William Rothenstein, Ernest Dowson, and others. But all this was after a lapse of years. In 1891 he went to New York. Cochran had always been a worshipper of the stars of the stage and circus. Money meant nothing to him—then or at any other time. It was as an actor that he hoped to make his name. In this he was unsuccessful, so much so that the Chicago World Fair found him selling fountain-pens. Eventually, he managed to secure a part with the actor-manager Richard Mansfield, who told him that he would never be a good actor, but, sensing his managerial ability, made Cochran his private secretary. Through this association came much experience and many stage contacts.

After some time Cochran quarrelled with Mansfield and in partnership with E. J. Henley opened a school of acting in New York. In 1897 he made his first production, Ibsen's *John Gabriel Borkman*. In the same year Cochran returned to London, working as a journalist and developing his natural flair for publicity. But the theatre won, as always, and seeing a production of *Cyrano de Bergerac* in Paris, he conceived the idea of Mansfield's playing it in New York. This was one of the earliest instances of Cochran's ability to star an actor in the right vehicle. The quarrel was quickly made up, and Cochran returned to the States as Mansfield's manager.

Yet again Cochran preferred to stand on his own feet. Returning once more to London, he set up as a theatrical agent, earning gradual success as a promoter of boxing and wrestling matches and outstanding music-hall acts such as Houdini the escapist and the great wrestler Georges Hackenschmidt, whom he matched at Olympia in 1904 against Ahmed Madrali, the 'Terrible Turk'. His first London production, a farce called *Sporting Simpson* at the Royalty Theatre in 1902, was a failure; so was his second attempt at the same theatre, *Lyre and Lancet*. By 1903 he had been made bankrupt for the first time, from which position he was quickly extricated by Hackenschmidt. Cochran's instinct for entertainment now induced him to promote all kinds of ventures, from pygmies to roller-skating (which became a craze from 1909 until the outbreak of war), as well as circuses at Earl's Court and Olympia in 1912–13. His greatest production of those years was Max Reinhardt's *The Miracle* which opened at Olympia on Christmas Eve, 1911. This tremendous spectacle was not the immediate success it should have been until Lord Northcliffe hammered it home every day in the *Daily Mail*. From that time on the eulogies Cochran received from the Northcliffe press were offset by his more critical reception by other popular newspapers.

From boxing, roller-skating, and spectacle, Cochran turned to revue, still a novelty during the war years. Beginning in a small way with *Odds and Ends* (1914) at the Ambassadors Theatre, which introduced Alice Delysia to London audiences, he continued at the Empire with Irving Berlin's *Watch Your Step* (1915). As an antidote, he produced two sociological plays by Brieux, *Damaged Goods* (1917) and *The Three Daughters of M. Dupont* (1917). In 1917, at the Oxford Theatre, he put on *The Better 'Ole*, the farce by Bruce Bairnsfather, which attained the run of 811 performances, exceeded only by *Bless the Bride* in 1947–9, Cochran's longest run. Both shows started slowly and built up. In 1918 Cochran redecorated and re-opened the London Pavilion, with *As You Were*, followed during the ensuing decade by a whole string of successful revues, including *London, Paris and New York* (1920); *Fun of the Fayre* (1921); *Dover Street to Dixie* (1923), featuring the American singer Florence Mills; *One Dam Thing After Another* (1927), with a score by Rodgers and Hart; and *Cochran's 1930 Revue*, with many members of the lately defunct Diaghilev ballet. Between these activities, Cochran presented *The League of Notions*, a revue introducing the Dolly Sisters at the New Oxford Theatre in 1921. The redecorating of the theatre alone cost £80,000 of his own money. The sumptuous *Mayfair and Montmartre* (1922), a revue containing a sketch debunking the dramatic critics, who resented it, showed losses amounting to £20,000. In order to recoup, he put on six successful American productions in 1923—including Eugene O'Neill's *Anna Christie*—none of which was particularly successful in London. In 1925 Cochran was made bankrupt for the second time. Such was his personal magnetism that both Alice Delysia and the Dolly Sisters offered to sell their jewels in order to save him.

Prior to this Cochran had given London Sarah Bernhardt's last season, at the Prince's Theatre; Eleanora Duse at matinées and Sacha Guitry in the evenings at the New Oxford; two Chaliapin appearances at the Albert Hall; the Chauve Souris company at the Pavilion, and a season of Diaghilev ballet at the Prince's, in which Stravinsky's music met with much critical disapproval. In boxing, he promoted the Wells-Beckett and the Beckett-Carpentier fights at the Holborn Stadium (1919), and preliminary negotiations for the famous Carpentier-Dempsey fight (1921). Disgusted by the crookedness of boxing promotion and after an unfortunate rodeo season at Wembley (1924), and an equally unprofitable presentation of Suzanne Lenglen in tennis exhibitions all over the country, Cochran in future confined himself, more or less, to the stage. His enthusiasms were easily aroused, but once damped, nothing could rekindle them.

Discharged from bankruptcy, penniless but ebullient, Cochran wrote his first book of memoirs, *The Secrets of a Showman* (1925). With the proceeds, a cabaret at the Trocadero, and backing which was never lacking, Cochran began his association with (Sir) Noël Coward with *On With The Dance* (1925) at the London Pavilion (the first show to feature 'Mr. Cochran's

Young Ladies'). Then came their brilliant partnership in *This Year of Grace* (1928) and *Bitter Sweet* (1929). In 1930 came *Private Lives*, with Noël Coward and Gertrude Lawrence in the leads, and in the same year New York saw all three shows. The climax of this association was reached in 1931 with *Cavalcade* at Drury Lane. Meanwhile Cochran had presented a Pirandello season; Sean O'Casey's *The Silver Tassie* (1929); the Lunts in a play called *Caprice* (1929) at the St. James's; the revue *Wake up and Dream* (1929) which also went to America; and *Evergreen* (1930), with Jessie Matthews, and the first use of a revolving stage in London.

Next came Cochran's association and friendship with (Sir) A. P. Herbert, beginning in 1932 with the production of *Helen* at the Adelphi, with Evelyn Laye in the title role, (Sir) George Robey, and superb décor by Oliver Messel. Five other shows in that season alone were *Dinner at Eight, The Cat and the Fiddle, Words and Music*, the Sacha Guitry season, and a revival of *The Miracle*, with Lady Diana Cooper as the Madonna. The year 1933 saw Elisabeth Bergner in *Escape Me Never* and Cole Porter's *Nymph Errant*; 1934, Coward's *Conversation Piece*, the revue *Streamline*, the end of the London Pavilion as a theatre and the break with Coward, both bitter blows.

Then came the lean years. *The Boy David* (1936), Barrie's last play, with Elisabeth Bergner, was not a success. Nor, in 1937, were the coronation revue, *Home and Beauty*, and Lehar's *Paganini*, with Richard Tauber. A trip to America proved financially abortive. His wartime shows did not fare well. Frank Collins, his stage director for twenty-eight years, took a job with E.N.S.A. Cochran wrote more books of reminiscence: his usual practice when things were at a low ebb. He and his wife faced the London blitz from a furnished flat in St. James's Court. Crippled by arthritis, he was full of plans for the future. Gone were the house in Montagu Street, the crowds of hangers-on, the Impressionist pictures (bought long before Impressionism was fashionable), the butler and the exquisite china; but he remained the *grand seigneur*, investing a sugarless bun with jam while his wife apologized for the tea cups.

After the war Cochran staged his last great come-back. In 1946, with some money for a film of his life which, characteristically, was never made, he commissioned Sir A. P. Herbert and Vivian Ellis to write the light opera *Big Ben*. The opening night at the Adelphi was attended by the Princess Elizabeth, the prime minister and half the Cabinet, in fact by everyone except the inspiration of it all who lay desperately ill at his flat. A fortnight after the removal of a kidney, still in bed, weak but ever courageous, he commissioned *Bless the Bride* by the same team for the same theatre. By 1947 he had a partner, Lord Vivian. 'My enthusiasm over *Bless the Bride* mounts hourly—I have a terrific hunch', wrote Cochran, after a famous actress and an equally well-known producer had utterly condemned it.

That is a measure of the man's dogged enthusiasm at the age of seventy-four. His faith was rewarded by a run of 886 performances which would have been even longer had not Cochran, always impatient to produce something new, withdrawn *Bless the Bride* to make way for *Tough at the Top* in 1949. This, the last of his big spectacular shows, was a failure.

Cochran was at various times the chairman and managing director of the Palace Theatre, manager of the Royal Albert Hall, president of the Actors' Benevolent Fund, and a governor of the Shakespeare Memorial theatre. He was knighted in 1948 and appointed a chevalier of the Legion of Honour in 1950. In appearance rubicund but urbane, he was always immaculately dressed. He usually wore a trilby hat at an angle. In later years he sported a monocle and, of necessity, a walking-stick. Somewhat awesome to meet, he disarmed the timid by his courteous manner. He always answered letters. He was calm in a crisis and seldom raised his voice. He was nothing if not generous, and like most of his friends a *bon viveur*. When things were good, he resembled a rooster; when bad, a benign bishop. At one time he used a rooster as a monogram. His friends called him 'Cockie', his enemies a snob, but he himself preferred to be known as 'C.B.' He was an authority on art and all things beautiful, including the feminine. Without any great musical training, he possessed a natural musical appreciation; but he had a limited sense of humour and his productions, always appealing to the eye and ear, were somewhat weak in comedy. By contrast, Lady Cochran was a well-known wit. In a runaway marriage in 1903 Cochran married Evelyn Alice (died 1960), daughter of the late Charles Robert Dade, captain in the Merchant Service. There were no children.

Unable, owing to his crippled condition, to turn off the hot tap, Cochran was scalded in his bath and died in London a week later, 31 January 1951. His vitality, in spite of his arthritis, was so great, his personality so vivid, that it seemed impossible he could be dead. The press, the B.B.C., and all the celebrities of the stage paid him tremendous tributes. He expressly asked that there should be no memorial service. 'Everything', he would say, 'is a nine days' wonder'. But in the words of W. Macqueen-Pope 'the last link with the golden Edwardian era has been snapped'. With the passing of Cochran, the English theatre lost much of its taste and most of its willingness to elevate as well as entertain the public. The things he created were of their nature transient—a roller-skating craze; the golden age of boxing and wrestling; seasons of acting and ballet which brought the London stage into touch with the best of European art; but the sponsorship of talent in authorship, acting, singing, and dancing added lustre to the theatrical scene, even if it did not always profit the managerial pocket.

A bust of Cochran by Peter Lambda was placed in the foyer of the Adelphi Theatre and there is a memorial panel in St. Paul's church, Covent Garden. The National Portrait Gallery has a drawing by Powys Evans, and a drawing by Wyndham Lewis is included in his *Thirty Personalities and a Self-Portrait*, 1932.

[Charles B. Cochran, *The Secrets of a Showman*, 1925, *I Had Almost Forgotten . . .*, 1932, *Cock-a-Doodle-Do*, 1941, *Showman Looks On*, 1945; Charles Graves, *The Cochran Story*, 1951; Vivian Ellis, *I'm on a See-Saw*, 1953; personal knowledge.]

VIVIAN ELLIS

*published 1971*

## COMPTON Fay

(1894–1978)

Actress, was born in West Kensington, London, 18 September 1894, the fifth and youngest child and third daughter of Edward Compton (Mackenzie), actor and manager, and his wife, the actress Virginia Bateman, daughter of Hezekiah Linthicum Bateman, of Baltimore. Fay was a stage name; she was christened Virginia Lilian Emmiline. Her elder brother was (Sir) E. Montague Compton Mackenzie, the author.

Educated at Leatherhead Court School, Surrey, and in Paris, Fay Compton's professional début was at the Apollo Theatre in August 1911, acting and singing with the Follies, a troupe created by Harry Gabriel Pélissier, who had a rare talent for revue. Before the programme opened, and after a seven-week engagement, Fay Compton was married to Pélissier. The marriage lasted only two years, for Pélissier died in the early autumn of 1913, aged thirty-nine, leaving an infant son.

Almost at once his young widow got the small part of a German girl in a comedy called *Who's the Lady?* at the Garrick Theatre and she went on to appear in various musical comedies, one of them (in December 1914) in New York. From the first this red-haired beauty was an assured professional; no actress of her time was more versatile. She earned an early reputation by performing in the works of Sir J. M. Barrie; but she went on to every type of play, from Shakespeare to romantic drama, high and light comedy, farce, and even as principal boy in pantomime.

She had a small part in the revival at the Savoy by H. B. Irving of *The Professor's Love Story* (1916). She acted the title-role in Barrie's *Peter Pan* at

Christmas 1917. In April 1920, at the Haymarket, which would always be her favourite theatre, she experienced her first real triumph when she played Mary Rose in Barrie's fantasy of the girl who vanishes on a Hebridean island and returns after many years as a ghost. Fay Compton acted the ghost scenes with an enchanted stillness. Now recognized as a leading lady, presently she had a long and improbably contrasted sequence of West End parts, among them the runaway wife in *The Circle* by W. Somerset Maugham (March 1921), Phoebe Throssel in *Quality Street* by Barrie (August 1921), and two characters in the complex and long-running *Secrets* (1922), in which she had to alter her age several times.

During 1923 she moved to the declining Ruritanian drama, as Princess Flavia in a Haymarket revival of *The Prisoner of Zenda*. She was happy as Lady Babbie in Barrie's *The Little Minister* (revived at the Queen's in November 1923); less so as Yasmin in *Hassan* by James Elroy Flecker, directed by Basil Dean at His Majesty's where she succeeded Cathleen Nesbitt in the spring of 1924. In February 1925 she had her first major classical opportunity: to appear at the Haymarket as Ophelia to the American John Barrymore's Hamlet, a performance of which the critic James Agate wrote: 'She was fragrant, wistful, and had a child's importunacy unmatched in my time.'

In spite of the number of her later parts (more than eighty in several genres) Fay Compton never quite recaptured her early brilliance. At the Haymarket (1925) she had the voice and technique for the Lady in the felicitous dialogue of a comedy set in a Regency inn, *The Man With a Load of Mischief* by Ashley Dukes. In April 1926 she was aptly cast as the girl in a man's world in *This Woman Business* by Benn Levy. With a generous professionalism that seldom failed, she employed in very many plays her stage sense, her emotional powers, and her swift comedy. Twice more she was Ophelia, to Henry Ainley at the Haymarket (1931), and to (Sir) John Gielgud in the final performances (1939) at the Lyceum, and afterwards in Elsinore, Denmark. She was often in Shakespeare, notably several times at the Old Vic where she appeared as Regan (1940) in the Gielgud *King Lear* which was guided by Harley Granville-Barker. She also appeared in such long-running West End plays as *Autumn Crocus* (1931), *Call it a Day* (1935), *Blithe Spirit* (1941), *No Medals* (1944), and *Bonaventure* (1949). Her last Barrie role was the Comtesse in *What Every Woman Knows* (Old Vic, 1960). She acted small parts at the opening of the Chichester Festival (1962) and the Yvonne Arnaud Theatre, Guildford (1965), and she was much applauded for her Aunt Ann in the television serial of *The Forsyte Saga* (1967). In 1975 she was appointed CBE.

Fay Compton's second husband, the actor Lauri de Frece, died in 1921 when he was only forty-one, and in 1922 she was married to Leon

Quartermaine (died 1967), with whom she had acted in *Quality Street*. Her third marriage was dissolved in 1942, and in that year she married Ralph Champion Shotter (Ralph Michael, the actor); this marriage was dissolved in 1946. There were no children of these last three marriages.

It was only towards Fay Compton's last decade that a strenuous life told on her and her memory wavered. She will be remembered most as Barrie's Mary Rose, from her youth, and over nearly fifteen years, in various productions, as the supreme Ophelia of her time. Fay Compton died at Hove 12 December 1978.

[Fay Compton, *Rosemary: Some Remembrances*, 1926; James Agate, *The Contemporary Theatre*, 1925; personal knowledge.]

J. C. Trewin

*published 1986*

## COOPER Dame Gladys Constance

(1888–1971)

Actress and theatre manager, was born at Lewisham 18 December 1888, the eldest of the three children (all daughters) of Charles William Frederick Cooper, journalist and editor of *Epicure*, founded by himself, and of his second wife, Mabel, daughter of Captain Edward Barnett of the Scots Greys. She was educated first at home by a French governess, then briefly at school in Fulham and from the age of seven began regular photographic modelling for the studio of Downey's in Ebury Street.

In the autumn of 1905 she was taken by a schoolfriend to an open audition at the Vaudeville Theatre and somewhat to her own surprise was offered the title role in a tour of *Bluebell in Fairyland* by (Sir) E. Seymour Hicks, which opened at Colchester on her seventeenth birthday. Within another year she had joined George Edwardes's company at the Gaiety, signing a contract for £3 (rising to £5) a week to play as cast, primarily small singing and dancing roles in such musicals as *The Girls of Gottenberg* (1907), *Havana* (1908), and *Our Miss Gibbs* (1909).

Gladys Cooper was not however the kind of Gaiety girl taken to Romano's by wealthy young men about town, her ambition was to be a serious actress, though all thoughts of a career were interrupted when one night she was seen on stage by Herbert John Buckmaster, a twenty-six-year-old Boer war soldier then working for Ladbroke's. Within days he had arranged an introduction to her, and they were married on 12 December 1908 much to the disapproval of her parents who felt that at nineteen she was still too young to leave home.

For a year or so after the marriage she continued to work at the Gaiety but then came the birth (in July 1910) of Joan, the first of her two children by Buckmaster, and when she returned to the stage after that it was at last to the straight theatre; she began to get small roles in comedy at the Royalty Theatre and then joined Sir George Alexander for a revival of *The Importance of Being Earnest* (1911) at the St. James's. Her first real break came in 1912 with a small but showy last-act role in *Milestones* by E. Arnold Bennett and Edward Knoblock, which ran for eighteen months during which time she would also take on many other roles at other theatres in other plays provided they finished early enough in the evening to allow her to get back to the Royalty for her entrance in *Milestones*. When that run ended she went into *Diplomacy* (1913) at Wyndham's which lasted another year, throughout which she played for the first time with the man who was to become the most constant and beloved of her stage partners, (Sir) Gerald du Maurier. By now she was earning £40 a week, and the strain was beginning to show on her marriage to a man still only earning about half that from Ladbroke's; then however came World War I. 'Buck' joined the cavalry and went to France with the Royal Horse Guards, while his wife spent the Christmas of 1914 also at the front, though with a concert party organized by Seymour Hicks. By now she was carrying her second child John (born June 1915).

It was in the following year, 1916, that she first began to act at the theatre she was later to manage, the Playhouse on the corner of the Embankment and Northumberland Avenue by Charing Cross, a building that was for the next fifteen years to become her professional home. By 1917 she had joined Frank Curzon in its management, thereby becoming the only woman other than Lilian Baylis at the Vic to run a London theatre before World War II, and the plays that she presented, acted in, and sometimes unofficially directed there were to include four W. Somerset Maugham premières (*Home and Beauty, The Letter, The Sacred Flame*, and *The Painted Veil*) as well as revivals of *My Lady's Dress*, *The Second Mrs Tanqueray*, and *Magda*.

Herbert Buckmaster returned from the war in 1918 to find that the chorus girl he had married a decade earlier had now become a professional actress and theatre manager, neither of them attributes he was looking for in a wife. Accordingly and amicably they were divorced in 1921; he was to marry twice more and make an eventual home at Buck's Club which he had founded in Clifford Street and where fifty years after their divorce she would still frequently be found at parties given by him to celebrate yet another first night. They were always to be the best of friends.

Gladys Cooper spent the 1920s bringing up her two children and running the Playhouse; in 1928 came a second marriage (to Sir Neville Arthur Pearson, second baronet); by him she had her third and last child Sally, but it was to be a short-lived marriage (dissolved in 1937) and by the early 1930s there was little to keep her in England. Changing theatrical tastes brought an end to her years of success at the Playhouse; Maugham had ceased to write plays, and despite her discovery of such interesting new works as *The Rats of Norway* (which gave Laurence (later Lord) Olivier one of his early stage successes in 1933) and a West End success in *The Shining Hour* (1934) Gladys Cooper began to feel that she had lost touch with London theatre-goers. The bright young things for whom she had worked so hard and successfully in the 1920s were no longer thronging the stalls, and she herself had by now fallen in love with the actor Philip Merivale who was to become her third and last husband and whose already successful career on Broadway encouraged Gladys to try her luck there too.

Hers was always a cut-and-run philosophy, and by the middle 1930s the London where she had once been a definitive *Peter Pan*, where she had run her own theatre and brought up her elder children, was a place of the past. America was where she would now live and despite a catastrophic Broadway start in which she played (unsuccessfully) both Desdemona and Lady Macbeth opposite Merivale (whom she married in Chicago in April 1937) it was indeed America that was to become her home for the second half of her long life.

She returned to London in 1938 for another brief and unsuccessful Shakespeare season (this in the Open Air Theatre, Regent's Park) and a West End run in *Dodsworth*, by now always appearing in partnership with Merivale. They returned to New York for Dodie Smith's *Spring Meeting* (1938) on Broadway and then, in the autumn of 1939, came an offer from (Sir) Alfred Hitchcock. He was making his first-ever Hollywood film, *Rebecca* (1940), and wanted Gladys Cooper for the small role of Laurence Olivier's sister; she went out to California for three weeks and stayed thirty years.

She fell immediately and totally in love with the sun, the sea, and the surroundings of California; though she was never there to get the leading roles that an actress of her stage distinction might have expected, she went under contract to MGM and played in a total of thirty films between 1940 and 1967, of which the most distinguished were *Now Voyager* (for which she got an Oscar nomination in 1943), *Separate Tables* (1958), and *My Fair Lady* (1964). Though Philip Merivale died in California in 1946, Gladys Cooper was to live on there alone, making a home for herself and those of her many relatives and friends seeking however temporarily a place in the Californian sun.

But during the 1950s and 60s she also began with increasing frequency to return to the London stage, first in *Relative Values* (1951) by (Sir) Noël Coward and then in such later successes as *The Chalk Garden* (1955) and the revival of Maugham's *The Sacred Flame* (1967). She bought a house on the regatta stretch of the Thames at Henley and, as the old English colony in California began to disappear, spent more and more of her time back home again amid children, grandchildren, and great-grandchildren. In 1967 she was appointed DBE, a year later she celebrated her eightieth birthday, and 17 November 1971, having just played in another revival of *The Chalk Garden*, she died at home in Henley only a month away from the start of her eighty-fourth year.

She left one son (John Buckmaster, himself for some time an actor), two daughters both of whom married actors (Joan married Robert Morley in 1940; Sally married Robert Hardy in 1961), five grandchildren, two great-grandchildren, just over £34,000, and the unforgettable memories of one of the most remarkable and resilient actresses of her generation.

[Sheridan Morley, *Gladys Cooper*, 1980; Gladys Cooper, *Gladys Cooper*, 1931; Sewell Stokes, *Without Veils*, 1953; personal knowledge.]

Sheridan Morley

*published 1986*

## COWARD Sir Noël Peirce

**(1899–1973)**

Actor, playwright, composer, lyricist, producer, author, occasional poet, and Sunday painter, was born 16 December 1899 at Teddington, Middlesex, the second in the family of three sons (the eldest of whom died at the age of six) of Arthur Sabin Coward (described as a clerk, but whose passion was music) and his wife Violet Agnes, daughter of Henry Gordon Veitch, a captain in the Royal Navy. His grandfather was James Coward, organist and chorister. Both parental backgrounds had a strong influence on the boy and the man. His mother was also musical—the parents met as members of the local church choir—and was an ardent and knowledgeable theatre-goer. Coward was soon to be a chorister himself, but was frustrated by the absence of applause after his solos. His birthday treats were invariably visits to the theatre; and by the time he was 'rushing towards puberty' he could play accurately by ear numbers from the show he had seen that day. His formal education was sporadic, not helped by a quick temper—he left one school after biting the headmistress in the arm; and though he attended the Chapel Royal choir school at Clapham in 1909, he failed surprisingly, but perhaps providentially, to be accepted for the choir. The start of his professional career was less than a year away—27 January 1911—playing Prince Mussel in *The Goldfish* as one of a 'Star Cast of Wonder Children'. (Indeed, they included Michael MacLiammóir, and (Dame) Ninette de Valois.) His success led to a number of engagements with (Sir) Charles Hawtrey, from whom he learned much about playing comedy, and—quite as important—gained an insight into the anatomy of writing plays. In 1913 he appeared as an angel in *Hannele* by Hauptmann with the fifteen-year-old Gertrude Lawrence. (And so began a very special personal and professional relationship which lasted until her death in 1952.) Christmas 1913 saw a dream realized when he played Slightly in *Peter Pan* with Pauline Chase.

Throughout 1914–15 there was little work and some anxiety about his health. However the period was not uneventful. Worldly-wise for his years, his sophistication was purely theatrical; but in June 1915 an invitation to visit a Mrs Astley Cooper at Hambleton Hall gave Coward a first exciting view of that undiscovered country of high society, in which he would become increasingly at home, as welcome as he was at ease, and from which, both as writer and actor, he was to develop an important element of his comedy. Also from this period comes that distinctive mark of self-awareness—a new and durable signature, described by Sir John Betjeman at the Coward memorial service: 'Noël with two dots over the "e", and the firm decided downward stroke of the "l".' At Christmas 1915 he at last worked again, in *Where the Rainbow Ends*; followed by a tour in the thankless part of Charley in *Charley's Aunt* (1916). After a two-week run in *Light Blues*, singing and dancing with the newly-wed Jack Hulbert and (Dame) Cicely Courtneidge, he had his first solo number in *The Happy Family* (1916), of which one critic wrote: 'He combined the grace of a Russian dancer with the manner of an English schoolboy'. In 1916 he wrote the lyrics and music of his first song; by 1917 he had written three plays. The best of them, *The Rat Trap* (produced in 1924), was described as 'lousy in construction' by American impresario Gilbert Miller. Dialogue is not enough, was Miller's message. Coward took it to heart. Miller was enthusiastic about his acting however, and engaged him for the juvenile lead in a star-studded production of *The Saving Grace* (1917). Before that he appeared in his first film, *Hearts of the World*, directed by the legendary D. W. Griffith.

In the spring of 1918 began a frustrating nine-month 'engagement' in the army. Though at home with the rigorous discipline of the theatre, and already recognizing the no less demanding self-discipline required of the writer, Coward found that the military equivalent actually made him ill. (Would it have been the same, one wonders, if his call-up had been to the navy?) Although personally little affected by 'the war to end war' Coward shared the hectic relief of his contemporaries that it was over; and was soon considered by press and public as typical of the Bright Young Things, and also paradoxically, of the cynically disillusioned minority as well. The epithet 'brittle' was first applied to him now; it was to haunt him and his reputation to the grave and beyond.

Through his friendship with the tragically short-lived Meggie Albanesi he came to know Lorn Macnaughtan, who as Lorn Loraine became his secretary and 'one of the principal mainstays' of his life until her death forty-six years later. (It was she who first called him 'master'—as a joke.) In 1920 he first appeared in London in a play of his own, *I'll Leave It to You*, which, despite good notices, closed in five weeks. Undaunted, he went abroad for the first time, visiting Paris, and going on to Alassio to Mrs Astley Cooper, where he met another lifelong member of his inner circle—Gladys Calthrop, who was to design sets and costumes for a host of his plays. A rapid escape abroad, when his contribution to a production was over (whatever its fate), became hereafter part of the pattern of his life. 'Like a window opening in my head', he called it.

In *The Young Idea* (1922) Coward shamelessly borrowed his brother and sister from the twins in *You Never Can Tell* by George Bernard Shaw. Shaw was not offended, but wrote Coward a most constructive letter, including the advice 'never to see or read my plays. Unless you can get clear away from me you will begin as a back number, and be hopelessly out of it when you are forty'. (In 1941, when Coward had unwittingly breached the currency regulations and received much bad publicity, Shaw was his doughty champion, reminding him that there was no guilt without intention, and telling him to plead 'not guilty' despite his lawyers' advice. He did; and received a minimal fine.) He was composer and part-author of *London Calling* (1923), a revue starring himself and Gertrude Lawrence. As with *The Young Idea* the majority of critics preferred his writing to his performances. The rest would only accept him as a performer in the works of others—a contradiction only explicable by the hostility of both factions to versatility. (Meanwhile in 1921 he had paid his first exciting but impoverished visit to New York, meeting Alfred Lunt—Lynn Fontanne he already knew from London; and also Laurette Taylor and family, whose absent-minded hospitality and parlour games gave him the idea for *Hay Fever*.)

In November 1924 *The Vortex*—his play about drug addiction—put Coward triumphantly and controversially on the map, winning the allegiance of the beau monde led by the Mountbattens; confirming the worst fears of the stuffier elements of society. During its seven-month run—the longest he would ever permit himself—his output included *On With the Dance* (1925), a revue for (Sir) C. B. Cochran, an association which lasted for nine years (to see its Manchester opening Coward left *The Vortex* briefly to his understudy—(Sir) John Gielgud); *Fallen Angels* (1925) with Tallulah Bankhead—another *succès de scandale*; and *Hay Fever* (1925) with (Dame) Marie Tempest, which ran for a year. In September 1925 *The Vortex* took New York by storm, and Coward bought his first Rolls-Royce. *Easy Virtue* (1925) was written and produced while he was there. There were two consequences of this astonishing burst of successful activity, neither surprising. In 1926 he suffered a severe breakdown; and he yielded to the temptation to allow the production of three plays from his bottom drawer. All were failures—the most notorious being *Sirocco* (1927), which starred his great friend Ivor Novello. It was the only time they worked together.

Thanks to Cochran, Coward soon bounced back, with his most successful revue *This Year of Grace* (1928). *Bitter Sweet* (1929) followed—its most famous number 'I'll see you again' being composed in a taxi in a New York traffic jam. Even a Far Eastern holiday was productive. Alone in Shanghai, he had a mental picture of 'Gertie' in a white Molyneux dress in the South of France. Four hours later *Private Lives* had been mapped out; the actual writing took four days. It opened in London in 1930—Laurence (later Lord) Olivier playing a minor role—and was sold out for its three-month season, as it was in New York. Arnold Bennett called Coward 'the Congreve of our day'. 'Thin' and 'brittle' replied the critics. *Cavalcade* (1931) was his most ambitious production, suggested to his ever fertile mind by a photograph of a troop-ship leaving for the Boer war. It gave him the opportunity to proclaim in a brilliant mixture of pageantry and understatement his intense patriotism, coupled with a warning that 'this country of ours which we love so much' was losing its way. His enemies found it obscene that the author of *The Vortex* should treat such a subject. The nation and the English-speaking world responded differently. *Design for Living* (1932) was written in South America to redeem a promise made to the Lunts. It was so successful that he broke his three-month rule and played five in New York, using the mornings to write his first volume of autobiography *Present Indicative* (1937). From a Caribbean cruise with the navy he emerged with the libretto of *Conversation Piece* (1934), his last collaboration with Cochran. 1935 saw the writing of the nine playlets, some with music, which were presented in three programmes as *To-night at 8.30* (1936). *Operette* (1938) broke this long run of success, despite the hit number 'The Stately Homes of England'. Coward spent the summer of 1939 writing *Present Laughter* and *This Happy Breed*, but their production was postponed until 1942 by the outbreak of war, and by Coward's prearranged war job in Paris. This and a proposed intelligence assignment in America came to nothing, due in part, he believed, to the hostility of Lord Beaverbrook. Angry and frustrated, he turned with relief to his own field. The results included his longest running comedy *Blithe Spirit* (1941); his finest film script *In Which We Serve* (1942) about the sinking of Mountbatten's destroyer *Kelly*; and one of his most enduring songs 'London Pride'.

Cole Lesley, who died in 1980, writer of the best biography of Coward, came to work for him in 1936; Graham Payn joined the resident 'family' in 1947, completing with Joyce Carey, Lorn Loraine, and Gladys Calthrop the inner circle, which apart from Lorn Loraine's death in 1967, remained unchanged until his own. But if the domestic background was serene, Coward for the next twenty years was to endure much professional disappointment and disparagement. Between 1946 and 1964 six musicals and two plays fell short of Coward's highest hopes; fortunately *Relative Values* (1951), *Quadrille* (1952), *South Sea Bubble* and *Nude With Violin* (1956), though not his own favourites, were box-office successes.

In 1948, after a disastrous New York revival of *To-night at 8.30*, Coward took Graham Payn, who had starred in it with Gertrude Lawrence, to Jamaica. He fell in love with the island, built a house by the sea called Blue Harbour, and later, on the hill above ('piling Pelléas on Mélisande' he called it) a small retreat—Firefly Hill (where he died, and is buried). Also in 1948 he performed *Present Laughter* (*Joyeux Chagrins* in French) in Paris—a remarkable achievement, which failed dismally. His French was too good, they said, and the humour did not translate.

In 1951 he accepted an engagement which led to lifelong financial security. He appeared singing his own songs in cabaret at London's Café de Paris. Three more sell-out seasons followed; and then one in 1955 at Las Vegas, at 35,000 dollars a week for four weeks. From this in turn came highly lucrative American television and film engagements; and the difficult decision to emigrate, first to Bermuda and later to Switzerland, to mitigate the depredations of the Inland Revenue, and because, intending to perform less in future, 'I might as well do it for double the appreciation and ten times the lolly'. In any case, as Sir Winston Churchill told him, 'An Englishman has an inalienable right to live wherever he chooses'.

In 1953 he had a great success as King Magnus in Shaw's *The Apple Cart*; in 1960 his only novel *Pomp and Circumstance* was predictably more successful in America than Britain.

In 1964 an invitation by Sir Laurence Olivier to direct Dame Edith Evans in *Hay Fever* for the National Theatre marked the beginning of the last sunlit years of Coward's career, demonstrating once again that the British only feel comfortable with talent or genius when their possessors are 'over the hill'. Coward decided to risk his new reputation as 'demonstrably the greatest living English playwright' (Ronald Bryden) by appearing one last time in the West End. The result was *A Song at Twilight* and a double bill *Come Into the Garden, Maud*, and *Shadows of the Evening* (1966). Though seriously weakened by the onset of arterio-sclerosis, and by amoebic dysentery caught in the Seychelles, and for the only time in his life suffering the indignity of occasionally drying up, the season was a triumphant sell-out. There was only one bad notice. 'Good', he said reading it, 'I thought I might be slipping.' Professionally that was the final curtain. What followed was a trip round the world with Cole Lesley and Graham Payn; the seventieth birthday celebrations, culminating in an emotional midnight tribute by his fellow professionals; his long delayed and much deserved knighthood (1970); in America a special Tony award (1970)—his first—for services to the theatre; an honorary D.Litt. from Sussex University (1972); peaceful days in Switzerland and Jamaica with his friends, and finally, without warning, the end in Jamaica 26 March 1973.

How to assess him? His staccato speech, developed, it is said, to penetrate his mother's deafness, became the instrument of both his comedy and of his conversation. A hostile journalist once asked him for what he would be remembered after his death. 'Charm', he replied. T. E. Lawrence called him 'a hasty kind of genius'. In 1930 W. Somerset Maugham predicted that he would be responsible for the manner in which plays would be written for thirty years. He said himself that it was only natural that 'my writing should be appreciated casually, because my personality, performance, music and legend get in the way'. Of his homosexuality Dame Rebecca West, a close and clear-sighted friend, wrote: "There was impeccable dignity in his sexual life, which was reticent but untainted by pretence.'

A quintessential professional himself, he could be a scathing and witty critic of the second-rate; but he was outstandingly generous in his praise, never standing on dignity because of his position. He had the capacity to inspire great devotion. Gertrude Lawrence's last letter to him ended: 'It's always you I want to please more than *anyone*'—a sentiment that would be widely echoed among those who knew him.

There are portraits of him by Edward Seago in the Garrick Club and the Phoenix Theatre and by Clemence Dane in the National Portrait Gallery. In 1984 a black memorial stone, with the words 'A talent to amuse', was unveiled in Westminster Abbey.

[*Noël Coward Autobiography*, 1986 (ed. Sheridan Morley); Cole Lesley, *The Life of Noël Coward*, 1976; Charles Castle, *Noël*, 1972; Sheridan Morley, *A Talent to Amuse*, 1969; *Who's Who in the Theatre* (15th edn.) for a comprehensive list of his writings and performances; personal knowledge.]

MICHAEL DENISON

*published 1986*

## CRAIG (Edward Henry) Gordon

**(1872–1966)**

Artist and stage designer, was born 16 January 1872 at Stevenage, the only son and second child of Edward William Godwin, architect, and (Dame) (Alice) Ellen Terry, actress. His parents were unmarried; Ellen Terry had been separated but not divorced from her first husband, the artist George Frederic Watts. Godwin left her in 1875; free by then from Watts, she married an actor, Charles Clavering Wardell, whose stage name was Charles Kelly, from whom she was judicially separated in 1881.

'Teddy' and his sister Edith were brought up by their mother who in 1878 became (Sir) Henry Irving's leading lady at the Lyceum Theatre, London. The boy, known first as Edward Wardell, entered a preparatory school near Tunbridge Wells in 1883; just before his thirteenth birthday (1885), and during a Christmas holiday with his mother, then touring in the United States, he acted at Chicago the small part of a gardener's boy in Irving's production of *Eugene Aram*. At fourteen he went to Bradfield College, and later to a school at Heidelberg from which in 1888 he was expelled for breaches of discipline: Irving ('as kind as a father', said Craig) engaged the tall, good-looking youth for the Lyceum where he played Arthur in *The Dead Heart* (28 September 1889) and remained, off and on, until 1896. He adopted Craig as a stage name, afterwards legalized by deed poll. Christened when he was sixteen, 'Teddy' had received the additional names of Henry and Gordon from his godfather and godmother, Henry Irving and Lady Gordon. He chose Craig from the island named Ailsa Craig.

Besides minor work at the Lyceum he made various summer repertory tours where he could play such leading parts as Hamlet (1894) and Macbeth. In 1893 he married an actress, May, daughter of Robert Gibson, of St. Albans. Ellen Terry said of him as an actor: 'I have never known anyone with so much natural gift.' Some of his later antagonists would forget that, never simply an unattached theorist, he was bred to the stage.

Ceasing to act after 1897, he started a magazine, *The Page*, in which he published many of his earliest wood-engravings; though now he had four children—three sons and a daughter—he was on bad terms with his wife and conducting one of the many liaisons familiar throughout his career, relationships which frequently resulted in the birth of a child. Already, as actor and artist, he had radical views on the theatre. Encouraged by Martin Shaw, in 1900 he designed and directed at the Hampstead Conservatoire of Music Henry Purcell's *Dido and Aeneas*, for its time a startlingly original production in terms of light and colour, with an oblong stage opening and lit from above: a break with popular pictorial realism that foreshadowed later experiment as 'a supreme master of the theatre of the clouds' (H. Granville-Barker's phrase).

By 1902 he was in love with Elena Meo, a twenty-two-year-old violinist, daughter of Gaetano Meo, a Hampstead painter. That year, at the Great Queen Street Theatre, his production of Purcell's *Acis and Galatea* was 'an ever-shifting maze of colour, form, and motion'. Living now with Elena, he turned to other theatre work, particularly for his mother, newly in management (1903) at the Imperial in Tothill Street and preparing to do Henrik Ibsen's *The Vikings at Helgeland* and Shakespeare's *Much Ado About Nothing*.

An American critic, James Huneker, wrote of the first: 'Abolishing foot and border lights, sending shafts . . . from above, Mr Craig secures unexpected and bizarre effects.' The second, equally a commercial failure, contained a well-known scene in which Craig indicated the church by a widening, many coloured light that streamed through an unseen stained-glass window to illuminate a huge crucifix. His fame had developed among artists but not with the established theatre; he left for Berlin and produced contentious designs of two scenes for *Venice Preserved* at the Lessing (1905). Thereafter he rarely returned to England for any sustained visit. His wife May had divorced him; Elena's first child had died but she had a second daughter and in 1905 gave birth to a son, Edward.

Craig began in 1905 his association with the extravagantly temperamental dancer Isadora Duncan. This was at the heart of a complex period, rich in his visionary ideas of a unified theatre experience under one master-mind. During the autumn of 1906 (shortly after Isadora had given birth to a daughter) he was contemplating his designs for Ibsen's

*Rosmersholm*, staged by Eleonora Duse at the Teatro della Pergola in Florence: an extraordinary visual conception that the Italian designer, Enrico Corradini, described as 'a new architecture of great height, ranging in colour from green to blue . . .; it portrayed a *state of mind*'. Parting from Isadora in 1907, the unbiddable Craig settled for seven years in Florence; he brought over Elena (to whom he was never married) and the children, and began a theatre magazine, *The Mask*, which (except for a gap in World War I) lasted until 1929. European managers, even Sir Herbert Beerbohm Tree, London's high priest of naturalism, were anxious for his work, but a proposed *Macbeth* for Tree got no further; in spite of Craig's imaginative mastery he could ignore simple practical problems and minimize the actor.

His most influential book, *On the Art of the Theatre*, which grew from an earlier one, appeared in 1911, about the time that he designed *Hamlet* for Constantin Stanislavsky at the Art Theatre, Moscow; this was a triumph, especially its first court scene with Claudius and Gertrude enthroned at the back of the stage in a glittering sea of gold, and Hamlet, a lonely black-clad figure, sitting far downstage, a silhouette under a great shadow. A school for the art of the theatre, founded by Craig in Florence, had to close when war came. Craig lived temporarily in Rome; there in 1917 Elena and the children joined him from England, and they went to live at Rapallo where steadily he wrote, drew, and engraved. *The Theatre Advancing* appeared in England during 1921; his etchings, *Scene*, in 1923; *Woodcuts, and Some Words*—Sir Max Beerbohm's title—in 1924. For an elaborate final venture, the staging of Ibsen's *The Pretenders* in Copenhagen (1926), he received the Order of the Knights of Dannebrog in 1930, the year in which the designs were published by the Oxford University Press. In 1937 he was appointed RDI of the Royal Society of Arts.

After 1930 he concentrated on his books. The Cranach Press, Weimar, had published in 1929 *Hamlet*, with his superb woodcuts. He wrote an acutely detailed study of his idol, *Henry Irving* (1930), and in the following year one of his mother, *Ellen Terry and Her Secret Self*. Presently, still a handsome amorist, he left Elena and moved to Paris to live with his secretary and their daughter. Squalidly interned for a period during the German occupation, they were released and Craig continued his work. He travelled, alone, after the war, settling finally at Vence where he was living in 1957 at the publication of the only volume of his memoirs, *Index to the Story of My Days* (1872–1907). It contained an affectionate tribute to Elena. Just before Christmas 1957 she died suddenly in her English home, and her daughter Nelly went out to Vence to live with Craig.

Many devotees visited him during the last years of his self-exile. In 1958 he was made a Companion of Honour, and in 1964 became president of the Mermaid Theatre, London. He lived on, quietly but zestfully, remembering the high days of his youth, until two disastrous strokes, one in the winter of 1965 and a second in the ensuing summer. On 29 July 1966 he died at Vence aged ninety-four, having seen the best of his former revolutionary ideas pass into general theatre practice.

A wood-cut self-portrait is at the university of Hull, a drawing by Sir Max Beerbohm in the Victoria and Albert Museum, London, and a drawing by Sir William Rothenstein in the Manchester City Art Gallery.

[Edith Craig and Christopher St. John (eds.), *Ellen Terry's Memoirs*, 1933; Janet Leeper, *Edward Gordon Craig: Designs for the Theatre*, 1948; Edward Gordon Craig, *Index to the Story of My Days, 1872–1907*, 1957; Marguerite Steen, *A Pride of Terrys*, 1962; Denis Bablet, *Edward Gordon Craig*, Paris 1962, London 1966; Edward A. Craig, *Gordon Craig: The Story of His Life*, 1968; personal knowledge.]

J. C. Trewin

*published 1981*

## CROFT (John) Michael

(1922–1986)

Founder and director of the National Youth Theatre, was born in Oswestry 8 March 1922, the child of Constance Croft, who was unmarried. As a young child he moved with his elder sister to live with his mother's sister in Manchester, where he was educated at Burnage Grammar School from 1933 to 1940. His adolescence was dominated by two passions, for literature (in particular, poetry, for which he had an almost photographic memory), and for team games, which he played with extreme gusto, but at which he achieved a limited effectiveness only in cricket, the rich lore of which always fascinated him.

He had little satisfaction or security from his home. He soon developed an uncompromising individualism and volunteered for aircrew duties in the Royal Air Force in 1940. He became a sergeant-pilot and took part in daylight bombing raids over occupied France, but his manual dexterity proved unequal to the demands of flying, and he was offered the option of a discharge.

He had a variety of casual occupations, as an actor, professional 'fire-watcher' in ARP (Air Raid Precautions), credit salesman, and lumberjack, before he volunteered for the navy in 1943. After service in Mediterranean convoys, he finished the war as a radar operator on merchant ships.

In 1946 he went to Keble College, Oxford, to read English. He was a member of an exceptionally talented generation of ex-service students, and revelled in being able to indulge his love of literature, theatre, writing, and sport, while, at the same time, breaking university regulations by living in licensed premises. He took a special short-course degree and achieved a third class in English in 1948.

An unsettled period followed graduation. He did occasional journalism, poetry writing, broadcasting, and acting, and worked as a private tutor and a supply-teacher. From teaching, he gathered the material for his novel, *Spare the Rod* (1954), a minor *cause célèbre* amongst liberal educationists, which, after skirmishes with the Board of Censors, was filmed in 1961 with Max Bygraves as the sexually ambivalent schoolteacher. He also wrote *Red Carpet to China* (1958). Croft's final teaching post was at Alleyn's School, Dulwich (1950–5), where he staged a series of epic Shakespearian productions, involving the majority of the school's pupils, that aroused the interest of the London press and the professional theatre. His work was characterized by spectacle, vigour, commitment, and an unusual concern for verse-speaking: he wanted to envelop everybody in his huge enthusiasm and to make them share his fascination with the works of Shakespeare.

*Spare the Rod* gave him sufficient financial independence to resign from teaching, ostensibly to devote himself to writing, but it seems that he was persuaded by a group of ex-pupils, disconsolate at the loss of their Shakespeare play, to direct them in an out-of-term production of *Henry V* at Toynbee Hall in 1956. In effect, this was the first 'Youth Theatre' production and it determined the course of the rest of his life. The venture was self-supporting: ticket sales and donations were the only funding until, in 1958, King George's Jubilee Fund gave a grant which was continuous. Subsequently, the British Council and the Department of Education and Science provided support. There was a long and fairly acrimonious battle with the Arts Council before any funding was secured, only for it to be withdrawn after a few years. By 1970, Croft was able to claim, 'We have three companies touring in Europe, four in London, and one in the north-east of England—the whole being run by a full-time staff of four, with a handful of voluntary helpers.' Ahead lay the televising and broadcasting of youth theatre productions, the commissioning of new works (significantly from Peter Terson and Barrie Keeffe in the 1970s), the visit to America, the acquiring of the Shaw theatre (1971), and, in 1977, official recognition of the National Youth Theatre of Great Britain.

Croft gained an increasing reputation as an internationally respected director, and his companies added to the lustrous reputation of the English theatre, but the NYTGB struggled against inadequate funding. He saw his creation as the victim of national parsimony to the arts and he became more obviously an abrasive, militant publicist, enjoying a bare-knuckle approach to negotiation. He had a flair for discovering stars, such as Derek Jacobi, Helen Mirren, Ben Kingsley, and Diana Quick.

He was appointed OBE in 1971. After the straitened circumstances of his early days, his later success introduced him to an expansive lifestyle, which he delighted in sharing generously with his vast number of friends and acquaintances. He was homosexual, but he had many friends of the opposite sex and, particularly in his early years, led a bisexual existence. He had few intimates, apparently finding it difficult to break down his core of loneliness. He was a man of gargantuan appetites in every way, especially for food and drink, and his eventual failure to control these proclivities, allied to a dread of surgery, contributed to his comparatively early death. He died of a heart attack at his home in Kentish Town, 15 November 1986. A characteristic instruction in his will provided a party for a vetted list of some hundreds of his friends, 'at which the food shall be wholesome—and the drink shall not be allowed to run out'.

[Michael Croft's papers in private hands; personal knowledge.]

Geoffrey Sykes

*published* 1996

## DEVINE George Alexander Cassady

(1910–1966)

Actor and theatre director, was born 20 November 1910 in Hendon, the only child of Giorgios Devine, bank clerk, of Hendon, and his wife, Ruth Eleanor Cassady. He was educated at Clayesmore School, of which the founder and headmaster was his uncle Alexander Devine, and at Wadham College, Oxford, where he read modern history. One of his tutors was Lord David Cecil. As president of the Oxford University Dramatic Society in his last year, he established a foothold in the professional theatre by inviting (Sir) John Gielgud to direct the 1932 OUDS production of *Romeo and Juliet* in which Devine played Mercutio in company with (Dame) Peggy Ashcroft's Juliet and (Dame) Edith Evans's Nurse, and Christopher Hassall's Romeo.

Devine left Oxford without taking Schools to embark on a London acting career. At the same time, he attached himself as business manager to the firm of Motley, the stage design partnership of Elizabeth

Montgomery, Margaret Harris, and her sister (Audrey) Sophia Harris (died 1966), who later became Devine's wife (1939) and the mother of his only child, Harriet.

It was in the Motley studio that he first met Michel Saint-Denis, director of the Compagnie des Quinze, whom for the rest of his life he acknowledged as his master. With Saint-Denis and others he set up the London Theatre Studio (1936–9) which attempted a revolution in British stage training. After the war (which Devine spent mostly in Burma as a captain in the Royal Artillery, and during which he was twice mentioned in dispatches), he resumed his alliance with Saint-Denis at the Old Vic Centre: a tripartite offshoot of the Old Vic Company, comprising a school (directed by Glen Byam Shaw), the Young Vic touring troupe (directed by Devine), and a never-completed experimental theatre (in the charge of Saint-Denis). From its opening in 1947 the Centre produced an astounding crop of young actors, directors, and designers, and when the governors of the Old Vic closed it down in 1952 their action provoked a storm of professional outrage and parliamentary criticism.

Up to this time Devine had spent most of his working life as a teacher-administrator, but with the break-up of the Vic Centre, he turned to freelance directing: partly of opera at Sadler's Wells and Covent Garden (where he directed the première of Sir William Walton's *Troilus and Cressida*, 1954), and partly of the Shakespeare repertory at Stratford-upon-Avon (collaborating with Gielgud and Isamu Noguchi in the 'Japanese' *King Lear*, 1955).

In 1956 he resumed his reformist mission as artistic director of the newly formed English Stage Company at the Royal Court Theatre. The ESC's original policy was to persuade established novelists to write for the stage, a policy abandoned after the production of John Osborne's *Look Back in Anger* (1956) which released a tidal wave of new plays by hitherto unknown young playwrights including John Arden and Arnold Wesker. Until the end of the decade the Court was the spearhead of the so-called 'breakthrough' movement, challenging the reigning conventions of dramatic craftsmanship and reasserting the theatre's role as a platform for radical opinion.

Throughout this spectacular period Devine remained personally inconspicuous. After the first season he directed very few new plays himself (excepting those by his close friend Samuel Beckett); and when he acted on the Court stage it was usually to save money. His purpose was to create a free space where the best talents could collaborate in pushing the theatre from the periphery to the centre of English cultural life: a purpose partly acknowledged in 1958 when he was appointed CBE 'for services to drama'.

Devine's 'writers' theatre' was a place where material of a kind formerly restricted to club performances found a public outlet. He was not the originator of this idea, but he was the first English director to make it work. He succeeded through an unshakeable determination, entirely untouched by narrow obsessiveness. In opening his doors to unknown writers and directors he also kept them open to eminent pre-war colleagues like Ashcroft and Laurence (later Lord) Olivier: and in keeping an open space for the rebel artists under his roof he took great care not to play the rebel with his own management committee. He remained a dedicated teacher, and the creator of an exemplary theatre in which the technician was respected no less than the actor and the writer. His final years were spent with his former London Theatre Studio pupil, the designer Jocelyn, daughter of Sir A. P. Herbert. In her company he died in London 20 January 1966.

[Irving Wardle, *The Theatres of George Devine*, 1978.]

IRVING WARDLE

*published 1981*

## DEXTER John

(1925–1990)

Stage director, was born 2 August 1925 in Derby, the only child of Harry Dexter, plumber, and his wife, Rosanne Smith. There were music, painting, and home theatricals in the family, but Dexter's only formal education was at the local elementary school (Reginald Street), which he left at the age of fourteen. He then took a factory job before joining the army as a national serviceman. Not having attended a university was a source of lifelong regret, particularly as his entry into the professional theatre coincided with the rise of the graduate director. For the same reason, he developed into a compulsive autodidact, a passionate scholar of stage history who never undertook a classical text without exhaustive research.

His career began in the Derby Playhouse, in a company that also included John Osborne. Osborne recommended Dexter to the English Stage Company's artistic director, George Devine, who engaged him in 1957 as an associate director. Dexter had no previous directing experience, but he rapidly gained it at the Royal Court theatre, which he subsequently described as his university; there he forged relationships with working-class writers, notably Michael Hastings and Arnold Wesker. At the same time he formed his long alliance with the designer Jocelyn Herbert, crucially in the 1959 production of Wesker's *The Kitchen*, an elaborately choreographed show on a defiantly undecorated stage, where even the lighting rig was exposed to the audience. This marked the beginning of the text-centred, visually austere style which was to become his trademark.

At the Royal Court Dexter gained a double reputation: as an electrifying animator of spectacle and crowd movement, and as a 'playwright's director', who could spot not only the defects of a script but also the hidden potential, and coax the writer into achieving it. The success of his subsequent partnership with Peter Shaffer (*The Royal Hunt of the Sun*, 1964; *Black Comedy*, 1966; *Equus*, 1973) depended as much on pre-rehearsal textual analysis as on the physical staging.

In 1963 Dexter left the Royal Court to become assistant director to Sir Laurence (later Baron) Olivier at the National Theatre when it was in its honeymoon phase. He began widening his range with productions of *Saint Joan* (1963), *Hobson's Choice* (1964), and the Olivier *Othello* (1964), shows that went lastingly into public memory. He also began another fertile partnership with the poet Tony Harrison, whose versions of Molière and Racine (*The Misanthrope*, 1973, and *Phaedra Britannica*, 1975) set a dazzling new standard for creative translation.

By the late 1960s Dexter was building a parallel career as a director of opera: a natural move given his flair as an animator and innate musicality (coupled with his temporary withdrawal from the National Theatre following disagreements with Olivier). His first venture, Berlioz' *Benvenuto Cellini* at Covent Garden (1966), was untypically ornate; but with Verdi's *I Vespiri Siciliani* at the Hamburg State Opera three years later he declared himself in a production of characteristically austere magnificence. Staged on Josef Svoboda's gigantic staircase between two vast watch-towers, this production carried his name round the world as a new force on the operatic scene; and although he maintained his connection with Hamburg until 1973 (Verdi's *Un Ballo in Maschera*), the main focus of his work during the 1970s was at New York's Metropolitan Opera House, where he was appointed director of productions in 1974. Dexter saw the Met. as a Babylonian anachronism, and he made it his mission to drag it into the twentieth century through simplified staging, technical reform, and enlargement of repertory. Against the odds, he won over the conservative public with a series of non-standard works, from Meyerbeer's *Le Prophète* and Poulenc's *Dialogues of the Carmelites* (both 1977) to *Parade* (1981), a French triptych which he assembled from Satie, Poulenc, and Ravel. By this time, however, his relationship had soured with the Met.'s administration and its musical director, James Levine; and during the early 1980s he returned to freelance work.

He continued to direct major productions in London and New York, but never achieved his ambition of running a house and company of his own; and his final attempt to do so—with a classically based West End troupe—fell apart after its opening production of *The Cocktail Party* by T. S. Eliot (Phoenix theatre, 1986).

Dexter was a stocky figure of medium height, with chubby features and a domed head that became increasingly prominent as he lost his hair. He had a biting tongue, which could wound actors and alienate patrons; he also suffered from declining health, due to diabetes and the aftermath of youthful polio, before his final heart attack. He was a homosexual and suffered a brief term of imprisonment for homosexuality in the 1950s. A collection of his writings, *The Honourable Beast: a Posthumous Autobiography*, was published by his friend Riggs O'Hara in 1993. Dexter died 23 March 1990 in London, following a heart operation.

[John Dexter, *The Honourable Beast: a Posthumous Autobiography*, 1993; private information; personal knowledge.]

Irving Wardle

*published 1996*

## DOLIN Sir Anton

(1904–1983)

Ballet dancer, was born (Sydney Francis) Patrick (Chippindall Healey) Kay in Slinfold, Sussex, 27 July 1904, the second of three sons (there were no daughters) of Henry George Kay, amateur cricketer, and later master and owner of the South Coast Harriers and Staghounds, and his wife, Helen Maude Chippindall Healey, from Dublin. Patrick Kay took his first dancing lessons at the age of ten, in Hove, after much pleading with his reluctant father. He went to a Miss Clarice James, then to the two Cone sisters Lily and Grace. His parents moved to London to further his stage training and he auditioned successfully for the Black Cat in *Bluebell in Fairyland* at Christmas 1915. This role was followed by that of John in *Peter Pan*. Dolin then trained as an actor and dancer at the Italia Conti School, which arranged engagements and tours for him.

In August 1917 he began serious ballet training with Seraphine Astafieva. He studied with her for five years during which he was engaged, under the name 'Patrikéeff', by Diaghilev to appear in his 1921 production of *The*

*Sleeping Princess*. More commercial engagements followed and on 26 June 1923 he appeared for the first time as Anton Dolin at the Royal Albert Hall in the 'Anglo-Russian Ballet'. He was by now also studying with Nicolas Legat, who had recently escaped from Russia. In November 1923 he joined Diaghilev's Ballets Russes.

He immediately established himself as an outstanding dancer and was particularly successful as Beau Gosse in *Le Train Bleu* for his Paris début in the summer season of 1924. He made his London début that autumn in the same role.

Less than two years later he left Diaghilev, whose favourite had become Serge Lifar, during the Paris summer season of 1925. He undertook many engagements in revues and musicals in England. In 1927 he danced with Tamara Karsavina at the Coliseum, and with (Dame) Ninette de Valois, in *Whitebirds* at His Majesty's. He also undertook a continental tour with Vera Nemchinova, with whom in 1927–8 he founded the first English Ballet Company, which included (Sir) Frederick Ashton, Harold Turner, Mary Skeaping, and Margaret Craske. Dolin created several ballets for his company, the best being *The Nightingale and the Rose*, Chopin's *Revolutionary Étude*, and George Gershwin's *Rhapsody in Blue*. By the end of 1928 he had rejoined Diaghilev in Monte Carlo and danced with more great ballerinas—Olga Spessivtseva in *Lac*, Karsavina in *Petrushka*, and Alexandra Danilova in *Le Bal*. It was while filming in *Dark Red Roses* with Lydia Lopokova in August 1929 that news of Diaghilev's death reached him and he was forced to become free lance again. That autumn he performed at the London Coliseum with Anna Ludmilla, to whom he became engaged. Later she terminated the engagement.

During the 1930s Dolin appeared in various revues and as a soloist in the new Vic-Wells Ballet from 1931 to 1935. He helped to launch the Camargo Society in 1930, for which he created Satan in *Job* (1931). In 1935 he and (Dame) Alicia Markova founded their own ballet company with Bronislava Nijinska as the ballet mistress and Dolin as a director and first soloist. The company, which was financed by Laura Henderson who ran the Windmill Theatre, lasted until December 1937. During the next two years Dolin danced in Paris, Blackpool, Australia, New Zealand, Honolulu, and London.

He spent the war years in America and Australia. He helped build up the American Ballet Theatre for whom he restaged several of the classical ballets and danced the lead in Michel Fokine's *Bluebeard* in Mexico City in 1941. He returned to London in 1948 as a guest star with the Sadler's Wells Ballet. In August 1950 Julian Braunsweg founded the London Festival Ballet, of which Dolin was artistic director and first soloist until 1961. The company travelled extensively, with the young John Gilpin as one of its dancers. Dolin and Gilpin formed a lasting friendship, Dolin outliving Gilpin by only three months.

After leaving the Festival Ballet Dolin directed the ballet at the Rome Opera for two seasons and then became a freelance producer all over the world. He was hospitalized in New York in 1966 for a hernia, but later in 1967 performed as the Devil in Stravinsky's *The Soldier's Tale*. He taught at summer schools, adjudicated at festivals, and acted in his own one-man show *Conversations with Diaghilev.* In 1979 he played the part of the ballet teacher Enrico Cecchetti in Herbert Ross's film *Nijinsky*. He remounted *Giselle* in Iceland in 1982 and taught in Hong Kong and China in 1983. His last engagement was in Houston before he returned to London and Paris where he had a medical check-up in a Paris hospital which pronounced him in good health before he collapsed and died immediately afterwards in Paris 25 November 1983.

Knighted in 1981, Dolin was the recipient of the Royal Academy of Dancing's Queen Elizabeth II award in 1954 and the Order of the Sun from Peru in 1959. He was the author of several books, including autobiographies. He spotted and sponsored many talented young dancers, to whom his generosity was remarkable. He partnered many great ballerinas who knew him as a most courteous partner. He was one of the best *danseurs nobles* in classical ballet and was the first British male dancer to be acclaimed internationally. He was also anxious to take his art to the widest possible public and managed to combine strict classicism with the instinct of a showman. He was unmarried.

[Anton Dolin, *Autobiography*, 1960; Andrew Wheatcroft (compiler), *Dolin, Friends and Memories*, 1982; *The Times*, 27 February 1980; personal knowledge.]

BERYL GREY

*published 1990*

## DONAT (Friederich) Robert

(1905–1958)

Actor, the fourth and youngest son of Ernst Emil Donat, civil engineer of Polish origin, and his wife, Rose Alice Green, was born at Withington, Manchester, 18 March 1905. He went to the Central School, Manchester, and later took stage-training under James Bernard of the same city. In 1924 he joined Sir Frank Benson whose company was not then so constantly on tour as it had been; thus Donat could alternate continuing membership with seasons in provincial repertory. This was well-varied and helpful schooling: the Shakespearian apprenticeship was valuable, for among Donat's enduring distinctions was the purity of his diction and the beauty of his voice. He worked for a while with Alfred Wareing whose repertory seasons at the Theatre Royal, Huddersfield, had unusual ambition and quality. In 1928 he began a year at the Playhouse in Liverpool and this was followed by important work at Terence Gray's Festival Theatre in Cambridge where plays by Euripides, Pirandello, Sheridan, and Shakespeare gave him opportunities to experiment in a range of widely different and challenging leading roles.

He made his mark decisively in London in 1931 when he created the part of Gideon Sarn in a dramatization of *Precious Bane* by Mary Webb. His handsome features and beautiful delivery, together with the equipment of technique acquired in his repertory years, promised promotion to the front rank and there was confirmation of his powers in the Malvern Festival of 1931. Again at Malvern, in 1933, he played the two Camerons in *A Sleeping Clergyman* by James Bridie; the piece was transferred to London and had a long run at the Piccadilly Theatre. Donat's performance of the two roles, the dying consumptive and his son the brilliant doctor, was memorable and repeated in a revival of 1947. To the simulation of a man with lung-trouble he brought his own knowledge of pain, for he was himself a sufferer from asthma and his later career was much impeded by illness.

His success carried him to important film work, especially with (Sir) Alexander Korda who was then recruiting remarkable casts from the leading players of the living stage. His notable appearances were in *The Private Life of Henry VIII* (in which Charles Laughton played the king), *The Ghost Goes West*, and as another Scottish doctor, Andrew Manson, in a screen-version of A. J. Cronin's *The Citadel*. Perhaps his most widely appreciated film-role was that of Mr. Chips, the ageing schoolmaster well known to readers of the novel by James Hilton.

Donat continued to mingle screen-work with important returns to the stage, taking on the cares and risks of management at the Queen's Theatre in 1936 when he presented J. L. Hodson's *Red Night*. During the war he gave vigour and volume to the eloquence of Captain Shotover in a revival of Shaw's *Heartbreak House* (1943). At the Westminster Theatre in 1945 he was much liked in a plebeian comedy part in *The Cure for Love* by Walter Greenwood. His last venture as a manager was at the Aldwych Theatre in 1945 when he staged *Much Ado About Nothing* with himself as Benedick. His spirited rendering of the wordy warfare with Beatrice was exemplary at a time when the speaking on the British stage was much criticized. He gave another lesson in delivery when he joined the Old Vic company in 1953 to play Becket in a production of T. S. Eliot's *Murder in the Cathedral*. Directed by (Sir) Robert Helpmann, this was one of the most effective renderings of a play frequently revived. Donat was far from being a player attached to one type of character. He was, however, seen at his best in parts which asked for splendour of voice and dignity of bearing and his Becket was held by those who knew the scope of his work to have a singular beauty. Asceticism was a quality which came naturally to his delicacy of feature, but he had learned in his repertory years to be richly versatile. In naming his favourite roles he included the two gusty, outspoken Camerons of *A Sleeping Clergyman*. Here, and in *Murder in the Cathedral*, were perhaps the summits of his achievement on the living stage.

During the last five years of his life Donat was a constant invalid. He did not mind the seclusion since he was of a shy and retiring disposition and had never sought the bright lights of publicity. But the frustration was galling for an actor who was only just entering his fifties and should have been at the height of his powers. He died in London 9 June 1958.

In 1929 Donat married Ella Annesley Voysey, by whom he had two sons and one daughter, but the marriage was subsequently dissolved. In 1953 he married the actress Dorothy Renée Ascherson.

[J. C. Trewin, *Robert Donat*, 1968; private information; personal knowledge.]

Ivor Brown

*published 1971*

## DORS Diana

(1931–1984)

Actress, was born Diana Mary Fluck 23 October 1931 in Swindon, Wiltshire, the only child of Albert Edward Sidney Fluck, of Swindon, a railway clerk and former army captain, and his wife, Winifred Maud Mary Payne. She was educated at local schools and when she was nine she wrote in a school essay, 'I am going to be a film star, with a swimming pool and a cream telephone.' At thirteen, pretending to be seventeen, she entered a beauty contest and came third, and during World War II she entertained troops at camp concerts.

At fifteen she enrolled at the London Academy of Dramatic Art, where she was spotted in a production and put into films, making her début in a thriller, *The Shop at Sly Corner*, in 1946. After other parts she was offered a ten-year contract by the Rank Organization and she joined the Rank Charm School, which had been set up to discover and groom British stars. She changed her surname to Dors, after her maternal grandmother.

Though as the cousin in the popular Huggett films she hinted at a flair for comedy, her screen career failed to develop and the Rank contract lapsed in 1950. But the publicity machine was already starting to take over. With her long, platinum blonde hair, sensational figure, and colourful private life, she was projected as the British answer to Marilyn Monroe; and for the rest of her life her professional achievements came a very poor second to her status as a celebrity.

The early publicity stunts were masterminded by her first husband, Dennis Hamilton, whom she married in 1951. Born Dennis Hamlington Gittings, he was the son of Stanley Gittings, manager of a public house in Luton. A Svengali figure, ruthless and domineering, he fed the gossip columns with a stream of Dors stories, many of them fabricated. The couple took off for Hollywood. Diana Dors continued to appear in films, most of them forgettable. An exception was *Yield to the Night* (1956), loosely based on the Ruth Ellis case, in which Dors eschewed her usual glamour roles to play a condemned murderess.

It showed her potential as a serious actress, though the public found the switch from blonde bombshell difficult to take. Her marriage foundered, and ended, in the now customary blaze of publicity, in 1957. Dennis Hamilton died in 1959 and in the same year she married in New York an American comedian, Dickie Dawson. They had two sons, Mark and Gary. In 1960 she was paid £35,000 for her memoirs by the *News of the World*. Lurid by the standards of the time, the series ran for twelve weeks. The archbishop of Canterbury denounced her as a wayward hussy.

By now the film parts were getting smaller. She put on weight and the erstwhile sex symbol gave way to a middle-aged mother figure. She had to return to England in 1966 to support her family, for she was sole breadwinner. She played Prince Charming in pantomime and did a cabaret act in the northern clubs. Her private life continued to make the headlines. Her marriage to Dawson ended after eight years and she lost custody of her two sons. In 1968 she married an actor, Alan Lake, son of Cyril Foster Lake, glaze maker. They had a son, Jason. In 1967 she was declared bankrupt, owing the Inland Revenue £48,413 in tax. She admitted to being hopeless with money. In October 1970 Lake was sent to prison for eighteen months for his part in a public house brawl.

Her acting career enjoyed a brief revival when she played a brassy widow in *Three Months Gone* at the Royal Court Theatre in London (1970) and there was a strong part in Jerzy Skolimowski's film, *Deep End* (1970). But a television series written for her, *Queenie's Castle* (1970), proved disappointing. Her Jocasta in Sophocles' *Oedipus* at the Chichester Festival in 1974 was a brave, but isolated, stab at the classics.

In 1974 she came close to death from meningitis and she underwent operations for cancer in 1982 and 1983. Resilient and cheerful in the face of such adversity, she produced further instalments of her memoirs (1978 and 1979), ran an agony column in a daily newspaper, and, by now well over fourteen stone, did a slimming series for breakfast television. A celebrity to the end, she died of cancer in hospital at Windsor, Berkshire, 4 May 1984. Her death was widely and genuinely mourned. Vulgar she may have been but there was admiration for her courage and tenacity. Alan Lake never got over his grief and he killed himself on 10 October 1984, the sixteenth anniversary of their first meeting.

[*The Times*, 7 May 1984; Joan Flory and Damien Walne, *Diana Dors: Only a Whisper Away*, 1987; personal knowledge.]

PETER WAYMARK

*published 1990*

## D'OYLY CARTE Dame Bridget

(1908–1985)

Theatrical manager and proprietor of the D'Oyly Carte Opera Company, was born in London in Suffolk Street, Pall Mall, 25 March 1908, the only daughter and elder child of Rupert D'Oyly Carte, proprietor of the D'Oyly Carte Opera Company, and his wife, Dorothy Milner, third daughter of John Stewart Gathorne-Hardy, second Earl of Cranbrook. Her second forename was Cicely but she later abandoned this name by deed poll. Educated privately in England and abroad, she later went to Dartington Hall, Totnes, where her artistic talents and abiding interest in the arts were much encouraged. At the age of eighteen, in 1926, she married her first cousin, John David Gathorne-Hardy, fourth Earl of Cranbrook, but the marriage was dissolved in 1931. There were no children. In 1932 she resumed her maiden name by deed poll and helped her father in the Savoy Hotel. From 1939 to 1947 she worked in the poorer districts of London in child welfare.

However, a great change in her life became inevitable when, as the granddaughter of Richard D'Oyly Carte, she unexpectedly became the inheritor of a great theatrical tradition, as a result of the death of her brother Michael in a motor accident in Switzerland in 1932. Becoming, as a consequence, her father's sole heir when he died in 1948, there passed to her the proprietorship of the D'Oyly Carte Opera Company, and all the family rights in the Gilbert and Sullivan operas. This was a challenge she accepted, and with marked accomplishment she continued without a break the presentation of the operas, both in Britain and in the United States and Canada, until thirteen years later the copyright expired, fifty years after the death of Sir W. S. Gilbert, and, with that, the performing rights owned by her family.

When the lapse of the copyright drew near, she at first thought it would be right that the long reign of her family, begun by her grandfather and faithfully continued and developed by her father, should be discontinued, and she gave no support to a petition to Parliament seeking a privileged position for the operas by a perpetuation of the copyright under some public body. However, those near to her suggested that she should continue to present the operas, for which there was still a great following, wherever the English language prevailed, and to this she consented.

The result was the formation of the D'Oyly Carte Opera Trust, a charitable organization, which she endowed, giving it her company's scenery, costumes, band parts, and other assets, worth then at least £150,000, to which she added £30,000 in cash. Later, she gave the trustees the original score of *Iolanthe*, which had been presented to her grandfather by Sir Arthur Sullivan.

The new trust, which took over in 1961, included representatives of the three families, D'Oyly Carte, Gilbert, and Sullivan, and, guided by A. W. Tuke, then chairman of Barclays Bank, who became chairman, it assigned to Bridget D'Oyly Carte the theatrical presentation of the operas by a company formed for this purpose, Bridget D'Oyly Carte Ltd., of which she became chairman and managing director. In this capacity, she continued to present the operas until their last season in London in 1982, and, having succeeded Tuke as chairman of the trustees, she held this office until her death. In 1975 she was appointed DBE.

By nature shy and retiring, characteristics she inherited from her father, but always entertaining in her methods of expression, she invariably gave evidence of her shrewd observation and artistic judgement and ability. It was these qualities which made her of exceptional value to the Savoy group of hotels and restaurants, founded by her grandfather, of which her father was the chairman, and of which she became a director when he died. In this additional capacity, she actively controlled with considerable talent the furnishing and decoration departments.

At the time of her death she was president of the Savoy Company, in which she was a large shareholder, and at the same time she maintained her family connection with the Savoy Theatre, built by her grandfather, of which she herself was a director. She was also chairman of Edward Goodyear Ltd., the royal florists.

She had a great love of gardening and when her father died, leaving her their beautiful family home in Devon (now the property of the National Trust) between Brixham and Kingswear, she decided to part with it and acquired instead the estate of Shrubs Wood in Buckinghamshire, which remained her home for more than thirty years. There, as her parents had done in Devon, she transformed the grounds with rare trees and shrubs of exceptional beauty. She also spent some time in Scotland, where she lived in the seventeenth-century castle of Barscobe in the stewartry of Kirkcudbright.

She died at her Buckinghamshire home 2 May 1985. When her will was published, her benefactions were seen to be munificent. After leaving her shares in the Savoy Company, worth several million pounds, to the D'Oyly Carte Charitable Trust, which she had established in her lifetime, she bequeathed to the D'Oyly Carte Opera Trust the residue of her estate, which amounted to a gift of £1½ million, for the future presentation of the operas, with which her family had been identified for over one hundred years.

[Personal knowledge.]

HUGH WONTNER

*published* 1990

## DU MAURIER Sir Gerald Hubert Edward Busson

(1873–1934)

Actor-manager, was born 26 March 1873 at Hampstead, where he lived all through his boyhood and young manhood until his marriage in 1903, and whither he returned in 1916 and remained until he died. He was, as he himself said, essentially a cockney, but he was a Hampstead cockney, a cockney entirely different from all others. He was extraordinary among these unique cockneys for several reasons. His father, George Louis Palmella Busson du Maurier, although the son of a naturalized British subject, was a Frenchman, born in Paris and married to an Englishwoman, Emma, daughter of William Wightwick.

Gerald du Maurier, the younger son and youngest child in a family of five, was educated at Harrow. At first indeterminate about his career, he decided that as he had been successful in amateur theatrical performances, he might as well go on to the professional stage. The decision was as casual as his style of acting, a deceptive style, since it caused shallow-minded people to think that he 'was always himself' and to overlook the remarkable technique which he brought to this easy, casual performance. His first appearance was made at the Garrick Theatre on 6 January 1894, as Fritz a waiter, in *An Old Jew* by Sydney Grundy. The management was that of (Sir) John Hare, and du Maurier appeared under it because his father and Hare were friends. He remained with Hare for six months, went on tour with (Sir) Johnston Forbes-Robertson, and then in September 1895 joined (Sir) Herbert Beerbohm Tree at Manchester, to play the part of Dodor in the dramatic version of his father's novel, *Trilby*, which was brought to the Haymarket Theatre, London, in October. He stayed with Tree for just over four years, steadily perfecting his nonchalant style. Two years (1899–1901) with Mrs. Patrick Campbell followed his long engagement with Tree. It was not, however, until November 1902 that he established himself truly. In that month, at the Duke of York's Theatre, he played the part of the Hon. Ernest Woolley in *The Admirable Crichton*, a comedy by (Sir) J. M. Barrie, and his nonchalance was now seen to be power. Thus he began an association with Barrie which was to be highly beneficial to both men: his tally of Barrie pieces was eight, including *Peter Pan* (in which he 'created' the parts of Captain Hook and Mr. Darling), *What Every Woman Knows*, and *Dear Brutus*. In 1910 du Maurier joined Frank Curzon in the management of Wyndham's Theatre where he remained for fifteen years, except for a short break in 1918 when he became a cadet in the Irish Guards. After his separation from Curzon, he joined Gilbert Miller at the St. James's Theatre, his first production, Frederick Lonsdale's *The Last of Mrs. Cheyney* (1925), being immensely successful.

Du Maurier was knighted in 1922, and died in London after an operation 11 April 1934. His wife, Muriel, herself an actress, daughter of Harry Beaumont, a solicitor, was playing with him in *The Admirable Crichton* at the time of their engagement. They had three daughters, of whom the second, Daphne, is a widely popular novelist and has written successful plays.

Du Maurier, who, in addition to introducing a style of acting which is now overcommon and almost routine, was a very skilful producer of plays, had a singularly successful career in the theatre. His daughter Daphne wrote of him 'he did not know what it was to wait at stage doors to interview managers and beg for a part in a new production'. If his good fortune began to flicker in the last year or two of his life, it was because he became careless of his performance. His moods were unusually variable, but he rallied easily from despondency and was good company, especially when he exercised his gift of mimicry. His family affection was strong, and he was deeply distressed by the death in action in 1915 of his brother Guy, a professional soldier who had, unexpectedly, written a play, *An Englishman's Home*, which was remarkably successful when Gerald produced it in 1909; and the deaths of his sisters and of his mother distressed him no less. His standard, as a theatre manager, was good, although not of the highest order. His profile, he declared, was against him, and debarred him from poetic drama and tragedy. But he read poetry aloud very charmingly, and might, if he had trusted himself more, have aspired to greater heights than he achieved.

There are portraits of du Maurier by Harrington Mann and John Collier in the possession of his widow. Another portrait by Collier is in the Public Library at Hampstead. A portrait by Augustus John was last heard of in the United States of America. A cartoon by 'Spy' appeared in *Vanity Fair*, 25 December 1907.

[*The Times*, 12 April 1934; Daphne du Maurier, *Gerald: A Portrait*, 1934; personal knowledge.]

ST. JOHN ERVINE

*published 1949*

## EDWARDS James Keith O'Neill ('Jimmy') (1920–1988)

Entertainer, was born 23 March 1920 in Barnes, London, the fifth of five sons and eighth of nine children of Reginald Walter Kenrick Edwards, professor of mathematics at King's College, London, and his wife, Phyllis Katherine Cowan, who was from New Zealand. He was educated at St Paul's Cathedral Choir School and King's College School, Wimbledon, where he first developed what was to become a lifelong enthusiasm for brass instruments and learned to play the trombone. In 1938 he went to St John's College, Cambridge, where he read history and developed a mock 'professor' act for the Cambridge Footlights, in which he gave a musical lecture on the trombone.

His university career was interrupted by World War II and in 1939 he joined the Royal Air Force, eventually succeeding in his ambition to become a pilot. In 1944 he was flying a hazardous mission towing gliders and dropping supplies to the beleaguered troops at Arnhem when his Dakota was badly hit by a German Focke-Wulf. He made a successful landing, saving the lives of two men on board and sustaining burns to his face which he later disguised by growing the magnificent 'handlebar' moustache that was to become his trademark. He was awarded the DFC in 1945 for his skill and bravery.

Throughout his RAF career he had successfully entertained the troops with his 'professor' act, and so after demobilization in 1946 he contemplated life as an entertainer. He served his apprenticeship at London's Windmill theatre, where he met Frank Muir, who with Denis Norden was to write his most successful comedy material. In 1948 Muir and Norden created one of Edwards's best loved characters, the bibulous belligerent Pa Glum in the BBC radio comedy programme *Take It From Here*. *Take It From Here* ran from 1948 until 1959, commanding audiences of over twenty million and making Edwards a wealthy man. He bought polo ponies, an aeroplane, and a farm in Fittleworth, Sussex, which was run by his elder brother Alan while Edwards played the local squire. Fox-hunting was one of his favourite pastimes and he was proud to be made master of foxhounds of the Old Surrey and Burstow Hunt. In 1951 he was elected lord rector of Aberdeen University, an appointment he held until 1954.

From 1957 until 1977 he appeared in *Does the Team Think?*, a radio panel game he had devised in which four comedians answered light-hearted questions from a studio audience. He attempted some 'straight' acting, turning in a creditable Sir Toby Belch in *Twelfth Night* and Falstaff in *The Merry Wives of Windsor* for BBC radio (both 1962). On television he found a tailor-made role in the series *Whack-O!* (1957–61 and 1971–2), in which he played the corpulent, conniving headmaster of Chiselbury School. His films included *Three Men in a Boat* (1957), *Bottoms Up* (1960), *The Plank* (1979), and *It's Your Move* (1982). Perhaps most surprising of all, in 1964 he stood as Conservative candidate for Paddington North, and although he did not win his seat, he polled 10,639 votes—more than his predecessor had gained.

His private life was less satisfactory. In 1958 he married Valerie, a British Overseas Airways Corporation ground stewardess, daughter of William Seymour, small landowner. They had no children and eventually divorced in 1969. She later told the press that on their honeymoon he had admitted that he was a homosexual 'trying to reform'. In 1976 Ramon Douglas, an Australian female impersonator, told the tabloid newspapers that for the past ten years he and Edwards had shared a 'loving relationship'. Even though he was personally devastated by the resulting publicity, Edwards found that his career did not suffer and in 1978 he was invited to reinvent his Pa Glum character when the Glums were revived for television. In 1984 he published his memoirs, *Six of the Best*, which followed an earlier autobiography, *Take It From Me* (1953).

By the early 1980s Edwards's blustering style of comedy was going out of fashion and he concentrated on touring in plays such as *Big Bad Mouse* with his friend Eric Sykes. He spent more time in the house he had bought in Perth, Western Australia, and it was there in 1988 that he became ill with bronchial pneumonia. He returned to England and died in the Cromwell Hospital, London, 7 July 1988.

[Jimmy Edwards, *Take It From Me*, 1953, and *Six of the Best*, 1984 (autobiographies); information from family and friends.]

VERONICA DAVIS

*published* 1996

## EVANS Dame Edith Mary

(1888–1976)

Actress, was born 8 February 1888 in Ebury Square, London, daughter of Edward Evans, a minor civil servant, and his wife, Caroline Ellen—a son born in 1886 died at the age of four. She was educated at St. Michael's Church of England School, Pimlico, until in 1903, at the age of fifteen, she was indentured as a milliner to a Mr Blackaller in the Buckingham Palace Road.

Her first appearance on the stage, as an amateur, was with Miss Massey's Streatham Shakespeare Players in the role of Viola in *Twelfth Night* in October 1910. In 1912 she was discovered by the noted producer William Poel, and made her first professional appearance for Poel at the Cambridge University Examination Hall in August of that year, playing the role of Gautami in an obscure sixth-century Hindu classic, *Sakuntala*. Her talents were then noted by novelist George Moore who became her passionate mentor and was responsible for her being engaged at the Royalty Theatre, Dean Street, in February 1914 on a year's contract at a salary of two pounds ten shillings a week. Previous to this she had created considerable attention by her performance as Cressida in *Troilus and Cressida* directed by Poel for the Elizabethan Stage Society in the King's Hall, Covent Garden, and subsequently at Stratford-upon-Avon. Thus her extraordinary career spanned sixty-six years and she performed without a break until a few months before her death—her final public appearance being a BBC radio programme before an invited audience in August 1976. From the outset she was a leading player ('God was very good to me', she once remarked, 'he never let me go on tour') and was dedicated to the truth, saying that 'I don't think there is anything extraordinary about me except this passion for the truth', and indeed it is difficult to call to mind any other leading actress of this century who had such single-minded application towards her profession. She played over 150 different roles in the course of her long career and created six of the characters of George Bernard Shaw, namely the Serpent, the Oracle, the She-Ancient and the Ghost of the Serpent in *Back to Methuselah* (1923); Orinthia in *The Apple Cart* (1929); and Epifania in *The Millionairess* (1940). She gave what many consider to be definitive performances as Millamant in *The Way of The World* (1924), Rosalind in *As You Like It* (1926 and 1936), the Nurse in *Romeo and Juliet* (1932, 1934, and 1961) and, most notably, as Lady Bracknell in *The Importance of Being Earnest* (1939). Indeed she became so identified with Lady Bracknell in the public eye that she grew to hate the role.

She commenced her film career in a silent film called *A Welsh Singer*, made for Henry Edwards at Walton-on-Thames studios in 1915, but then concentrated on stage roles until Emlyn Williams directed her in his own film *The Last Days on Dolwyn* in 1948, the same year as she appeared in Thorold Dickinson's widely admired *The Queen of Spades*. Although she recreated two of her most famous stage roles for the cinema—Lady Bracknell and Mrs St. Maugham from Enid Bagnold's *The Chalk Garden*—they are but pale versions of the originals and she herself was not proud of them. Perhaps her most rounded screen performance was as Mrs Ross in *The Whisperers* (1966), for which she received the Golden Bear for best actress at the Berlin Film Festival, the British Academy award, the New York Film Critics award, and was nominated for an American Oscar and other international prizes. Her last screen performance (in which she sang and danced) was in *The Slipper and The Rose* (1975), when she was eighty-seven.

Her most widely admired asset was her voice, a highly individual instrument, often imitated but never surpassed. She often professed herself unaware of the extraordinary effect it had on her audiences, but she set great store by clear diction and in her later years was openly critical of the slovenly standards of speech prevalent in the theatre. Belonging as she did to the old school, she imposed severe disciplines on herself and, although she liked to be in complete control of her audiences, always kept them at a distance, becoming over the course of the years a remote and finally very lonely figure. She had a love for and natural feeling for poetry; her taste was catholic and when she felt unable to undertake the task of learning any new roles, she embarked upon a highly successful one-man show of poetry readings (1973) and indeed her last appearance on any West End stage took place during a revival of this entertainment on 5 October 1974.

She was the complete actress, dedicated, always professional, sublimating all other aspects of her life in the service of the theatre. A prime mover and lifelong supporter of British Actors' Equity, though not actively political, she was honoured by being appointed DBE in the New Year's list of 1946. She also received four degrees *honoris causa* from the universities of London (1950), Cambridge (1951), Oxford (1954), and Hull (1968). Walter Sickert painted her, Shaw flirted with her, playwrights queued to write for her, but she remained curiously untouched by fame and whenever she was not active in the theatre or the film studios, retired to her Elizabethan manor house in Kent, there to tend her garden, read, 'recharge my batteries', and watch football on television.

She was a Christian Scientist, a devout woman, a woman who frequently did good by stealth, and when she died she left the bulk of her considerable estate for the benefit of the Actors' Charitable Trust. James Agate wrote of her 'there has never been a more versatile actress' and indeed she had a way of acting that was unique in the annals of our theatre and must place her amongst the immortals. She said of herself 'I can't imagine going on when there are no more expectations' but she fulfilled those expectations to the very end of her days and died in harness. 'Marking ages', she said, 'is a sign of deterioration. Age has nothing to do with me.'

In 1925 Edith Evans married George ('Guy') Booth, whom she had known since she was sixteen. The marriage was childless and Booth died in 1935. Edith Evans died at her home in Kilndown, Kent, 14 October 1976.

[Bryan Forbes, *Ned's Girl*, 1977; J. C. Trewin, *Edith Evans*, 1954; Jean Batters, *Edith Evans*, 1977; personal knowledge.]

BRYAN FORBES

*published 1986*

## FAY William George

(1872–1947)

Actor and producer, was born in Dublin 12 November 1872, the second son of William Patrick Fay, a civil servant, and his wife, Martha Dowling. Fay was educated at Belvedere College, Dublin. He and his elder brother Frank started life with united aims and affections. They loved the theatre with a deep-rooted love and set themselves with concentrated energy and dogged persistence to train themselves and others for a theatrical career. By 1902 Fay had his own company playing in small halls in Dublin and in the country. In 1903 he joined forces with AE (G. W. Russell), and a year later he joined W. B. Yeats and Lady Gregory, a combination which led to the creation of the Abbey Theatre with the help of Miss A. E. F. Horniman. Fay was a man of the theatre through and through and the importance of the work he did for the Irish theatre from 1904 until January 1908 cannot be too greatly emphasized. His brother Frank was a beautiful verse-speaker; William was more interested in character and comedy, and the brothers made a perfect combination. When differences of opinion with the directors of the Abbey Theatre led Fay to resign in 1908 Yeats wrote: 'We are about to lose our principal actor. William Fay has had enough of it, and we don't wonder, and is going to some other country where his exquisite gift of comedy and his brain teeming with fancy will bring him an audience, fame, and a little money.'

At the Abbey Theatre he created such great parts as Martin Doul in *The Well of the Saints* by J. M. Synge; Shan Grogan in William Boyle's *The Building Fund*; Jeremiah Dempsey in Boyle's *The Eloquent Dempsey*, which is said to have been his favourite part although from another source we learn that he preferred his creation of Christy Mahon in Synge's *The Playboy of the Western World*.

After he left the Abbey Theatre Fay had a distinguished career on the English stage, beginning with *What the Public Wants*, *John Bull's Other Island*, and *The O'Flynn* with Sir Herbert Tree. During the latter part of the war he produced plays for the Navy and Army Canteen Board, and he was afterwards producer for the repertory theatres in Nottingham (1920–21) and Birmingham (1925–7). Although he never retired from the stage or from production, in later years he appeared more often in films, notably in *The Blarney Stone*, *General John Regan*, *Oliver Twist*, *London Town*, *Spring Meeting*, and, very late in life, perhaps his best screen part as Father Tom in *Odd Man Out*. He touched no part which he did not adorn, for although he had not a striking stage personality he had a genius for character and comedy, and he excelled in Lady Gregory's one-act comedies. In 1935 he published his reminiscences in collaboration with Catherine Carswell under the title *The Fays of the Abbey Theatre*. A fine portrait of him painted by J. B. Yeats is at the Abbey Theatre, and another by the same artist is in the Municipal Gallery of Modern Art, Dublin.

Fay married in 1906 Anna Bridget (died 1952), daughter of Thomas Joseph O'Dempsey, lawyer, of Enniscorthy, county Wexford; they had one son. Fay died in London 27 October 1947.

[Private information; personal knowledge.]

LENNOX ROBINSON

*published 1959*

## FIELDS Dame Gracie

(1898–1979)

Music-hall artiste and film star, was born Grace Stansfield in Rochdale, Lancashire, 9 January 1898, the eldest of four children (three daughters and a son) of Fred Stansfield, engineer, and his wife, Sarah Jane Bamford. Her education, at Rochdale Parish School, was disrupted by her mother's attempts to put her on the stage, and ceased when she was thirteen. It was at this time that she changed her name to Gracie Fields.

Her stage career began with singing competitions, brief appearances at local music halls, and membership of various juvenile troupes, but in 1913, when she was fifteen, she became a member of a touring music-hall company, and began a full-time career as a singer and *comédienne*. In 1916, Archie Pitt, another member of the company, broke away to form a company to perform his own revues, and invited Gracie Fields to be his leading lady. She toured with Pitt for eight years, acquiring a tremendous depth of experience in all aspects of music-hall and revue work. She was naturally versatile, and Pitt worked hard to exploit her many talents—dancing, singing, mimicry, acting, improvisation—and to reinforce in her that dedication to her work and to the show which her mother had instilled in her at an early age. Archie Pitt exercised an almost complete control over Gracie's life, and in 1923 they married—an arrangement of convenience on both sides. Pitt (a stage name) was the son of Morris Selinger. There were no children of the marriage.

In 1924 Pitt's company, which had been touring continuously since 1916, was invited to stage its current revue, 'Mr Tower of London' in the West End. This was the company's first exposure to the London critics, and the production was widely acclaimed. Gracie Fields found that she had become a star, literally overnight.

Her fame spread rapidly—she became known to millions as 'Our Gracie'—and soon she was in demand everywhere. As well as starring in

Pitt's revues, she also performed in cabaret after each nightly show, and made records during the day. Pitt guided her career and used her vast earnings to create a lifestyle of luxury and display which Gracie Fields, always a simple Lancashire girl at heart, neither desired nor enjoyed. Their marriage, which had never been a close one, deteriorated further, but although by 1931 separation was imminent, the professional partnership flourished, and Pitt seized the opportunity to launch Gracie Fields into the most recent development in popular entertainment—film-making.

In this new venture Gracie Fields was instantly successful with the film *Sally in our Alley* (which included the famous song). The plots of the early films were weak, and the direction poor, but in spite of this the public flocked to see them. In 1935 Monty Banks (Mario Bianchi), an Italian director, was brought in, the quality of the films improved, and in 1938 Gracie Fields began to make films in Hollywood, with a contract which made her the best paid film star in the world.

In 1939 Gracie Fields underwent major surgery for cancer, and it is a measure of her popularity at this time that prayers were said for her in the churches, and newspapers and radio carried daily bulletins. She made a complete recovery, but the outbreak of war a few months later led to an event in her life which overnight changed public adulation into almost universal condemnation.

In 1938 Gracie had agreed to marry Monty Banks, and in 1940 she followed him into voluntary exile in America (Banks's Italian nationality meant that he ran the risk of internment if he remained in Britain) and, after a divorce from Archie Pitt in 1940 (the year in which he died) they were married there the same year. The popular press immediately accused Gracie Fields of deserting Britain in its moment of need, and of taking her wealth with her. Although the accusations were unfounded, her reputation was tainted for many years: her dedicated work for ENSA throughout the war did little to redeem her in the eyes of the British public.

After the war, Gracie Fields settled at her home in Capri. She was gradually taken back into the favour of the British, and she returned home periodically to record and give concerts. In 1950 Monty Banks died, and in 1952 she married Boris Alperovici (died 1983), a Bessarabian radio engineer living in Capri. With him she at last found real contentment and she led a peaceful life in Capri. She had no children.

Gracie Fields's career cannot be fully appreciated without recognizing that her roots lay in the music hall, where she received her training and formulated her act. When the music halls died, and she progressed to films, records, and variety work, it was the grounding in the music hall which gave her the strength and the ability to project herself, which was the key to her success. The great talent which she undoubtedly had, combined with her excellent training and her dedication to her work meant that, whatever the medium, she could win her audience and allow them to share a memorable experience.

On stage she was exceptionally versatile, her only prop a headscarf, held in her hand during romantic or sentimental songs, but tied over her head for the comic Lancashire songs which had made her famous. Even her voice changed according to the song—her lovely, clear singing voice became in the comic songs coarse and raucous. Her hold over her audience was so great that she could move in a moment from a comic to a religious song, and change laughter into tears. Only Gracie Fields could offer 'The Lord's Prayer' and 'Ave Maria' alongside 'The Biggest Aspidistra' and, 'Walter, Walter, lead me to the Altar'.

In her personal life, Gracie Fields never allowed her success to affect her. She remained open, affectionate, home-loving, generous with both time and money, and with a deep religious faith. She gave thousands of pounds to charity and in 1935 endowed and maintained the Gracie Fields Orphanage at Peacehaven, Sussex. She was also very humble—and touchingly unsure of herself when meeting other stars, almost unable to believe their respect for her.

Gracie Fields was appointed CBE in 1938 and DBE in 1979. In 1937 she received the freedom of Rochdale. She made over 500 records and fifteen films and she appeared in eleven Royal Variety performances. Her portrait, by Sir James Gunn, hangs in Rochdale Art Gallery.

She died in Capri 27 September 1979.

[Gracie Fields, *Sing As We Go* (autobiography), 1960; private information; personal knowledge.]

Elizabeth Pollitt

*published 1986*

## FLANAGAN Bud

(1896–1968)

Comedian, was born Chaim Reeven Weintrop 14 October 1896 in Hanbury Street, London, the fifth son and the youngest of the ten children of Polish immigrants, Wolf Weintrop, the owner of a barber's shop and tobacconist's in Whitechapel, and his wife, Yetta, or Kitty, Price. The 'Weintrop' became Winthrop on the birth certificate, and Bud's Hebrew names, Chaim Reeven, became Robert. He went to school in Petticoat Lane. At the age of ten he was a call boy at the Cambridge Music Hall, and at the age of twelve he made his theatrical debut in an amateur talent contest at the London Music Hall in Shoreditch, performing conjuring tricks as Fargo, the Boy Wizard.

In 1910, inspired by the American vaudeville acts he had seen, he walked to Southampton, and passing himself off as an electrician, sailed on the SS *Majestic* for New York. There he jumped ship, and spent the years that followed earning his living variously as a Western Union messenger boy, in a feather-duster factory, and selling newspapers. He had a one-line part in a play called *The Wild Beast*, and in 1911 he joined a vaudeville act called *Campus Days* which toured America. The following year he acquired a partner, and their double act appeared in New Zealand, Australia, and South Africa.

In 1915 he decided to return to England, and in Birmingham he joined the Royal Field Artillery. In an *estaminet* in the village of Poperinghe in France, he met his future partner, an actor named Chesney Allen, but they did not meet again until after the war. On 21 March 1918, at Vandelle Wood, Flanagan was gassed and temporarily blinded. He was sent to 14 General Hospital in Deauville.

Returning home in February 1919, he formed a double-act called Flanagan and Roy (with Roy Henderson). He had decided to call himself Flanagan as an act of revenge against a sergeant-major of that name who had made his life miserable in the artillery. This act, and another called Flanagan and Poy, were both unsuccessful, and by 1922 he was back in London driving a taxi.

In 1923 the urge to perform reasserted itself, and he walked all the way to Glasgow in search of work. In 1925 he met and married his wife Anne, 'Curly', daughter of Johnny Quinn who was well known in Ireland as the 'Singing Clown'. In 1926 their son, Buddy, was born. 1926 was the year when he again encountered Chesney Allen, who was then doing a double-act called Stanford and Allen in Florrie Forde's touring revue. They agreed to team up, and Flanagan and Allen, an act which was to endure for twenty years, came into being. It was not immediately successful; in fact, at one point, so discouraged were they that they decided to exploit a shared passion for horse-racing and became bookmakers.

But the act was improving all the time; Chesney Allen's patient dignity, perfectly wedded to Bud's gleeful roguery, was beginning to delight audiences, and in 1927 they attracted the attention of Valentine Charles Parnell, booking manager to the Variety Theatre Controlling Company and later director of the mighty Moss Empires, whose principal theatre was the London Palladium.

In 1929 Flanagan and Allen made their London début at the Holborn Empire. They were an immediate success, and the following year they appeared in their first royal command performance at the London Palladium, in the presence of King George V and Queen Mary.

Val Parnell had conceived the idea of combining the talents of Flanagan and Allen with those of a group of comedians: Nervo and Knox, Naughton and Gold, Carryl and Mundy, and Eddie Gray, in order to present a new kind of show at the Palladium. The first of these shows was an enormous hit, and soon this riotous assembly of comics was to become known as the 'Crazy Gang', with Bud Flanagan as its undisputed leader.

Between 1931 and 1939 Flanagan and Allen appeared in many shows, some with the Crazy Gang—they included *London Rhapsody* (1931) and *The Little Dog Laughed* (1939)—some without, including *Life Begins at Oxford Circus* (1935), *Many Happy Returns* (1937), and, in 1933, a musical comedy at the London Hippodrome, *Give Me a Ring*.

During the war years they appeared in *Black Vanities* (1941), at the Victoria Palace, and *Hi-De-Hi* (1943), at the Palace Theatre. Between shows, Flanagan and Allen toured the provinces, giving performances for the troops, which included a tour of France immediately after D-Day.

In 1945 ill health forced Chesney Allen to retire from the act, and Flanagan, encouraged by Jack Hylton, decided to carry on alone. In 1947 the Crazy Gang reassembled in *Together Again*, and from then until 1959 Flanagan appeared in an extraordinary succession of long-running shows: *Knights of Madness* in 1950, *Ring Out the Bells* in 1952, and *Jokers Wild* in 1954. In 1956 *These Foolish Kings* ran for 882 performances. At last, in 1959, Bud Flanagan, then sixty-three years of age, gave his last performance with the Crazy Gang. In that year's birthday honours list, he was appointed OBE.

Flanagan and Allen appeared in many films. Among them were: *A Fire Has Been Arranged* (1934), *Underneath the Arches* (1937), *Alf's Button Afloat* (1938), *Gasbags* (1940), *We'll Smile Again* (1942), and *Here Comes the Sun* (1945).

He wrote many of his own songs. They include: 'Free', 'Dreaming', and the song with which he is most closely associated, 'Underneath the Arches'.

During three reigns he was a great favourite with the royal family, and between the years 1932 and 1965 he appeared in no fewer than fifteen variety command performances.

He was a tireless worker for charity, both through the Grand Order of Water Rats, and through his own Leukemia Fund, which he initiated as a memorial to his son, Buddy, who died in 1955. Bud Flanagan himself died in a hospital in Sydenham, London, 20 October 1968.

There is a portrait of Bud Flanagan, by Robert O. Lenkiewicz, in the museum of the Grand Order of Water Rats.

[Bud Flanagan, *My Crazy Life*, 1961; Colin MacInnes in the *Spectator*, 25 October 1968; *The Times*, 21 October 1968; *Who's Who in the Theatre*.]

SID COLIN

*published* 1981

## FLANDERS Michael Henry

(1922–1975)

Actor, lyricist, and dramatic author, was the eldest of three children and the only son of Peter Henry Flanders and his wife, Rosa Laura ('Laurie') O'Beirne. He was born in Hampstead, London, 1 March 1922. His father had followed various occupations, including that of cinema manager; his mother was a professional musician. Flanders was educated at Westminster School, where he was one of a remarkable theatrical quartet—himself, Donald Swann, Peter Ustinov, and Peter Brook—but to anyone who remarked that the school performances must have been something to see, he explained that drama had been somewhat frowned upon apart from the annual Latin play, so that apart from Swann, the only accomplished Latinist among them, the rest had been little more than spear-carriers. In 1940 he went to Christ Church, Oxford, to read history. There he both acted and directed for the OUDS and the Experimental Theatre Club, playing among other roles Brabantio in *Othello*, Pirandello's Henry IV, in which he achieved a notable success, and Shawcross in *The Ascent of F6*. He also wrote witty drama criticisms for *Cherwell* and made his first professional appearance on the stage, in October 1941, at the Oxford Playhouse as Valentine in *You Never Can Tell*. A lean and long-striding six feet three, a fine oarsman and quarter-miler, he was by far the outstanding actor of his generation. With his height, athleticism, thin, handsome face, deep intelligence, and splendid voice, he was formidably equipped.

He left Oxford to join the RNVR, and in 1943 contracted poliomyelitis, which condemned him to spend the rest of his life in a wheelchair. His application to return to Christ Church to continue his studies was refused, something which he had difficulty in forgiving, and for the best part of a decade he was a sad figure, arranging small musical evenings at his parents' home with other amateur instrumentalists, including Gerard Hoffnung. Occasionally he took small parts in radio plays. None of his friends was prepared for the extraordinary career he was to carve out for himself after the age of thirty.

In 1951 the impresario Laurier Lister commissioned him to write songs and lyrics for a revue, *Penny Plain*. These were acclaimed, as were his contributions to Lister's subsequent revue, *Airs on a Shoestring*, in 1953. The same year he wrote the libretti for two operas, *Three's Company* and *A Christmas Story*; then, in 1954, he translated, with Kitty Black, Stravinsky's *The Soldier's Tale* for the Edinburgh Festival. In 1956 he collaborated with Donald Swann, who had written much of the music for the two previous Lister revues, in a third, *Fresh Airs*. They then decided to write a show between them which they would perform together, mainly comprising songs they had written which nobody had wanted to sing. The result was *At the Drop of a Hat*, which opened on 31 December 1956 for a fortnight's run at a small fringe theatre, the New Lindsey in Kensington. It was the first time either of them had appeared professionally on stage apart from Flanders's Valentine at Oxford. *At the Drop of a Hat* was so enthusiastically received that it transferred immediately to the Fortune Theatre, where it ran for no less than 759 performances. In October 1959 they took it to Broadway, where it was equally successful, and they toured it widely through the United States and Canada during 1960–1. The combination of Flanders's genial yet caustic lyrics and Swann's witty and tuneful music, and the contrast between Flanders's robust exuberance and the prim appearance of Swann, exerted a seemingly universal appeal.

In 1962 Flanders appeared at the Aldwych Theatre, still of course in his wheelchair, as the story-teller in the Royal Shakespeare Company's production of Brecht's *The Caucasian Chalk Circle*. He and Swann toured the United Kingdom and Eire in 1962–3 with *At the Drop of a Hat*; then in October 1963 they appeared at the Haymarket Theatre, London, in *At the Drop of Another Hat*, which proved as successful as its predecessor. They toured a combined version of the two 'Hat' programmes through Australia, New Zealand, and Hong Kong, then reopened *At the Drop of Another Hat* at the Globe Theatre, London. In 1968 Flanders appeared at the Queen Elizabeth Hall, London, as the narrator in *The Soldier's Tale*, and in 1970 at the Mayfair Theatre in a revue, *Ten Years Hard*. In 1969 he wrote the libretto for a cantata by Joseph Horowitz, *Captain Noah and his Floating Zoo*, which proved almost as popular as the 'Hat' shows. He was often seen on television, on the concert platform in such works as *Façade* and *Peter and the Wolf*, and especially enjoyed working on radio, in feature, documentary, and music programmes. He also appeared in several films, notably *The Raging Moon* (1970).

Flanders was one of the most popular stage personalities of his time, both with audiences and with his fellow professionals. Like the great music-hall comics, he had the rare talent of making every member of an audience feel that he was addressing him or her personally, and with his fine speaking voice he was a master of the aside. He was one of the few great lyric writers that the theatre has known, arguably the best since Sir W. S. Gilbert. His disability caused him much pain and sleeplessness, which he bore with fortitude and humour; far from exploiting it, he sought to persuade audiences to forget it, though outside the theatre he was tireless in championing the cause of disabled people. He developed unexpected skills from his chair: gardening (for which he invented ingenious implements, such as an apple corer wired on to a long stick for weeding), bar billiards, table tennis, and certain kinds of cooking. He was the warmest and wittiest of companions. He was appointed OBE in 1964.

In 1959 he married Claudia, the daughter of the journalist Claud Cockburn and stepdaughter of Robert Gorham Davis, professor of English at Columbia University, New York. There were two daughters of the marriage, which was very happy. On 15 April 1975 he died suddenly of a cerebral haemorrhage while on holiday at Betws-y-Coed in Wales. His ashes were scattered in the grounds of Chiswick House, London, where he had loved to sit on fine afternoons.

[*Who's Who in the Theatre*; private information; personal knowledge.]

MICHAEL MEYER

*published 1986*

## GILBERT Sir William Schwenck

(1836–1911)

Dramatist, born at 17 Southampton Street, Strand, the house of his mother's father, Dr. Thomas Morris, on 18 Nov. 1836, was only son in a family of four children of William Gilbert (1804–1890) by his wife Anne Morris. His second christian name was the surname of his godmother. As an infant he travelled in Germany and Italy with his parents. When two years old he was stolen by brigands at Naples and ransomed for 25*l*. In later days when visiting Naples he recognised in the Via Posilippo the scene of the occurrence. His pet name as a child was 'Bab', which he afterwards used as a pseudonym. He is said to have been a child of great beauty, and Sir David Wilkie was so attracted by his face that he asked leave to paint his picture. At the age of seven he went to school at Boulogne. From ten to thirteen he was at the Western Grammar School, Brompton, and from thirteen to sixteen at the Great Ealing School, where he rose to be head boy. He spent much time in drawing, and wrote plays for performance by his schoolfellows, painting his own scenery and acting himself.

In Oct. 1855 he entered the department of general literature and science at King's College, London (*King's Coll. Calendar*, 1855–6, p. 89). Alfred Ainger and Walter Besant were fellow students. Some of his earliest literary efforts were verses contributed to the college magazine. He remained a student during 1856–7, intending to go to Oxford, but in 1855, when he was nineteen years old, the Crimean war was at its height, and commissions in the Royal Artillery were thrown open to competitive examination. Giving up all idea of Oxford, he read for the army examination announced for Christmas 1856 ('An Autobiography' in *The Theatre*, 2 April 1883, p. 217). But the war came to an abrupt end, and no more officers being required, the examination was indefinitely postponed. Gilbert then graduated B.A. at the London University in 1857, and obtained a commission in the militia in the 3rd battalion Gordon highlanders.

In 1857 he was a successful competitor in an examination for a clerkship in the education department of the privy council office, in which 'ill-organised and ill governed office' he tells us he spent four uncomfortable years. Coming unexpectedly in 1861 into 300*l*., 'on the happiest day of my life I sent in my resignation'. He had already, on 11 October 1855, entered the Inner Temple as a student (Foster's *Men at the Bar*). With 100*l*. of his capital he paid for his call to the bar, which took place on 17 Nov. 1863 (cf. 'My Maiden Brief', *Cornhill*, Dec. 1863). With another 100*l*. he obtained access to the chambers of (Sir) Charles James Watkin Williams, then a well-known barrister in the home circuit, and with the third 100*l*. he furnished a set of rooms of his own in Clement's Inn, but he does not appear to have had any professional chambers or address in the 'Law List'. He joined the northern circuit on 15 March 1866, one of his sponsors being (Sir) John Holker (*MS. Circuit Records*). He attended the Westminster courts, the Old Bailey, the Manchester and Liverpool assizes, the Liverpool sessions and Passage Court, but 'only earned 75*l*. in two years'.

During the same period he was earning a 'decent income' by contributions to current literature. He appeared for the first time in print in 1858, when he prepared a translation of the laughing-song from Auber's 'Manon Lescaut' for the playbill of Alfred Mellon's promenade concerts; Mdlle. Parepa, afterwards Madame Parepa-Rosa, whom he had known from babyhood, had made a singular success there with the song in its original French. In 1861 Gilbert commenced both as author and artist, contributing an article, three-quarters of a column long with a half-page drawing on wood, for 'Fun', then under the editorship of Henry James Byron. A day or two later he was requested 'to contribute a column of "copy" and a half-page drawing every week' (*Theatre*, 1883, p. 218). He remained a regular contributor to 'Fun' during the editorship of Byron and that of Byron's successor, Tom Hood the younger (from 1865).

There is no evidence that he studied drawing in any school, but he was an illustrator of talent. In 1865 he made 84 illustrations for his father's novel, 'The Magic Mirror', and in 1869 he illustrated another of his father's books, 'King George's Middy'. His illustrations of his own 'Bab Ballads' have much direct and quaint humour. In 1874 'The Piccadilly Annual' was described as 'profusely illustrated by W. S. Gilbert and other artists'. One of the 'other artists' was John Leech.

Having already both written and drawn occasionally for 'Punch', Gilbert offered that periodical in 1866 his ballad called 'The Yarn of the Nancy Bell', but it was refused by the editor, Mark Lemon, on the ground that it was 'too cannibalistic for his readers' tastes' (*Fifty Bab Ballads*, pref., 1884). Gilbert's connection with 'Punch' thereupon ceased. 'The Nancy Bell' appeared, without illustrations, in 'Fun' on 3 March 1866. Gilbert's other work in 'Fun' may be traced by single figure drawings signed 'Bab'. A series of dramatic notices commencing 15 Sept. 1866 and 'Men we Meet, by the Comic Physiognomist' (2 Feb. to 18 May 1867) are thus illustrated. The first illustrated ballad was 'General John' (1 June 1867). From this date they became a regular feature of the paper. But not until 23 Jan. 1869, in connection with 'The Two Ogres', was the title 'The Bab Ballads' used. They were first collected in volume form in the same year. Further 'Bab Ballads' continued to appear in 'Fun', at varying intervals until 1871. A collected volume of 'More Bab Ballads' followed in 1873. The Bab Ballads established Gilbert's reputation as a whimsical humorist in verse.

At the same time Gilbert contributed articles or stories to the magazines—the 'Cornhill' (1863–4), 'London Society', 'Tinsley's Magazine', and 'Temple Bar'; he furnished the London correspondence to the 'Invalide Russe', and, becoming dramatic critic to Vizetelly's 'Illustrated Times', interested himself in the stage. In spite of these activities Gilbert found time to continue his military duties, and became captain of his militia regiment in 1867. He retired with the rank of major in 1883.

At the end of 1866 Gilbert commenced work as a playwright. To Thomas William Robertson, the dramatist, he owed the needful introduction. Miss Herbert, the lessee of St. James's Theatre, wanted a Christmas piece in a fortnight, and Robertson recommended Gilbert for the work, which was written in ten days, rehearsed in a week, and produced at Christmas 1866. The piece was a burlesque on 'L'Elixir d'Amore', called 'Dulcamara, or the Little Duck and the Great Quack'. Frank Matthews made a success in the title rôle, and it ran for several months and was twice revived. No terms had been arranged, and when Mr. Emden, the manager, paid Gilbert the 30*l.* that he asked, Emden advised him never again to sell so good a piece for so small a sum. Thenceforward Gilbert was a successful playwright, at first in the lighter branches of the drama. Another burlesque on 'La Figlia del Reggimento', called 'La Vivandière, or True to the Corps', was produced at the Queen's Theatre on 22 Jan. 1868, and in it John Lawrence Toole and Lionel Brough played. It ran for 120 nights. A third burlesque, on the 'Bohemian Girl', entitled 'The Merry Zingara, or the Tipsy Gipsy and the Popsy Wopsy', was produced at the Royal Theatre on 21 March 1868 by Miss Patty Oliver. On 21 Dec. 1868 the new Gaiety Theatre was opened by John Hollingshead with a new operatic extravaganza by Gilbert called 'Robert the Devil', in which Nellie Farren played the leading part. Next year, at the opening of the Charing Cross (afterwards Toole's) Theatre, on 19 June 1869, the performance concluded with a musical extravaganza by Gilbert, 'The Pretty Druidess, or the Mother, the Maid, and the Mistletoe Bough, a travestie of Norma'. Gilbert was much attached to second titles. Between 1869 and 1872 he also wrote many dramatic sketches, usually with music, for the German Reeds' 'entertainment' at the Gallery of Illustration, 14 Regent Street. His musical collaborator was Frederick Clay. On 22 Nov. 1869 they produced together 'Ages Ago', which was afterwards expanded into the opera 'Ruddigore'; on 30 Jan. 1871 'A Sensation Novel'; and on 28 Oct. 1872 'Happy Arcadia'. Arthur Cecil, Corney Grain, and Fanny Holland were the chief performers.

It was under the auspices of the German Reeds that Gilbert and (Sir) Arthur Sullivan first made each other's acquaintance. Sullivan was one of the composers of music for German Reed plays, and at the Gallery of Illustration in 1871 Clay introduced Sullivan to Gilbert (Lawrence's *Life of Sullivan*, p. 84, and E. A. Browne's *Gilbert*, p. 35). They soon were at work together on a burlesque, 'Thespis, or the Gods Grown Old', which was produced at the Gaiety Theatre on 26 Dec. 1871 (John Hollingshead's *Gaiety Chronicles*, 202–7). They often met at Tom Taylor's, and engaged together in amateur theatricals (Ellen Terry's *Story of My Life*, 1908), but for the present no further dramatic collaboration followed.

Meanwhile Gilbert was assiduously seeking fame in more serious branches of the drama. On 8 Jan. 1870 'The Princess', a respectful parody on Tennyson's poem, was produced at the Olympic with great success. This was afterwards the basis of the opera 'Princess Ida'. John Baldwin Buckstone now commissioned Gilbert to write a blank verse fairy comedy on Madame de Genlis's story of 'Le Palais de la Vérité'. This was produced on 19 Nov. 1870 at the Haymarket under the title of 'The Palace of Truth', with Buckstone, Madge Robertson (Mrs. Kendal), and W. H. Kendal in the cast. It ran for 230 nights. 'Pygmalion and Galatea', a rather artificial classical romance, was produced also at the Haymarket on 9 Dec. 1871. It proved a remarkable success. The play was revived at the Lyceum with Miss Mary Anderson in 1884 and later in 1888, at the same theatre, with Miss Julia Neilson in the part. Gilbert is said to have made 40,000*l.* out of this play alone (*Daily Telegraph*, 30 May 1911). 'The Wicked World', a fairy comedy, followed at the Haymarket on 4 Jan. 1873 and was not quite so successful as its forerunners.

In the meantime Gilbert wrote an extended series of comedies for Miss Marie Litton's management of the new Court Theatre in Sloane Square, London. This playhouse was opened by Miss Litton with Gilbert's 'Randall's Thumb' on 25 Jan. 1871; there followed during Miss Litton's tenancy 'Creatures of Impulse' (15 April 1871); 'Great Expectations' (28 May), an adaptation of Dickens's novel; 'On Guard' (28 Oct.); and 'The Wedding March' (under the pseudonym of F. Latour Tomline) (15 Nov. 1873). One of Gilbert's plays written for the Court Theatre, 'The Happy Land', which Miss Litton produced on 17 March 1873, caused much public excitement. It was a burlesque version of Gilbert's 'Wicked World', designed by himself, but mainly worked out by Gilbert Arthur à Beckett. Gilbert received 700*l.* for his share of the libretto (*W. S. Gilbert*, by Kate Field, *Scribner's Monthly*, xviii. (1879), 754). His name did not appear on the bill, where the piece was assigned to F. L. Tomline (i.e. Gilbert) and à Beckett. 'The Happy Land' was received with enthusiasm. But three of the actors, Walter Fisher, W. J. Hill, and Edward Righton (manager of the theatre), were made up to resemble respectively Gladstone, Robert Lowe (Lord Sherbrooke), and A. S. Ayrton, members of the liberal administration then in office. The lord chamberlain insisted on the removal of this feature of the performance.

Of more serious plays 'Charity', produced on 3 Jan. 1874 at the Haymarket, was the story of a woman redeeming her one mistake in life by an after career of self-sacrifice. It was denounced as immoral by the general public, and was withdrawn after a run of eighty nights. There followed a series of successful comedies in which sentiment predominated over Gilbert's habitually cynical humour. 'Sweethearts' was produced at the Prince of Wales's on 7 Nov. 1874 under Mrs. Bancroft's management; 'Tom Cobb' at the St. James's, on 24 April 1875; 'Broken Hearts' on 17 Dec. 1875 at the Court Theatre under (Sir) John Hare's direction. 'Dan'l Druce', a play of very serious tone, and 'Engaged' both came out at the Haymarket, on 11 Sept. 1876 and 3 Oct. 1877 respectively. 'Gretchen', a four-act drama in verse on the Faust legend, was produced on 24 March 1879 at the Olympic. In 1884 Gilbert wrote an ambitious sketch, 'Comedy and Tragedy', for Miss Mary Anderson to perform at the Lyceum Theatre (26 Jan. 1884).

Meanwhile Gilbert acquired a more conspicuous triumph in another dramatic field. The memorable series of operas in which he and Sullivan collaborated began with 'Trial by Jury', which was produced at the Royalty Theatre by Madame Selina Dolaro on 25 March 1875. A sketch of an operetta under this title had appeared in 'Fun' on 11 April 1868. The words now took a new shape, Sullivan supplied the music, and the rehearsals were completed within three weeks. Gilbert's libretto betrayed the whimsical humour of his early 'Bab Ballads', as well as the facility of his earlier extravaganzas and burlesques. Richard D'Oyly Carte was the manager of the Royalty. In view of the piece's success Carte formed a Comedy Opera Company, and gave Gilbert and Sullivan a commission to write a larger work together. The result was 'The Sorcerer', which was first played at the Opera Comique on 17 Nov. 1877, and introduced George Grossmith and Rutland Barrington to the professional stage. This opera proved the forerunner of a long series of like successes. 'The Sorcerer' was followed by 'H.M.S. Pinafore, or the Lass that loved a Sailor', under the same management on 25 May 1878. This ran for 700 nights and enjoyed an enormous popularity throughout the country. It was at once received in America with an 'enthusiasm bordering upon insanity' (Kate Field in *Scribner's Monthly*, xviii. 754), and after its first production in America Gilbert, with Sullivan, D'Oyly Carte, and Alfred Cellier, the musical conductor, went to New York (Nov. 1879) to give it the fresh advantage of Gilbert's personal stage management and Sullivan's own orchestral interpretation. While in New York they produced for the first time a new opera, 'The Pirates of Penzance, or the Slave of Duty', which was brought out at the Fifth Avenue Theatre on New Year's Eve, 31 Dec. 1879. The party returned to England in time to produce 'The Pirates of Penzance' at the Opera Comique on 3 April 1880. This ran for a year. 'Patience, or Bunthorne's Bride' came out at the Opera Comique on 23 April 1881, and at the height of its triumph, on 10 Oct. 1881, it was transferred to the 'Savoy'—the new opera house built by D'Oyly Carte for the Gilbert and Sullivan operas. 'Patience' was a satire on the current 'æsthetic movement' and enjoyed great popularity.

The succeeding 'Savoy operas' were 'Iolanthe, or the Peer and the Peri' (25 Nov. 1882); 'Princess Ida, or Castle Adamant', based on Gilbert's comedy 'The Princess' (5 Jan. 1884); and 'The Mikado, or the Town of Titipu' (14 March 1885). The last piece ran for two years, was played over 5000 times in America, and found favour on the Continent. It was the most popular of all Gilbert and Sullivan's joint works. It is said Gilbert, Sullivan, and Carte each made 30,000*l.* out of it. 'Ruddigore, or the Witch's Curse', an elaboration of the German Reed piece 'Ages Ago', followed on 22 Jan. 1887; 'The Yeoman of the Guard, or The Merryman and His Maid' on 3

Oct. 1888, and 'The Gondoliers, or The King of Barataria' on 7 Dec. 1889. The partnership was shortly afterwards interrupted. A disagreement on financial matters arose between Gilbert and Carte, and Gilbert thought that Sullivan sided with Carte. Separating for the time from both Sullivan and Carte, Gilbert wrote his next libretto, 'The Mountebanks', for music by Alfred Cellier. It was produced at the Lyric Theatre on 4 Jan. 1892.

In writing these operas Gilbert first wrote out the plot as though it were an anecdote, and this he expanded to the length of a magazine article with summaries of conversations. This was overhauled and corrected and cut down to a skeleton, and then broken up into scenes with entrances and exits arranged. Not until the fifth MS. was the play illustrated by actual dialogue. Sometimes a piece would after a fortnight's rest be re-written entirely afresh without reference to the first draft. In arranging the scenes, too, no trouble was too great. In 'H.M.S. Pinafore' Gilbert went down to Portsmouth and was rowed round about the harbour and visited various ships, and finally pitched upon the quarter-deck of the Victory for his scene, which he obtained permission to sketch and model in every detail.

Gilbert's partnership with Sullivan and Carte was resumed in 1893, when he and Sullivan wrote 'Utopia Limited, or the Flowers of Progress'. It was produced at the Savoy on 7 Oct. 1893, but was not so popular as its predecessors, although it ran till 9 June 1894. Gilbert's next opera, 'His Excellency', had music by Dr. Osmond Carr (Lyric, 27 Oct. 1894); it was followed by revivals of older pieces. In 'The Grand Duke', which came out on 7 March 1896 at the Savoy, Gilbert and Sullivan worked together for the last time. Thenceforth Gilbert pursued his career as a playwright spasmodically and with declining success. A fanciful drama, 'Harlequin and the Fairy's Dilemma', was produced without much acceptance by Mr. Arthur Bourchier at the Garrick Theatre (3 May–22 July 1904). On 11 Dec. 1909 his opera 'Fallen Fairies', with music by Edward German, came out at the Savoy. His final production was 'The Hooligan', a grim sketch of the last moments of a convicted murderer, played by Mr James Welch at the Coliseum in 1911.

Gilbert's successes as a dramatist brought him wealth, which he put to good purpose. He built and owned the Garrick Theatre in Charing Cross Road, which was opened in 1889. In 1890 he purchased of Frederick Goodall, R.A., the house and estate of Grims Dyke, Harrow Weald, Middlesex. The estate covered 100 acres and the house had been built for Goodall by Norman Shaw. Gilbert added an observatory and an open-air swimming lake. He was something of an astronomer as well as a dairy farmer, bee-keeper, and horticulturist. He was made J.P. in 1891 and D.L. for Middlesex, and devoted much time to his magisterial duties. In 1907 he was knighted. He was a well-known member of the Beefsteak, Junior

Carlton, and Royal Automobile Clubs, and was elected by the committee to the Garrick Club on 22 Feb. 1906.

Gilbert died from heart failure brought on by over-exertion while saving a young lady from drowning in his swimming lake at Grims Dyke on 29 May 1911. The body was cremated at Golder's Green and the ashes buried at Great Stanmore church, Middlesex.

Gilbert was, perhaps, the most outstanding figure among Victorian playwrights. Few if any contemporary writers for the stage made so much money from that source alone, none acquired so wide a fame. In all his writing there is an effort after literary grace and finish which was in his early days absent from contemporary drama. His humour consists mainly in logical topsy-turveydom in a vein so peculiar to Gilbert as to justify the bestowal on it of the epithet 'Gilbertian'. He himself disclaimed any knowledge of Gilbertian humour, stating that 'all humour properly so called is based upon a grave and quasi-respectful treatment of the ludicrous'. His satire hits current foibles with unvarying urbanity and with no Aristophanic coarseness. The success of his operas was largely due to their freedom from vulgarity and to the excellence of the lyrics, which not only were musical and perfect in form but applied mastery of metre to the expression of the most whimsical and fanciful ideas. He had little or no ear for tune, but a wonderful ear for rhythm. Gilbert's words and metre underwent no change in the process of musical setting.

Gilbert believed that the playwright should dominate the theatre. He was a master of stage management. In a privately printed preface to 'Pygmalion and Galatea' he pointed out that 'the supreme importance of careful rehearsing is not sufficiently recognised in England'. His experience, for which he vouched by statistics, taught him that when his pieces were carefully rehearsed they succeeded, and when they were insufficiently rehearsed they failed. A sufficient rehearsal for a play he then considered to be three weeks or a month. His conduct at the rehearsals of his adaptation of 'Ought we to visit her' (a comedy in three acts by Messrs. Edwardes and Gilbert), produced at the Royalty on 17 Jan. 1874, led to a quarrel with Miss Henrietta Hodson, which was renewed over the production of 'Pygmalion and Galatea' in January 1877. Miss Hodson published 'A Letter' in the same year complaining of Gilbert's dictatorial action, to which Gilbert replied in 'A Letter addressed to the Members of the Dramatic Profession'. Gilbert developed the practice of Tom Robertson, who was perhaps the first English playwright to impress his personal views at rehearsal on the actor. Gilbert rehearsed his pieces in his study by means of a model stage and figures, and every group and movement were settled in the author's mind before the stage rehearsals began. Until Gilbert took the matter in hand choruses were practically nothing more than a part of the stage setting. It was in 'Thespis' that Gilbert began to carry out his expressed determination to get the chorus to play its proper part in the performance.

Gilbert had in ordinary society a ready, subtle, and incisive wit. He was aggressive and combative and rarely let the discomfort of a victim deprive him and his companions of a brilliant epigram or a ready repartee. Nevertheless he had a kind heart, and was only a cynic after the manner of Thackeray. Many of the artists who worked under him bore testimony to his personal kindness. He was not interested in sport. He had a constitutional objection to taking life in any form. 'I don't think I ever wittingly killed a blackbeetle', he said, and added 'The time will come when the sport of the present day will be regarded very much as we regard the Spanish bull-fight or the bear-baiting of our ancestors' (William Archer, *Real Conversations*).

He married in 1867 Lucy Agnes, daughter of Captain Thomas Metcalf Blois Turner, Bombay engineers. His wife survived him without issue. A portrait painted by Frank Holl, R.A., in 1887 is destined for the National Portrait Gallery. He also owned a portrait of himself by Herman Gustave Herkomer and a bronze statuette by Andrea Lucchesi.

Besides the plays already mentioned, Gilbert wrote the following dramatic pieces: 'Harlequin Cock Robin and Jenny Wren, or Fortunatus, the Three Bears, the Three Wishes, and the Little Man who wooed the Little Maid', pantomime (26 Dec. 1866); 'Allow Me to Explain', farce, altered from the French (Prince of Wales's Theatre, 4 Nov. 1867); 'Highly Improbable', farce (New Royalty, 5 Dec. 1867); 'No Cards' (German Reeds, 29 March 1869); 'An Old Score', comedy-drama in three acts (Gaiety Theatre, 19 July 1869); 'The Gentleman in Black', opera bouffe in two acts, music by Frederick Clay (Charing Cross Theatre, 26 May 1870); 'Our Island Home' (Gallery of Illustration, 20 June 1870); 'A Medical Man', a comedietta (Drawing Room Plays, 1870); 'The Realms of Joy', farce by F. Latour Tomline, i.e. Gilbert (Royalty Theatre, 18 Oct. 1873); 'Committed for Trial', a piece of absurdity in two acts, founded on 'Le Réveillon' of H. Meilhac and L. Halévy (Globe Theatre, 24 Jan. 1874, revived at the Criterion, 12 Feb. 1877, as 'On Bail'); 'Topsy-turveydom', extravaganza (Criterion Theatre, 21 Mar. 1873); 'King Candaules' (1875); 'Eyes and No Eyes, or the Art of Seeing', a vaudeville, music by T. German Reed, founded on Hans Andersen's 'The Emperor's New Clothes' (St. George's Hall, 5 July 1875); 'Princess Toto', comic opera in three acts, music by Frederick Clay (Strand Theatre, 2 Oct. 1876); 'The Ne'er-do-Weel', drama (Olympic Theatre, 25 Feb. 1878); 'Foggerty's Fairy', a fairy comedy (Criterion, 15 Dec. 1881); 'Brantinghame Hall', drama (St. James's Theatre, 29 Nov. 1888); 'The Brigands', opera bouffe in three acts, music by Offenbach, adapted from

'Les Brigands' of Meilhac and Halévy (Avenue Theatre, 16 Sept. 1889); 'Rosencrantz and Guildenstern', a travesty on 'Hamlet', in three tableaux (Vaudeville Theatre, 3 June 1891); 'Haste to the Wedding', comic opera, music by George Grossmith (Criterion Theatre, 27 July 1892), a version of E. M. Labiche's 'Un Chapeau de Paille d'Italie', played at the Court Theatre as 'The Wedding March' on 15 Nov. 1873; 'The Fortune Hunter', drama (Theatre Royal, Birmingham, 27 Sept. 1897).

Collected editions of Gilbert's dramatic work appeared as 'Original Plays' (4 series, 1876–1911) and 'Original Comic Operas' (8 parts, containing 'Sorcerer', 'H.M.S. Pinafore', 'Pirates of Penzance', 'Iolanthe', 'Patience', 'Princess Ida', 'Mikado', and 'Trial by Jury', 1890). He also published 'Songs of a Savoyard', a collection of songs from the Savoy operas, illustrated by Gilbert (1890), and 'Foggerty's Fairy and other Tales' (1890).

[William Schwenck Gilbert, *An Autobiography in The Theatre*, 2 April 1883, pp. 217 seq.; Edith A. Browne, *W. S. Gilbert*, 1907; Arthur Lawrence, *Life of Sir Arthur Sullivan*, 1899, William Archer, *English Dramatists of Today*; William Archer, *Real Conversations*; Percy FitzGerald, *The Savoy Opera and the Savoyards*; *Daily Telegraph*, 30 May 1911; *The Times*, 30 May–2 June, 18 Aug. (will), 1911; John Hollingshead's *Gaiety Chronicles*, 1898; Kate Field's *W. S. Gilbert* in *Scribner's Monthly*, 1879, xviii. 754; Smalley's *London Letters*, 2vols., 1890; and his *Anglo-American Memories*, 1911; *The English Aristophanes*, art. by Walter Sichel, in *Fortnightly Review*, 1912; W. Davenport Adams, *Dict. of the Drama*.]

E. A. Parry

*published 1912*

## GINGOLD Hermione Ferdinanda

**(1897–1987)**

Actress, was born in London 9 December 1897, the elder daughter (there were no sons) of James Gingold, stockbroker, who had emigrated from Austria, and his wife, Kate Walter. She claimed Viennese, Turkish, and Romanian blood on her father's side. Her mother was Jewish.

La Gingold, or Herman or Toni, as she was often called in the theatre, first appeared on stage at the age of ten as the herald in *Pinkie and the Fairies*, produced by (Sir) Herbert Beerbohm Tree. She later played the title role on tour and was cast by Tree as Falstaff's page, in *The Merry Wives of Windsor*. In 1912, aged fifteen, she played Cassandra at Stratford-upon-Avon in *Troilus and Cressida*, adventurously produced by William Poel.

(Dame) Edith Evans was Cressida. For an actress who was subsequently to achieve fame for her flamboyant personality, her wit, her sophisticated but often grotesque comedy, and her basso profundo voice, described by J. C. Trewin as 'powdered glass in deep syrup', her surprising billing in the actor's directory *Spotlight* in the 1920s and early 1930s read 'Shakespearean and soprano'. She lost her high notes after suffering nodules on her vocal chords: 'One morning it was Mozart and the next "Old Man River".'

She played many parts in the theatre and on radio in the 1930s; but she found her true *métier* in revue. She was in *Spread It Abroad* at the Saville in 1936, *The Gate Revue* in 1939 which transferred to the Ambassadors theatre, and its sequel *Swinging the Gate* (1940). Her legendary partnership with Hermione Baddeley ('the two Hermiones'), which was shorter lived than memory usually allows, began at the Comedy theatre in 1941 with *Rise Above It* (two editions) and continued in *Sky High* at the Phoenix theatre. It was during this show that their rivalry escalated in the press into a famous feud. She moved back to the Ambassadors for *Sweet and Low* (1943), *Sweeter and Lower* (1944), and *Sweetest and Lowest* (1946). Gingold became a special attraction for American soldiers and 'Thanks, Yanks' was one of her most appropriate numbers. During the astringent, name-dropping 'Sweet' series she played 1,676 performances, before 800,000 people, negotiating 17,010 costume changes.

She followed with *Slings and Arrows* at the Comedy in 1948 and appeared in cameo roles in English films, notably in *The Pickwick Papers* (1952), capturing a wider radio following with her weekly show *Home at Eight*, which featured Sid Colin's Addams-like family, the Dooms.

However, in spite of success with Baddeley in 1949 in *Fallen Angels*, by (Sir) Noël Coward, achieved despite the author's disapproval of their overdoing the comic effects, she was determined to renew her American friendships. Her first significant appearance in New York was in *John Murray Anderson's Almanac* (Imperial, 1953). For the rest of her career she was based in America and became particularly well known on talk shows. She made other appearances in revue, toured in a number of plays and musicals—taking over from Jo Van Fleet the role of Madame Rose Pettle in Arthur Kopit's *Oh Dad, Poor Dad, Mama's Hung You in the Closet and I'm Feelin' So Sad*. She made many cameo appearances on television and in films, notably *Around The World in Eighty Days* (1956); *Bell, Book and Candle* (1958); and *The Music Man* (1962). She joined the San Francisco Opera to play the Duchess of Crackenthorp in Donizetti's *La Fille du Regiment* in 1975 and attacked the concert platform as a narrator.

There were two milestones in this period. She appeared with Maurice Chevalier in *Gigi* (1958), in which they sang Alan Jay Lerner and Frederick

Loewe's song 'I Remember It Well' with exquisite wit and pathos. In 1973 she played Madame Armfeldt in Stephen Sondheim's *A Little Night Music*, triumphing with 'Liaisons', the memoirs of a *grande horizontale*. Once again she reminded audiences of her gift for pathos and the power of her acting.

In 1977 she took over the narrator's role in *Side by Side by Sondheim* on Broadway. Over eighty, she stayed with it gallantly on the gruelling 'bus and truck' tour of one-night stands, travelling over 30,000 miles and visiting sixty cities until she tripped over an iron pole on Kansas City railway station in the small hours. A shattered knee and a dislocated arm effectively ended her performing career.

Hermione Gingold was an artist whose style and wit were unmistakable and who always held the promise of laughter and outrage. Adored as an icon and often underestimated as an actress, she is secure in her reputation as a queen of revue and one of the essential sights of London during World War II. She was a statuesque woman who exaggerated her gargoyle features for comic effect on the stage; but she could achieve a handsome aspect in repose.

In 1918 she married Michael Joseph (died 1958), publisher, the son of Moss Joseph, diamond merchant. They had two sons, the younger of whom, Stephen Joseph, pioneer of theatre in the round in Scarborough, later Alan Ayckbourn's base, died in 1967. They were brought up by her husband. The marriage was dissolved in 1926, and in the same year she married (Albert) Eric Maschwitz (died 1969), playwright, lyricist, and television executive, son of Albert Arthur Maschwitz, of Edgbaston. The marriage was dissolved in 1940. Hermione Gingold died of pneumonia and heart disease in the Lennox Hill Hospital, New York, 24 May 1987.

[Hermione Gingold, *How To Grow Old Disgracefully* (autobiography), 1989; G. Payn and S. Morley (eds.), *The Noël Coward Diaries*, 1982; Gerald Bordman, *American Musical Theatre*, 1978; personal knowledge.]

Ned Sherrin

*published 1996*

## GRANT Cary

(1904–1986)

Film actor, was born 18 January 1904 at 15 Hughenden Road, Ashley, Bristol, as Archibald Alec Leach, the son of Elias Leach, tailor's presser, and his wife, Elsie Maria Kingdon, daughter of a shipwright. An earlier baby brother had died before his birth. Years later, after he had left England, a half-brother was born. He attended Fairfield Secondary School, Bristol. When he was ten, his mother disappeared and he thought she had died. However, she had been committed to a mental hospital, where she remained for many years. Discovering the exciting life backstage at the Bristol Hippodrome, he was fascinated by Bob Pender's Knockabout Comedians, a visiting troupe of slapstick, acrobatic, and stilt artists, and joined them when he was fourteen. For two years they toured Britain, and then had a long run in New York in 1920, after which they spent a year touring the United States. When the troupe returned to England Leach, now eighteen, stayed on in America and took various jobs in vaudeville, at Coney Island and as a sandwich-board man on stilts. After a speaking part in revue, Arthur Hammerstein, the producer, cast him in an operetta by his nephew Oscar in 1927. He spent several years working in Broadway musicals, in theatrical touring companies, and in repertory. In the 1920s he went to and fro between England and America.

In 1931 he easily obtained a Hollywood contract with Paramount, adopted the name Cary Grant, and began five years as a handsome romantic lead in many unremarkable films. *Blonde Venus* (1932) with Marlene Dietrich and two Mae West films may not have been great pictures, but the exposure was good for his career. *Sylvia Scarlett* in 1935, although another indifferent film, was a turning-point for him as he began to evolve a style of his own.

In 1937 he became freelance, which he remained, choosing his films carefully and developing a light comedy touch. Over the next thirty years he was to make many huge box-office successes, taking a percentage rather than a fee. He changed his name legally in 1941 and became an American citizen in June 1942. Among his many sophisticated and 'screwball' comedies, romantic comedies, and comedy thrillers, perhaps the best remembered are *Bringing Up Baby* (1938) and *The Philadelphia Story* (1940). He worked with some of the best directors and with stars such as Katharine Hepburn, Irene Dunne, Ingrid Bergman, and Grace Kelly. Above all, it was (Sir) Alfred Hitchcock who saw beyond the light comedian and jaunty man-about-town, giving him more subtle parts and being responsible for three of his best films, *Suspicion* (1941), *Notorious* (1946), and especially *North by Northwest* (1959). In 1966, at the age of sixty-two, he appeared in a part other than romantic lead for the first time. Not relishing the role of elderly character actor, and perhaps bored after seventy-two films, he made no more.

For many years one of the most glamorous and wealthy stars in Hollywood, playing opposite top actresses from Jean Harlow in the 1930s to Leslie Caron over a generation later, he was widely seen as an amiable performer who always played himself and, somewhat unjustly, was not taken seriously as an actor. He was nominated for the Best Actor award in 1941 and 1944 but did not win the Oscar. He finally got recognition from his peers in 1969 when, his film career over, the Academy belatedly gave him the survivor's consolation prize, an honorary award. The public loved him, however, and most of his films did well at the box office, some of them spectacularly so. He remained busy in old age, having a number of active directorships, including of the cosmetic firm Fabergé and Metro-Goldwyn-Mayer.

A tall, well-dressed man with thick dark hair and a marked cleft in his chin, he had a charming screen personality and self-deprecatory wit. He modified his west country working-class tones to an accent all his own, clipped and acceptable to American ears as upper-class British. So distinctive was his screen presence that it was easily mistaken for the man himself, but his private life suggests a deeply troubled individual. Rumoured to be bisexual, he had four unhappy marriages which collapsed quickly, with acrimony. His damaged childhood and vagabond youth had not equipped him for good personal relationships. Only a fifth marriage, when he was seventy-seven, to a much younger woman, seems to have brought him some tranquillity.

Cary Grant was married to actress Virginia Cherrill, formerly wife of Irving Adler and daughter of James Edward Cherrill, of independent means, 1934–5; Woolworth heiress Barbara Hutton, daughter of Franklyn Laws Hutton and his wife Edna, one of Frank Winfield Woolworth's two daughters, 1941–5; actress Betsy Drake 1949–59; actress Dyan Cannon (whose true name was Samile Dyan Friesen, daughter of an insurance executive), by whom he had his only child, a daughter, 1965–8; and former public relations director Barbara Harris in 1981. The first four marriages ended in divorce. He died of a stroke in Davenport, Iowa, 29 November 1986.

[*The Times* and *Independent*, 1 December 1986; Nicholas Thomas (ed.), *International Dictionary of Films and Filmmakers*, vol. iii, 1992; Chuck Ashman and Pamela Trescott, *Cary Grant*, 1987; William Currie McIntosh and William Weaver, *The Private Cary Grant*, 1983; Charles Higham and Roy Moseley, *Cary Grant, the Lonely Heart*, 1989.]

RACHAEL LOW

*published 1996*

## GRANVILLE-BARKER Harley Granville

(1877–1946)

Actor, producer, dramatist, and critic, was born in Kensington 25 November 1877, the only son and elder child of Albert James Barker, who came of an old Warwickshire and Hereford family. He is spoken of as an architect, but the family was largely dependent on his wife, Mary Elisabeth Bozzi Granville, who was a well-known elocutionist and reciter of the Victorian type. She was the granddaughter of Augustus Bozzi Granville, the son of Dr. Carlo Bozzi, who in 1806 took the name Granville to commemorate his Cornish grandmother who had married an Italian, Rapazzini. There were therefore two strains of Italian blood in Harley, both on the maternal side.

There is no record of his schooling, but he grew up in an atmosphere of good speech and drama and at an early age had a thorough knowledge of Dickens and Shakespeare. A precocious child, he frequently assisted at his mother's recitals, and even deputized for her. He began his professional career in 1891 at Harrogate and in Sarah Thorne's famous stock company at Margate; his first London appearance was at the Comedy Theatre in 1892. A tour with (Sir) Phillip Ben Greet in 1895 brought him to the notice of William Poel for whom he played Richard II in 1899. An introduction to the Fabian set, with which the founders of the Stage Society were closely allied, led to his great friendship with G. B. Shaw which had a profound influence on his career and lasted until his second marriage in 1918. For the Stage Society he produced or acted in a number of first performances of plays such as *Candida*, and *Mrs. Warren's Profession*, and his own *Weather Hen* and *The Marrying of Ann Leete*. His position once established, he devoted himself to the task of raising the standard of English acting and drama, and accustoming the English actor and audience to the permanent repertory company: with the idea of a national theatre in view. With William Archer in 1904 he drew up in great detail *A Scheme and Estimates for a National Theatre* which was not made public until 1907. Meanwhile his own first great chance came when, at Archer's suggestion, he was invited to produce *Two Gentlemen of Verona* at the Royal Court Theatre in 1904. He accepted on condition that during the run he might present a set of matinées of *Candida*. These were so successful that in partnership with John E. Vedrenne, the manager of the Court Theatre, and in close association with Shaw, he embarked upon the famous Vedrenne-Barker season which lasted until 1907, made Barker's name as a director and Shaw's as a dramatist, and became a landmark in the history of the British theatre. A new standard of intelligence and social criticism was brought into the theatre and in both plays and acting there was an intense regard for truth to life rather than for meretricious theatrical effect. Some 950 performances were given of 32 plays by 17 authors, including 11 of Shaw's, first plays of Galsworthy, St. John Hankin, and Mr. John Masefield, and works by Euripides (in Gilbert Murray's translations), Ibsen, Maeterlinck, and Barker. Expenses, including the actors' salaries, were kept very low but the financial stability of the enterprise was largely dependent on the success of Shaw's plays, especially *You Never Can Tell, John Bull's Other Island*, and *Man and Superman*. For the two latter Miss Lillah McCarthy joined the company in 1905 and in 1906 she and Barker were married.

The growing success of the Vedrenne-Barker partnership prompted a move in the autumn of 1907 to a larger theatre, the Savoy, but expenses increased more than receipts, Barker's new play, *Waste*, was forbidden by the censor, there were internal disputes over casting, and something of the joyful pioneering spirit had gone. The season petered out at Christmas and the new plays in preparation, Masefield's *Nan* and Galsworthy's *Strife* and others, were produced by Barker with all his care and skill but for Sunday societies or short runs under other managements. He was offered but declined control of the Millionaires' Theatre (later the Century), just completed in New York, which he found too vast for his style of work. In 1910, at the instigation of (Sir) James Barrie, Charles Frohman mounted a season of real repertory at the Duke of York's Theatre, with Barker and Dion Boucicault sharing the productions. Galsworthy's *Justice* in Barker's hands made a great sensation, and among other plays was Barker's own *The Madras House*. Although business was quite good the theatre was unsuitable for repertory, the expenses enormous, and the venture failed in three months. Barker had increased his reputation but not his finances and to recoup them he appeared for a season at the Palace Variety Theatre in a series of Schnitzler's *Anatol* duologues translated and produced by himself. In 1911 his wife, with the help of Lord Howard de Walden, raised a small syndicate to take the Little Theatre where they produced *The Master Builder* and Shaw's *Fanny's First Play*. The latter was a great success and, transferred to the Kingsway Theatre, ran until 1912.

Plans were now maturing for building a national theatre in time for the Shakespeare tercentenary in 1916, and in preparation for this, with the backing of Lord Howard de Walden and others, Barker in 1912 mounted at the Savoy two plays by Shakespeare which set a completely new standard of production never since surpassed. Continuity of action, an apron stage, the full text spoken with great beauty and a new swiftness, an entirely new approach to the plays in intelligence, truth, and taste, a brilliant company headed by Henry Ainley and Miss Lillah McCarthy, and exquisite simple settings by Albert Rothenstein (afterwards Rutherston) and Norman Wilkinson, all contributed to Barker's achievement. He was perhaps too far in advance of his time; even the critics were startled by the violent changes from the accepted traditions, and the first play, *The Winter's Tale*, was a comparative failure. *Twelfth Night*, although almost as revolutionary, was a more familiar play and ran for a hundred nights. These two productions, with *A Midsummer Night's Dream* in 1914, have had a profound and permanent effect on the approach to Shakespeare in the theatre. Further productions proved impracticable but meanwhile in 1913 Barker achieved a great comedy success at the Kingsway Theatre with Ainley in *The Great Adventure* by Arnold Bennett which ran until after the outbreak of war. The same year (1913) saw the opening of a season at the St. James's Theatre with Shaw's *Androcles and the Lion*, followed by revivals of *Nan*, *The Doctor's Dilemma*, and plays of Ibsen and Maeterlinck. Barker was now at the height of his powers, and his productions, although costly to his backers, greatly enhanced his European reputation and marked him as the future director of the national theatre.

The war demolished all his hopes. Barker presented Hardy's *Dynasts* in an adaptation of his own with outstanding artistic success, but the theatre had turned to frivolity and the production failed completely. In 1915 he produced *Androcles and the Lion*, *The Doctor's Dilemma*, and *A Midsummer Night's Dream* in New York for an American syndicate of millionaires. A mutual attraction between Barker and the wife of Archer Huntington (one of the backers) broke his marriage, and as neither of their partners wished a divorce there ensued a period of great strain during which Barker worked first for the Red Cross in France and then enlisted, later undertaking military intelligence work. Eventually the divorces went through and in 1918 Barker married Helen Huntington (died 1950) who as Helen Gates was a poet and novelist of some distinction. Archer Huntington settled a large sum on her and Barker was able to live henceforth in luxury. His wife insisted on almost complete severance from his work in the theatre and all his friends, however old and intimate, connected with it, and above all from Shaw.

Potentially perhaps the most remarkable theatre personality of this century Barker's career thus proved on the whole a disappointment and his influence on the theatre of this country fell far short of the hopes inspired by his brilliant start. His remaining work for the theatre was mainly professorial and literary, although almost surreptitiously he did a certain amount of directing of his own plays and translations. His last acknowledged stage production was Maeterlinck's *The Betrothal* at the Gaiety Theatre in 1921. In 1919 he took up with enthusiasm the work of the

British Drama League recently founded by Geoffrey Whitworth, and was its valuable chairman for thirteen years. In 1920 he made a rather pathetic attempt to live as a country gentleman in south Devon and during this period wrote his last two plays and the first of his series of translations from the Spanish (with his wife) which introduced the Quintero brothers and Sierra to the British public. As a dramatist Barker was too meticulous a writer to be very prolific. He experimented in a number of styles and probably his best work is found in the high comedy of *The Voysey Inheritance* and *The Madras House* and in the tragedy of *Waste*. Although slow moving, the characterization is vivid and as social criticism of their time they have a cutting edge. The two plays written in retirement, *His Majesty* and *The Secret Life*, seem never to have been publicly performed and have the rarefied atmosphere of one who has detached himself from the task of satisfying an audience which has paid for its seats. His *Exemplary Theatre* (1922) shows how far his mind had travelled even then from the contemporary theatre.

In 1923 Barker undertook the part editorship of 'The Players' Shakespeare', and although the series was abandoned he continued until his death to write the prefaces he had begun for it. They will probably outlive all his other written work, for they are most valuable interpretations of the plays from the director's point of view, and as a director Barker may be regarded as the first and greatest of the moderns. As an actor he had too much critical intelligence to be really successful for, with a certain lack of common humanity, it showed vividly through his impersonations. This was valuable in detached parts such as Marchbanks and Keegan, or even John Tanner, but it marred his performance of more ordinary characters. His face lacked the true flexibility of the actor's mask and his expressive voice, probably from being overworked as a boy, had too little ground tone to carry its strong higher harmonics. Yet he was an actor to his finger-tips, and with this he combined a first-class analytical and administrative brain and an outstanding gift for leadership. As a producer he used all his varied gifts completely selflessly in the service of the dramatist to bring out and express the full emotional and intellectual content of the play. His mastery of the play before starting rehearsals inspired confidence in his actors and he had the power to stimulate and use their own imaginative ideas, blending and moulding them within the framework of the play as he saw it. His intuitive grasp, as a dramatist, of human motives, thought, and emotions, and his technical knowledge of how to express them were continually at the service of his cast with every device of witty metaphor and amusing illustration. He was a perfectionist but no dictator, criticizing to the last inch and the last rehearsal, always with good humour, every tiniest movement or vocal inflexion, until the whole play became a symphony in which every phrase, rhythm, melody, and movement reached as near perfection as he could make it.

In 1930 Barker was appointed to the Clark lectureship at Trinity College, Cambridge, and in 1937 he was Romanes lecturer at Oxford. He received honorary degrees from Edinburgh (1930), and from Oxford and Reading in 1937, in which year he became director of the British Institute in Paris where he had been living for some time. He continued to take some interest in the British theatre and in 1940 came over to take a major share of the direction of (Sir) John Gielgud's *King Lear* at the Old Vic, on condition that his name did not appear. He resigned from the British Institute in 1939 and when Paris fell he went to America where he was a visiting professor at Yale and Harvard. He returned to England in failing health in 1945 and to Paris in 1946 where he died 31 August and was buried in the cemetery of Père Lachaise. He had no children.

Of slight, wiry build, almost five feet eleven in height, until well past middle age Barker still gave an extraordinary impression of youth both in face and figure. He had a sensitive face, strong and masculine with humorous warm brown eyes, and a mouth always harder than the eyes, tending even to grimness in his later days. His thick red-brown hair was parted in the middle and thrown back. A curious feature was his very flabby handshake. The British Drama League has a bust in bronze by Clara Billing and a posthumous bust by David McFall; the National Portrait Gallery has a painting by J.-E. Blanche; a bronze by Lady Kennet is at the Shakespeare Memorial Theatre, Stratford on Avon, and a portrait statuette by the same artist is at the Garrick Club.

[Desmond MacCarthy, *The Court Theatre, 1904–7*, 1907; C. B. Purdom, *Harley Granville Barker*, with a complete catalogue of his known writings, 1955; *Who's Who in the Theatre*; private information; personal knowledge.]

Lewis Casson

*published 1959*

## GRENFELL Joyce Irene

(1910–1979)

Actress and broadcaster, was born in London 10 February 1910, the elder child and only daughter of Paul Phipps, an architect and a fellow of RIBA, and his wife, Nora Langhorne, from Virginia, USA, who was the sister of Nancy (later Viscountess) Astor, the first woman to sit in the House of Commons. Educated at Francis Holland School, London, and the Christian Science school Clear View in South Norwood, and then 'finished' in Paris, stage-struck Joyce Phipps, in the intervals of going to debutante dances, attended classes at the Royal Academy of Dramatic Art, but shortly abandoned her histrionic dreams to become the wife of Reginald Pascoe Grenfell, chartered accountant. They married in 1929, Joyce then being nineteen, and remained happily so until her death, fifty years later. They had no children.

Meeting J. L. Garvin, editor of the *Observer*, and conveying to him in all innocence, and with no ulterior motive, her interest in and affection for the radio, she found herself, much to her surprise, the radio critic on that paper, writing a weekly column from 1936 to 1939 when, also unsuspecting of the outcome, she met Herbert Farjeon, theatre critic of the *Tatler* and author of a current revue, *Nine Sharp*. At a party given by Stephen Potter, with whom she was later, in 1943, to broadcast the popular 'How' programmes, Joyce was persuaded to entertain the company with a rendering of a talk she had heard at a Women's Institute meeting. It was called 'Useful and Acceptable Gifts', and was the foundation stone upon which her stage career was built. For Farjeon was so amused by it that he invited her, absolute amateur though she was, to give this talk in his coming revue, *The Little Revue*, which was to open in March 1939. Feeling she had nothing to lose, and being of a fearless disposition, Joyce accepted.

Thus began Joyce Grenfell's long and successful career as an entertainer. Not only did she write a large number of monologues, many of which, notably the 'Nursery School' series, became classics, but lyrics as well, the music for which was, for the most part, composed by Richard Addinsell. Her monologue characters, ranging through every stratum of society, catching the tones and manners of, among others, a chairman of a north country ladies' choral society, a wife of an Oxbridge university vice-chancellor, a foreign visitor at a cocktail party, a country cottager, an American mother, and a cockney girl friend, were masterpieces of observation. Along with her songs, sung in a small but pretty and perfectly tuned voice, they provided evenings of rare entertainment.

She had an instantaneous success. There were two more Farjeon revues, *Diversion* and *Light and Shade*, and then, during World War II, she went on two long tours abroad for the Entertainments National Service Association, visiting hospitals and isolated units in fourteen countries. She was appointed OBE in 1946.

In 1945 she appeared in the revue *Sigh No More* by (Sir) Noël Coward, in 1947 *Tuppence Coloured*, and in 1951 *Penny Plain*. She also took part in a radio discussion programme, 'We Beg to Differ', in 1949, and over the years appeared in a variety of films: *Genevieve, The Happiest Days of Your Life, The Million Pound Note, The Yellow Rolls-Royce*, to name the better known; and the St. Trinian's series in which her interpretation of a much badgered games mistress brought her increased fame.

But it was in 1954 that she reached the height of her profession, for in that year she had her own show, *Joyce Grenfell Requests the Pleasure*, which led eventually to her handling a two-hour programme solo (like her well-known friend Ruth Draper) and touring the world with it. Her tours abroad were numerous and glorious. Canada, the USA, Australia, New Zealand, Hong Kong, Switzerland, (not South Africa), all saw her many times, and so of course did every part of Britain, her dearest local triumph being a short season at that most stylish of London theatres, the Haymarket. After nearly forty years of entertaining a grateful public composed of all classes, age groups, and nationalities, she retired from the stage in 1973, her final performance of songs and monologues being given before the Queen and her guests at the Waterloo dinner in Windsor Castle.

She continued to appear on television, making a particularly pleasing contribution to the musical quiz programme 'Face the Music' and giving a memorable TV interview to Michael Parkinson in September 1976.

Through the years Joyce Grenfell was committed to projects unconnected with show business. In 1957 she became president of the Society of Women Writers and Journalists; from 1960 to 1962 she served on the committee concerned with the 'future of the broadcasting services in the UK', chaired by Sir W. H. (later Lord) Pilkington; in 1972 she was appointed a member of the council of the Winston Churchill Memorial Fellowship Trust, the grants from which enable students to go overseas to study their special subjects.

A lifelong Christian Scientist she was deeply interested in metaphysics, and on a number of occasions spoke in the 'dialogues' initiated by the Revd Joseph McCulloch from the two pulpits in St. Mary-le-Bow church in London. She also spoke in Truro Cathedral and Westminster Abbey (in which latter church she was given, in 1980, the rare honour of a memorial service). She lectured on 'communication', about which she was naturally very experienced, to all sorts of groups, in universities, colleges, and technical institutes, being made an honorary fellow of the Lucy Cavendish College, Cambridge, and the Manchester Polytechnic, and often contributed to the BBC morning programme 'Thought for the Day'.

During her partial retirement from public life she wrote her autobiography in two volumes, *Joyce Grenfell Requests the Pleasure*, a bestseller published in 1976, and *In Pleasant Places*, published in 1979.

Joyce Grenfell's total enjoyment of life was the keynote to her character. She had a genuine love of goodness and sought it in all things, in music, literature, nature, and above all people. Her talent was unique in that although she caricatured her subjects and pin-pointed their idiosyncracies, there was never a hint of censure. Although she became a true professional she retained one attractive element of the amateur, in that she seemed to be doing it all for fun; and her manifest zest for living coupled with her artistry, kind-heartedness, and sense of humour had a cherishing effect upon her audiences. They loved her. On the stage, television, and radio she had a huge following and at her death, in London 30 November 1979, she had become in the nature of an institution. As the critic Clive James wrote in an obituary: 'Beyond those favoured hundreds who knew her in person are the thousands and the millions who could tell just from the look of her that she had a unique spirit.' She was to have been appointed DBE in the 1980 New Year honours list.

[Joyce Grenfell, *Joyce Grenfell Requests the Pleasure*, 1976, and *In Pleasant Places*, 1979; Reggie Grenfell and Richard Garnett (eds.), *Joyce*, 1980; personal knowledge.]

VIRGINIA GRAHAM

*published 1986*

## GROSSMITH George (the younger) (1874–1935)

Actor-manager and playwright, was born in London 11 May 1874, the elder son of the entertainer and singer in light opera George Grossmith, by his wife, Emmeline Rosa, only daughter of Edward Noyce, M.D. He was nephew of the comedian W. W. Grossmith. He was educated at University College School and in Paris, and it was originally intended that he should enter the army, but he failed in his examination at Woolwich. He first appeared on the stage at the Criterion Theatre, in July 1892, in *Haste to the Wedding*, a musical play adapted by (Sir) W. S. Gilbert, with music composed by Grossmith's father. Engagements followed at several London theatres until November 1894, when for the first time he was seen at the Gaiety Theatre in *The Shop Girl*. In the autumn of 1895 he made his first appearance in New York in this play. He appeared at the Comedy Theatre in 1899 in one of his own plays, *Great Caesar*, and at the Globe Theatre in 1900 in another, *The Gay Pretenders*. After acting for a short period at other theatres and in the United States of America, he returned to the Gaiety in 1901, under the management of George Edwardes, with whom he remained in association until 1913, appearing in a succession of popular musical plays, notably in *The Toreador* (1901), *The Orchid* (1903), *The Spring Chicken* (1905), *The Girls of Gottenburg* (1907), and *Our Miss Gibbs* (1909). During this period he also appeared at the Hicks (later Globe) Theatre in 1908 in *A Waltz Dream*, at the Alhambra Theatre in 1914, and in the United States. In 1914 he entered into management with Edward Laurillard, his productions with whom included *Potash and Perlmutter* (Queen's Theatre, 1914), *Tonight's the Night* (Gaiety, 1915), and *Theodore and Co.* (Gaiety, 1916).

During the war of 1914–1918 Grossmith was commissioned in the Royal Naval Volunteer Reserve (1916) and later served with the Royal Naval armoured cars. After the end of the war he became manager, with Laurillard, of the Winter Garden Theatre, which they opened in May 1919 with *Kissing Time*; this was followed by a number of other successful musical plays there and at the Adelphi Theatre, which, with other theatres, they also controlled. This partnership ended in 1921, when Grossmith entered into partnership with J. A. E. Malone. Grossmith appeared at His Majesty's Theatre in April 1923, under his own management, as Lord Quex in a revival of *The Gay Lord Quex* by Sir Arthur Pinero, his first venture into serious comedy. At the Palace Theatre in March 1925 he scored one of the greatest successes of his career in *No, No, Nanette*, and he also appeared there in *Princess Charming* in 1926. In 1929 he again visited America and appeared in several plays. He made his last appearance on the stage at His Majesty's Theatre, during October 1934, as Talma in *Josephine*.

In 1931 Grossmith became managing-director of Drury Lane Theatre, but resigned the position after twelve months, and in 1932 he became chairman of London Film Productions, Ltd.; he had himself appeared on the screen in several pictures from 1929 to 1931.

Grossmith wrote (both alone and in collaboration) or adapted more than thirty plays, many of which were eminent successes, including *The Spring Chicken, Rogues and Vagabonds, The Girls of Gottenburg, Havana, The Dollar Princess, Everybody's Doing It, The Bing Boys are Here, Theodore and Co., A Night Out, The Cabaret Girl*, and *Primrose*.

Grossmith originated the 'dude' or 'dandy' in musical comedy when he appeared as Lord Percy Pimpleton in *Morocco Bound* at the Shaftesbury Theatre in 1893, and he continued to play that type of character for nearly thirty years with almost unvarying success. To Grossmith must also be accorded the credit of introducing the modern type of revue to London with *Rogues and Vagabonds* at the Empire Theatre in 1905; and he was also the first to introduce 'cabaret' entertainment to this country, at the Whitehall Rooms, Hotel Metropole, in 1922.

Always a fluent French speaker, Grossmith appeared in Paris, in revue at the Folies Bergère in 1910, and also acted with Réjane, the famous French actress, at her theatre in 1911. He was created a chevalier of the Legion of Honour and an officer of Public Instruction by the French government, and also received decorations from the Greek government and from the pope.

In appearance Grossmith was lanky and of angular physique. He made capital out of his physical peculiarities, which, combined with the curious carriage of his arms and hands, and the fixed smile of his large mouth, helped to create a stage personality which few could forget. Although he had no voice for singing, he had the faculty of putting his songs across the footlights in an inimitable manner, and he was a very nimble dancer.

Grossmith married in 1895 Gertrude, youngest daughter of Henry Rudge, actor, of Edgbaston; she was known on the stage as Adelaide Astor. They had a son and two daughters, the elder of whom, Ena, adopted her father's profession with some success. He died in London 6 June 1935.

A portrait of Grossmith in uniform by Weedon Grossmith was exhibited at the Royal Academy in 1917.

[George Grossmith, *'G. G.'*, 1933; *Morning Post* and *News Chronicle*, 7 June 1935; *Who's Who in the Theatre*, 1933; personal knowledge.]

John PARKER

*published* 1949

## GUTHRIE Sir (William) Tyrone

**(1900–1971)**

Director and theatre designer, was born 2 July 1900 at Tunbridge Wells, the elder child and only son of Thomas Clement Guthrie, doctor and surgeon, and his wife, Norah Power. He had much theatrical blood in his veins, since his mother was the granddaughter of Tyrone Power, the first of a long line of popular actors, of whom Tyrone Power, the film actor, was Guthrie's cousin. He was educated at Wellington, and won a history scholarship at St. John's College, Oxford. He early showed that independence of spirit which later enabled him to transform the shape of theatre in Britain, Canada, and America by telling the authorities of St. John's that if he won a scholarship he did not need the money, which he hoped would be given to a poorer man. It was not until he had done this that he told his father of the magnanimous gesture he had made on his behalf.

He went up to Oxford at the time of the armistice in a state of high exhilaration. He declared that 'certainly we are living in the most marvellous times since the Reformation—if not since Christ. . . . For the young . . . it's an opportunity such as the world has never known before'. His Scots-Irish blood roused greater fires in him than were kindled by the gracious propriety of Tunbridge Wells. Immediately he left Oxford he plunged into the society of those as yet unknown, but who were, with him, to become famous. He joined the company of J. B. Fagan at the Playhouse, Oxford, which in the early 1920s had in it such young players as (Sir) John Gielgud, Richard Goolden, and (Dame) Flora Robson. He was to see Flora Robson frequently in subsequent years, and proposed to her, but the proposal came to nothing because they could not agree whether to have children. Guthrie was further dashed by his great height and comparatively small head, and so gave up acting.

After working in radio in Belfast and then with the BBC, and at one or two other indeterminate occupations, he at last found his vocation by directing *The Anatomist* by James Bridie at the Westminster Theatre (1931), with Henry Ainley as Dr Knox and Flora Robson as the unfortunate prostitute, Mary Paterson, a part which she considered the finest performance she ever gave. Guthrie immediately recognized that he had a great gift, aided by his commanding height, his gentle voice, and inflexible determination, for controlling actors, and two years later Lilian Baylis appointed him as director of plays at the Old Vic and Sadler's Wells.

His years at the Old Vic were a period of ambition, achievement, and frustration. He raised the standard of productions, but angered Lilian Baylis by bringing in outside stars like Charles Laughton (whom she resented as too expensive), Flora Robson, and Athene Seyler. After Lilian Baylis's death in 1937 Guthrie was appointed administrator. When war came he was much criticized for evacuating the Old Vic to Burnley. He developed his conviction that the director was a more important element in a production than the actor, but when the Old Vic came back to London in 1944, reaching tremendous success in a temporary West End home at the New (later Albery) Theatre, Guthrie was overshadowed by the performances of Laurence (later Lord) Olivier, (Sir) Ralph Richardson, and (Dame) Sybil Thorndike, who had now joined the company. He felt rebuffed when knighthoods were conferred on Richardson and Olivier in 1947, and he himself was passed over. He ended the war very depressed, quite different from his mood of 1918, and resigned from the Old Vic. He travelled restlessly, and produced a fine *Oedipus Rex* for the Habimah company in Tel Aviv.

The turning point in his life came in 1948, when he directed an adaptation of Sir David Lindsay's *Ane Satyre of the Three Estaits* in the Assembly Hall of the Church of Scotland at the second Edinburgh Festival. Guthrie had long felt dissatisfied with the separation of audience and players by the conventional proscenium arch, and the thrust stage of the austere Assembly Hall, with the audience on three sides of it, enabled him to bring about a sense of participation between players and audience which became the keynote of the work by which he was to change the nature and shape of theatre in the western world. Here he came into his kingdom, of which he felt he had been hitherto deprived. He suddenly saw the kind of theatre he wanted—a theatre of processions and banners and ritual, a theatre that was in itself a Festival, an Event, a Celebration, in which the actor played an important but essentially subordinate part in the pageantry and splendour of the director's conception of the play, which he insisted was essentially subjective and need not conform with the author's. Inspired by this revelation, he established the Stratford Ontario Festival in 1952, in the second largest theatrical tent in the western hemisphere, and in 1963 a theatre in Minneapolis based on the principles worked out at Edinburgh. Guthrie's theories have influenced the building of nearly all new theatres, and are particularly apparent in England in the construction of the Chichester Festival Theatre (1962) and the Olivier (1976). It was thus, rather than by individual productions, that Guthrie justified his conviction of 1918 that a new world was opening to those that could seize it.

Guthrie received many honours. He was knighted in 1961 and was chancellor of Queen's University, Belfast (1963–70). He was an honorary fellow of St. John's College, Oxford (1964). He received honorary degrees from Queen's University, Trinity College, Dublin, (1964), St. Andrews (1956), Franklyn and Marshall university (Pennsylvania), Western Ontario (1954), Ripon College (Wisconsin), and Citadel Military College, Charleston.

In 1931 he married Judith, daughter of Gordon Bretherton, solicitor, and Nellie Lacheur, and, as he himself said, lived happily ever after. She died in 1972. There were no children of the marriage. Guthrie died 15 May 1971 at his family estate in Newbliss, county Monaghan, Eire.

[*The Times*, 17 May 1971; James Forsyth, *Tyrone Guthrie*, 1976; Tyrone Guthrie, *A Life in the Theatre*, 1960; personal knowledge.]

Harold Hobson

*published 1986*

## HANCOCK Anthony John (Tony)

**(1924–1968)**

Comedian, was born at Small Heath, Birmingham, 12 May 1924, the second of three sons of John Hancock, hotelier, and his wife, (Lucy) Lilian Thomas. He was educated at Durlston Court, Swanage, and Bradfield College, Reading. Much of his youth was spent in Bournemouth where his father, himself a part-time professional entertainer, ran a hotel. Here he met many people from the lighter side of the entertainment world. Attempts to find employment in ordinary life were less than successful. He was, briefly, in the Civil Service and his subsequent job, at a Birmingham tailor's, lasted just under three hours.

Enlisting in the RAF in 1942, Hancock toured with ENSA (Entertainments National Service Association) and the Ralph Reader 'Gang Shows'. Demobilized in 1946, in 1948 he appeared at the Windmill Theatre, a variety house whose girl-predominated turns had much pleased the mainly male wartime audiences and whose proud motto was 'We Never Closed'.

But it was to be with the BBC, both in radio and on television, rather than on the stage that Hancock's name was to be made. Graduating from such wireless attractions as 'Workers' Playtime', 'Variety Bandbox', and 'Educating Archie', where his catchphrase of 'flippin' kids!' became well known and widely copied, he was given on 2 November 1954 his own programme, 'Hancock's Half-Hour', which was an immediate success.

To add incongruity to his fictional and somewhat squalid East Cheam background, his name was elaborated into Anthony Aloysius St. John Hancock. The programme owed much to the presence in the cast with him of Bill Kerr, Kenneth Williams, and, particularly, Sid James. It owed perhaps most of all, for Hancock was incapable of producing his own material, to Alan Simpson and Ray Galton, his scriptwriters. The strength of the Half-Hour lay in the fact that it relied on comedy of character and situation rather than on set jokes and it had none of the musical interludes with which such programmes were normally interrupted. Hancock played an unsuccessful actor, full of pretentiousness and snobbery and deeply prejudiced. In one of the John Freeman 'Face to Face' interviews on BBC television, he said: 'The character I play isn't a character I put on and off like a coat. It's a part of me and a part of everybody I see.'

Throughout the 1950s television was becoming increasingly efficient and popular and vastly expanding (ITV appeared in 1955) and in due course in 1956 the Hancock programme was transferred to this medium and to the huge audience which it by then commanded. Here the success was even greater and for a few years there was no comedian of comparable popularity. His face fitted to perfection the character which had up to then been purely a wireless voice. There were the heavy jowls, the creases, the sunken and pouchy eyes, the turned-down corners of the mouth. There was a fresh catchphrase ('Stone me!'). Sid James, his partner in the constant disasters—financial, social, and professional—which beset them, had a face along similar lines. The programme frequently found them, bored to tears, after lunch on a Sunday afternoon and with rain falling. One of the episodes began with the following series of groans, treasured by the whole viewing public, from Hancock: 'Ahh. Oh dear. Mm. Oh dear, oh dear. Ahh, dear me. Ahhh. Stone me, what a life.'

Bored indeed with his by now familiar comedy routines, his attempts to branch out into other comic realms brought real disaster with them. Seldom has such a dazzling career disintegrated so swiftly. He abandoned Sid James and Galton and Simpson. He made three poor films. There was an unsuccessful ITV series. He began drinking heavily and could not remember his lines. His first marriage (to Cicely Romanis in 1950) broke up in 1965 and his second marriage to 'Freddie' Ross, his public relations agent, in the same year ended in divorce a week before his death.

Tony Hancock was the last of a cherished line of English comedians whose stock-in-trade it has been to have about them a seedy air of vanished sartorial grandeur and of better times, Burlington Berties every one of them. There was George Robey's bowler hat and frock-coat, with the red nose and heavy, arched eyebrows to go with them. There was Billy Bennett ('Almost a Gentleman') with his defiant bow-tie and dickey and boots. And with Hancock it was the Homburg hat, the shabby fur-collared overcoat, and the grand manner, all so splendidly out of place either in a fish and chip parlour or at home at 23 Railway Cuttings, East Cheam. And to accompany the run-down clothing there was the look of total gloom and despondency and a deep resentment against life.

J. B. Priestley, writing enthusiastically on the special characteristics of purely English humour, a brand so incomprehensible to other nations, says that Hancock, in the television sketches written for him by Alan Simpson and Ray Galton and which suited him so perfectly, 'seemed to combine an unconscious despair and hatred of show business with more than a touch of genius for it, finally giving him deep at heart a deathwish'.

Priestley was sadly right and in the end Hancock died by his own hand in Sydney, Australia, 25 June 1968.

[Roger Wilmot, *Tony Hancock—'Artiste'*, 1978; Eric Midwinter, *Make 'em Laugh*, 1979; *The Times*, 26 June 1968.]

ARTHUR MARSHALL

*published 1981*

## HARE (John) Robertson

**(1891–1979)**

Actor, was born in London 17 December 1891 at 26 Cloudesley St., Islington, the family home, the younger child and only son of Frank Homer Hare, an accountant, and his wife, Louisa Mary Robertson. He was educated at Margate College and was then coached for the stage by Lewis Cairns James.

His first professional stage appearance was in 1911 when he played the Duke of Gallminster in *The Bear Leaders* in a provincial production. The following year he made his London début as one of the crowd in the Covent Garden production of *Oedipus Rex*, and in 1913 he had his first part in a metropolitan production, as Kaufman in *The Scarlet Band* at the Comedy Theatre. He then toured the provinces for a number of years, notably in the title role of *Grumpy*, which thereafter remained his favourite part. It commanded considerable success on tour during the early years of the war of 1914–18, after which Hare served for the last two years of the war with the army in France.

1922 was the crucial year of his career. He played James Chesterman in *Tons of Money* at the Shaftesbury Theatre under the joint management of Tom Walls and Leslie Henson. In February 1924 he transferred, with the same management, to the Aldwych, where he opened as William Smith in *It Pays to Advertise*. This inaugurated the era of the famous Aldwych farces, and, for over ten years, the outrageous comedies of Ben Travers offered their contribution to the madcap climate of the twenties and early thirties in London. Chief among Hare's parts were the Revd Cathcart Sloley-Jones in *A Cuckoo in the Nest* (1925), Harold Twine in *Rookery Nook* (1926), Hook in *Thark* (1927), and Ernest Ramsbotham in *A Cup of Kindness* (1929). In all, he featured in twelve consecutive farces at the Aldwych between 1924 and 1933. The pattern of his career was by then firmly established. Apart from an occasional appearance in revue—*Fine Fettle*, for instance, in 1959—or in 'period' farce in 1963, as Erronius in *A Funny Thing Happened on the Way to the Forum*, he was fairly strictly type-cast as the nervy and fussy innocent, continually trapped in awkward situations. Between 1933 and 1960 he created such a character in over twenty more farces, several of them at the Strand Theatre. Herbert Holly (*Aren't Men Beasts!*, 1936), Humphrey Proudfoot (*One Wild Oat*, 1948), and, very successfully, Willoughby Pink (*Banana Ridge*, 1938) are perhaps his best-remembered roles from this period. During the sixties his extraordinarily active stage appearances began to diminish as he rested on his well-earned laurels, although he toured in *Arsenic and Old Lace*—a rare example of his playing in a comedy already well-tried—and, after opening in the play at the Lyric in 1968, he visited South Africa as Dr Simmons in *Oh, Clarence!* in 1970, when he was almost eighty years old.

His cinema work was of early vintage. In 1929 Herbert Wilcox, production chief of British and Dominion Studios at Elstree, began the straightforward and uncomplicated filming of several of the Aldwych farces, and Hare also made a few film appearances in the post-war years. *Thark* (1932) is usually regarded as the pleasantest cinematic translation of a Travers comedy. Hare wrote, not too successfully, a couple of plays, and then, late in life, turned energetically to television. He will be most easily recalled by the seventies generation, who would scarcely have recognized him as a stage performer, for his playing of the archdeacon in *All Gas and Gaiters*, a creditable comedy series with a clerical orientation, starring Derek Nimmo as Noote, a young and naive clergyman.

Robertson Hare created a cosily familiar style and was identified completely with, in effect, one part, that of the prissy little man, constantly in a state of unease and agitation, invariably sucked into some maelstrom of domestic upset and dislocation, unfailingly compromised and often trouserless. The bald dome, with brows furrowing anxiously beneath it; the spectacles, emphasizing the shock and bewilderment with which he responded to his travails; the jerky, staccato movements as his distress grew—these made him a highly recognizable stage figure. In concert with the worldly wise Tom Walls and the affable Ralph Lynn and, later, in alliance, on stage or screen with the likes of Gordon Harker or Alfred Drayton, he became perhaps the premier exponent of English farce, particularly in the between-wars period. Above all, there was the somewhat archdeaconal, tremulous, and vacillating (although, from an audience stance, always clearly intelligible) voice. Rarely has a comic actor become so intimately associated with one word. Robertson Hare, faced with disaster, was wont to warble the five syllables of 'Oh, calamity' in a characteristic kind of plainchant. It is fitting that many should remember and identify him thus, and that 'Oh, calamity' should have passed into popular usage. His autobiography *Yours Indubitably* was published in 1957. He was appointed OBE in 1979, just before he died.

In 1915 Hare married Irene Mewton, who predeceased him in 1969. They had one daughter. He died in London 25 January 1979.

[*The Times*, 16 November 1979; *Who's Who in the Theatre*; personal knowledge.]

Eric Midwinter

*published 1986*

## HARRISON Sir Reginald Carey ('Rex') (1908–1990)

Actor, was born 5 March 1908 in Huyton, Lancashire, the youngest of three children and only son of William Reginald Harrison, stockbroker, and his wife, Edith Mary Carey. At the age of ten he adopted the name 'Rex', by which he was known for the rest of his life. He was a sickly child and a bout of measles left him with poor sight in his left eye. He was educated at Birkdale Preparatory School and Liverpool College. His appearances in school plays and regular visits to the Liverpool Playhouse confirmed an early desire to be an actor. At sixteen he was taken on at the Playhouse and after a year backstage made his acting début in 1924 in *Thirty Minutes in a Street*. After two and a half years playing small roles, he left Liverpool for London, where in 1927 he landed a part in a touring production of *Charley's Aunt*. Thus began six years of touring and repertory, in which he learned his craft. It was a five-month run as a caddish explorer in *Heroes Don't Care* in 1936 that provided his breakthrough. The critic of *Theatre World* proclaimed him 'one of the best light comedians on the English stage' and he maintained this position until his death.

On the basis of *Heroes Don't Care*, the producer (Sir) Alexander Korda signed a contract with Harrison at London Films, and he was launched on a cinematic career, which he was to continue henceforth in tandem with his stage career. He achieved an early success in the delightful comedy *Storm in a Teacup* (1936), where as a crusading reporter he was taught by the director Victor Saville how to relax in front of the camera. He consolidated his theatrical reputation with long runs in *French Without Tears* (1936), *Design for Living* (1939), and *No Time for Comedy* (1941). From 1942 to 1944 he served in the Royal Air Force Volunteer Reserve as a flying control liaison officer. Emerging from the forces, he established himself as a major

British film star in the screen version of *Blithe Spirit* (1945) and in *The Rake's Progress* (1945), in which he was excellent as a charming, feckless, parasitic playboy, who expiates a worthless life with a heroic death on the battlefield.

Hollywood inevitably beckoned and Twentieth Century-Fox signed a seven-year contract with him. They saw him not as a light comedian but as a character actor. The vehicles they provided for him, if not always to his taste, were invariably superbly mounted and stretched him as an actor. In *Anna and the King of Siam* (1946), Harrison was both comic and touching as the capricious but dedicated King Mongkut. In *The Ghost and Mrs Muir* (1947), playing the spirit of an old sea dog, he took to being blasphemous and bad tempered with evident glee. In *Unfaithfully Yours* (1948) he played an autocratic and egocentric orchestral conductor with a memorable line in vituperation. But his continuing unhappiness in Hollywood, his unflattering comments on the film capital, poor box-office returns on his later Fox films, and an unsavoury scandal surrounding the suicide of actress Carole Landis, with whom he was having an affair, led Harrison and Fox to terminate the contract by mutual consent. He returned to Broadway to play King Henry VIII in Maxwell Anderson's *Anne of the Thousand Days* (1948) at the Shubert theatre, New York, and promptly won a Tony award as best actor. Then in London and on Broadway he did John Van Druten's play *Bell, Book and Candle* (1950) and directed and starred in (Sir) Peter Ustinov's play *The Love of Four Colonels* (1953). He won the 1961 *Evening Standard* Best Actor award for his performance in Anton Chekhov's *Platonov* at the Royal Court theatre in 1960.

Harrison resolutely avoided Shakespeare, but became the supreme interpreter of the plays of Bernard Shaw, bringing the necessary quality of civilized intelligence to his performances both on stage (*Heartbreak House* 1983, *The Devil's Disciple* 1977) and film (*Major Barbara* 1940–1). He will forever be associated with the role of Professor Henry Higgins in *My Fair Lady*, the Lerner and Loewe musical based on Shaw's *Pygmalion*. Harrison played the part for three years on stage in New York and London (1956–9), winning a second Tony award, and an Oscar for his performance in the film version (1964). So much did he make the part his own that he later said: 'For years I could never bear to see anyone else do it—Higgins has become so much a part of me and I, of him.'

Harrison's success in *My Fair Lady* made him a major international star and led to appearances in several screen epics in the 1960s. There was more than a touch of Shaw's Julius Caesar in his drily witty and very human performance as the Roman conqueror in *Cleopatra* (1963). When Caesar expired half-way through, so did the film. The ponderous film about Michelangelo, *The Agony and the Ecstasy* (1965), was almost redeemed by Harrison's engaging interpretation of Pope Julius II as an urbane schemer.

In the late 1960s there was a string of expensive flops—*The Honey Pot* (1965), *Doctor Doolittle* (1966), *A Flea in her Ear* (1967)—and in the 1970s and 1980s Harrison's film appearances were mainly cameos, though he played Don Quixote in a notable 1973 BBC TV production. He concentrated his energies on the stage, displaying his gifts in London and New York in a series of Edwardian revivals: *Heartbreak House* 1983, *Aren't We All?* 1984–5, *The Admirable Crichton* 1988, and *The Circle* 1989. He was appearing in *The Circle* when his final illness was diagnosed.

Harrison was married six times, and allegedly mistreated all his wives. His first wife (1934) was the fashion model Collette Thomas (her real name was Marjorie). They had one son, the actor and singer Noel Harrison, born in 1935, and were divorced in 1943. His second wife was the émigré German Jewish actress Lilli Palmer (whose real name was Lilli Peiser), whom he married in 1943. They had one son, the playwright Carey Harrison, born in 1944, and were divorced in 1957. His third wife (1957) was the English actress Kay Kendall, who died of leukaemia in 1959 at the age of thirty-two. Their relationship was the basis of the play *After Lydia*, by Sir Terence Rattigan, in which Harrison starred on Broadway in 1974, playing the role based on himself. He married his fourth wife in 1962, the Welsh actress Rachel Roberts, daughter of the Revd Richard Rhys Roberts. They divorced in 1971 and she committed suicide in 1980. His fifth wife (1971) was Mrs (Joan) Elizabeth Rees Harris, daughter of David Rees Rees-Williams, first Baron Ogmore, PC, and ex-wife of actor Richard Harris. They divorced in 1976. He married finally in 1978 an American, Mercia Tinker. Harrison wrote two volumes of autobiography and three of his wives left their impressions of him in their autobiographies.

Harrison was a man of enormous charm and this often compensated for the personal and professional self-centredness and perfectionism that sometimes tried the patience of colleagues and associates. He was perhaps the last Edwardian, compeer of Sir Gerald du Maurier, Sir Charles Hawtrey, and Sir (E.) Seymour Hicks, actors who contrived to give the impression that they had just popped into the theatre for a spot of acting on the way to the club. Harrison had admired and closely studied the style and technique of the great Edwardians and had come to embody the same combination of elegance, authority, wit, and grace. He was appointed commendatore of Italy's Order of Merit in 1967, awarded an honorary degree by the University of Boston in 1973, and knighted in 1989. He died of cancer of the pancreas in New York, 2 June 1990.

[Rex Harrison, *Rex*, 1974, and *A Damned Serious Business*, 1990; Allen Eyles, *Rex Harrison*, 1985; Nicholas Wapshott, *Rex Harrison*, 1991; Alexander Walker, *Fatal*

*Charm*, 1992; Lilli Palmer, *Change Lobsters and Dance*, 1976; Rachel Roberts and Alexander Walker, *No Bells on Sunday*, 1984; Elizabeth Rees Harrison, *Love, Honour and Dismay*, 1976.]

JEFFREY RICHARDS

*published 1996*

## HARTY (Fredric) Russell

(1934–1988)

Broadcaster, was born 5 September 1934 in Blackburn, the only son and elder child of Fred Harty, greengrocer (who, his son claimed, introduced Blackburn to the avocado pear), and his wife, Myrtle Rishton. He was educated at Queen Elizabeth's Grammar School, Blackburn, and Exeter College, Oxford, where he read English and was taught by Nevill Coghill, who noted of an early essay on 'Sex in the Canterbury Tales', 'Energetic and zealous but very naïve'. He took a third-class degree (1957) and taught briefly at Blakey Moor Secondary Modern School in Blackburn before moving in 1958 to Giggleswick School in Yorkshire. Giggleswick was a school and a village with which he was to have close connections for the rest of his life. In 1964 there followed a spell at City College, New York, and at Bishop Lonsdale College of Education, Derby, but with many of his friends and contemporaries busy in the theatre and broadcasting he was increasingly dissatisfied with teaching.

In 1966 he made his first foray into television, an inglorious appearance as a contestant on Granada TV's *Criss Cross Quiz*; the only question he answered correctly was on Catherine of Braganza. It was such a public humiliation that his mother refused to speak to him. Still, it was a beginning and in 1967 he was taken on by BBC Radio as an arts programmes producer, his hankering to perform whetted by the occasional trip to the studio down the corridor whenever *Woman's Hour* wanted a letter read in a northern accent.

As an undergraduate Harty had invited Vivien Leigh round for drinks and this precocious appetite for celebrity stood him in good stead when, in 1969, he became producer and occasional presenter of London Weekend TV's arts programme, *Aquarius*. He might not have seemed the best person to film Salvador Dalí, but the elderly surrealist and the boy off Blackburn market took to one another and the programme won an Emmy award; in another unlikely conjunction he set up an encounter on Capri between the eminent Lancashire exiles Sir William Walton and Gracie Fields. Harty was never abashed by the famous (his critics said that was the trouble), but it was his capacity for provocative half-truths and outrageous overstatement, which made him such a good schoolmaster, that now fitted him for a career as the host of a weekly talk show (*Eleven Plus* and later *Russell Harty*) and made him one of the most popular performers on television. Plump, cheerful, and unintimidating, he was particularly good at putting people at their ease, deflating the pompous and drawing out the shy.

In 1980 he returned to the BBC, but his output remained much as it had been for the last ten years, the same mixture of talk shows varied by occasional films like *The Black Madonna*, and his *Grand Tour*, shown in 1988. He wrote regularly for the *Observer* and the *Sunday Times*, publishing a book of his television interviews, *Russell Harty Plus* (1976) and also *Mr Harty's Grand Tour* (1988). He was a regular broadcaster on radio besides presenting the Radio 4 talk show, *Start the Week*.

'Private faces in public places are wiser and nicer than public faces in private places' (W. H. Auden) did not anticipate television, where the distinction is not always plain. For his friends Harty was naturally a private face but for the public he seemed a private face too and one that had strayed on to the screen seemingly untouched by expertise. That was why, though it infuriated his critics, so many viewers liked him and took him to their hearts as they never did more polished performers. He giggled, he fumbled and seldom went for the right word rather than the next but two, and though his delivery could be as tortured as his mother's on the telephone, it did not matter. It was all part of his ordinariness, his deficiencies, his style.

Harty never made much of a secret of his homosexuality. He did not look on it as an affliction, but he was never one for a crusade either. His funniest stories were always of the absurdities of sex and the ludicrous situations it had led him into, and if he was never short of partners, it was because they knew there would always be laughs, sharing a joke being something rarer than sharing a bed.

In the second half of the 1980s the spread of AIDS enabled the tabloid press, and in particular those newspapers owned by Rupert Murdoch, to dress up their muckraking as a moral crusade, and they systematically trawled public life for sexual indiscretion. Harty, who had not scrupled to question his more celebrated interviewees about their sex lives, knew that he was in a vulnerable situation. Early in 1987 a young man, who had had a previous fling with Harty, was wired up with a tape recorder by two *News of the World* reporters and sent to call on Harty at his London flat. To the reporters' chagrin nothing newsworthy occurred, but the paper fell back on printing the young man's account of the previous association, thus initiating a campaign of sporadic vilification in the tabloid press, which only ended with Harty's death just over a year later.

The cause of his death was liver failure, the result of hepatitis B, but in the hope that he was suffering from AIDS the press laid siege firstly to his home in Giggleswick and then to St James's Hospital in Leeds, where he was in intensive care. A telescope was trained permanently on the window of his ward and a reporter tried to smuggle himself into the ward disguised as a junior doctor, in order to look at his case notes. When Harty was actually on his deathbed one of the journalists responsible for the original 'scoop' could not be restrained from retelling the tale of her exploits on television.

He died in Leeds 8 June 1988 and is buried in Giggleswick, the gravestone evidence of the vulgarity from which he never entirely managed to break free.

[Private information; personal knowledge.]

Alan Bennett

*published 1996*

## HAWTREY Sir Charles Henry

(1858–1923)

Actor, the fifth son and eighth of the ten children of the Rev. John William Hawtrey, by his first wife, Frances Mary Anne, daughter of Lieutenant-Colonel George Procter, historical writer and superintendent of studies at the Royal Military College, Sandhurst, was born at Eton 21 December 1858. His father, a first cousin once removed of Edward Craven Hawtrey, provost of Eton, was then a house master at Eton, the lower school of which Charles Hawtrey entered at eight years old. In 1869 his father left Eton and founded St. Michael's School, Aldin House, Slough; and there Hawtrey was educated until he returned to Eton in 1872. In 1873 he left Eton for Rugby, where he played cricket for the school. Intended for the army, he went in 1875 to a crammer's in London, but he abandoned the intention, and from 1876 to 1879 was a private tutor. In February 1881 he matriculated at Pembroke College, Oxford, but in November following his name was taken off the books, since in October he had gone on the stage.

Hawtrey made his first appearance under the name of Charles Bankes at the Prince of Wales's Theatre, London, in the part of Edward Langton in

*The Colonel* by (Sir) Francis Cowley Burnand. With his brother William, who had also gone on the stage (as did another brother, George), Hawtrey took a company on tour in the spring of 1883; but he had been a professional actor for less than two years when he came upon the play which began his very successful career in farce and comedy. This was an English version of a German farce, *Der Bibliothekar*, by Gustav von Moser. Rewritten by Hawtrey, who entitled it *The Private Secretary* and later revised it, the play was first staged at the Prince's Theatre on 29 March 1884, and transferred on 19 May 1884 to the Globe Theatre, where W. S. Penley succeeded (Sir) Herbert Beerbohm Tree in the title-part, and Hawtrey, under his own name, took the part of Douglas Cattermole. The play ran for two years, and Hawtrey claimed that he inaugurated the 'queue' for pit and gallery in order to control the crowds which came to see it.

Thereafter for nearly forty years Hawtrey worked hard at his profession. He managed the Globe Theatre till the autumn of 1887; then the Comedy Theatre till the beginning of 1893 and again from April 1896 to April 1898. At one time and another he managed sixteen other London theatres and produced about one hundred plays. Of these the most memorable by reason of their success and of his performances in them, were two more adaptations from von Moser, *The Pickpocket* by George Hawtrey, and *The Arabian Nights* by Sydney Grundy; *Jane* by Harry Nicholls and William Lestocq; *One Summer's Day* by H. V. Esmond; *Lord and Lady Algy* by R. C. Carton; *A Message from Mars* by Richard Ganthony; *The Man from Blankley's* by 'F. Anstey'; *Dear Old Charlie* by C. H. Brookfield; *Jack Straw* by W. S. Maugham; *The Little Damozel* by Monckton Hoffe; *General John Regan* by 'George Birmingham', and *Ambrose Applejohn's Adventure* by W. Hackett.

Hawtrey was a good producer of plays and teacher of acting. In staging farce and light comedy he showed a mastery of fine shades and the polish which belonged to the school of the Bancrofts and W. S. Gilbert; but now and then he proved himself efficient in producing more serious drama. As actor, he had the wit to make his greatest strength out of what had been the bane of his youth, his immobility of face. He learned so to charge that immobility with expression that he excelled in the characters of liars, selfish men, and erring husbands, in which imperturbability was necessary, and any break in it came with great effect. Better than any of his contemporaries he achieved by art an air of being entirely natural. He seldom attempted the pathetic; but in *One Summer's Day* he showed that his method was capable of giving a signal moment of it.

In 1901 and in 1903 to 1904 Hawtrey paid professional visits to the United States. He was knighted in 1922. He was twice married: first, in 1886 to Madeline Harriet, daughter of Thomas Sheriffe, of Henstead Hall, Suffolk, who divorced him in 1893 and died in 1905; and secondly, in 1919 to Katherine Elsie, daughter of the Rev. William Robinson Clarke, and widow of the Hon. Albert Henry Petre, son of William Henry Francis, eleventh Baron Petre. He had no children by either marriage. He died in London 30 July 1923.

Off the stage and on, Hawtrey was a charming man, and had many friends of both sexes. He was a good cricketer and golfer; but the chief interest of his life (an interest shared by his father) was horse-racing. He began betting when at Eton; in 1885 he won £14,000 on a single race, and in 1885 and 1886 he had horses of his own in training.

[*The Times*, 31 July 1923; Charles Hawtrey, *The Truth at Last*, 1924; Florence Molesworth Hawtrey, *The History of the Hawtrey Family*, 1903; *Who's Who in the Theatre*, 1912.]

H. H. CHILD

*published 1937*

## HELPMANN Sir Robert Murray

(1909–1986)

Ballet dancer and choreographer, was born 9 April 1909 in Mount Gambier, South Australia, the elder son and eldest of three children of James Murray Helpman (the original spelling), a rich sheep farmer, and his wife Mary, daughter of Robert Gardiner, a sea captain in the whaling business. Helpmann attended Prince Alfred's College, Adelaide, but his education was marred by his habitual truancy and his parents finally withdrew him from the college, engaging a private tutor. This gave Helpmann the opportunity to concentrate on his two passions, dancing and acting; even at this early age he described himself as 'the complete show-off'.

His appearance was certainly unusual. His head was large, with a bulging forehead and wide, protruding eyes: beneath a normally shaped nose an exceptionally long upper lip culminated in a small, thin mouth which revealed many long, rather alarming teeth. Narrow shoulders, a large diaphragm, and thin, unmuscular legs completed an image which he later used to great effect in character roles, both balletic and dramatic. Romantic performances were less successful and, in modern dress, he seemed too fantastic to be believable. He added the final 'n' to Helpman to avoid having a name of thirteen letters for his theatrical career.

His first engagement was as a student-dancer on the 1921 Australian tour by the company run by Anna Pavlova. He then appeared in J. C. Williamson's productions of musicals and revues until 1927. In pantomime in 1931 he was seen and admired by the English actress, Margaret Rawlings, then touring Australia. He joined her company in New Zealand and sailed with her for England in 1932.

Margaret Rawlings introduced Helpmann to (Dame) Ninette de Valois, director of the recently formed Vic-Wells (later Sadler's Wells) Ballet. Intrigued by his appearance rather than his ability as a dancer, she employed him and, in 1933, he replaced (Sir) Anton Dolin as Satan in de Valois' barefoot masque-ballet, *Job*. He created his first role in *The Haunted Ballroom* in 1934 and, in the following year, gave the first of many outstanding performances as the Rake in *The Rake's Progress*. In 1937, while forming his long partnership with the young ballerina, (Dame) Margot Fonteyn, he created another superb characterization as the old Red King in *Checkmate*.

These four de Valois ballets—and a fifth, *The Prospect Before Us* (1940), in which he played a wonderfully drunken stage manager—gave Helpmann the best roles of his career. His classical technique was barely adequate and none was required; all dancing and movement was in character, tragic or comic, and his superlative talent for mime was given full rein. No other actor-dancer matched him in this field.

His restlessness and determination for wider horizons took him to the Old Vic in 1937 to play Oberon in *A Midsummer Night's Dream*, his first essay into the English dramatic theatre. His light tenor voice had neither range nor power but his exotic appearance in this supernatural role was a success. He returned to the ballet and, while touring, met an Oxford undergraduate, Michael Pickersgill Benthall (died 1974). Helpmann, a flamboyant homosexual, made a lifelong companion of Benthall, who became a leading stage director and a major contributor to their partnership. He was the son of Sir Edward Charles Benthall, director of the Reserve Bank of India.

Leading the Sadler's Wells Company, Helpmann branched out into choreography. It was unsurprising that his few classically based ballets were pallid and derivative while his dramatic, character works were of genuine substance. Most notable were *Hamlet* in 1942 and *Miracle in the Gorbals* in 1944. In these, and in his future stage direction, he was guided by the taste and expert advice of Benthall. In 1950 Ninette de Valois, who had been fortunate to have Helpmann in her company in World War II because, as an Australian, he was unavailable for call-up into the armed services, gave Helpmann another perfect role for his talents in her ballet,

*Don Quixote*. On an American tour later that year he resigned, abruptly and inexplicably, from the company.

Turning to the dramatic theatre, Helpmann played Hamlet, King John, Shylock, and Richard III at Stratford and the Old Vic; he appeared with Sir Laurence (later Baron) Olivier and his wife Vivien Leigh in the George Bernard Shaw and Shakespeare *Cleopatras* in 1951 and with Katharine Hepburn in *The Millionairess* in 1952. He played supporting roles in films, including Olivier's *Henry V* (1944), *The Red Shoes* (in which he also choreographed the ballet sequence, 1948), and *The Tales of Hoffmann* (1951). He directed *The Tempest* and *Murder in the Cathedral* (1953) at the Old Vic; *Madame Butterfly* (1950) and *Le Coq d'Or* (1956) at Covent Garden, and a number of plays, musicals, and pantomimes.

He returned to Australia to tour with the Oliviers and, later, with Katharine Hepburn. This experience was so successful and enjoyable that he decided, in 1962, to live many months of each year in his own country, visiting London less and less frequently. In 1965 he joined (Dame) Peggy van Praagh as an artistic director of the Australian Ballet and choreographed four productions for the company. His energy remaining undiminished, he acted in several Australian films and directed plays and musicals in New York and London. His last success was a production of Franz Lehár's *The Merry Widow* as a ballet at the Sydney Opera House in 1975.

Helpmann was the most theatrical of performers both on and off stage. He held court, always the centre of attention, and was considered a wit by close colleagues. Many found him amusing but not witty; his humour was always sharply malicious, at the expense of others, and, perhaps because of this, he evoked more wariness than affection. He was neither a great actor nor a great dancer, but he brought a singular and effective presence to the theatre, particularly the ballet stage. He was appointed CBE in 1964 and knighted in 1968. He died in the Royal North Shore Hospital, Sydney, 28 September 1986.

[D. C. Abrahams, *Robert Helpmann, Choreographer*, 1943; Anthony Gordon, *Robert Helpmann*, 1946; Kathrine S. Walker, *Robert Helpmann*, 1957; Elizabeth Salter, *Helpmann*, 1978; personal knowledge.]

MOIRA SHEARER

*published 1996*

# HENSON Leslie Lincoln

(1891–1957)

Actor-manager, was born in Notting Hill, London, 3 August 1891, the eldest of the three children of Joseph Lincoln Henson, tallow chandler, of Smithfield, and his wife, Alice Mary, daughter of William Squire, of Glastonbury. He was educated at Cliftonville College and Emanuel School, Wandsworth. His parents, realizing where his talents lay, wisely swallowed their disappointment at his reluctance to stay in the family business and sent him to study acting under Cairns James. Beginning his professional career in 1910 as a member of a concert party called 'The Tatlers', he continued for the next five years to be engaged in concert-party work, alternating this with touring in musical comedy. He made his first London success at the Gaiety Theatre, 28 April 1915, as Henry in *To-Night's the Night*. It was appropriate that his success, which was instantaneous, should have been made at a theatre so closely identified with the reputations of many famous comedians.

All actors reflect, with varying degrees of distortion, the times in which they live. Henson was no exception. His cockney alertness, his bubbling humour, and his india-rubber face which never ceased to underline or embroider the lines he was speaking, exploded like a catherine wheel, in a theatre grown accustomed to the heavier humours of Edmund Payne and his contemporaries. Here was a different, a livelier talent.

Henson's emergence as a star of musical comedy was put into temporary eclipse by the war of 1914–18. Before joining the army, he flung himself into the work of entertaining the troops. Early in 1916 he appeared in a revue of his own contriving in the new garrison theatre at Park Hall Camp, Oswestry, one of the first of the new hutted camps soon to be dotted over the countryside. The building of this theatre out of the soldiers' regimental funds was the genesis of the system of government-sponsored entertainment in wartime which reached its full development in the war of 1939–45 under the aegis of E.N.S.A. The company, which included Melville Gideon, Stanley Holloway, and Davy Burnaby, and six girls from the Gaiety chorus, all of them destined to achieve success in one direction or another, left the Gaiety Theatre after the Saturday night performance, wrote the revue on the night mail to Chester, rehearsed it on the garrison theatre stage on the Sunday morning, and performed it twice that same evening: the kind of gay, chaotic improvisation in which Henson delighted. Later, he joined the Royal Flying Corps, was sent to France, commissioned, and put to work organizing entertainment for the Fifth

Army. The little company of actors which he gathered round him, some professional, some amateur, soon became famous as The Gaieties, making their headquarters at the municipal theatre in Lille.

Following demobilization Henson achieved a series of outstanding successes in musical comedy at the Winter Garden, of which *Sally* (1921) and *Kid Boots* (1926), both American importations, were best remembered. In 1935 he returned to the Gaiety to appear in a series of musical plays containing parts specially written for him, and to share in the management. He was also associated in management with Tom Walls. Together they were responsible for the production of the farce *Tons of Money* (1922), followed by the series of plays known as the Aldwych farces, a generic title acquired from the theatre in which they were presented. Henson also made a number of films. His star was now at its zenith and he was fully occupied until the outbreak of war in 1939.

Henson's sense of obligation towards the audiences who had welcomed him with such acclaim found its full expression in his untiring efforts throughout the war, when he worked almost continually for E.N.S.A., first in France, and later in North Africa, the Middle East, Italy, and India. Welcomed in every mess and canteen, raising uproarious laughter like clouds of desert dust wherever he went, this was Leslie Henson at his most fulfilled. He was a droll, a cockney clown, of unmistakable genius. Representing the art of the ridiculous in the theatre, he was at his best when pursuing the golden thread of absurdity through a maze of commonplace situations. His humour was as characteristic of the years in which he flourished as many of the gritty jokes of the television artists reflect the nervous hilarity of a later day. One of the best ways of remembering him is by the widely published photograph of King George VI roaring with laughter at a Henson joke during a performance for the Fleet at Scapa Flow.

The time came, after the war and coinciding with the natural decline in his own powers, when his brand of humour began to stale. The last production in which he may be said to have appeared in a characteristic part, largely of his own fashioning, was *Bob's Your Uncle*, at the Saville Theatre in 1948. Thereafter, he was forced to abandon the musical-comedy eccentricities in which he had made his name and to appear in plays where his inability to create a part otherwise than in terms of his own drollery became a serious handicap. His performances in the revivals of such plays as *1066 and All That* (1947), in *Harvey* (1950), and in the musical play about Samuel Pepys called *And So To Bed* (1951) had only equivocal success.

Like all great comic actors Henson took his work seriously, and he cheerfully accepted the responsibilities which success brought him. He was president of the Royal General Theatrical Fund from 1938 and remained to the last indefatigable in charitable causes.

Henson married in 1919 Madge Saunders, actress; the marriage was dissolved in 1925. His subsequent marriage to Gladys Gunn was also dissolved; and in 1944 he married Mrs. Harriet Martha Day, by whom he had two sons. He died at Harrow Weald 2 December 1957. A portrait by Frank O. Salisbury is in the possession of the family, and one of the actor as Mr. Pepys by Maurice Codner is in the hands of the artist's son.

[*The Times*, 3 and 9 December 1957; Leslie Henson, *My Laugh Story*, 1926, and *Yours Faithfully*, 1948; personal knowledge.]

Basil Dean

*published 1971*

## HICKS Sir (Edward) Seymour (George) (1871–1949)

Actor-manager and author, was born at St. Helier, Jersey, 30 January 1871, the son of Lieutenant (later Major) Edward Percy Hicks of the 42nd Highlanders, and his wife, Grace Seymour. Hicks had no ancestral call to the theatre, although his younger brother, Stanley Brett, followed his example. Educated at Prior Park College, near Bath, and at Victoria College, Jersey, he was only sixteen when he 'walked on' in *In the Ranks* at the Grand Theatre, Islington. It was the two years he then spent with W. H. and (Dame) Madge Kendal, in both England and America, taking parts in early plays by (Sir) Arthur Pinero like *The Money Spinner* and *The Squire* and other classics of the period—all before he was twenty-one—that gave him an invaluable grounding. On his return, thanks to a recommendation from (Dame) Irene Vanbrugh and adopting a Scottish accent, he went to see (Sir) James Barrie, who immediately gave him the part of Andrew McPhail, the young Scottish medical student, in *Walker, London*, at Toole's Theatre, 1892, in which he made a great hit, the play running for over a year. Then in 1893, whilst at the Court Theatre, he engaged in and wrote with Charles H. E. Brookfield and Edward Jones what was really the first London revue, *Under the Clock*. It contained burlesques of current plays and was called a 'musical extravaganza'. Another visit to the United States, in *Cinderella*, was followed by his first appearance under George Edwardes's banner at the Gaiety Theatre as Jonathan Wild in *Little Jack Sheppard* in 1894, and afterwards, until 1897, in *The Shop Girl* and *The Circus*

*Girl*. In 1899 he was the Duc de Richelieu—quite a new type of part for him—in *A Court Scandal* at the Court, paid another visit to America, and on his return registered another success as the Mad Hatter in *Alice in Wonderland* at the Vaudeville (1900). At the same theatre in 1901 he gave a performance of the utmost tenderness and charm in Basil Hood's *Sweet and Twenty*. Here also he appeared as Scrooge in John Baldwin Buckstone's play of that name and as Dicky in his own *Bluebell in Fairyland* with Walter Slaughter's music. His Valentine Brown in Barrie's *Quality Street* came at the Vaudeville in the next year, succeeded by an astonishing portrait of Edmund Kean in Gladys Buchanan Unger's one-act play of that title, and Moonshine and Happy Joe in his own *The Cherry Girl* to Ivan Caryll's music in December 1903. In September 1904 came his great Vaudeville success, *The Catch of the Season*, written by himself with Cosmo Hamilton, which ran until 1906.

Hicks now went in for the building of new west-end theatres. He built the Aldwych which he opened in December 1905 with *Bluebell in Fairyland*, playing there the following year in his own and Cosmo Hamilton's *The Beauty of Bath*. With this he also opened the Hicks—later the Globe—in Shaftesbury Avenue, built for Charles Frohman. His next adventures, alike as actor and author, were *The Gay Gordons* at the Aldwych in 1907 with music by Guy Jones, followed by *The Dashing Little Duke* with music by Frank E. Tours at the Hicks in 1909, in which he appeared as his old friend, the Duc de Richelieu, a part also played by his wife. Finding himself in financial difficulties he went next to the Coliseum at the invitation of (Sir) Oswald Stoll. In 1914 he organized a concert party and gave a series of performances to the British forces at the front in France. In 1922 he had a memorable season at the Garrick Theatre, which he opened with himself as *The Man in Dress Clothes* which he had adapted from the French. He was afterwards seen in *Vintage Wine*, adapted from the Hungarian by himself and Mr. Ashley Dukes, and presented, with himself as Charles Popinot, at Daly's Theatre in 1934. In 1938 he appeared as Captain Hook in *Peter Pan* at the Palladium, and at the Coliseum in 1939 appeared in *You're Telling Me*, an adroit Franco-British sketch, with Sacha Guitry as his companion. Though his ready laugh and blinking eyes made comedy his natural vehicle, his flashes of tragic expression when called for—as in *Edmund Kean*—were unforgettable. Hicks was, needless to say, extremely popular in films.

Hicks was knighted in 1935 and was made a chevalier of the Legion of Honour in 1931, largely for his services to French drama in London. He was elected president of Denville Hall in 1935. He published *Twenty-Four Years of an Actor's Life* in 1910 and many volumes, mostly anecdotal, in his later career, and *Me and My Missus—Fifty Years on the Stage*, in 1939.

Throughout his entire career Hicks owed an incalculable deal to the inspiration of his beautiful, talented, and devoted wife, the charming actress Ellaline Terriss (Mary Ellaline Lewin, daughter of William Terriss). They married in 1893. He died at his home at Fleet, Hampshire, 6 April 1949, survived by his widow and one daughter. A son died at birth. Hicks was the most versatile and brilliant comedian of his time, and a delightfully intelligent and imaginative personality. A portrait of him as Lucien in *The Man in Dress Clothes* painted by Maurice Codner has hung on loan from the artist at the Garrick Club, of which Hicks was a leading member.

[His own writings; Ellaline Terriss, *Just a Little Bit of String*, 1955; private information; personal knowledge.]

S. R. Littlewood

*published* 1959

## HITCHCOCK Sir Alfred Joseph

(1899–1980)

Film director, was born 13 August 1899 in Leytonstone, London, the second son and youngest of the three children of William Hitchcock, a greengrocer and poulterer, and his wife, Emma Jane Whelan. He was educated at various Catholic boarding schools in London, and always spoke of his childhood as lonely and protected. But the memory of the period he most often quoted as having shaped his attitude towards authority, fear, and guilt, was being sent by his father at the age of five with a note addressed to the superintendent of the local police station, where he was locked in a cell for ten minutes and then released with the words, 'That is what we do to naughty boys'.

His father died when Hitchcock was fourteen and he left St. Ignatius's College, a Jesuit institution in Stamford Hill, to study at the School for Engineering and Navigation, and then became a draughtsman and advertising designer with a cable company. After some free-lance work designing silent-movie titles, he obtained a full-time job at Islington Studios in 1920, and under its American owners, Famous Players–Lasky, and their British successors, Gainsborough Pictures, he gained a knowledge of all aspects of the business before the producer (Sir) Michael Balcon gave him the opportunity to direct his first picture, the extravagant melodrama *The Pleasure Garden*, in 1925.

The following year Hitchcock drew on his fascination with the classic English murders to make a movie about a man suspected of being Jack the Ripper, *The Lodger*, which was his first thriller and the first time he 'signed' a film by making a brief personal appearance. In 1929 he directed the first British talking film, *Blackmail*, another thriller. With its plot of a police officer in love with an accidental murderess, its innovative use of sound, and a finely staged climactic chase in the British Museum, *Blackmail* had all the characteristics of his mature work.

Although he directed adaptations of *The Manxman* (1928) by (Sir) T. H. Hall Caine, *Juno and the Paycock* (1930) by Sean O'Casey, and *The Skin Game* (1931) by John Galsworthy, Hitchcock soon came to specialize in thrillers, and after the success of *The Man Who Knew Too Much* (1934), only one film—a version of the Broadway comedy *Mr and Mrs Smith* (1941)—took him away from his chosen *métier*. Starting in the late 1920s, he cultivated the acquaintance of journalists and cinephiles, becoming one of the most articulate and frequently quoted exponents of his craft and winning the title 'master of suspense'. His pictures were meticulously planned before they went into production and he often said that the real interest lay in the preparation, the actual shooting being a necessary chore. The performers, however eminent their reputations, were there simply to realize his and his screenwriters' conception. This is what he meant when he said: 'Actors should be treated like cattle.'

Through such films as *The Thirty-Nine Steps* (1935), *Sabotage* (1936), and *The Lady Vanishes* (1938), the comedy-thriller many consider the finest achievement of his English period, Hitchcock became the most successful and highly regarded director in Britain. But he was increasingly attracted by the greater technical facilities, larger budgets, and more substantial international fame that working in America would bring him. Equally the apparent classlessness of American society afforded opportunities for social acceptance denied him in the hide-bound Britain of that time. So in 1939, after completing a film of (Dame) Daphne du Maurier's *Jamaica Inn*, he left for Hollywood where his first assignment for his new employer, David O. Selznick, was to adapt Daphne du Maurier's *Rebecca* (1940). It won an Academy award for the best film of the year.

Except for three brief sojourns in Britain—first making as a patriotic gesture two short films in French in 1944 for distribution by the Ministry of Information in newly liberated France, next directing *Under Capricorn* (1949) and *Stage Fright* (1950), then later his penultimate picture *Frenzy* (1971)—Hitchcock remained in Hollywood. A number of his early American films, however, had English settings, and most of his Hollywood productions featured British actors in key roles. He remained deeply attached to his native country and did not take out American citizenship papers until 1955.

During the 1940s and 1950s, Hitchcock developed a fascination for solving technical problems. His wartime melodrama *Lifeboat* (1943) is confined to the inside of a lifeboat after an American merchant ship has been torpedoed by a German U-boat. His version of Patrick Hamilton's play *Rope* (1948) is shot in a series of ten-minute takes so that the whole picture appears seamless and unedited. In 1954 he filmed another play, *Dial M for Murder*, using the three-dimensional camera, and in the same year he restricted the point of view of *Rear Window* to what a temporarily crippled photographer could see from the window of his New York apartment.

In the decade between his psychological thriller *Strangers on a Train* (1951) and his influential horror film *Psycho* (1960), Hitchcock produced within the perimeters of his chosen genre an extraordinarily varied range of work. It included *I Confess* (1952), the story of a Canadian priest prevented by the confidences of the confessional from clearing his name of a murder charge; *The Wrong Man* (1957), the reconstruction of a true story of a New York musician falsely accused of robbery; and *North by Northwest* (1959), an immaculate comedy-thriller that recaptured the light touch of his pre-war British films.

In this period his reputation advanced on two quite different fronts. In 1955 he began a ten-year association with television through his series of tales of mystery, crime, and the occult, *Alfred Hitchcock Presents* (1955–61) and *The Alfred Hitchcock Hour* (1961–5), some editions of which he directed, and all of which he introduced in his gentle, even London accent, and with his own brand of deadpan, often rather macabre, humour. This regular exposure on television, added to those eagerly awaited glimpses of him in the feature films, helped make his short portly figure (his weight varied between fourteen and twenty stones) and chubby face immediately recognizable and beloved by film-goers the world over. He became the only director in the history of the cinema to be instantly recognizable to the general public.

On another front, Hitchcock became the idol of the young French critics of the monthly journal *Cahiers du Cinéma* who were later to become the directors of the *nouvelle vague*. They regarded him as not merely a master film-maker with a unique ability to manipulate audiences, but also a profound psychologist, social observer, and Catholic moralist. A full-length study by Claude Chabrol and Eric Rohmer in the 'Classique du Cinéma' series (1957) was the foundation-stone for what by the end of Hitchcock's life was to be a substantial body of scholarship.

The English-speaking world at first resisted these larger claims that were being made for a man thought of largely as a skilled entertainer. But as film studies grew on the campuses of America, Hitchcock was accorded a similar status in his adopted and native countries. Honorary doctorates came his way, he received the Irving G. Thalberg memorial award (1972) from the American Film Academy, the Life Achievement award from the American Film Institute (1979), and finally in the 1980 New Year's honours list a KBE.

After *The Birds* (1963), the story of a mysterious avian attack on a small Californian community that initiated a cycle of ecological horror films, there was something of a decline in Hitchcock's work. His old-fashioned psychological melodrama *Marnie* (1964) was a throwback to the Freudian thrillers of the 1940s he had inspired with *Spellbound* (1945); his cold-war espionage pictures, *Torn Curtain* (1966) and *Topaz* (1969), and his film about a psychopathic murderer in London, *Frenzy* (1971), seemed dated, the products of a man not really living in the contemporary world. Then in 1976, working with a cast of mostly young American actors in the sprightly *Family Plot*, he showed himself once more the unchallenged master of the comedy-thriller, his set pieces as ingenious as ever, the Hitchcock touch as deft and definite. He was still discussing projects and planning a new film when he died in Los Angeles 29 April 1980.

In 1926 Hitchcock married Alma Reville (died 1982), the daughter of an employee of Twickenham Film Studio and herself a script girl and assistant editor. She collaborated on the screenplays of many of her husband's films. This man who took a gleeful delight in terrifying audiences with movies that were often violent, sadistic, and erotic in character (he often spoke of taking film-goers for an emotional roller-coaster ride), lived a happy, quiet domestic life of impeccable rectitude. When not busy filming, he devoted much of his spare time to indulging a gourmet's taste for good food and wine. The Hitchcocks had one child, a daughter Patricia, born in 1928, who trained as an actor at RADA in London and appeared in three of her father's films.

[John Russell Taylor, *Hitch*, 1978; *The Times*, 30 October 1980; private information.]

Philip French

*published 1986*

## HOLLOWAY Stanley Augustus

(1890–1982)

Actor and singer, was born 1 October 1890 in Manor Park, London, the younger child and only son of George Augustus Holloway, a law clerk, and his wife, Florence Bell. His family was fairly prosperous, and he attended the Worshipful School of Carpenters, where local engagements as a boy soprano encouraged him to contemplate a career in singing. As soon as his voice matured after breaking, he took a teenage plunge into the world of entertainment. He studied singing in Milan and then served with the Connaught Rangers during World War I.

With other stars, such as Leslie Henson, he was a successful concert party entertainer after the end of the war. In 1921 he became a utility-man–cum–baritone for a West End success—the Co-Optimists pierrot show. The show waned in 1927; two years later it revived.

In 1927 he first introduced the monologue into his work, with the story of 'Sam "pick oop tha musket" Small'. He delivered comic narratives such as these in a flat, unemotional Lancastrian fashion. The droll accounts, both in variety and on twelve-inch records, of Albert Ramsbottom, who was swallowed by the lion at Blackpool zoo, and other such tales, ensured Holloway a deep and lasting popularity.

Holloway also appeared in light theatre. His first West End showing was in 1919 as Captain Wentworth in *Kissing Time*, and his first pantomime was in Birmingham in 1934, where he was Abanazar in *Aladdin*. He starred on variety bills as well as in musical comedy and revue, and his personable and dominating presence was much in demand.

Next, there were his legitimate theatre successes, notably in Shakespeare, as First Gravedigger in *Hamlet* (with (Sir) Alec Guinness, 1951) and Bottom in the Old Vic's Edinburgh Festival and American coast-to-coast tour of *A Midsummer Night's Dream* (1954). In the Shaw Festival at Niagara-on-the-Lake, Canada, he appeared as Burgess in *Candida* (1970) and William in *You Never Can Tell* (1973). He also played Pooh Bah in an impressive USA television production of *The Mikado*. As late as 1977 he toured Australia and Hong Kong with Douglas Fairbanks jun.

A generation of cinema audiences also learned to appreciate his delightful comedy acting, and he appeared in over thirty films, among them *This Happy Breed* (1944), *Brief Encounter* (1945), *The Way to the Stars* (1945), *The Lavender Hill Mob* (1951), and *The Titfield Thunderbolt* (1952). On American television he appeared with his son, Julian, in the series *Our Man Higgins* (1962–3).

Ultimately, he crowned a satisfying career by his legendary creation of Alfred Doolittle, the philosophic dustman, in *My Fair Lady*, Lerner and Loewe's musical version of *Pygmalion* by G. B. Shaw. In a jubilant hat-trick, he starred in the Broadway première (1956–8), the London production at Drury Lane (1958–9), and the film version of 1964. With his cockney authenticity, his splendid baritone voice, and his wealth of comedy experience, he seemed, in this one superb role, to encapsulate all the exuberance and gusto that had marked his long years of well merited achievement. Few actors so bestrode the world of entertainment and mastered so many of its facets. Above all, Holloway's expansive personality relaxed and pleased audiences of all kinds. He evoked for them what the critic (Sir) Harold Hobson called 'a maelstrom of uncomplicated happiness'.

He was appointed OBE in 1960, and was awarded the Variety Club of Great Britain special award in 1978. He published his autobiography, *Wiv a Little Bit o' Luck* in 1967 and three anthologies of monologues in 1979, 1980, and 1981.

In 1913 he married Alice Mary-Laure ('Queenie') Foran (died 1937), daughter of John Thomas Foran, who lived on the income from inherited property. They had three daughters and a son. In 1939 he married Violet Marion Lane, actress, daughter of Alfred Lane, civil engineer. They had one son. Holloway died at Littlehampton, Sussex, 30 January 1982.

[*The Times*, 1 February 1982; Stanley Holloway, *Wiv a Little Bit o' Luck*, 1967; private information; personal knowledge.]

ERIC MIDWINTER

*published 1990*

## HOPE-WALLACE Philip Adrian

(1911–1979)

Music and theatre critic, was born in London 6 November 1911, the only son (there were two elder sisters) of Charles Nugent Hope-Wallace MBE, charity commissioner, and his wife, Mabel, daughter of Colonel Allan Chaplin, Madras Army, of Dorking. He grew up a tall boy but with a weak constitution, and after schooling at Charterhouse he was sent to a sanatorium in Germany and then to lodge with a Protestant pastor in Normandy. By the time he went up to Balliol College, Oxford, to read modern languages he had already acquired a thorough grasp of French and German and a lifelong passion for Racine and Goethe. He graduated with a third class honours degree (1933) at the worst point of the great depression and for a while found it impossible to obtain congenial employment, or indeed any at all. He worked briefly and disastrously (1933–4) for the International Broadcasting Co. in France, at Fécamp radio station, and then (1935–6) as press officer for the Gas Light & Coke Co. In later life he claimed he had hawked appliances as a door-to-door salesman.

In 1935 he got his first chance as a critic, covering song recitals for *The Times*. By the time war came he had established himself as a sensitive and exceptionally knowledgeable judge of theatre and music (especially opera), being sent to Zurich in 1938 for the world première of Paul Hindemith's *Mathis der Maler* and to Frankfurt for the drama festival. Ill health prevented active war service, and he spent six years in the Air Ministry press office. With peace he became, and remained to his death, one of the most prolific and influential arts critics in the West, first with the *Daily Telegraph* (1945–6) and with *Time and Tide* (1945–9), and then for a quarter-century (1946–71) on the arts staff of the *Guardian*. He was for many years the paper's chief drama critic, though for the last decade of his life he concentrated almost exclusively on opera. He was also a mainstay of the *Gramophone*, a member of the editorial board of *Opera*, and a frequent contributor to the *Listener*, the *New Statesman*, and other journals. For thirty-five years he broadcast with great success, especially on such key programmes as *The Critics* and *Music Magazine*. In 1958 he was president of the Critics' Circle, and in 1975 he was appointed CBE for services to the arts.

Hope-Wallace was the least assertive of men but he had an imperturbable confidence in his own artistic judgement and so remained serenely impervious to fashion. As a young critic he championed Handel and Verdi, then little regarded, and he always admired uncerebral but theatrical masters like Gounod, Massenet, and Bizet. In the theatre he appreciated a good Shavian argument but anything which smacked of dogma, ideology, or 'message' filled him with dismay; from the mid-sixties he quite lost sympathy with most contemporary playwrights. He was concerned, above all, with what actually happened on stage, and was perhaps the last great British critic to regard assessment of the performance as his chief function. He did not see the critic as a privileged high priest but as spokesman for the theatre-goers. 'The best critic', he wrote, 'will be the epitome of the best part of any given audience, its head, heart and soul.' Hence, though mandarin in mind, he was democratic at heart, and in spirit always close to the ordinary London theatre and opera patron. Loving skilled performance, he enjoyed Chinese acrobats, Kabuki players, or the Royal Tournament almost as much as great actors and singers. He admitted he was easily moved to tears: by Emlyn Williams reading the death of Paul Dombey, for instance, or by Irina's line 'They are gone away' from *The Three Sisters*.

Hope-Wallace's sense of theatrical occasion, his intuitive sympathy with performers, his vast experience and wonderful memory made him the outstanding judge, in his generation, of dramatic celebrities, especially women. He wrote with superb precision of such fine actresses as (Dame) Edith Evans, Edwige Feuillère, (Dame) Peggy Ashcroft, and (Dame) Sybil Thorndike. But his greatest enthusiasm was for the diva: 'I love a soprano', he wrote, 'a loud soprano, even a lame one'. He treasured the personalities, follies, triumphs, and misadventures of the prima donna, and much of his best writing revolved around stars like Elisabeth Schwarzkopf, Birgit Nillson, Kirsten Flagstad, Maria Callas, and (Dame) Joan Sutherland.

He was close to Bloomsbury in its silver age, but he was essentially a journalist rather than a literary man. His only books were *A Key to Opera* (written in collaboration with Frank Howes), published in 1939, and *A Picture History of Opera* (1959), though a selection of his notices and essays, *Words and Music*, was published posthumously in 1981. He gently rejected the entreaties of his friends to write an autobiography. For him, immediacy of impression was everything: many of his best notices were dictated straight to the copy-takers from a call-box. He worshipped words but drew no hard distinction between their written and spoken form. Indeed his real genius lay in conversation. For many years some of the best talk in London could be heard at his favourite table at El Vino's in Fleet Street. His noble head, his mellifluous voice, his thesaurus of anecdotes and the shafts of wit, sharp but never cruel, which he played on the personalities of the day, attracted a gifted circle of writers, editors, lawyers, and public men, over which he presided with grace, generosity, and a quiet but unmistakable moral authority. To his younger admirers, who were legion, he epitomized the best characteristics of the pre-war generation: breadth of culture, fine breeding, flawless manners, and delightful urbanity. At the age of sixty-seven a visit to a health farm led to a fall and a broken hip, providing him with his last, ironic joke; he never left Guildford hospital and died there 3 September 1979. With his death, his circle broke up, and it contained, alas, no Boswell. He was unmarried.

[Private information; personal knowledge.]

PAUL JOHNSON

*published 1986*

## HORNIMAN Annie Elizabeth Fredericka (1860–1937)

Pioneer of the modern theatre repertory movement, was born at Forest Hill, London, 3 October 1860, the only daughter of Frederick John Horniman, founder of the Horniman Museum and liberal member of parliament for Falmouth and Penryn from 1895 to 1904, by his first wife, Rebekah, daughter of John Emslie, of Dalton. She was educated privately, and studied for five years at the Slade School of Fine Art under Alphonse Legros, and for five years acted as secretary to W. B. Yeats. A woman of considerable wealth, with very determined views, she interested herself originally in the theatre merely because her relatives strongly disapproved of it. Doubtless, however, she was to some extent influenced by her association with Yeats.

Miss Horniman's first connexion with theatrical affairs was in March 1894 when, at the Avenue Theatre (on the site of the Playhouse), London, she produced John Todhunter's play *The Comedy of Sighs* and Yeats's *The Land of Heart's Desire*; these were followed in April by Mr. Bernard Shaw's comedy *Arms and the Man.* She incurred heavy financial loss in this initial venture, which she described as a 'fruitful failure'. She was not deterred by this early setback, and it in no way damped her enthusiasm, but it was ten years before she made her next move. It was an important decision. She determined to subsidize the Irish national theatre movement. In 1904 she took over the old theatre of the Mechanics' Institute in Abbey Street, Dublin, and lent it rent free for six years to the Irish National Theatre Society. The gift amounted to £12,000 and the Abbey Theatre, Dublin, presented many fine plays and produced several brilliant players.

Miss Horniman transferred her activities to Manchester in 1907, when she acquired the Midland Theatre, which she opened in September of that year with *David Ballard* and *His Helpmate* both written by Charles Evoy. She produced several modern plays here. Her policy was thoroughly catholic, her object being to produce plays by authors of all ages, with especial emphasis on new writers; they were to be performed by a permanent company of picked, front-rank artists, and at prices within the reach of all.

The immediate appreciation of Miss Horniman's efforts was such that in 1908 she purchased the old Gaiety Theatre, Manchester, and practically rebuilt the house. She opened the new Gaiety (the first modern repertory theatre in this country) in September with *When the Devil was Ill*, by Evoy, and *Marriages are made in Heaven*, by Mr. Basil Dean. From that date until

1921 she presented over 200 plays, more than a hundred of which were original. The early promise of catholicity in the selection of authors was amply fulfilled. Euripides, Shakespeare, Beaumont and Fletcher, Ben Jonson, Goldsmith, Sheridan, Ibsen, Sudermann, Maeterlinck, Galsworthy, St. John Hankin, Rostand, Arnold Bennett, Mr. Bernard Shaw, Harley Granville-Barker, Barrie, and Mr. St. John Ervine were all represented. Among the new writers of the 'Manchester school' whose works she presented were Evoy, W. S. Houghton, Allan Monkhouse, Mr. Harold Brighouse, Mr. Basil Dean, Harold Chapin, and Miss Elizabeth Baker. Among the successful modern plays presented were *Hindle Wakes, The Mob, The Younger Generation, Jane Clegg, Chains*, and *Mary Broome*. She made one solitary appearance on the stage, when she 'walked on' in *Nothing Like Leather* at the Gaiety in September 1913.

To the great regret of lovers of the repertory movement all over the country the enterprise collapsed after fourteen years, and in 1921 Miss Horniman was forced to sell out. She received the sum of £52,000 for her interest, but out of this amount a large overdraft at the bank had to be met. When she relinquished her management, she presented her entire library of plays to the Drama League.

Manchester University recognized the value of Miss Horniman's work by conferring upon her the honorary degree of M.A. in 1910, and she was appointed C.H. 'for services to the drama' in 1933. She was deeply interested in astrology, had a great knowledge of Wagnerian opera, and a wide understanding of art and architecture. She was an interesting lecturer, and was widely esteemed as a generous personality. At one time she was an ardent supporter of the suffragette movement, but the stage was her ruling passion. She died at Shere, Surrey, 6 August 1937.

A portrait of Miss Horniman by Emma Magnus hangs in the Chorlton Repertory Club.

[*The Times*, 9 August 1937; *Who's Who in the Theatre*, 1936; personal knowledge.]

John Parker

*published 1949*

## HOWARD Trevor Wallace

(1913–1988)

Actor, was born Trevor Wallace Howard-Smith in Cliftonville, Kent, 29 September 1913, the only son and elder child of Arthur John Howard-

Smith, who worked as Ceylon representative for Lloyd's of London, and his Canadian wife, Mabel Grey Wallace, nurse. Until he was five he lived in Colombo, but then travelled with his mother until the age of eight, when he was sent to school at Clifton College, Bristol. He was an isolated child and when neither of his parents returned to England holidays were spent either in seaside bed-and-breakfast accommodation or in the home of one of the housemasters. At school Howard was not strongly academic and it was sport that caught his interest, particularly boxing and cricket. The latter became one of the great loves of his life, together with jazz. Towards the end of his school career he started visiting the local theatre, and he left Clifton to become an actor, getting into the Royal Academy of Dramatic Art without any previous stage experience.

His first paid work was in the play *Revolt in a Reformatory* (1934), before he left RADA in 1935 to take small roles. That year he was spotted by a Paramount talent scout but turned down the offer of film work in favour of a career in theatre. This decision seemed justified when, in 1936, he was invited to join the Stratford Memorial Theatre and, in London, given the role of one of the students in *French Without Tears* by (Sir) Terence Rattigan, which ran for two years. He returned to Stratford in 1939. At the outbreak of war he decided to enlist, but both the army and the Royal Air Force rejected him. However, in 1940, after working at the Colchester repertory theatre, he was called up into the Royal Corps of Signals, Airborne division, becoming a second lieutenant before he was invalided out in 1943. The stories of Howard's war heroism were fabricated, without his consent, for publicity purposes.

Howard moved back to the theatre in *The Recruiting Officer* (1943). A short part in one of the best British war films, *The Way Ahead* (1944), provided a springboard into cinema. This was followed by *The Way to the Stars* (1945), which led to the role for which Howard became best known, the doctor in *Brief Encounter* (1945), in which his co-star was Celia Johnson. Directed by (Sir) David Lean, the film won an award at the Cannes festival and considerable critical acclaim for Howard. Next came two successful Frank Launder and Sidney Gilliat thrillers, *I See a Dark Stranger* (1945) and *Green for Danger* (1946), followed by *They Made Me a Fugitive* (1947), in which the roots of British realism in cinema can be traced. In 1947 he was invited by Sir Laurence (later Baron) Olivier to play Petruchio in an Old Vic production of *The Taming of the Shrew*. Despite *The Times* declaring 'We can remember no better Petruchio', the opportunity of working again with David Lean, in *The Passionate Friends* (1948), drew Howard back to film and, although he had a solid reputation as a theatre actor, his dislike of long runs, and the attractions of travel afforded by film, made him concentrate on cinema from this point.

Howard's film reputation was secured in *The Third Man* (1949). He played the character type with which he became most associated, the British military officer, but his capabilities were stretched by his role in this story of postwar Vienna by Graham Greene. Howard had a certain notoriety as a hell-raiser, based on his drinking capacity. Under the influence of alcohol he could embark on celebrated exploits, one of which led to his arrest in Vienna, for impersonating an officer. Despite his drinking, however, he always remained reliable and professional, never allowing alcohol to affect his work.

During the 1950s, while often eliciting good notices for his work, he frequently appeared in flawed films like *Odette* (1950) and *An Outcast of the Islands* (1951). An exception was *The Heart of the Matter* (1953), another Graham Greene story, in which he produced his best screen performance. Such opportunities were rare even though he shifted into the American market. In 1958 he received the Best Actor award from the British Film Academy for his performance in *The Key*, but this film, too, failed to meet his high standards.

Although *Sons and Lovers* (1960), for which he received an Oscar nomination for his performance as the father, and *Mutiny on the Bounty* (1962), in which he worked with Marlon Brando, enabled him to move away from playing military stereotypes, *Von Ryan's Express* (1965) and *The Long Duel* (1967), with Yul Brynner, saw a return to playing officer figures. Even the role of the pugnacious Cardigan in *The Charge of the Light Brigade* (1968) revisited military territory, and in this uneven yet innovative film Howard gave a fine performance. Working with Brando and Brynner proved frustrating experiences, leaving him with a mistrust of Hollywood. After the 1960s cinema gave him fewer opportunities to display his ability. His performance as the cynical priest in *Ryan's Daughter* (1971) is one of the most memorable in this over-long film, but for much of the 1970s he was increasingly relegated to cameo appearances in films such as *Ludwig* (1973) or disappointing movies such as *Persecution* (1974) and *Conduct Unbecoming* (1975). However, in 1978 he played a choric-narrator figure in *Stevie* with Glenda Jackson, an experience he found satisfying.

In television he began to find more substantial roles. In 1962 he played Lovborg in *Hedda Gabler* with Ingrid Bergman, and in 1963 won an Emmy award as Disraeli in *The Invincible Mr Disraeli*. In the 1970s he was acclaimed for his playing of an abbot in *Catholics* (1973) and in 1975 he received an Emmy nomination for his role as Abbé Faria in a television version of *The Count of Monte Cristo*. The decade ended with him reunited with Celia Johnson, giving a moving performance in the nostalgic *Staying On* (1980), written by Paul Scott.

The 1980s saw a resurgence of Howard as a film actor. The exhilarating role of a Cheyenne Indian in *Windwalker* (1980) revitalized his acting. However, as was the case with *Sir Henry at Rawlinson End* (1980), a low budget, black and white film, this impressive movie never reached a wide audience. He continued with cameo roles, including Judge Broomfield in *Gandhi* (1982). His final films were *White Mischief* and *The Old Jest*, both released in 1988. Howard did not abandon the theatre altogether in 1947, returning to the stage on occasions, most notably as Lopakhin in *The Cherry Orchard* (1954) and the captain in *The Father* (1964). His last appearance on the British stage was in *Waltz of the Toreadors* in 1974.

Howard made seventy-four films. He embodied the traditional Englishman. His tight-lipped features and quiet, well-bred speaking voice caught the mood of postwar Britain while, in later years, his craggy face and gravelly voice animated the crusty character roles he played. He lacked the looks and physique to be an archetypal male hero, and his tall frame suited military roles. He failed to fulfil his potential, for he rarely played the lead roles he deserved. Supporting some of the most notable names in the world of cinema, he often received the highest critical acclaim.

In 1944 he married an actress, Helen, daughter of William Cherry, who retired from the army at the end of World War I. They had no children. Howard died 7 January 1988, at Bushey Hospital in Hertfordshire, of bronchitis complicated by jaundice.

[Michael Munn, *Trevor Howard, the Man and his Films*, 1989; Vivienne Knight, *Trevor Howard: a Gentleman and a Player*, 1986; *The Times* and *Guardian*, 8 January 1988; *Observer*, 10 January 1988; private information.]

LIB TAYLOR

*published* 1996

## IRVING Sir Henry

**(1838–1905)**

Actor, whose original name was John Henry Brodribb, was born at Keinton Mandeville, Somerset, on 6 Feb. 1838. His father, Samuel Brodribb, came of yeoman stock, and was a small and not prosperous shopkeeper; his mother, Mary Behenna, was a Cornishwoman. When their only child was four years old, the parents moved to Bristol; later, on their leaving Bristol for London, the boy was sent to live at Halsetown, near St. Ives in Cornwall, with his mother's sister, Sarah, who had married Isaac Penberthy, a Cornish miner, and had three children. The household was methodist and religious, and Mrs. Penberthy a woman of stern but affectionate nature. The life was wholesome and open-air. In 1849, at the age of eleven, the boy joined his parents, who were living at 65 Old Broad Street (on the site of the present Dresdner Bank), and attended school at Dr. Pinches' City Commercial School in George Yard, Lombard Street. Here he acted with success in the school entertainments. In 1851 he left school, and entered the office of Paterson and Longman, solicitors, Milk Street, Cheapside, whence, at the age of fourteen, he went to be clerk in the firm of W. Thacker & Co., East India merchants, Newgate Street. A year later he joined the City Elocution Class, conducted by Henry Thomas. Here he won a reputation among his fellows as a reciter, and was always 'word-perfect' in the parts he acted. His first visit to a theatre had been to Sadler's Wells, to see Samuel Phelps play Hamlet; and he took every opportunity of seeing Phelps act, studying each play for himself before going to the theatre. At sixteen he made the acquaintance of a member of Phelps's company, William Hoskins, who gave him tuition in acting, and later introduced him to Phelps, who offered him an engagement. Brodribb had, however, determined to begin his career in the provinces: he continued to read, to study plays, to learn fencing and dancing, and to carry on his office work until, in 1856, Hoskins introduced him to E. D. Davis, who engaged him for the stock company at the Lyceum Theatre, Sunderland.

At this theatre, under the name of Henry Irving, Brodribb made his first public appearance on the stage on 18 Sept. 1856, he being between eighteen and nineteen years old. His part was Gaston, Duke of Orleans, in Lytton's 'Richelieu'. On one occasion he broke down in the part of Cleomenes in 'The Winter's Tale', because the religious notions imbibed at Halsetown prevented him from learning the part on a Sunday. This was said to be the only time in his career in which he failed for lack of previous study. He received no salary for the first month, and 25*s.* a week during the remainder of his engagement, and out of this he contributed to the support of his parents. In Feb. 1857, when just nineteen, he left Sunderland for Edinburgh, where he remained two and a half years under the management of R. H. Wyndham. Among the parts he played there were Horatio, Banquo, Macduff, Catesby, Pisanio (to the Imogen of Helen Faucit) and Claudius in 'Hamlet'; while he appeared with success also in pantomime and burlesque. His reception by the Edinburgh public and press was by no means altogether favourable. From the outset he was praised for his 'gentlemanly' air, his earnestness, and the care he took over his costume and 'make-up'; but he was often taken to task for the mannerisms of which much was to be heard later.

From Edinburgh Irving passed to his first engagement in London. On 24 Sept. 1859 he appeared in a small part in Oxenford's 'Ivy Hall', produced by Augustus Harris, the elder, at the Princess's Theatre, Oxford Street. The parts allotted him being beneath his ambition, he obtained a release from his contract. Readings of 'The Lady of Lyons' and 'Virginius' at Crosby Hall in the following winter and spring led to a four weeks' engagement at the Queen's Theatre, Dublin, which began in March 1860. Replacing a popular actor who had just been dismissed, Irving was received by a section of the audience with three weeks of active hostility. When the nightly disturbances had at last been stopped, his Laertes, Florizel, and other performances won him general favour. From Dublin he went to Glasgow and Greenock, and in Sept. 1860 obtained an engagement at the Theatre Royal, Manchester, under Charles Calvert.

In Manchester Irving spent nearly five years. His progress was slow and disheartening. Calvert, however, was a staunch friend and adviser, and in time the good qualities of Irving's acting—his earnestness, his intelligence, and the effort to be natural—made themselves felt. It was at the Theatre Royal, Manchester, that he first appeared as Hamlet. In April 1864 he had impersonated Hamlet (or rather J. P. Kemble as Hamlet) in one of a series of tableaux illustrating a reading by Calvert. On 20 June following he chose the part for his benefit. For his 'make-up' on this occasion he copied that of Fechter and wore a fair wig. Lack of physical and vocal power were the chief faults urged by the critics. The periods during which the theatre was closed Irving spent in giving readings in various places, and the vacation of 1864 was spent at Oxford, where he acted Hamlet and other parts. In October 1864 Calvert moved from the Theatre Royal to the new Prince's Theatre. Irving remained at the Theatre Royal, playing unimportant parts, till the early part of 1865. In February of that year he and two others gave in public halls in Manchester an entertainment burlesquing the spiritualistic *séances* of the Davenport Brothers; and his refusal to demean (as he considered) the leading theatre by repeating this entertainment on its stage was the ostensible reason for the termination of his engagement. For a few weeks he played under Calvert at the Prince's, and then returned to Edinburgh. Between April and Dec. 1865 he acted at Edinburgh, Bury, Oxford, and Birmingham. Having received and refused an offer to join Fechter's company at the Lyceum Theatre, London, he began in Dec. 1865 an engagement at Liverpool. In the summer of 1866 he went touring with his lifelong friend, John Lawrence Toole, whom he had first met at Edinburgh in 1857, and in July 1866 he created at Prince's Theatre, Manchester, the part of Rawdon Scudamore, the villain in Boucicault's drama

'The Two Lives of Mary Leigh', afterwards called 'Hunted Down', His arrangement with Boucicault was that, should he succeed in the part, he should be engaged to play it in London; and the arrangement was duly carried out.

When he joined Miss Herbert's company at the St. James's Theatre in Oct. 1866 Irving was twenty-eight and a half years old, had been on the stage ten years, and had played nearly 600 parts (Brereton, ii. 345). His first part at the St. James's was not Rawdon Scudamore, but Doricourt in 'The Belle's Stratagem'. Boucicault's play 'Hunted Down' was produced in November, and Irving's performance made a favourable impression. In Feb. 1867 there followed Holcroft's 'The Road to Ruin', in which he played Young Dornton. A brief engagement with Sothern to play Abel Murcott in 'Our American Cousin' at the Théâtre des Italiens, Paris, was followed by a tour with Miss Herbert in England, and in Oct. 1867 Irving returned to the St. James's, now under the management of J. S. Clarke, only to leave it very soon for the new Queen's Theatre in Long Acre. Here, under Alfred Wigan, he appeared in Dec. 1867 as Petruchio in 'Katherine and Petruchio', the Katherine being Miss Ellen Terry, whom he then met for the first time. His Petruchio was not liked, but during his engagement at the Queen's, which lasted till March 1869, he played with success three villains, two in plays by H. J. Byron, the third being Bill Sikes in Oxenford's 'Oliver Twist'. Like Macready, he was almost confined for a time to villains, for after a brief and unsuccessful engagement at the Haymarket in July, in August 1869 he was playing yet another villain at Drury Lane. In April 1870 he joined the company at the Vaudeville, and here, on 4 June, he made his first notable success in London, in the part of Digby Grant in Albery's 'Two Roses'. The run was a long one, and on his benefit night in March 1871 Irving added to his fame by reciting 'The Dream of Eugene Aram'.

In this year, 1871, the Lyceum Theatre was taken by an American, H. L. Bateman, whose daughters, Kate and Isabel, were actresses. Irving, rather against his will, left the Vaudeville to join the newly formed company, of which Miss Isabel Bateman was the leading lady. On the opening night, 11 Sept. 1871, he played Landry Barbeau in 'Fanchette', an adaptation from the German by Mrs. Bateman, the manager's wife. On 23 Oct. this play gave place to Albery's 'Pickwick', in which Irving took what proved to be the leading character, Alfred Jingle. Bateman's resources were now almost exhausted; and as a measure of despair he accepted Irving's urgent entreaty to put on 'The Bells', a version by Leopold Lewis of Erckmann-Chatrian's 'Le Juif Polonais'. 'The Bells', produced at the Lyceum on 25 Nov. 1871, was a complete success. Irving, now between thirty-three and thirty-four, 'woke to find himself famous'. In place of the easy-going, comfortable Burgomaster represented in the original and other versions of the play he created a conscience-haunted wretch, and made horror the chief emotion of the play. 'The Bells' ran till the middle of May 1872 and during its run Irving acted nightly, in addition to Mathias, first Jingle and later Jeremy Diddler. On 28 Sept. 1872 Bateman put up 'Charles I' by W. G. Wills. Despite much protest against the dramatist's treatment of Cromwell, the play was successful, and the pathos and dignity of Irving's performance of the King increased his fame. On 19 April 1873 Bateman put on Wills's 'Eugene Aram', in which Irving took the title-part; and on 27 Sept. he appeared as the Cardinal in Lytton's 'Richelieu'. Here, for the first time, he came into comparison with Macready and Phelps. In spite of his nervousness, the originality of his conception, and the inadequacy of his support, his success was almost complete, only one critic of importance accusing him of monotony and feebleness of voice. On 7 Feb. 1874 'Richelieu' gave place to Hamilton Aïdé's 'Philip', where Irving snatched a personal success from a poor play.

Meanwhile, somewhat against Bateman's wishes, Irving was preparing a bolder stroke; and on 31 Oct. 1874 he appeared as Hamlet. The excitement among playgoers was great; and though the play was cheaply mounted and the audience failed during the first two acts to see the drift of a very quiet and original performance, in the end the rendering was a triumph. The play ran for 200 nights. Tennyson and others liked the new Hamlet better than Macready's, and Irving had now attained the supreme position among living actors. Criticism and even scurrilous attack were not wanting, and they broke into greater activity when in September 1875 he appeared as Macbeth. His Macbeth was not the robust butcher to whom the public were accustomed, and in bringing out the imagination in Macbeth, Irving doubtless, in this his first rendering, brought out too strongly his disordered nerves. The play ran for eighty nights. In February 1876 'Othello' was produced. Salvini had appeared as Othello in London only the year before, and Irving's very different reading of the character was even more hotly attacked than his Macbeth, while with this play his mannerisms of voice and movement probably reached their worst. In Tennyson's 'Queen Mary', which followed in April 1876, they were less obvious; but the part of Philip of Spain was, by comparison, a small one, and the play, as staged, uninteresting, and in June 'The Bells' was revived, together with 'The Belle's Stratagem', in which Irving played Doricourt. The autumn was spent in a tour, during which the graduates and undergraduates of Trinity College, Dublin, presented him in the dining-hall of the university with an address. On 29 January 1877 Irving appeared at the Lyceum as Richard III in Shakespeare's play, which then for the first time ousted Colley Cibber's version from the stage. In the following May came 'The Lyons Mail', Irving taking the two parts of Lesurques and Dubosc; and this play, which ran till the end of July, remained in his repertory till the end of his career. His next appearance in a new part was in May 1878, when he played the King in Boucicault's 'Louis XI', and enthralled his audiences in the death scene. In June came the unsuccessful production of 'Vanderdecken', by Wills and Percy FitzGerald, to be followed in July by 'The Bells' and 'Jingle', the latter being a new version by Albery of his 'Pickwick'. Bateman had died in June 1875; and the theatre had since been managed, not illiberally, by his widow, who naturally desired that her daughters should have good opportunities, and retained Miss Isabel Bateman as leading lady. The time had now come when Irving felt the necessity of choosing his own company and conducting his own management. On his proposing to leave the Lyceum, Mrs. Bateman resigned in August 1878, and the theatre passed into Irving's hands. He was then a few months over forty years old.

During his autumn tour in 1878 the theatre was altered and improved. For his leading lady he engaged Miss Ellen Terry, who began a famous association of twenty-four years when she appeared as Ophelia to his Hamlet on the opening night of his management, 30 Dec. 1878. Joseph Knight summed up in the 'Athenæum' (4 Jan. 1879) the aims of the new manager: 'Scenic accessories are explanatory without being cumbersome, the costumes are picturesque and striking and show no needless affectation of archæological accuracy, and the interpretation has an *ensemble* rarely found in any performance, and never during recent years in a representation of tragedy'. Irving's second production was 'The Lady of Lyons' (27 April 1879), of which only forty performances were given, and which he never afterwards played. His summer holiday he spent cruising with the Baroness Burdett-Coutts in the Mediterranean, where he gathered some ideas for a production of 'The Merchant of Venice'. In the season of 1879–80 a short run of 'The Iron Chest', by George Colman the younger, was followed by a hurried (Stoker, chap. 9) but brilliant production of that play, in which Irving showed a new Shylock, the grandest and most sympathetic figure in the play. The season of 1880–1 was opened with 'The Corsican Brothers'; and on 3 Jan. 1881 came Tennyson's 'The Cup', one of the most beautiful stage productions that Irving achieved. In May began a series of twenty-two performances of 'Othello', in which Irving and the American actor, Edwin Booth (who had just before been playing with ill-success at the Princess's Theatre, and who came to the Lyceum on Irving's invitation), alternated weekly the parts of Othello and Iago. During Irving's autumn tour the theatre was once more altered and improved; and in March 1882 came the production of 'Romeo and Juliet', to which Irving restored the love of Romeo for Rosaline. This play was even more finely mounted than 'The Merchant of Venice'; it was Irving's first really elaborate production, and here for the first time he showed his ability in handling a stage crowd, having possibly taken some hints from the visit to London in the previous year of the Meiningen company. Though Romeo was not a part in which Irving excelled, the play ran till the end of the season and opened the season of 1882–3. In Oct. 1882 he produced 'Much Ado about Nothing', playing Benedick to the Beatrice of Miss Terry, and the comedy was at the height of its success when it was withdrawn in June 1883.

In Oct. 1883 Irving and his company set sail for the first of his eight tours in America. The tour lasted till March 1884, and included New York and fifteen other towns, the repertory containing eight plays. Everywhere he was received with enthusiasm by press and public. At the end of May 1884 he was back at the Lyceum, where in July he produced 'Twelfth Night'. His Malvolio was not generally liked, and the run of the play was brief. In September he sailed for his second American tour (which at the time he intended should be his last), during which he played in the chief towns of Canada, as well as in those of America. His return to the Lyceum in May 1885 was marked by a mild disturbance owing to his attempt to introduce the practice of 'booking' seats in the hitherto unreserved pit and gallery, an attempt which he surrendered in deference to the objections raised. After a few revivals he put on, towards the end of the month, a slightly altered version of Wills's 'Olivia', in which Miss Terry had appeared with great success elsewhere. Irving took the part of Dr. Primrose, and the play ran till the end of the season. Once more the theatre was redecorated and altered. On 19 Dec. came one of the greatest financial successes of Irving's management, Wills's 'Faust'. In this production Irving for the first time indulged in scenic effects for their own sake, and used them rather as an amplification of the author's ideas than as a setting for the drama. His Mephistopheles was one of his weirdest and most striking impersonations, and the play ran continuously for sixteen months, that is, till April 1887, new scenes of the students' cellar and the witches' kitchen being introduced in the autumn of 1886. In June 1887 Irving gave two special performances: one of Byron's 'Werner' (as altered by F. A. Marshall), in which he played Werner, and one of A. C. Calmour's 'The Amber Heart', in which he did not appear. From Nov. 1887 to March 1888 he and his company made their third tour in America, 'Faust' being the principal thing in the repertory. In the week before he sailed for home, Irving gave at the Military Academy, West Point, a performance of 'The Merchant of Venice' without scenery. 'Faust', 'The Amber Heart', and 'Robert Macaire', in which Irving played the title part, filled the short summer season of 1888 at the Lyceum, and the winter season opened with a revival of 'Macbeth'. The production was sumptuous, and Irving was now capable of expressing his idea of Macbeth more fully and with less extravagance than in 1875. In April 1889 a command performance at Sandringham enabled Queen Victoria, who was a guest there, to see Irving and Miss Terry for the first time. The programme consisted of 'The Bells' and the trial scene from 'The Merchant of Venice'. For his first production in the autumn of 1889 Irving chose Watts Phillips's drama, 'The Dead Heart', as re-modelled by Mr. W. H. Pollock. He played Landry, and induced Sir Squire (then Mr.) Bancroft, who had retired in 1881, to play the Abbé Latour. On 20 Sept. 1890 he opened his winter season with 'Ravenswood', a new version by Herman Merivale of 'The Bride of Lammermoor'. The play was too gloomy to be popular. After this there was no new production at the Lyceum till 5 Jan. 1892, when 'King Henry VIII' with music by Edward German was mounted with more splendour than Irving had allowed even to 'Faust'. The cost of production, which exceeded 11,000*l.* was too great to be profitable, though the piece remained in the bill for six months. In November 'King Lear' was put on; and in Feb. 1893 came the performance of Tennyson's 'Becket'. This play had been sent to Irving by Tennyson in 1879 (*The Theatre*, Oct. 1879, p. 175); and Irving, though he refused it at first (*Alfred, Lord Tennyson*, ii. 196), had frequently thought it over. Not till 1892 (Stoker, i. 221–2; but see *Alfred, Lord Tennyson, loc. cit.*) did Irving decide to produce it; he then obtained Tennyson's approval of his large excisions, and persuaded him to write a new speech for Becket for the end of act i. sc. iii. Produced on 6 Feb. 1893, four months after the poet's death, 'Becket' proved to be one of Irving's greatest personal and financial triumphs; its first run lasted till 22 July, and it was frequently revived. Soon after its first production it was acted by command before Queen Victoria at Windsor.

Irving's fourth American tour lasted from Sept. 1893 till March 1894, 'Becket' being the piece most often played. This was Irving's most successful tour, the total receipts being over 123,000*l.* In the provincial tour which occupied the autumn of 1894 Irving appeared for the first time as Corporal Gregory Brewster in A. Conan Doyle's 'A Story of Waterloo', or 'Waterloo', as it was afterwards called. On 12 Jan. 1895 he produced at the Lyceum Comyns Carr's 'King Arthur', which was followed in May by a bill consisting of Pinero's 'Byegones', 'Waterloo', and 'A Chapter from the Life of Don Quixote', a condensed version of a play written to Irving's order by Wills in 1878. The fifth American tour occupied the months from Sept. 1895 to May 1896, and included towns in the south which Irving had not before visited, 'King Arthur' being the principal piece in the repertory. The following September saw him back at the Lyceum, where he produced 'Cymbeline', himself playing Iachimo. On 19 Dec. 1896 he revived 'King

Richard III'. On his return to his rooms after the play he fell and injured his knee, and it was not till the end of Feb. 1897 that he was able to return to work and resume the interrupted run of that play. In April 1897 he played Napoleon in Comyns Carr's adaptation of Sardou and Moreau's 'Madame Sans-Gêne'. The year 1897 had not been a successful one; the year 1898 was disastrous. 'Peter the Great', a tragedy by Irving's son Laurence, and 'The Medicine Man', by H. D. Traill and Robert Hichens, both failed outright; and in February Irving's immense stock of scenery, comprising the scenes of all his productions except 'The Bells' and 'The Merchant of Venice', was destroyed by fire. During his autumn tour he was taken with pleurisy and lay dangerously ill at Glasgow. The result of these heavy losses was the sale of his library by auction in Feb. 1899, and the transference, early in the same year, of his interest in the Lyceum Theatre to a company. Not till April was Irving well enough to reappear on the stage; he then produced Laurence Irving's translation of 'Robespierre', a play written for him by Sardou. After a brief autumn tour he sailed for his sixth tour in America, which lasted from October 1899 to May 1900, the company visiting more than thirty towns, and playing five plays in addition to 'Robespierre'. In April 1901 he produced at the Lyceum 'Coriolanus'—his last new Shakespearean production. In October began his seventh American tour, which lasted till March 1902. It was at the conclusion of this tour that Miss Ellen Terry left Irving's company, though she appeared once or twice at the Lyceum in the next London season, and took part in the autumn provincial tour of 1902. In April 1902 Irving revived 'Faust' at the Lyceum and closed the season on 19 July with a performance of 'The Merchant of Venice'. This was his last performance in that theatre. The company which had taken over the Lyceum Theatre had lost so much money over their ventures during his tours that they were unable to carry out certain structural alterations demanded by the London County Council. The contract was annulled; the Lyceum Theatre remained empty till it was converted into a music-hall, and Irving had to find a house elsewhere.

It was at Drury Lane that he produced on 30 April 1903 'Dante', written for him by Sardou, and translated by Laurence Irving. The expenses of production and running were enormous, and the play failed to attract either in England or in America, where Irving made his eighth and last tour from Oct. 1903 to March 1904. In April he began a provincial tour which ended in June, and in September another, which he intended to be his last. 'Becket' was the play chiefly performed. Broken by a brief holiday at Christmas, the tour went on till Feb. 1905, when ill-health compelled Irving to rest. In April he revived 'Becket' at Drury Lane, and played it, with other pieces, with success till June. This was his last London season, and the last performances of it were, as if prophetically, scenes of enthusiasm as wild as any that had attended him in his early popularity. On 2 Oct. he resumed at Sheffield his provincial tour. In the following week he was at Bradford. On the evening of 13 Oct. 1905 he played 'Becket', and on returning to his hotel collapsed and died almost immediately. His age was sixty-seven years and eight months. His body was taken to the London house of the Baroness Burdett-Coutts, where it was visited by crowds of mourners; and after cremation the ashes were buried in Westminster Abbey on 20 Oct. 1905.

Irving occasionally gave recitations and readings. His recitation of Lytton's poem, 'The Dream of Eugene Aram', was his most famous *tour-de-force*. His earlier readings have been mentioned; of those given later and for public objects the most important were his reading of 'Hamlet' in the Birkbeck Institute in Feb. 1887, of scenes from 'Becket' in the chapterhouse at Canterbury in May 1897, and at Winchester during the celebration of the tercentenary of Alfred in Sept. 1901. Among the many addresses he delivered were the following: 'Acting: an Art', before the Royal Institution in February 1895; 'The Theatre in its Relation to the State', the Rede Lecture for 1898 to the University of Cambridge; and 'English Actors', delivered before the University of Oxford in June 1886. The last was published in 1886, and, together with three other addresses, was reprinted, under the title of 'Four Great Actors', in 'The Drama, by Henry Irving' (1893). 'The Stage', an address delivered before the Perry Bar Institute in March 1878, was published in the same year. To the 'Nineteenth Century' he contributed short articles, under the collective heading of 'An Actor's Notes', in April and May 1877, Feb. 1879, and June 1887, a note on 'Actor Managers' in June 1890, and 'Some Misconceptions about the Stage' in Oct. 1892.

Irving also published acting editions of many of his productions, including 'Becket', and himself prepared with the assistance of Francis Albert Marshall and many other coadjutors the text, with suggestions for excisions in performance, of the 'Henry Irving Shakespeare', to which he contributed an essay on 'Shakespeare as a Playwright' (1888).

Irving opened many memorials, among them the Shakespeare fountain presented to Stratford-upon-Avon by G. W. Childs in Oct. 1887, the memorial of Marlowe at Canterbury in Sept. 1891, and the statue of Mrs. Siddons on Paddington Green in June 1897.

His degrees and honours included the LL.D. of Dublin (1892), the Litt.D. of Cambridge (1898), the LL.D. of Glasgow (1899), and the Komthur Cross of the Ernestine Order of the second class, conferred upon him by the Dukes of Saxe-Coburg-Gotha and Saxe-Meiningen. In 1883 he was approached on the subject of a knighthood, and declined the honour (*The Times*, 24 Oct. 1905, p. 12); in 1895 he accepted it, and thus, being the first actor to be knighted for his services to the stage, obtained for his profession the 'official recognition' which he had declared to be its due. He was the first actor to speak at the annual banquet of the Royal Academy, and the inclusion of the toast of 'The Drama' dates from that occasion.

Irving married on 15 July 1869 Florence, daughter of Daniel James O'Callaghan, surgeon-general in the East India Company, and niece of John Cornelius O'Callaghan, author of 'The Green Book, or Gleanings from the Desk of a Literary Agitator'. There were two children of the marriage: Henry Brodribb, born on 5 Aug. 1870, and Laurence Sidney Brodribb, born on 21 Dec. 1871. Early in 1872 the husband and wife ceased to live together, and a deed of separation was executed in 1879. During the greater part of his London career Irving lived in rooms at 15A Grafton Street, Bond Street; in 1899 he moved to a flat at 17 Stratton Street, Piccadilly.

In figure Irving was tall and very thin, in constitution wiry and capable of great and prolonged exertion. The beauty and nobility of his face and head increased with years (on his appearance in youth see Ellen Terry, *The Story of my Life*, pp. 147–8, and *The Bancrofts*, p. 324); and he had expressive features and beautiful hands. In character he was ambitious, proud, lonely, and self-centred ('an egotist of the great type' is Miss Terry's phrase for him), but gentle, courteous, and lavishly generous. His personal magnetism was very strong; he inspired devotion in those who worked with him and adulation in his admirers. His resentment of parody and caricature may probably be ascribed to his jealousy for the dignity of his art as much as to sensitiveness in himself; of direct attack (and perhaps few actors have been so virulently attacked as Irving was in his earlier years at the Lyceum) he took little notice. Though open to suggestion, he relied almost entirely upon his own mind, and had sufficient power of genius and will to force acceptance of his always sincere and original views. As an actor, he had many disabilities, natural and contracted, a voice monotonous and not powerful, a peculiar pronunciation, a stamping gait, and a tendency to drag his leg behind him, angular and excessive gesture, and a slowness of speech which became more marked when powerful emotion choked his utterance. These mannerisms, which were at their height between 1873 and 1880, were less pronounced after his second American tour in 1884; and through most of his career he may be said to have either kept them in check or made good use of them. It has been said that in all his parts he was 'always Irving'; this is true inasmuch as his physical characteristics and commanding personality could not be disguised, but his assumptions of character were nearly always complete 'from the mind outwards'. He has been called an intellectual actor. If the phrase is meant to state that he could not express great passion, it is unjust: unsurpassed in the portrayal of fear, horror, scorn or malignity, he could draw tears as freely as any 'emotional' actor. His intellectuality lay in the thought which he brought to bear on any part or play he undertook. The dregs of the old school in tragedy still lingered on the stage when he forced his audiences to think out Shakespeare's characters anew, and helped forward the revolution begun by Fechter, a revolution which aimed, no less than did that of Garrick, at restoring nature and truth. Irving's bent led him towards the bizarre and fantastic, and touches of these appeared in all his work. He kept it, however, in check, and his distinction of appearance and manner, with a power of donning a noble simplicity, enabled the impersonator of Mathias and of Mephistopheles to be admirable also as Charles I, Dr. Primrose, or Becket. Of his Shakespearean characters, his finest was probably his Hamlet in which his thought, his princely air, his fantasy, his tenderness, and his power of suggesting coming doom, all had play. His much debated Macbeth, his Iago, and his Shylock were also very fine; as Othello and Romeo he was less successful. A sardonic humour and a raffish air were the best things in such comic parts as Jingle and Robert Macaire.

For the modern drama of his own country Irving did little or nothing. It did not appeal to him, nor did it suit his large theatre or his love of beautiful production. His excursions into it were few and ill judged; but he has the honour of having staged Tennyson's 'The Cup', 'Queen Mary', and 'Becket'. The other dramatists whom he employed gave him nothing of permanent value.

The sumptuousness and elaboration of his mountings have been exaggerated. In the early days of his management they were very modest. As time went on they grew more complete and splendid; but, if they left little to the imagination, and if his example has led to subsequent extravagance and vulgarity, Irving himself never mangled Shakespeare in order merely to make room for more scenery (though he altered him in order to secure the kind of dramatic effects demanded by the modern stage). Not himself a man of wide culture or trained taste, he took advantage of the contemporary revival in art, and knew where to go to find beauty; and among those who designed scenes or costumes for him were Burne-Jones, Alma-Tadema, and Seymour Lucas, while his music was supplied by the leading composers of the time. In rehearsing he was even more fixed than Macready (though more courteously so) in his own opinion on the smallest details; and the result was a perfection in the *ensemble*, a single artistic impression, which in tragedy had not been known before, even in the accurate archæology of the Shakespeare productions of Charles Kean. By these means and by his own acting, he drew back to the theatre the intelligent and distinguished people who had deserted it. He numbered among his personal friends the leading men in the country, was invited to meet royalty at country houses, and entertained magnificently (indeed, almost officially as head of the English stage) in his own theatre. The effect was to fulfil one of his dearest wishes, that the drama might be raised to an acknowledged place of honour among the arts and influences of civilisation. Its maintenance there he believed to be impossible without an endowed national theatre.

The portraits of Irving in oil, statuary, and other media are very many. The principal oil-portraits are (1) full-length as Philip II by Whistler (about 1875), now in the Metropolitan Museum, New York; an etching after this picture was made by the painter; (2, 3, and 4) as Richard Duke of Gloucester (1878), as Hamlet (1880), and as Vanderdecken (1880), all by Edwin Long, and in the collection of Mr. Burdett-Coutts; (5) three-quarter length, seated, in modern dress, by J. Bastien-Lepage (1880), in the National Portrait Gallery; (6) half-length, seated, in modern dress, by the Hon. John Collier (1886); (7) three-quarter length, standing, in modern dress, by Millais (1884), in the Garrick Club (engraved by T. O. Barlow, 1885); a copy of this picture, presented by the Garrick Club to the National Portrait Gallery, is on loan to the Shakespeare Memorial Gallery, Stratford-upon-Avon. Oil-portraits of Irving as Mathias and as Charles I, by James Archer, R.S.A., were exhibited in the Royal Academy in 1872 and 1873 respectively. An oil portrait by J. S. Sargent, R.A., which was exhibited in the Royal Academy in 1889, was afterwards destroyed by Irving (*The Bancrofts*, p. 337). In statuary the following portraits are known: (1) a marble statue by R. Jackson, exhibited in the Royal Academy in 1874; (2) a marble bust, by W. Brodie (1878), in the possession of Mr. Burdett-Coutts; (3) a marble statue of Irving as Hamlet, by E. Onslow Ford, R.A. (1883–5), in the Guildhall Art Gallery; (4) a bronze bust by Courtenay Pollock, R.B.A. (1905), in the Garrick Club; (5) a small figure as Tamerlaine, by E. Onslow Ford, forming part of the Marlowe Memorial at Canterbury; (6) a colossal statue in academic robes, by Thomas Brock, R.A., erected by subscription of actors and actresses in front of the north side of the National Portrait Gallery and unveiled by Sir John Hare on 5 Dec. 1910. Many sketches and studies of Irving were made by Bernard Partridge; among these, one, a pen-and-ink sketch of Irving as Richard III, is in the possession of Mr. Burdett-Coutts, who also owns sketches and drawings of Irving by F. W. Lawson and James Pryde, and miniatures of Irving at twenty-five and at thirty-seven by an artist unknown. Drawings by Fred Barnard are frequent. A pastel of Irving as Dubosc, by Martin Harvey, is in the possession of Mr. Charles Hughes of Kersal, Manchester, and a drawing by Martin Harvey is in the possession of Sir George Alexander. Mr. Gordon Craig owns a pencil head of Irving by Paul Renouard; and drawings by Val Bromley and Gordon Craig, a lithograph by W. Rothenstein, and wood engravings by

James Pryde and W. Nicholson are also known. A cartoon by 'Ape' appeared in 'Vanity Fair' in 1874.

[The authoritative biography of Irving is that by Mr. Austin Brereton, 2 vols. 1908 (with bibliography). In 1906 Mr. Bram Stoker, many years his manager, published 2 vols. of *Personal Reminiscences of Henry Irving*. The most vivid portrait of the man and the actor is to be found in Miss Ellen Terry's *The Story of my Life*, 1908. Mr. Percy FitzGerald published a life of Irving in 1906, and presented to the Garrick Club a very large collection of press-cuttings and other papers concerning him. See also William Archer, *Henry Irving, Actor and Manager: a critical study*, 1883; F. A. Marshall (pseud. Irvingite), *Henry Irving, Actor and Manager*, 1883; John Hollingshead, *My Life*, 2 vols. 1895; Clement Scott, *Some Notable Hamlets of the Present Time*, 1905; Bernard Shaw, *Dramatic Opinions and Essays*, 1907; W. H. Pollock, *Impressions of Henry Irving*, 1908; *The Bancrofts, by Sir Squire and Lady Bancroft*, 1909. On his knighthood, see *Neue Freie Presse*, 20 Oct. 1905, and *The Times*, 24–27 Oct. 1905.]

H. H. Child

*published 1912*

## JACKSON Sir Barry Vincent

(1879–1961)

Theatre director, was born at Northfield, a Birmingham suburb then in the county of Worcester, 6 September 1879, the second son and the youngest child by ten years of George Jackson, provision merchant, and his wife, Jane Spreadborough. His father, founder of the Maypole Dairies, was a wealthy man who loved the arts; he named his younger boy after the actor Barry Sullivan. Unusually for that time, Barry Jackson was encouraged to go to the play; he never forgot his earliest experiences in Birmingham, particularly Shakespeare by the company of (Sir) Frank Benson and by such artists as Wilson Barrett, Ada Rehan, and Hermann Vezin. Even before going to a preparatory school, he was taken abroad; later, except for eighteen months in Geneva, studying French and the theatre when he was sixteen, he was educated entirely by a tutor. In adolescence he began to paint; but his father wished him to be an architect. For five years he worked in a Birmingham office until he decided at twenty-three that this was not his vocation.

Thenceforward his life was in the theatre. In 1907 he and several of his friends, notably two young insurance officials, H. S. Milligan and a tall, black-haired youth, John Drinkwater, then beginning to write poetry, founded the Pilgrim Players. From the work of this amateur company which within five years presented twenty-eight plays of literary and aesthetic worth, there rose in February 1913 the Birmingham Repertory Theatre, later among the most honoured institutions of its kind in Britain; one intended, in Jackson's words, 'to serve an art instead of making that art serve a commercial purpose'.

After more than three years in planning, the Repertory took only four months to build. Once the site behind New Street Station had been secured in June 1912 and the plans had been completed that October, Jackson's life and the story of his theatre would be inextricably linked. In February 1913 the Repertory Company opened, with *Twelfth Night*, in the house—holding 464 people and called in a Drinkwater poem 'the captive image of a dream'—that would be used for over fifty years; a building ahead of its time, its auditorium descending to the stage in sharply raked steps. The money was Jackson's; he sent off the première by reading, 'rather bashfully', the rhymed iambics of Drinkwater's prologue and its often-quoted phrase, 'We have the challenge of the mighty line; / God grant us grace to give the countersign'.

A grey-eyed, urbane man, six feet tall and a conspicuous figure at any gathering, Jackson seemed, outwardly, to change little during his life. Although only a moderate actor (and he gave this up after the first Repertory years), he was always naturally authoritative. In those early days he would sometimes direct the play or design the sets. The programme he chose had an uncommon range; he saw his theatre not as a West End annexe but as 'a revolving mirror of the stage'. Birmingham, where some people spoke slightingly of 'a rich man's toy', responded sluggishly. Jackson, to begin with, was uncompromising; although it was the period of the theatre theatrical, he had no orchestra at the Repertory and even banned curtain-calls. Slowly the theatre did collect a following; when, mid way through the war, Jackson was commissioned in the navy, Drinkwater carried on the work, and his own *Abraham Lincoln* (Birmingham, 1918) was the first of many Repertory plays to reach London (1919). On Jackson's return his life again became inseparable from the changes and chances in Station Street. He saw such a triumph as the opera *The Immortal Hour* (1921) by Rutland Boughton, which he presented later in London (1922); and in 1923 there arrived the famous production of the pentateuch *Back to Methuselah* by G. B. Shaw, directed by H. K. Ayliff, which established a lasting friendship between dramatist and manager. Earlier, Jackson had experimented with the then radical idea of Shakespeare in modern dress by presenting *Cymbeline* (1923).

Birmingham remained oddly aloof. At length, among startled protests, Jackson—who for all his urbanity could be resolute—closed the theatre until an audience was guaranteed. Meanwhile, he devoted himself to London and to the presentation of *The Farmer's Wife* (1924), the Dartmoor comedy by Eden Phillpotts, done long before in Birmingham and now a steady success at the Royal Court. The Repertory was reprieved; but Jackson continued a London career which was progressively complex. In 1925 he leased the Kingsway as well as the Royal Court; during that year, when he was knighted for services to the stage, he put on the modern-dress *Hamlet*, known popularly as *Hamlet* in plus-fours', and in the next year *The Marvellous History of Saint Bernard*, his own version of a French mystery play by Henri Ghéon.

The period from the mid twenties to the early thirties was Jackson's most strenuous time. At Birmingham his theatre prospered artistically. He believed in the inspiration of youth; no friend of the star system, he yet made his own stars. The Repertory had produced such players as Gwen Ffrangcon-Davies, (Sir) Cedric Hardwicke, (Sir) Ralph Richardson, and Laurence (later Lord) Olivier; people were speaking of it as the university of the English stage. In 1929, besides his active London management, Jackson increased his responsibilities by planning the Malvern summer festival with the lessee of the local theatre. Living now on the Malvern Hills, he thought the town would be unexampled for a festival, which he dedicated at first to Shaw. When Jackson left the London stage in 1935 he had still two or three Malvern seasons before he concentrated on Station Street. Birmingham had had another scare; in the spring of 1934, after spending not less than £100,000 on the Repertory within twenty-one years, Jackson insisted that the city must finally prove itself. After a year he was able in 1935 to transfer his interest to a local trust, giving the theatre, in effect, to the city, although he remained its governing director. In 1938, tired of apathy among the townsfolk of Malvern, he withdrew from the festival after nine years of ardent and costly toil.

Generous and sensitive, Barry Jackson could not forgive ingratitude; several times he was sharply hurt. The last occasion came in 1948 when, after he had restored the fortunes of the Shakespeare Memorial Theatre at Stratford-upon-Avon during three celebrated post-war seasons of re-organization (which also established Paul Scofield as an actor and Peter Brook as a director), his contract was not renewed. Thereafter he gave himself entirely to the Birmingham Repertory, putting on, among other successes, the three parts of the rarely staged *Henry VI* (1953) and in 1956 a *Caesar and Cleopatra* which went to Paris. He relied more and more on a trusted staff. After severe illness he was in his theatre for the last time during the first two acts of *Antony and Cleopatra* at a matinée on 15 March 1961; on Easter Monday, 3 April, he died in Birmingham. He was unmarried.

Barry Jackson, practical visionary, connoisseur, and philanthropist, asked, above all, for style and for living speech. He wrote, translated, or adapted, several plays himself, among them *The Christmas Party* for children (1914), *The Marvellous History of Saint Bernard* (1925), and *Doctor's Delight* (from Molière, 1945). He was an honorary freeman of Birmingham (1953); he held the honorary degrees of MA and D.Litt. from the university of Birmingham, the LLD from St. Andrews, and D.Litt. from Manchester. A lover of opera, in 1949–55 he was a director of the Royal Opera House, Covent Garden. A portrait of him by Harold Knight is in the London offices of the Actors' Benevolent Fund; and the new Birmingham Repertory Theatre (opened in 1971) has portraits by Harold Knight and Sir A. J. Munnings.

[John Drinkwater, *Discovery*, being the second book of an autobiography, 1897–1913, 1932; George W. Bishop, *Barry Jackson and the London Theatre*, 1933; J. C. Trewin, *The Birmingham Repertory Theatre: 1913–1963*, 1963; private information; personal knowledge.]

J. C. Trewin

*published 1981*

## KARLOFF Boris

**(1887–1969)**

Actor, was born William Henry Pratt in Camberwell 23 November 1887, the son of Edward John Pratt, of the Indian Salt Revenue Service, and his wife, Eliza Sara Millard. He was the youngest of nine children, eight of them boys; one brother became a judge in the high court of Bombay and another was Sir John Thomas Pratt, an expert on China for the Foreign Office. Young William gained his first interest in the stage from a third brother, who acted under the name of George Marlowe.

In 1894 the family moved to Enfield, and William was educated at Merchant Taylors' School and Uppingham; in 1906 he moved to King's College, London, and studied for the Consular Service. In fact he elected instead for a stage career, but in deference to family feeling sailed to Montreal before beginning it. Despite his striking looks and inimitable voice, his young manhood was not a period of great success. He acted with repertory companies all over Canada, and when jobs were hard to find he worked on farms and fairgrounds. In 1911 he adopted Karloff, an old family name, adding Boris because it seemed to fit. The new name got him a steady job at Kamloops, where he worked until 1912, subsequently joining a company in Prince Albert, Saskatchewan. In 1917 he joined a touring company of the play *The Virginian* starting in Chicago and ending in Hollywood, where he stayed.

Gradually extra work came his way, and by 1919 he was playing villains in Douglas Fairbanks films. During the twenties he worked fairly steadily without being at all well known. His best role in silent films was as the mesmerist in *The Bells* (1926), but the first years of sound found him again reduced to playing bandits and minor gangsters. In 1930 he was fortunate to find a good stage role in Los Angeles in *The Criminal Code*. When this was filmed he was offered the same part, of a convict who, with gait and gestures which were to become very familiar, kills a stool-pigeon. This led to several roles in 1931, including the unexpected one of the hypocritical effeminate reporter in *Five Star Final*.

When James Whale was casting *Frankenstein*, he saw something unusual about the shape of Karloff's head which might make him effective as the monster. Weighed down under much uncomfortable make-up, Karloff was sensationally effective in the role, extracting pity as well as revulsion for the monster. His name did not appear on the credits, the intention being to surround the role with mystery, but immediately the film was released he was a star, and in his next films, *The Old Dark House* (in which he played the deaf mute butler) and *The Mummy*, his name appeared on the bills in larger letters than the titles. In 1932 he was the Chinese villain in *The Mask of Fu Manchu*, and in 1933 he returned to England for *The Ghoul*. This period, though exciting, had typecast him, and in his occasional non-horror roles (*The Lost Patrol, The House of Rothschild*) he showed that he had become an over-emphatic actor.

Returning to horror films, he was successful in *The Black Room* and *The Bride of Frankenstein*, although he himself felt that the monster should not have been allowed to talk. Lean years followed, horror films being unfashionable, and he was reduced to playing Mr Wong in a low-budget series of detective films. In 1939 *Son of Frankenstein* revived his stature somewhat, though he played the monster, for the last time, rather disappointingly as a soulless killer. The popularity of horror films revived during the war, and Karloff starred in a series of 'mad doctor' films, in which his intentions at least were always honourable. It was clear that he was never to find another role like the monster, and that Hollywood regarded him as no more than a useful addition to low-budget offerings; yet ironically his name was known throughout the world.

Karloff determinedly made a name for himself in other fields, notably the Broadway stage. He successfully caricatured his own image in *Arsenic and Old Lace* (1941), was a kindly professor in J. B. Priestley's *The Linden Tree*

(1948), and Captain Hook in *Peter Pan* (1950). He also issued several recordings, in which he recited fairy tales and ghost stories, and edited volumes of similar material; and he was a noted Hollywood cricketer.

At the end of World War II Hollywood began to offer him more distinguished roles, such as the leading part in his first colour film, *The Climax* (1944), smooth comedy villainy in *The Secret Life of Walter Mitty* (1947) and, curiously, an Indian chief in *Unconquered* (1947). He had also some success with Val Lewton, a producer of 'intellectual horror' films: *The Body Snatcher* (after Robert Louis Stevenson) (1945), *The Isle of the Dead* (1945), and *Bedlam* (1946). Thereafter he was unsuccessful in Hollywood, except in television.

In Britain he played patch-eyed Colonel March of Scotland Yard in a 1955 TV series, and in 1958 secured two thrillers better than Hollywood was likely to offer: *Corridors of Blood* and *Grip of the Strangler*. In 1959 he retired to a Sussex village to enjoy cricket. He died at Midhurst, Sussex, 2 February 1969, shortly after completing a moving performance in a TV series, *The Name of the Game*, as a Czech writer caught in the cold war.

Karloff's deep and cultured voice was widely imitated. He deserved better roles, although his acting range was limited.

He was married three times, in 1923 to Helene Vivian Soule, in 1929 to Dorothy Stine, and in 1946 to Evelyn Helmore (*née* Hope), who survived him. There was one daughter of the second marriage.

[Richard Bojarski and Kenneth Beals, *The Films of Boris Karloff*, 1974; Peter Underwood, *Horror Man*, 1972; Denis Gifford, *Karloff, the Man, the Monster, the Movies*, 1973.]

LESLIE HALLIWELL

*published* 1981

## KENDAL Dame Margaret Shafto (Madge)

**(1848–1935)**

Better known as Madge Kendal, actress, was born at Grimsby, Lincolnshire, 15 March 1848. She belonged to a family, originally domiciled in Scotland, which had been connected with the stage for two hundred years. Her great-great-grandfather, James Shafto Robertson, was a theatre-manager at Peterborough, his company touring a circuit of towns in the vicinity of that city; her father, William Robertson, although he had been intended for a solicitor, managed this theatre after his father's death and, in addition, acted in a great many parts; her eldest brother, Thomas William Robertson, originally an actor, became a celebrated dramatist, the founder of a new, naturalistic style of play, sometimes, derisively, described as 'the teacup and saucer drama', or 'bread and butter school', which included *Caste* (1867); and she herself, in addition to two of her brothers and four of her sisters, went on the stage. Her husband was an actor, and two of her daughters became actresses. Her father married a young actress, Margharetta Elisabetta Marinus, the daughter of a Dutchman who taught languages in London. It was while she was with her husband's company on the Lincoln circuit that Madge, her twenty-second and last child, was born.

The failure of the Lincoln circuit sent the Robertsons to London, where William Robertson became the partner of J. W. Wallack in leasing the Marylebone Theatre, and it was in this theatre, on 20 February 1854, that Madge, then not quite six years of age, made her first appearance as an actress. Her part was Marie in *The Struggle for Gold*. By the time she was fifteen she was a seasoned actress, and had performed in London, Bristol, and Bath. It was while she was appearing at the reopening of the Theatre Royal, Bath, in March 1863 that Ellen Terry, then aged sixteen, and she appeared together for the first time. The play was *A Midsummer Night's Dream*. Ellen Terry was Titania, Madge Robertson the second singing fairy. Her songs were 'Over hill, over dale' and 'I know a bank'. The Oberon of this production was Ellen's sister, Kate Terry. After another engagement at Bristol had ended, Madge, now turned seventeen, returned to London where, on 29 July 1865, she made her real London début, playing Ophelia to the Hamlet of Walter Montgomery at the Haymarket Theatre. This production was a failure, and was soon succeeded by *King John*, with Madge Robertson as Blanche of Spain. It, too, was a failure, and it was followed by *Othello*, with Madge as Desdemona, Montgomery as Iago, and a negro, named Ira D. Aldridge, as the Moor. This was strenuous training for a girl of seventeen, but it is not the entire tally of her training, for in the same year, or early in 1866, she played Lady Macbeth to the Macbeth of Samuel Phelps at Hull and later, in London, Lady Teazle to his Sir Peter at the Haymarket. By the time she was married, when she was twenty-one, she had acted over fifty parts in productions as various as Shakespeare and pantomime.

In 1869 Madge Robertson married the actor-manager William Hunter Kendal, with whom thenceforth her whole life was identified. As an actor, he was in no wise comparable to his wife, as an actress: he was dull and pompous, both as a player and a private person, a solemn, sententious man whose heavy utterances were received by his wife as the most delicious sallies of wit; and he made a cult of respectability which, although it earned appreciation for him and his far abler wife, made them both disliked in many quarters because of the ostentation with which the respectability was displayed. Mrs. Kendal was called the 'matron of the English theatre', and the title sat very heavily upon her. Her marriage, so far as it related to Kendal and herself, was happy, but it was far from happy in respect of their five children, two sons and three daughters, the divorce of one being a heavy grief to Kendal. After Kendal's death the influence which he had exercised over his wife's opinions seemed to become more severe. She grew publicly censorious, and all her utterances, often witty, whether they referred to the times in general or to the theatre in particular, were acid and denunciatory. Acting had declined, the drama was degenerate, the young had neither morals nor manners. Her reproaches were rendered more grim by the style of dressing which she now affected; a style which was ostentatiously old-fashioned, but, nevertheless, suited her appearance and was attractive.

Madge Kendal was an accomplished, but not a great, actress. Her verve was immense, as a result, in part, of extraordinary vitality, and her gaiety, on occasions, was charming and infectious. It is arguable that she might have been a greater *comédienne* than she was, had she forgotten her husband's passion for respectability. But even under his oppressive influence she was delightful to watch, on the stage or off it. Her stature was tall, and she had a serene look that fitted her especially for elderly parts. Her character was firm and robust, too firm, perhaps, for family affection to survive, too robust to make her easy to work with. But the long line of actors and actresses who went to the making of her were able, at times, to resist and even to overthrow her husband's influence; and it was when they were in the ascendant that she was at her best. She was familiar to playgoers in her last years on the stage mainly in amiable, unexacting, sentimental pieces, such as *A Scrap of Paper, Still Waters Run Deep*, and *The Elder Miss Blossom*, but in June 1902, at His Majesty's Theatre, when she and Ellen Terry played respectively Mrs. Ford and Mrs. Page in *The Merry Wives of Windsor* to Beerbohm Tree's Falstaff, she showed her happiest spirit. Those who had the good fortune to see her and Ellen Terry in this production, realized what great *comédiennes* they were. As they had begun together, almost forty years earlier, so they ended together, in Shakespeare.

In 1908 Mrs. Kendal retired from public work. In 1926 she was appointed D.B.E. and in 1927 G.B.E. Her birthplace did not forget her: in 1932 she was made an honorary freewoman of Grimsby. Her autobiography, *Dame Madge Kendal*, in writing which she was assisted by Rudolph de Cordova, was published in 1933, but it is an untidy, inaccurate work, as was, perhaps, inevitable, for she was eighty-five when it appeared. She died at her home at Chorley Wood, Hertfordshire, 14 September 1935.

A portrait of Madge Kendal, painted in her eightieth year by Sir William Orpen, was presented to her on behalf of a number of old friends by Sir Johnston Forbes-Robertson, and is now in the Tate Gallery.

[*The Times*, 16 September 1935; *Dame Madge Kendal*, by herself, 1933; *Who's Who in the Theatre*, 1933; personal knowledge.]

ST. JOHN ERVINE

*published 1949*

## KOMISARJEVSKY Theodore

(1882–1954)

Theatrical producer and designer, born in Venice 23 May 1882, was the son of Theodore Komisarjevsky (who was first tenor of the St. Petersburg Opera and taught Stanislavsky) and his wife, the Princess Kourzevich. Vera Komisarjevskaya, the actress, was his sister.

Educated at a military academy and the Imperial Institute of Architecture in St. Petersburg, Komisarjevsky directed his first production in his sister's theatre in 1907. In 1910, the year of her death, he founded his own school of acting in Moscow, to which in 1914 he added a studio-theatre in her memory. From 1910 to 1913 he was producer at the Nezlobin Theatre in Moscow, and after an interlude with the Imperial Grand Opera House he became producer at Ziminne's Opera House, with which he remained when it became the Soviet Opera House. After the revolution he was also appointed director of the Moscow State Theatre of Opera and Ballet (previously the Imperial Grand Opera) and he was allowed to continue to direct his own small theatre. In 1919, believing that he was about to be arrested by the Cheka, he fled to Paris, where Diaghilev advised him to go to England. Within four weeks of his arrival he was entrusted by Sir Thomas Beecham with a production of *Prince Igor* at Covent Garden, which immediately led to further opera productions in Paris and New York. On his return to London he began, at a time when the English theatre was inclined to insularity, a series of productions of plays by Russian authors including Chekhov, Gogol, Andreyev, Tolstoy, and Dostoevsky.

In 1925 he converted a small cinema at Barnes into a theatre with its own company which included (Sir) John Gielgud, Charles Laughton, Jean

Forbes-Robertson, Jeanne de Casalis, and Martita Hunt. The standard of production in the English theatre (to quote from *The Times* of that day) was 'sloppy and slovenly'; there was little attempt at ensemble playing and the settings and lighting were dull and unimaginative. Komisarjevsky's productions at Barnes (1925–6) had an immediate effect on the English theatre by making the critics aware of its deficiencies. At a time when English acting had a glossy veneer which concealed its shallowness, Komisarjevsky demanded from his actors a new intensity of feeling and a deeper understanding of the characters they were playing. He introduced a method of acting based on the theories of Stanislavsky, although he never accepted them unconditionally and to some of them he was strongly opposed.

In 1932 Komisarjevsky became a British subject. It was the year of the first of his productions at Stratford on Avon; productions which were unorthodox and provocative, sometimes brilliant, sometimes merely wayward; all of them valuable as a means of making critics and audiences realize how conventional and humdrum had been the routine Stratford productions of Shakespeare. As a Shakespearian producer Komisarjevsky's weakness was that he had little respect for the text and small appreciation of the rhythms of the verse.

Komisarjevsky saw little to attract him to the ordinary west-end theatre, although Sir C. B. Cochran managed to persuade him to produce three plays there. He preferred to spend his time producing an extraordinary variety of plays in London, in the provinces, and on the Continent for any theatre or society (such as the Stage Society) which was leading rather than following theatrical tastes. His productions included *The Pretenders*, in Welsh, in a gigantic marquee at Holyhead; two productions at Oxford for the O.U.D.S.; *The Cherry Orchard* at the Leeds Civic Playhouse; *The Wild Duck* in Riga; *Peer Gynt* in New York; *The Dover Road* (in English) in Paris; and *Cymbeline* in an open-air theatre in Montreal.

Besides being a great producer, Komisarjevsky was also a brilliant stage designer. Almost invariably he designed his own sets and costumes. He had nothing in common with the photographically realistic English designers. His settings reduced factual realism to a minimum, stressing mood rather than detail. The effectiveness of his settings was enormously enhanced by the skill and subtlety of his lighting which made dramatic use of highlights, shadows, and halftones to give emphasis to his beautifully composed groupings.

Komisarjevsky was a small man with a completely bald head, a beak nose, inscrutable brown eyes set in a pale face which seemed all the paler because of the small bright red scarf which he invariably wore around his throat at rehearsals. His rather melancholy air concealed a mischievous sense of humour which had a streak of cruelty in it. At work he was the quietest of producers. He would seldom give an actor an intonation or say how a line should be spoken. He preferred to discuss what a character was thinking or feeling, and leave it to the actor to work it out. Unfortunately, if he decided that an actor had no particular talent he would take no trouble over his performance but concentrate all his attention on the better actors, with the result that under his direction good actors usually surpassed themselves while dull actors seemed duller than ever.

In 1939, when war broke out, he was working in the United States. He felt that as he had become a British subject he should return to England, so he offered his services to E.N.S.A. But he was unable to get back and spent the rest of his life in America, devoting his time mainly to lecturing and teaching. He died at Darien, Connecticut, 17 April 1954.

In the twenty years during which he worked in the English theatre he had a greater influence than any other producer on methods of direction, acting, setting, and lighting. On his death, Sir John Gielgud described him in a letter to *The Times* as 'a great *metteur en scène*, an inspiring teacher, and a master of theatrical orchestration . . .'.

Komisarjevsky was three times married: first, to Elfriede de Jarosy; secondly in 1934, to (Dame) Peggy Ashcroft; thirdly, to Ernestine Stodelle. The first two marriages were dissolved. He had two sons and one daughter.

[*The Times*, 19 April 1954; Theodore Komisarjevsky, *Myself and the Theatre*, 1929; personal knowledge.]

Norman Marshall

*published 1971*

## KORDA Sir Alexander

(1893–1956)

Film producer, whose original name was Alexander Laszlo Kellner, was born 16 September 1893, at Pusztaturpaszto, Hungary. He was the eldest of the three sons of Henry Kellner, land agent to a large estate, and his wife, Ernestine Weisz. He was educated at Protestant gymnasiums in Nagykoros and Kecskemet and at a commercial school in Budapest. His father died when he was thirteen and to augment the family income he gave lessons in the evenings. Leaving school at seventeen, he became a proof-reader and newspaper reporter in Budapest and published a novel under the name of Alexander Korda. In 1911 he went to Paris where he became proficient in French but could find no work. Back in Budapest he had his first introduction to the infant film world by translating sub-titles from French into Hungarian. In 1912 he founded a film magazine, the first of its kind to appear in Budapest, and in 1913 with some friends he started to write and direct short film comedies.

Owing to his eyesight which was always weak Korda was not called up after the outbreak of war and was able to continue as a film director. In 1915, with the director of the Kolozsvar National Theatre in Transylvania, he formed a plan to make films with that company, using their actors, scenery, and costumes. The course of the war enforced a return to Budapest where he took over the company and built a studio, the Corvin. His first full-length film, *The Man of Gold* (1918), taken from M. Jokai's novel, was highly successful.

In 1919 there was unrest in Hungary and Korda, together with many other citizens, was arrested; by a fortunate chance he shortly obtained his release, and on returning home he took a bath, changed his clothes, and departed from Hungary for ever. In Vienna he joined the Sascha studios which at that time were making advanced films, and there he matured his film-craft. Among his films of this period were *The Prince and the Pauper* (1920) and *Samson and Delilah* (1922). In 1923 he moved to Berlin and in 1926 to Hollywood where amongst the films he made was *The Private Life of Helen of Troy* (1927) in which his wife, Maria Corda, played the title role.

Returning to Europe in 1930 Korda found work in Paris with the Paramount Film Company, for whom he made the classic film *Marius* (1931) from the play by Marcel Pagnol, in which Raimu played the leading part. In 1931 he went for Paramount to London to direct *Service for Ladies* which was an outstanding success and proved the turning-point in Korda's career, for he settled in London, formed his own company, London Film Productions, with Big Ben as trademark, and built the Denham studios and laboratories which when completed in 1937 were the most advanced in Europe. In the meantime Korda had become one of the most notable personalities of the film world with a series of pictures which obtained world-wide fame. They included *The Private Life of Henry VIII* (1933), *The Private Life of Don Juan* (with a script by Frederick Lonsdale, 1934), *The Ghost Goes West* (1935, directed by René Clair and starring Robert Donat), *The Scarlet Pimpernel* (1935, starring Leslie Howard), *Things to Come* and *The Man Who Could Work Miracles* (scripts by H. G. Wells, 1936), *Rembrandt* (1936), *Knight Without Armour* (1936), *Elephant Boy* (1936–7), *Fire Over England* (Vivien Leigh's first film, 1937), and *The Four Feathers* (1939).

No one in this country before or since Korda has equalled his range and brilliance of faculties for film-making. Building studios and making pictures need large sums of money and Korda seemed at this period to conjure them out of the air. His sense of romance and gift of story-telling produced excellent scripts; his knowledge, direction, and camera-work brought to his service the finest technicians, among whom were his two younger brothers, Zoltan and Vincent. His tact and talent, together with his generosity and personal magnetism, drew to him the best actors in the world.

With the worsening international situation financial backing was gradually withdrawn and in 1939 Korda had to give up the Denham studios. But he continued his film-making with *The Thief of Baghdad* (1939–40) and, immediately after the outbreak of war, the documentary *The Lion has Wings*. During the war years he moved between London and Hollywood where he directed *Lady Hamilton* (1941) and with his brother Zoltan produced *Jungle Book* (1941); in Britain he made *Perfect Strangers* (1944). After the war he revived London Films as an independent company, built studios at Shepperton, and once again under his management there came forth fine films, including *An Ideal Husband* (1947), *The Fallen Idol* (1948), *The Third Man* (1949), *The Wooden Horse* (1950), *Sound Barrier* (1952), and *Richard III* (1955). Working to the last, Korda died in London 23 January 1956.

In 1921 Korda married Maria Farkas, who acted under the name of Maria Corda, by whom he had one son, Peter. The marriage was dissolved in 1931. His second marriage (1939), to Merle Oberon, was dissolved in 1945. In 1953 he married a Canadian, Alexandra Irene Boycun (died 1966). Korda was naturalized in 1936 and knighted in 1942. He was made an officer of the Legion of Honour in 1950.

[Paul Tabori, *Alexander Korda*, 1959; private information; personal knowledge.]

Ralph Richardson

*published* 1971

## LANE Lupino

(1892–1959)

Actor and theatre-manager, was a member of a family of acrobats, dancers, and clowns whose record goes back to the eighteenth century. He was the elder son of Harry Lupino and his wife, Charlotte Sarah Robinson. So many of his cousins were already on the stage under the family surname that there was a danger that Henry William George Lupino might go unremarked. The 'Lane' half of his stage name was assumed in honour of his maternal great-aunt, Sarah Lane, whose management of the Britannia Theatre, Hoxton, had brought her wide fame and a great fortune.

Born in London 16 June 1892, the future Lupino Lane was bred to the stage as a matter of course, and made his first public appearance at the age of four, in a benefit performance for Vesta Tilley at the Prince of Wales's Theatre, Birmingham. This was no more than a preliminary canter; but by 1903 he was far enough on in his profession to make his London début, under the name of 'Nipper' Lane, at the London Pavilion. From then onwards he proved a worthy upholder of his family tradition, and the various skills which he learned so thoroughly in those early days were invaluable to him when, with the years, he began to show himself a comedian with an endearing personality of his own.

The name 'Nipper' had suggested a creature small, quick, and neat; and small, quick, and neat he remained throughout his career. He was the very embodiment of cockneydom (it is the characteristic of the Lupinos that, although their name betokens a foreign origin, they became Londoners in grain). He had the true clown's gift of pathos, while the brilliantly executed struggles in which he could involve himself with inanimate objects—for instance, the peer's robe in which he fell from the stage into the orchestra in *Me and My Girl*—were a tribute both to his clown's instinct and his acrobat's immaculate sense of timing.

His progress towards a leading position in the world of revue and pantomime was not at first spectacular, but it was steady. In 1915 he appeared at the Empire in a successful *Watch Your Step*, and he remained there for the next two productions, and from then onwards he was seldom out of an engagement, playing 'funny man' parts of increasing importance in London, in New York, or in Manchester and the other principal cities in the then well-established touring network. Gradually the versatility of his talent became more clearly manifest. He tried his hand here at management or direction, there at authorship. He made a successful New York appearance as Ko-Ko in *The Mikado* in 1925. By the time he was forty he was well established as a leading comedian on both sides of the Atlantic.

It was not, however, until the part of the cheerful little cockney character, Bill Snibson, was written for him that his years of triumphant progress began. Snibson made his first appearance in *Twenty to One*, a musical farce by L. Arthur Rose and Frank Eyton, with music by Billy Mayerl, which opened at the London Coliseum on 12 November 1935, presented jointly by Lupino Lane and Sir Oswald Stoll. Lane as Snibson took the public fancy at once, and the piece ran for nearly a year and subsequently went on a long tour. This was success on a considerable scale, and turned Lane into a star performer as well as into a manager of substance; but it was swiftly put in the shade by the second Snibson play, *Me and My Girl*, in which L. Arthur Rose had Douglas Furber as collaborator and the music was composed by Noel Gay.

This piece, directed as well as presented by Lane, opened at the Victoria Palace 16 December 1937 and had the phenomenal run of 1,646 performances, for the first 1,550 of which Snibson, now raised to the peerage but still an irrepressible cockney, was played by Lane. Nor was this the end of it. The play was several times revived; and in 1942 the first Snibson play, *Twenty to One*, was revived at the Victoria Palace with Lane again in the part, and had a longer run than at first.

At the heart of the triumph of *Me and My Girl* lay, undoubtedly, the dance which swept the world—'The Lambeth Walk'. It was created by Lane to a happy little tune by Gay, and was the distilled essence of the cockney spirit. When the play was filmed (Lane yet once again playing Snibson), 'The Lambeth Walk' was chosen as title.

The result of all this was to make Lane a very rich man and a power in the world of the theatre. He was never again to enjoy success on the stage on the grand, or even on a noteworthy, scale; but he came spectacularly into the public eye in 1946 when he bought for £200,000 the Gaiety Theatre, with which his family had been connected for a hundred years. He failed, however, to find the financial backing necessary to reopen the theatre, and he resold the property in 1950.

In 1917 Lupino Lane married an actress, Violet, daughter of John Propert Blyth, sea captain; they had one son. Lane died in London 10 November 1959.

[James Dillon White, *Born to Star*, 1957; *The Times*, 11 November 1959; *Who's Who in the Theatre*; personal knowledge.]

W. A. Darlington

*published* 1971

## LANG (Alexander) Matheson

**(1877–1948)**

Actor-manager and dramatist, was born in Montreal, Canada, 15 May 1877, a cousin of Cosmo Gordon Lang, archbishop of Canterbury, a notice of whom appears below, and youngest of the seven children of the Rev. Gavin Lang, minister of the Scottish Presbyterian church of St. Andrew's, Montreal, and his wife, Frances Mary Corbett.

Educated at Inverness College and St. Andrews University, Lang, after watching Sir Henry Irving, finally decided to go on the stage. He made his first appearance with Louis Calvert in 1897, and afterwards joined the company of (Sir) Frank Benson. In 1902 he played with Mrs. Langtry at the Imperial Theatre in a royal command performance, and toured with her through America. At the Imperial, too, in 1903, he played Benedick to the Beatrice of (Dame) Ellen Terry. He later toured with her in repertory. In 1907, after an excellent Othello at Manchester, he was with (Sir) George Alexander in *John Glayde's Honour* at the St. James's Theatre, and with John E. Vedrenne and Harley Granville-Barker at the Savoy Theatre in the same year, when he played Dick Dudgeon in *The Devil's Disciple*. Also in 1907 he took part in a great adventure of popular drama with Ernest Carpenter, the manager of the Lyceum Theatre. He played John Storm in *The Christian*, and Romeo in 1908. At this time he took great interest in the promotion of a national theatre. In March 1909, still at the Lyceum, he played Hamlet; but unfortunately with the death of Carpenter in that year the Lyceum organization broke up.

Lang next toured in Australia and in 1911 started his own management, taking an extensive repertory, largely Shakespearian, to South Africa and the Far East. On his return, Sir Herbert Tree asked him to play Charles Surface in *The School for Scandal*. Lang's next personal success was as Wu Li Chang in *Mr. Wu* by Harry M. Vernon and Harold Owen, at the Strand Theatre, 1913, and in 1914 he played Hotspur in *King Henry IV, Part I*. At the New Theatre, 1920, he presented *Carnival*, which he had adapted from the Italian with H. C. M. Hardinge, and he was remarkable as Matathias in E. Temple Thurston's drama, *The Wandering Jew*, which ran for twelve months. At the New he presented matinées as Othello—an extremely fine and memorable performance—to the Iago of Arthur Bourchier. In 1926–7 Lang toured Canada with a repertory company and in 1928 played his favourite part of Count Pahlen in *Such Men are Dangerous*, adapted by Mr. Ashley Dukes from the German play by Alfred Neumann and presented at the Duke of York's Theatre. He next produced *The Chinese Bungalow* by Marion Wallace Osmond and James Corbett—a *nom de plume* of his own. Then, at the Duke of York's, he produced *Jew Süss* (1929) adapted by Mr. Ashley Dukes from the book by Dr. Lion Feuchtwanger. This play, which included a charming little ballet by Marie Rambert (Mrs. Ashley Dukes), for which music was arranged and conducted by Constant Lambert, made a unique attraction.

In 1916 Lang began his screen career, which included nearly all his stage successes, with a remarkable performance of Shylock in a film of *The Merchant of Venice*. Although he never claimed the credit which was his due, he was one of the chief helpers of Lilian Baylis in her early efforts at the Old Vic. He made Shakespearian production possible, as a member of her first committee, by granting her for nothing a loan of any scenery or costumes she required.

Lang was helped all his life by a personality of marked dignity, thanks to his tall figure and commanding features. The grand manner came naturally to him, without any need for affectation. Owing to illness he was not seen in London for the last eleven years of his life, and it was only ill health which prevented him from achieving the supreme position to which he was in so many ways entitled. He married in 1903 Nellie Hutin Britton, who was with him as a member of the Benson company and with Ellen Terry and played many principal parts in his productions. She was keenly interested in the Old Vic and was a member of the governing body for many years. Lang wrote an autobiography, *Mr. Wu Looks Back* (1940), and died at Bridgetown, Barbados, 11 April 1948. There were no children of the marriage.

A portrait of Lang as Hamlet, by Somerled MacDonald, is in the possession of the family.

[Private information; personal knowledge.]

S. R. Littlewood

*published* 1959

## LAUDER Sir Harry

**(1870–1950)**

Comedian, was born in Portobello, near Edinburgh, 4 August 1870, the eldest of the seven children of John Lauder, potter, of Musselburgh, by his wife, Isobella Urquhart Macleod, daughter of Henry MacLennan, of the Black Isle, Ross-shire. Lauder's assumption for stage purposes of Highland dress of a fanciful order was not therefore without ancestral justification. Before Lauder was twelve his father died, and the boy had to take what jobs he could, including work in a flax-mill in Arbroath as a half-timer (one day at work, the next at school), and in a pit-head in Hamilton. He subsequently became a miner, but his voice and his skilful, genial use of it were obviously his fortune. He was soon well known in his area through local concerts, and in a short time became a professional entertainer, at first travelling in concert-parties, and later appearing in the smaller music-halls. He was thirty before he reached London, but once there his conquest of the capital was immediate, rewarding, and unbroken. He began his London triumphs at a hall called Gatti's-in-the-Road, but soon he was the acknowledged 'bill-topper' of the central halls, including the Tivoli, Oxford, and London Pavilion. Such favourite ditties as 'Tobermory' and 'The Lass of Killiecrankie' were already in his repertory.

Lauder's vehicle was the song with an interlude of patter. With his growing popularity his turn became longer and would include four or five 'numbers'. He usually wrote the words and music himself, drawing with instructive shrewdness on traditional airs for the simple, ear-catching lilts which were so easily and widely remembered and so joyously re-sung—and not by Scotsmen only. As time went on, he developed a serious, almost a religious note. He liked to end his performance with 'Rocked in the Cradle of the Deep' or 'The End of the Road', and it was a sign of his genius that he could carry his music-hall audience easily from such frivolities as 'Stop your tickling, Jock' to the more serious ballad of his finale and even into listening patiently while he gave them what was almost a sermon.

At the height of his popularity Lauder was often 'working' four houses a night at an extremely high salary, and he was canny in his handling of the immense sums which he earned. He publicized his own thrift with good humour and some of the Harry Lauder stories were generally supposed to have been invented by himself.

Lauder gave a command performance before King Edward VII in 1908 and came increasingly to be the first citizen, as well as the first favourite, of the vaudeville stage. From 1907 he made nearly every year an immensely successful tour of the Empire and the United States. In the war of 1914–18, in which his only son was killed in action in 1916, he was an ardent recruiter, in speech and song, and a tireless contributor to troop concerts, at home and on the western front; he energetically renewed these efforts in 1939. He was knighted for his services in 1919, and in 1927 received the freedom of the city of Edinburgh. He published several volumes of memoirs.

In later years the serious youth of Scotland began to resent what was deemed to be Lauder's exploitation of a quaint, old Caledonia wherein a laughing wee man, in fantastic tartans and carrying a crinkly cromach, indulged in the sentimentalities and humours of the 'Kailyard School' which was in growing disrepute. Lauder's antics and equipment had indeed little to do with the real Scotland, but they were enormously pleasing to the expatriate Scots all over the world who richly enjoyed a nostalgic heart-glow at the thought of 'Roamin' in the Gloamin'', and would happily fill a glass to the strain of 'A Wee Deoch-an-Doris'. The Scots are not notably a musical nation, but even those who were almost tone-deaf could appreciate, and even share without disgrace, a Harry Lauder chorus.

'Star-quality' on the stage is indefinable; roughly it means that its possessor has a magnetic, even a mesmeric, power which holds the audience immediately and maintains that grasp whatever the performer may be saying or doing. Lauder had that quality to the full. His patter, like his songs, had an elemental nature: he was never bawdy (at a time when the music-hall often was), never subtle, and never ingenious in the smart, 'wise-cracking' way which was to come. He wore his heart on his sleeve, and it seemed to be a heart of gigantic size. He sometimes executed part of his turn in the plain clothes of a trousered working-man; there was, for example, the unforgettable loon who lay in his bed crooning 'It's nice to get up in the morning' while his brother Jock the baker rose soon after midnight and was stumbling off to his ovens. In these features he struck a veracity absent from his gurgling, rollicking, absurdly kilted Highlanders. But the latter were the darlings of his public.

Lauder's strutting figure, short, broad, and tough, was that most common in the Lowland industrial districts, but his accent was more of Scotland in general than of any particular area. It was broad enough to give character, but not so broad as to puzzle any southern ear, a valuable factor in his music hall victories.

Lauder married in 1890 Annie (died 1927), daughter of James Vallance, underground manager of a mine in Hamilton. When not working Lauder lived for a long while near Dunoon and later at Strathaven, nearer the scene of his pit-work and of his first successes as an amateur. He had a bad fall at the age of sixty-eight, but overcame a fractured thigh; he was taken very seriously ill in the autumn of 1949, but lived on beyond expectation until his death at Strathaven 26 February 1950. He had willed to 'keep right on to the end of the road', as he had so often counselled others in song. His friends in all ranks of life were countless; he had built up the reputation, in a half-humorous way, of never 'banging a saxpence' without much careful cogitation, but his kindnesses were quiet, many, and 'known to his own'. A portrait by James McBey is in the Glasgow City Art Gallery.

[*The Times*, 27 February 1950; Harry Lauder, *Harry Lauder at Home and on Tour*, 1907, *A Minstrel in France*, 1918, and *Roamin' in the Gloamin'*, 1928.]

Ivor Brown

*published* 1959

## LAUGHTON Charles

(1899–1962)

Actor and film star, was born 1 July 1899 at the Victoria Hotel, Scarborough, the eldest of three sons (there were no daughters) of Robert Laughton, a prosperous hotelier, and his wife Elizabeth Conlon. Laughton spent a childhood largely tormented by a glandular problem which made him constantly overweight and therefore unpopular at school and indeed at home, where his early determination to become an actor met severe parental opposition.

Brought up as a Catholic, he was educated at Stonyhurst, where even one of his few school friends described him as 'the ungainliest of boys with a huge head'. Laughton was sent, against his wishes, to study the hotel trade at Claridge's in London before being called up at the end of World War I; he was rapidly invalided out of the army after being gassed on the western front in 1918.

Returning to his parents in Scarborough, he continued to train in hotel management until in 1925 he at last defied the family and enrolled as a drama student at the Royal Academy of Dramatic Art in London, where two years later he won the gold medal and was immediately given his start in the professional theatre by one of his teachers, the Russian director Theodore Komisarjevsky. His earliest stage roles at Barnes and the Everyman in Hampstead in 1926 were in classic Russian plays but in 1928, at the Little Theatre in London, he first made his name in the type of role which was to become his hallmark: that of the neurotic, greedy, sinister villain in *A Man with Red Hair* by Hugh Walpole. From there Laughton progressed to two more familiar roles, Poirot and Pickwick, before scoring another big success as the Chicago gangster loosely modelled on Al Capone in *On the Spot* (1930) by Edgar Wallace. He then made his New York début in 1931 as the squalid murderer in *Payment Deferred*, before accepting a Hollywood offer which took him to California for *The Old Dark House* (1932) and his first Nero in *The Sign of the Cross* (1932).

It was back in England for (Sir) Alexander Korda in 1933 that Laughton made his screen name in *The Private Life of Henry VIII* at the start of a sequence of major cinema biographies (*The Barretts of Wimpole Street* (1934), *Mutiny on the Bounty* (1935), *Rembrandt* (1936), and the unfinished *I Claudius* (1936)), which were to see him at the very peak of his reflective, anguished talent for larger-than-life monsters of reality.

In 1933 he joined the Old Vic Company for an impressive range of stage work (*Henry VIII* again, *The Cherry Orchard*, *Macbeth*, *Measure for Measure*,

*The Tempest*) and in 1936 he was the first English actor ever to be invited to appear at the Comédie Française in Paris, where he played Molière's *Le Médecin Malgré Lui*. He then settled in California, where despite occasional returns to the theatre (notably in the first production of Bertolt Brecht's *The Life of Galileo* in 1947, which he also adapted) he focused mainly on such films as *Jamaica Inn* (1939), *The Hunchback of Notre Dame* (1939), *Witness for the Prosecution* (1957), *Spartacus* (1960), and *Advise and Consent* (1962), returning only rarely to Britain and only notably for David Lean's *Hobson's Choice* in 1954.

But then, as if aware that his time was running out and that his film career was waning, he returned to Britain in 1959 for one last remarkable Stratford season in which he played both *King Lear* and Bottom in *A Midsummer Night's Dream*: his last London appearance was in *The Party* (1958).

In 1929 he married the actress Elsa Lanchester, daughter of James Sullivan, an Irish worker in a black-lead factory, and Edith Lanchester, a Cambridge graduate and active speaker and member of the Social Democratic Federation. They had no children. Throughout his long marriage his homosexuality caused him great unhappiness, and if there was any one key to Laughton's greatness as an actor then it was surely his sense of being a misfit, uneasy in his own skin and forever on the outside of the social, sexual, and familial demands of his upbringing and conditioning. An American citizen from 1950, Laughton died in Hollywood 15 December 1962.

[*The Times*, 17 December 1962; Simon Callow, *Charles Laughton: a Difficult Actor*, 1988; Charles Higham, *Charles Laughton, an Intimate Biography*, 1976; Kurt D. Singer, *The Charles Laughton Story*, 1954; Elsa Lanchester, *Charles Laughton and I*, 1938; personal knowledge.]

SHERIDAN MORLEY

*published 1993*

## LAUREL Stan

(1890–1965)

Comic, was born Arthur Stanley Jefferson at his grandfather's house in Ulverston, Lancashire, 16 June 1890, the second son in the family of four sons and one daughter of Arthur Jefferson, known as 'A.J'., of Bishop Auckland, theatre manager, and his wife Margaret ('Madge') Metcalfe, actress, of Ulverston. He attended schools in Bishop Auckland, Gainford, and Glasgow, after which his family connections helped him to gain entry to the music-hall, as a 'boy' comedian. It was while touring the United States with Fred Karno in 1912 that he tried his luck on American vaudeville, principally in a duo with his common-law wife, Mae Dahlberg, who suggested his stage name, Laurel, although he did not adopt it legally until 1934. In 1916 he saw the opportunities for music-hall pantomimists in the silent movies, and sought a mixed fortune in films and the stage. He lived in the USA from this period.

He became acquainted with Oliver 'Babe' Hardy in the early 1920s, but it was 1927, under the auspices of the Hal Roach studio, before they were first paired with any success. From that point they were to make over a hundred films together, some thirty of them silent ones, and with their best work probably deriving from the phase 1929–35, when they were engaged in creating coherent and sparse twenty-minute cameos.

The Laurel and Hardy set piece was the ordinary situation from which sprang a coiling spiral of disaster. Nervy, flustered, even tearful, Stan Laurel, 'the thin one', exacerbated these accumulating troubles, to the growing chagrin of 'the fat one', the ever-earnest Oliver Hardy. Laurel, in effect, made two contributions to the partnership: as Hardy was quick to concede, Laurel was the creator and rigorous controller of their comedy, as well as a member of what was widely recognized as the best comic double act of its time. An important reason for this was their eschewal of the conventional 'straight' man, two-dimensional and irritable. Each developed a detailed and complete persona of his own. The endearing bathos and crassness of Laurel found an admirable foil in the elephantine smugness of his rotund partner.

Laurel's marital toils were convoluted and confusingly reported. The nearest to an exact listing would be to record that he was married to Lois Neilsen in 1926; to Virginia Ruth Rogers in 1935 (after a possibly illegal ceremony in Mexico the previous year); to Illeana Shuvalova in 1938; to Ruth Rogers again in 1941; and to Ida Kitaeva Raphael, who survived him, in 1946. His only children were a daughter, Lois, who survived him, and a son, Stanley Robert, who lived but a few days: both were by his first wife. He died 23 February 1965 in Santa Monica, Hollywood, USA.

[Laurel and Hardy Museum, Ulverston; F. L. Guiles, *Stan*, 1980.]

ERIC MIDWINTER

*published 1993*

## LEIGH Vivien

**(1913–1967)**

Actress, was born Vivian Mary Hartley in Darjeeling, India, 5 November 1913, the only surviving child of Ernest Richard Hartley and his wife, Gertrude Robinson Yackje. She spent the first six years of her childhood in India, where her father was a junior partner in a firm of exchange brokers in Calcutta. Her mother, who was of French-Irish descent, carefully superintended her small daughter's upbringing, and the books and music which early appeared in the nursery had a warm welcome. In 1920 the Hartleys returned to England and placed their daughter in the Convent of the Sacred Heart in Roehampton, where Maureen O'Sullivan was a fellow boarder. Even as a child, Vivian Hartley was a leader in style, and her beautifully chosen clothes not a little coveted. Although bored by conventional school lessons, Vivian Hartley lost no opportunity in absorbing what interested her, and her letters home urged many extra lessons in ballet, piano, and violin. Visits to the theatre fed the child's dramatic instinct, and she took part each term in school productions, making her début as Mustardseed in *A Midsummer Night's Dream*.

When Vivian Hartley was thirteen, her parents extended her education by taking her on a European tour. This decision, which included study in schools and convents in France, Italy, and Bavaria, gave her fluency in three languages, and a liberal experience of great value. She made the utmost use of her five years abroad, visiting the great art galleries, attending opera, concerts, and the theatre, while her natural taste for beauty and quality was nourished by the international fashion designers. When she returned to England at eighteen, she was abundantly prepared to conquer the theatre world. Her clear green-blue eyes, chestnut hair, and delicate features were enhanced by a flawless complexion, and she walked with an assured grace.

Scarcely had she enrolled as a student at the Royal Academy of Dramatic Art, when she announced her engagement to a young barrister, Herbert Leigh Holman. The fashionable wedding which followed in December 1932 at St. James's, Spanish Place, and the establishment of a new pattern of living engrossed her until after the birth of her daughter in October 1933. Characteristically, this was recorded in her diary—'Had a baby—a girl'. Gradually, however, her ambition to become an actress again grew restless, and in August 1934 she interrupted a family yachting cruise to return home, just in case she should be called for a small part in a film. Her reward came in one line in the film *Things are Looking Up*, with

(Dame) Cicely Courtneidge. More small parts now began to come her way, and she decided upon the stage name Vivien Leigh.

Less than a year after her entry into films, Vivien Leigh was given the stage opportunity she needed, when casting had been held up for a young actress to play a leading part in *The Mask of Virtue* by Carl Sternheim. Since the first requirement was exceptional beauty, Vivien Leigh conquered everyone concerned at the first interview. The play, produced at the Ambassadors Theatre in 1935, was not a success, but the young actress was acclaimed 'a star of unusual promise'. It was very much to her credit that the adulation she received did not turn her head, but like the good professional that she wished to be she took the exposure of her inexperience intelligently and began to learn her craft.

Within twenty-four hours of her successful press reviews, Vivien Leigh had signed a five-year contract with (Sir) Alexander Korda, but she had to wait another year before Korda was ready to cast her: in *Fire Over England* (1937). The occasion, when it came, was fateful, bringing her into professional relationship with Laurence (later Lord) Olivier. They were soon very much in love. She was already an admirer of his acting, and the four months working daily together on the film was deeply influential in her subsequent development. Aware of her limitations, and working constantly to overcome them, Vivien Leigh eagerly accepted the challenge to play Ophelia to Olivier's Hamlet, when the Old Vic production was invited to appear in Elsinore, Denmark, in June 1937. Under expert tuition, her voice—which had been light and small—gained in strength, and her willingness to learn so won her director's admiration that she was cast for Titania in the Old Vic production of *A Midsummer Night's Dream* at Christmas 1937.

With the offer to play Scarlett O'Hara in the film *Gone with the Wind* (1939), Vivien Leigh saw her first chance to break the image of a Dresden china shepherdess—a comparison she despised. Although she had no sympathy for Scarlett, the actress could recognize 'a marvellous part' when she saw one, and she seized and exploited every facet of her heroine, who gave her both an Oscar award and international status as a film star.

Following the dissolution of their previous marriages, Vivien Leigh and Laurence Olivier were married in California in August 1940. They made the film *Lady Hamilton* (1941), then returned to England—Olivier to service in the navy, and Vivien Leigh to establish a wartime home for them both. She was eager to return to the theatre, making her appearance in *The Doctor's Dilemma* by G. Bernard Shaw at the Haymarket in 1942. This was followed a year later by a three-month tour of North Africa, in which she appeared in a concert party with Beatrice Lillie for the armed services. In a letter home she confesses to 'one of the most exciting and often the most moving experiences I have ever had'.

Vivien Leigh had been an actress for almost ten years before her capacity to carry the action of a play was tested. In Thornton Wilder's *The Skin of Our Teeth* (Phoenix, 1945), as Sabina, she showed a new authority in her work, and evidence that she could now stand unsupported. In 1947 her husband was knighted. In a demanding ten-month tour of Australia and New Zealand with Olivier with the Old Vic Company, in 1948, she had abundant classical opportunities to prepare her for the tragic role of Antigone, in which she made a great impression when they returned to London in 1949. Critics, who had been cautious over her early successes, observed that 'this is a new Miss Leigh altogether', and complimented her on her extended vocal range and 'fanatical force of character'.

The actress was now seen in full maturity; and when she appeared as Blanche in *A Streetcar Named Desire* at the Aldwych in October of the same year she received a storming ovation for a performance of uncommon subtlety, and filled the theatre for eight months. Another Oscar award was given her for her film performance in the same role.

While she appreciated her film successes, it was more important to her to succeed as her husband's equal in the theatre. Her great joy was to act with Olivier, and in spite of her fears that she was not yet ready for the demanding variety of Cleopatra, she accepted the challenge to appear under their joint management in the two plays on alternate nights: *Caesar and Cleopatra* by Shaw and *Antony and Cleopatra* by Shakespeare, at the St. James's, 1951. Under her husband's direction, she gave a performance which satisfied both scholars and the general public.

The Oliviers' first season together at Stratford-upon-Avon in 1955 culminated in a powerfully effective production of *Titus Andronicus* by Peter Brook. In May 1957 this production was selected to represent the Memorial Theatre Company on a prestige tour of European capitals for the British Council. On such occasions, Vivien Leigh appeared in her natural element—a distinguished guest, a gracious hostess, and totally professional. Colleagues paid warm tribute to the unvarying quality of her performances, which remained constant throughout a gruelling social programme. Her tact and consideration for the press were tireless and individual. However, she repeatedly began to suffer from manic phases in which she lost physical control of herself and abused her husband verbally in public. Olivier finally decided that he could no longer tolerate the situation.

In 1957 Vivien Leigh and Laurence Olivier appeared together for the last time, at the Stoll Theatre in *Titus Andronicus*. It was during this run that

Vivien Leigh interrupted a debate in the House of Lords to protest—without avail—against the projected demolition of the St. James's Theatre.

The last decade of her life, although marked by the same high level of performance, in plays by Jean Giraudoux and (Sir) Noël Coward, among others, had lost its radiance. Her marriage to Olivier was dissolved in 1960; they had no children. She continued to act, making a new reputation for herself in the musical *Tovarich* in New York, 1963, but her delicate constitution could not sustain a career single-handed; the fire of a shared grand passion for the theatre had gone out. Her career had been interrupted from time to time by nervous collapse when she drove herself too hard and by the tuberculosis which caused her death 8 July 1967, in London, during preparations for her appearance in Edward Albee's *A Delicate Balance*. That night the exterior lights of London's West End theatres were darkened for an hour.

Portraits of Vivien Leigh include an oil-painting (unfinished) by Augustus John, held in a private collection in America; an oil-painting, as Blanche DuBois in *A Streetcar Named Desire*, 1950, by A. K. Lawrence, given to the British Theatre Museum at Leighton House, London; and an oil-painting as Henriette in *The Mask of Virtue* by Diet Edzard, 1935, privately owned.

Vivien Leigh received the knight's cross of the Legion of Honour in 1957.

[Anne Edwards, *Vivien Leigh, A Biography*, 1977; *Who's Who in the Theatre*; Felix Barker, *The Oliviers*, 1953; Alan Dent, *Vivien Leigh—a Bouquet*, 1969; Gwen Robyns, *Light of a Star*, 1968; *Observer*, 16 February and 16 October 1949; private information.]

FREDA GAYE

*published 1981*

## LENO Dan

**(1860–1904)**

Music-hall singer and dancer, was born as George Galvin on 20 Dec. 1860 at 4 Eve Court, Somers Town, afterwards demolished to make room for St. Pancras terminus. His father and mother, who were known professionally as Mr. and Mrs. Johnny Wilde, were itinerant music-hall performers who trained the child as a tumbler and contortionist. The father at any rate was Irish, and to that circumstance and the boy's occasional sojourns in Ireland may be attributed his marked Irish voice, which was no small part of his attraction in later years. He made his first appearance as early as 1864 as 'Little George, the Infant Wonder, Contortionist and Posturer' in the Cosmotheca off the Edgware Road, since destroyed. His father dying about this time, his mother married another member of the same profession, named Grant, whose stage name was Leno. The boy with his mother, stepfather, and a brother, also an acrobat, began to tour the United Kingdom and to some extent the continent. Described as 'The Great Little Lenos', the brothers were performing in various places in 1867. The brother soon disappeared, and in 1869 Dan, who had been forced through an accident to substitute clog-dancing for tumbling, was known as 'The Great Little Leno, the Quintessence of Irish Comedians', and had presumably added singing and patter to his agility. In 1869 he was in Belfast, among the audience being Charles Dickens, then lecturing in Ireland, who is said to have spoken to the boy and prophesied success for him (Jay Hickory Wood, *Dan Leno*, 1905).

The boy's name was changed from George to Dan owing to a misapprehension on the part of either the printer or deviser of a playbill. The boy's stepfather appreciated the accidental change and saw the value of it, and as Dan Leno the stage name was crystallised. For many years the touring life continued, with moderate success, and then in 1880 Dan Leno, now nearly twenty, entered for a clog-dancing competition and the championship of the world silver belt at the Princess's Music Hall, Leeds, and won it. He subsequently lost it, but recaptured it in 1883, at the People's Music Hall, Oldham, and emerged from the contest into the successful period of his life. In 1883, in St. George's Church, Hulme, Manchester, he married Miss Lydia Reynolds, a music-hall singer, and not long afterwards made his first appearance as Dan Leno in London, at the Foresters' Music Hall, where at a salary of 5*l*. a week he sang and danced. His first song, 'Going to Buy the Milk for the Twins', a mixture of singing and monologue such as he practised to the end, was so successful that he obtained an engagement at the Oxford Music Hall and there attracted the attention of George Conquest, of the Surrey Theatre, who engaged Leno and his wife at a joint salary of 20*l*. a week to play in the 1886–7 pantomime of 'Jack and the Beanstalk'. Dan accepted, and played Jack's mother. From this point his career was a triumph.

In 1887 he made his appearance at the Empire theatre, Leicester Square, on the occasion of its being converted into a music hall, and sang one of his earliest successes, a parody of 'Queen of My Heart' in 'Dorothy'. Next year Sir Augustus Harris engaged him for the Drury Lane pantomime of 1888–9—'Babes in the Wood'—for which he worked so acceptably as the Wicked Aunt that it ran from 26 Dec. until 27 April, and his engagement was renewed for a term of years which ended only with his death. Every winter he was the particular star of Drury Lane; while during the rest of the year he made a tour of the principal music halls in the United Kingdom. No other comedian of his time had drawing power to compare with him. On 26 November 1901 the culminating point of his success was reached when he was commanded to Sandringham to sing before King Edward VII, Queen Alexandra, and their guests—the first music-hall performer to be thus honoured.

In September 1902 Dan Leno's health broke down. His continuous and excitable activity exhausted his strength. He was able to return to the stage during the early months of 1903 and for the Drury Lane pantomime of 1903–4; but he died at Balham from general paralysis of the brain on 31 Oct. 1904 at the early age of forty-three. His funeral on 8 Nov. at Lambeth cemetery, Tooting, was attended by an immense crowd of admirers.

Dan Leno throughout the best years of his career, which covered his connection with Drury Lane, signally excelled all other music-hall comedians in intelligence, humour, drollery, and creativeness. He used the words provided for him only as a basis, often suggested by himself, on which to build a character. Although essentially a caricaturist, with a broad and rollicking sense of fun which added myriad touches of extravagance beyond experience, the groundwork of his creations was true, and truth continually broke through the exuberance of the artist. His most memorable songs in his best period were a mixture of monologue and song, in male or female character, but the song came gradually to count for less and less. 'The Shop-walker' perhaps first convinced the great public of his genius. Leno's long series of largely irresponsible but always human pantomime figures at Drury Lane differed from all pantomime figures by their strange blend of fun and wistfulness. It was his special gift to endear himself to an audience, and compel its sympathies as well as applause.

The recipient of large salaries, he was correspondingly lavish. He was President of the Music Hall Benevolent Fund, and himself the distributor of much private charity. He carried his fun into private life and was much addicted to practical jokes. His hobbies were farming live stock in the meadow attached to his house at Balham and painting or modelling in the wooden studio in his garden. For one evening in 1902 he edited the 'Sun', a short-lived newspaper then under Mr. Horatio Bottomley's ownership. He also wrote a burlesque autobiography entitled 'Dan Leno: his Book' (1901), which is not wholly without nonsensical merit.

He left a widow and several children, among them a married daughter, Georgiana, who had appeared on the stage. A bust of the comedian is in the entrance hall of Drury Lane Theatre.

[*The Times*, 1 Nov. 1904; *Daily Telegraph*, 1 Nov. 1904; *Era*, 5 Nov. 1904. *Dan Leno*, by Jay Hickory Wood, 1905; James Glover, *Jimmy Glover his book*, 1911; pp. 74 seq. (with portrait of Leno from bust by himself).]

E. V. LUCAS

*published 1912*

## LILLIE Beatrice Gladys

(1894–1989)

*Lady Peel*

Actress and singer, was born 29 May 1894 in Toronto, the younger daughter (there were no sons) of John Lillie, cigar seller, of Lisburn in Ireland, and his wife, Lucie Ann, eldest daughter of John Shaw, a Manchester draper. Following her parents' emigration to Toronto, the family grew up there and 'Bea' was educated at St Agnes' College in Belleville, Ontario; she began to appear in amateur concerts there with her mother and sister as the Lillie Trio. At the outbreak of World War I they all returned to London, and it was at the Chatham Music Hall in 1914 that Bea made her professional stage début.

Already it was clear that the Lillie Trio was not much of a success, and that if Beatrice Lillie was to succeed in the theatre it would have to be as a solo act. Almost immediately after her London début she formed an alliance with the leading World War I producer of intimate revues, André Charlot, who saw in her not the serious singer she had set out to become, but a comedian of considerable if zany qualities. Charlot at this time was also fostering the very early careers of Gertrude Lawrence (who for a time was Lillie's understudy), W. J. ('Jack') Buchanan, and (Sir) Noël Coward. In World War I Lillie became a favourite of troops on leave from the front, relying on spontaneity and an improvised response to her audiences, which Charlot had to restrain when it threatened to go too far. Lillie's great talents were the arched eyebrow, the curled lip, the fluttering eyelid, the tilted chin, the ability to suggest, even in apparently innocent material, the possible *double entendre*.

In 1920 she married Robert Peel, son of Robert Peel and great-grandson of Sir Robert Peel, prime minister. He succeeded his father as fifth baronet in 1925. He died in 1934, leaving his wife with one beloved son, Robert, sixth and last baronet, who was killed in World War II, in 1942. The loss of first husband and then son comparatively early in her life (she never married again) left Lillie with a constant private sadness that she seemed able to overcome only on stage. Her career encompassed some fifty stage shows in the West End and Broadway as well as a dozen films, but she excelled in live performance, demolishing scripts and songs alike with her own particular brand of solo eccentricity. (Sir) Charles Cochran, Coward, and Florenz Ziegfeld all employed her in their revues, but in 1932 American audiences saw her as the Nurse in the New York première of *Too Good to be True* by Bernard Shaw, one of the comparatively few 'straight' roles she undertook: others were in Robert Morley's first play, *Staff Dance* (1944), and the non-musical version of *Auntie Mame*, which she brought to London after the war.

She made her cabaret début at the Café de Paris in 1933, worked in revue and troop concerts throughout the war, and made her own television series, based on her cabaret routines, as early as 1951. She then developed, and toured for many years around the world, a solo show called simply *An Evening with Beatrice Lillie*, which ranked alongside those of Joyce Grenfell and Ruth Draper. Her career in films began with the silent film, *Exit Smiling*, in 1927 and continued intermittently right through to *Around the World in Eighty Days* (1956) and *Thoroughly Modern Millie* (her last, in 1967). But in films as on radio something was missing, the live audience to which she could respond and which she often made part of the act. She was excellent as the mad Auntie Mame, or as Madame Arcati in *High Spirits* (1964), a Broadway musical version of Coward's *Blithe Spirit*. Coward called her 'the perfect comedienne' and wrote his 'Marvellous Party' for her to sing, while Cole Porter wrote her 'Mrs Lowsborough-Goodby'. Her entire career was a sustained monument to anarchic alternative comedy before those terms had ever been invented, and hers was a triumph of manic high spirits. With her long face, tall brow, lively eyes, natural poise, and radiant personality, she was one of the great female clowns.

Her last years were overshadowed by illness; she lived in Henley-on-Thames, a virtual recluse had it not been for her devoted manager John Philip, who shared the house with her for twenty years and who died of a stroke only a matter of hours after her death. She died 20 January 1989 in Henley.

[Beatrice Lillie, *Every Other Inch a Lady*, 1973; *The Times*, 21 January 1989; private information.]

Sheridan Morley

*published 1996*

## LOPOKOVA Lydia Vasilievna

**(1892–1981)**

*Lady Keynes*

Ballerina, was born 21 October 1892 at St Petersburg (Leningrad), the third of five children (three sons and two daughters) and second daughter of Vasili Lopukhov, impassioned theatre lover and an usher at the Imperial Alexandrinsky Theatre, and his wife, Rosalia Constanza Karlovna Douglas, daughter of the clerk to the municipality of Riga, of Scottish ancestry. Lopokova was educated at the Imperial Ballet School, St Petersburg, which she entered shortly before her ninth birthday in 1901. She graduated into the Imperial Ballet at the Maryinsky Theatre, St Petersburg, in 1909. Although a demi caractère dancer she could also shine in the purely classical roles because of her strong technique, extreme lightness in jumping, and stylistic sensitivity.

In 1910 Serge Diaghilev included Lopokova in the company he had formed for the second summer running to tour European capitals. Although only seventeen when thrust among Diaghilev's exalted group of artists Lopokova quickly established herself and successfully danced Tamara Karsavina's roles, including those in *Firebird* and *Carnaval* (with Nijinsky) when Karsavina was away fulfilling other contracts.

Following the tour Lopokova, with her sister and elder brother, both dancers, sailed for America on eight-month contracts. She never returned to the Imperial Ballet nor danced again in Russia. When her brother and sister went home she chose to stay on to dance in assorted ballet groups, shows, and musicals, making a name for herself. She also ventured into straight acting.

In 1916 Diaghilev sent his Ballets Russes to America and Lopokova rejoined the company as the leading ballerina. During the tour she married in 1916 Randolfo Barocchi, Diaghilev's business manager and an older man of great charm. Thus Lopokova returned to Russian ballet and with it to Europe for the first time in six years. There followed seasons in Europe and North and South America but it was not until 1918 that Lopokova first danced in London. Her triumphs were now crowned by the roles created for her by Léonide Massine in *The Good-Humoured Ladies* (1917–18) and *Le Boutique Fantasque* (1919). Such was her fame that when she abruptly left her husband and the ballet company simultaneously in July 1919 her mysterious disappearance caused banner headlines in the London press. Once again Lopokova had abandoned the Russian Ballet as though it meant nothing to her. Yet two years later she returned to Diaghilev's company in Paris and then starred among five important ballerinas in Diaghilev's 1921 London production of *Sleeping Beauty*.

At this time the economist (John) Maynard (later Lord) Keynes became her ardent admirer. He was the brother of (Sir) Geoffrey Keynes, and the son of (John) Neville Keynes, registrary of Cambridge University. Belonging to the Bloomsbury Group, he brought Lopokova into the circle—which was difficult at times for her, and for its members. When Keynes began to think of marriage some of his friends were filled with foreboding. They tended to find Lopokova bird-brained. In reality she was intelligent, wise, and witty, but not intellectual. E. M. Forster, T. S. Eliot, and Picasso were among her close friends. She artfully used, and intentionally misused, English to unexpectedly comic and often outrageous effect. Keynes was constantly amused and enchanted. Lopokova idolized him and they married in 1925, the year of her divorce from Barocchi. They had no children. When they were apart they wrote daily if only between King's College, Cambridge, of which Keynes was the bursar, and Bloomsbury.

Lopokova continued to dance and act intermittently, playing Ibsen, Molière, and Shakespeare, albeit with her charming Russian accent; and she helped the burgeoning British Ballet tremendously. But from when Keynes suffered his first serious illness in 1937 until his death in 1946 the total dedication she had never quite mustered for her career came to flower. She was a devoted wife, forsaking all interests save her husband's health and work while entertaining him and their friends with her unpredictable remarks. They now lived mostly at Tilton in Sussex, sharing their love of poetry, literature, and the countryside. Lopokova accompanied her husband on his economic missions abroad.

Lopokova was a diminutive figure with the natural air of an eager, enquiring child which caused her to hold her head tilted up towards anyone with whom she was conversing. This could give the impression that her nose, too, was up-tilted whereas, unusually, just the tip turned down as a Picasso drawing of 1919 clearly shows. Her face was round with alert eyes under perfectly curved eyebrows; her mouth was a well-defined feature. Both her face and hands were remarkably expressive. On or off the stage her vitality, originality, humour, and youthful enthusiasm were irresistible. Gaiety and good humour prevailed. In addition she was devoid of jealousy, malice, vanity, meanness, or pretension.

After her husband's death she adopted a retired way of life but lost none of her originality and charm. She died in a home near Tilton 8 May 1981.

[Milo Keynes (ed.), *Lydia Lopokova*, 1983; Polly Hill and Richard Keynes (eds.), *Lydia and Maynard: Letters between Lydia Lopokova and John Maynard Keynes*, 1989;

Lydia Yoffe, 'The Lopukhov Dynasty', *Dance Magazine*, New York, January 1967; Anatole Chujoy in *Dance Encyclopedia*, A. S. Barnes & Co., New York, 1949; personal knowledge.]

MARGOT FONTEYN

*published 1990*

## MCCARTHY Lillah

(1875–1960)

Actress, was born in Cheltenham 22 September 1875, the third daughter and seventh of the eight children of Jonadab McCarthy, furniture broker, and his wife, Emma Price. When she was eight her father, a handsome imaginative Irishman, whose interests ranged between furniture and astronomy (he was a fellow of the Royal Astronomical Society), decided to teach her himself. She studied with him at home until, on the advice of the young actor-manager (Sir) Frank Benson whose company had already begun to achieve its status as a 'touring university of the theatre', Jonadab McCarthy moved to London so that his daughter might be trained in elocution with Hermann Vezin and voice production with Emil Behnke. As an amateur she appeared during May 1895 as Lady Macbeth in a Shakespeare Society production at St. George's Hall, the occasion on which she first used the stage name of Lillah, her real names being Lila Emma. G. B. Shaw, who went to the play for the *Saturday Review* of which he had not long been dramatic critic, wrote of her: 'She is as handsome as Miss [Julia] Neilson; and she can hold an audience whilst she is doing everything wrongly . . . I venture on the responsibility of saying that her Lady Macbeth was a highly promising performance, and that some years of hard work would make her a valuable recruit to the London stage'.

She began at once the years of hard work by appearing in Shakespeare with the touring manager (Sir) P. Ben Greet, and in playing Berenice in the London production of *The Sign of the Cross* (Lyric, 1896) for Wilson Barrett, the melodramatic actor with whom she spent eight years, off and on, touring England, Australasia, and South Africa. Her parts included Mercia in *The Sign of the Cross*, Virginia in *Virginius*, Desdemona in *Othello*, and Ophelia in *Hamlet*. Barrett had intended to set her up in her own company, but died before he could do so. After working with (Sir) Herbert Beerbohm Tree in the theatrically sumptuous surroundings of His Majesty's (among her parts was Calpurnia in *Julius Caesar*), she called upon Shaw to tell him that the years of apprenticeship were up. In consequence she was cast presently as Nora in a revival of *John Bull's Other Island* (May 1905) and Ann Whitefield in the original production of *Man and Superman* (May 1905), each play produced at the Court Theatre by Harley Granville-Barker whom she had met while touring with Greet. She played through the Court season of 1906, succeeding Tita Brand as Gloria in *You Never Can Tell* and creating Jennifer Dubedat (whose Celtic quality she could suggest with ease) in *The Doctor's Dilemma*. By now this tall, statuesque young woman with the dark velvet voice was bringing to every part a sure theatrical instinct: her fault was a certain heaviness. In a preface to her autobiography Shaw wrote: 'Lillah McCarthy's secret was that she combined the executive art of the grand school with a natural impulse to murder the Victorian womanly woman; and this being just what I needed I blessed the day when I found her'.

In 1906 she married Granville-Barker. She went on to use her tragic gift in the title-part of John Masefield's Gloucestershire *Nan* (Royalty, 1908). Later, in marked contrast, she created the drawling Lady Sybil in Barrie's *What Every Woman Knows* (Duke of York's, 1908); and she appeared at the same theatre during the repertory season of 1909 as Madge Thomas in Galsworthy's *Strife*. Lillah McCarthy needed sustained tragic intensity: hence her success (Court, 1911) as Anne Pedersdotter in *The Witch*, adapted by John Masefield from the Norwegian of H. Wiers-Jenssen. During her personal management of the Little Theatre in the Adelphi during 1911, she played, among other parts, Hilde in Ibsen's *The Master Builder*, and Margaret Knox in Shaw's *Fanny's First Play*, described as 'a strong, springy girl of eighteen, with large nostrils, an audacious chin, and a gaily resolute manner'. Greek tragedy, which became one of her passions, occupied her at the beginning of 1912: Jocasta in *Oedipus Rex*, presented by (Sir) John Martin-Harvey at Covent Garden in January, and Iphigenia in *Iphigenia in Tauris* at the Kingsway in March. It was almost immediately after this that she entered, with her husband, upon the management of the Savoy Theatre, and later of the St. James's, in a sequence of provocative and historic productions.

At the Savoy in the autumn and winter of 1912 she was Hermione in *The Winter's Tale* and Viola in *Twelfth Night*, revivals from which all stock Shakespearian business was eradicated. During 1913 her major part at the St. James's was Lavinia in Shaw's *Androcles and the Lion*; she returned to the Savoy in February 1914 as Helena in her husband's third Shakespeare production, *A Midsummer Night's Dream*. She was a beautiful and moving actress, but not an intellectual match for Barker, although she did much for him by finding backers. During 1915 she went with him to America, acting a few parts. Then in 1916—when she used her lesser gift of comedy as Maude in Somerset Maugham's *Caroline* (New)—she heard from Barker that he did not wish to return to her. It was a grave blow; but for a time, with the counsel and encouragement of Shaw, she went on working after the divorce in 1918. In April 1919, during a brief management of the Kingsway Theatre, she played Judith in Arnold Bennett's Apocrypha-based drama of that name, a second-rate work which she could not lift.

Lillah McCarthy did little more in the theatre after two showy parts with Matheson Lang at the New: Joanne in Temple Thurston's *The Wandering Jew* (1920) and Doña Sol in Tom Cushing's *Blood and Sand* (1921). Later, after her second—and intensely happy—marriage to (Sir) Frederick Keeble in 1920 she settled down near Oxford. During the thirties she undertook a number of recitals in various parts of the country (scenes, for example, from *Twelfth Night* and *Iphigenia in Tauris*) and her voice was the first to be heard on the stage of the second Shakespeare Memorial Theatre at Stratford on Avon on its opening afternoon, 23 April 1932: she spoke John Masefield's prologue, with its line, 'The acted passion beautiful and swift'. Her husband died in 1952 and she was living in London when she died 15 April 1960. She had no children.

Her autobiography, *Myself and My Friends* (in which Granville-Barker forbade any mention of his name), published in 1933, is the record of a warm-hearted woman and a potentially fine actress. Owing to the breaking of her first marriage, she never did what had been expected of her, although she won the loyalty of such diverse figures as Masefield and Shaw.

Two portraits of Lillah McCarthy by Charles Shannon are in the Cheltenham Art Gallery. These represent her as Doña Ana in the dream scene (sometimes detached as *Don Juan in Hell*) of Shaw's *Man and Superman*, and as the Dumb Wife in Anatole France's *The Man Who Married a Dumb Wife* which she acted in the Ashley Dukes version. Charles Ricketts added the butterfly on the veil of the high head-dress.

[*The Times*, 16 April 1960; Lillah McCarthy, *Myself and My Friends*, 1933; Desmond MacCarthy, *The Court Theatre 1904–1907*, 1907; C. B. Purdom, *Harley Granville Barker*, 1955; G. B. Shaw, *Our Theatres in the Nineties*, vol. i, 1932; personal knowledge.]

J. C. Trewin

*published* 1971

## MARSHALL (Charles) Arthur (Bertram) (1910–1989)

Humorist, writer, and broadcaster, was born 10 May 1910 in Barnes, London, the younger son of Charles Frederick Bertram Marshall, consulting engineer, and his wife, Dorothy Lee. His father was a loving husband, but although he quite liked the idea of children, to Arthur's disappointment he preferred to be where they were not. In 1920 the family moved to Newbury and Arthur was sent away to boarding school. First he went to Edinburgh House, an uncomfortable but enjoyable preparatory school in Lee-on-Solent, and then to Oundle. He was happy at Oundle—he seems to have been happy almost everywhere—and during a debate in his last winter term a great burst of laughter at something he said gave him such a whiff of power and pleasure that he decided to make the raising of laughter the prime consideration of his life. He then went to Christ's College, Cambridge, where he obtained a second class (division II) in part i of the modern and medieval languages tripos (French, 1929, and German, 1930) and a third class in part ii (1931).

He acted at every opportunity at Oundle and at Christ's and was determined on a career in the theatre. He mostly played female parts at university, for which he collected some excellent press notices, notably for his playing of Lady Cicely, opposite (Sir) Michael Redgrave, in *Captain Brassbound's Conversion*. He became president of Cambridge's Amateur Dramatic Society.

Down from Cambridge, armed with his glowing press cuttings, he had his heart set on going to the Royal Academy of Dramatic Art, but his mother pointed out that the acting profession would hardly give an ecstatic welcome to an amateur female impersonator. She persuaded him to go back to Oundle instead and make a career as a schoolmaster. In 1931 Oundle offered him a job as a house tutor and teacher of French and German, which he accepted, quaking in his shoes. To his own surprise he turned out to be a good teacher and, as the terms sped happily by, he spent a good deal of his free time writing and performing to friends what were then called 'turns', three-minute comic monologues in which, inspired by Angela Brazil's girls' school stories which he found hilarious when read aloud, he impersonated hearty botany mistresses and stern school matrons.

In 1934 a BBC radio producer saw Arthur perform his botany-mistress turn at a party and booked him to broadcast it on *Charlot's Hour*. Thus his professional career began by his becoming the world's first radio drag act.

In the same year (C.) Raymond Mortimer, literary editor of the *New Statesman*, asked Arthur to review a clutch of schoolgirl stories. His review was much enjoyed and for many years was a popular Christmas feature of the magazine.

During World War II Marshall, like many a schoolmaster, was drafted into intelligence and he had a busy time, surviving the evacuation of Dunkirk in the British Expeditionary Force and working with Combined Operations headquarters and SHAEF (Supreme Headquarters, Allied Expeditionary Force). In 1945 he was a lieutenant-colonel on General Dwight D. Eisenhower's staff. He was appointed MBE in 1944. In 1943, still in uniform, he wrote and starred in a BBC comedy series on the radio, *A Date with Nurse Dugdale*, which was a wartime success.

After the war Marshall returned to Oundle in 1946 as a housemaster, but his fascination with the theatre was still strong and, afraid that he might end up as a rotund Mr Chips before his time, he left Oundle in 1954 at the age of forty-four and became a social secretary to his old friend, Victor, third Baron Rothschild. In 1958 he changed jobs again and went to work as a script reader for one of the leading figures of Shaftesbury Avenue's commercial theatre, H. G. ('Binkie') Beaumont of H. M. Tennent Ltd. Marshall was in his element at last. He was such pleasant company that everybody in the theatre seemed to know and like him and this charming, funny, and non-competitive person was invited everywhere. He spent many long weekends at W. Somerset Maugham's Villa Mauresque at Cap Ferrat and months with Alfred Lunt and Lynn Fontanne in the USA. No doubt part of his attraction as a guest was that when conversation sagged his host would call upon him to entertain the company with a turn, and he was delighted to oblige.

In 1953 he began to publish his humorous prose pieces in book form, beginning with *Nineteen to the Dozen* (1953); there were many more. He also published some gratifyingly successful compilations from the *New Statesman* competitions and his own book reviews, *Salome Dear, Not in the Fridge!* (1968), *Girls Will Be Girls* (1974), *Whimpering in the Rhododendrons* (1982), and *Giggling in the Shrubbery* (1985). In 1975 he started writing a regular column for the *New Statesman* and another for the *Sunday Telegraph*. He also became a regular broadcaster and chat-show guest and in 1979 was enlisted as a team captain in the BBC TV game *Call My Bluff*, which he graced for ten years. A measure of his aggressive nature and will to win was evident in his first appearance on *Call My Bluff*. He led his team to an 8–0 defeat and laughed so much he was unable to say 'goodnight' to camera.

In the world of broadcast humour in the 1980s it was Arthur Marshall who was the 'alternative comedian'. This was the era dominated by young writers and comics, who appealed to young viewers and readers with a stunning display of aggressive, sexual, and politically simplistic routines nurtured on the students' union circuit. For those for whom this sort of comedy ceased to appeal much after the first excitement, Marshall's charming, intelligent, witty, *affectionate* humour came as a breath of fresh air. He was, perhaps, the last flowering of the humour which Joseph Addison and Sir Richard Steele pioneered in the early eighteenth century and called 'polite comedy'.

With his unconventional attitudes towards such things as religion and erudition, his distaste for foreigners (the 'Boche' and 'Frogs'), and his eyes sparkling and chins a-wobble at some absurdity he had noticed, a line of Rupert Brooke's should be bent to Arthur Marshall, this happiest of humorists, as 'an English unofficial sunbeam'.

He was unmarried. His last years were spent in Devon and during his final illness he was fortunate to have an old friend, Peter Kelland, a retired schoolmaster, to look after him and share his life. He died 27 January 1989.

[Arthur Marshall, *Life's Rich Pageant* (autobiography), 1984; private information.]

FRANK MUIR

*published 1996*

## MARTIN-HARVEY Sir John Martin

**(1863–1944)**

Actor-manager, was born at Wivenhoe, Essex, 22 June 1863, the eldest son to survive infancy and fourth of the seven children of John Harvey, a noted builder of yachts and other craft, whose family had been connected with the town for generations. Martin-Harvey's mother was Margaret Diana Mary, daughter of the Rev. David George Goyder, Swedenborgian minister, of the Carmarthenshire family of Gwydyr. Martin-Harvey was brought up as a Swedenborgian, but while still a boy joined the Church of England. He was educated at a succession of schools ending with King's College School, London. The one subject he was good at was drawing. In later years he drew many excellent sketches and believed that he would have succeeded as a professional artist. Instead, he became an apprentice to his father at Wivenhoe.

His decision to go on the stage was due to a chance remark of his father after a performance of *H.M.S. Pinafore* by children. It was on the advice of

(Sir) W. S. Gilbert, for whom Harvey was building a yacht, that his son became the pupil of John Ryder, Macready's former leading man. Martin-Harvey appeared in 1881 as a boy in *To Parents and Guardians* at the Royal Court Theatre, afterwards touring in *Betsy* and then in 1882 joining the company of (Sir) Henry Irving at the Lyceum Theatre, walking on in *Romeo and Juliet*. He remained with Irving for fourteen years, playing small parts, but doing so with peculiar charm, particularly as the Dauphin in *Louis XI* and as Lorenzo in *The Merchant of Venice*. He went with Irving four times to the United States, and each summer from 1888 to 1894 toured with a repertory company in conjunction with William Haviland and Louis Calvert.

On leaving the Lyceum in 1896 Harvey appeared in several plays at the Royal Court Theatre, including *The Children of the King*. At the Prince of Wales's Theatre his Pelléas in Maeterlinck's *Pelléas and Mélisande* moved the author to declare: 'Il a volé mon âme, ce M. Harvey'. It was in the following year (1899) that 'little Jack Harvey' as (Dame) Ellen Terry still called him, astonished the playgoing world by presenting *The Only Way* at the Lyceum with complete success. This simple and frankly sentimental adaptation of Dickens's *Tale of Two Cities*, made by two Irish clergymen, Freeman Crofts Wills and Frederick Langbridge, was destined to become a stage classic. Much of its appeal was due to the insight and initiative of Martin-Harvey's wife, whom he married in 1889, when both were junior members of the Lyceum company. She was Angelita Helena Margarita (died 1949), daughter of Don Ramón de Silva Ferro, and her name suggests her distinguished Spanish parentage; but she also had Stewart blood through the Earls of Seaforth. She suggested, planned for years, and finally named *The Only Way*. The perfect fitness of the parts of Sydney Carton and Mimi to the Martin-Harveys made its arrival one of the most memorable theatrical events of its time. Martin-Harvey was to present many other productions in the course of a subsequent career of half a century. To the end *The Only Way* remained a never-failing attraction throughout the English-speaking world.

Martin-Harvey's productions of *Hamlet* (1904), *Richard III* (1910), and *The Taming of the Shrew* (1913) were full of original touches and fine work. His Lieutenant Reresby, 'The Rat', in *The Breed of the Treshams* (1903) had a rakish vigour in conscious contrast to sensitive and beautiful studies like his Count Skariatine in *A Cigarette Maker's Romance* (1901) and the natural dignity of his performance in Maeterlinck's *The Burgomaster of Stilemonde* (1918). His *Œdipus Rex* (1912) at Covent Garden was a profoundly impressive performance and an epoch-making production.

Martin-Harvey, who was one of the early supporters of the scheme for the establishment of a national theatre, was knighted in 1921, and received the honorary degree of LL.D. from the university of Glasgow in 1938. He died at East Sheen 14 May 1944. His *Autobiography* (1933) is a delightful record of all that went to the making of an abundantly fruitful life. In it he made no secret of his ungrudged homage to Irving and of his debt to his wife's faith and vision. His sister May (Mrs. Helmsley), who died in 1930, was leading lady to Sir John Hare. He had one son, and a daughter, Muriel, who went on the stage.

There are portraits of Martin-Harvey by Frank O. Salisbury as Richard III, by Harrington Mann as Sydney Carton, and by Arthur Hacker as Hamlet, all reproduced in the autobiography; a number of other portraits and drawings are in the possession of the family and a bust by Sir George Frampton is at Stratford on Avon.

[Sir John Martin-Harvey, *Autobiography*, 1933; *The Book of Martin Harvey*, compiled by R. N. Green-Armytage, 1932; *The Times*, 15 May 1944; *Who's Who in the Theatre*; private information; personal knowledge.]

S. R. LITTLEWOOD

*published 1959*

## MASON James Neville

(1909–1984)

Actor, was born 15 May 1909 at Huddersfield, the youngest of three sons (there were no daughters) of John Mason, a textile merchant of that town, and his wife, Mabel Hattersley, only daughter of J. Shaw Gaunt, also of the west riding of Yorkshire. He was educated at Marlborough College and Peterhouse, Cambridge, where he took a first in architecture in 1931. At Cambridge he discovered a taste for acting and the theatre. His performance as Flamineo in a Marlowe Society production of *The White Devil* by John Webster was well reviewed by the theatre critic of the London *Daily Telegraph*. Thus encouraged, he began to reconsider his decision to become an architect (he was skilful at drawing for the rest of his life). He was stage-struck, of course, but also shrewd about himself. He knew that he had a good voice, a true ear, and other graces of body and mind. He also knew that in acting, as in the other performing arts, a broad gulf divides the talented amateur from the employable professional. He believed, though, that he could bridge it. His interest in films was that of a young intellectual. The thought of working in them (except, possibly, as an avant-garde director) had not yet occurred to him.

He had no formal training as an actor, but served an older, informal kind of apprenticeship: that of answering advertisements in the *Stage*, of presenting himself for auditions, of living cheaply, of taking ill-paid jobs in provincial touring and repertory companies, of making friends in the theatre, of doing the best he could with unsuitable parts and of making the suitable ones seem better. He made his professional début at the Theatre Royal, Aldershot, in 1931 playing the Grand Duke Maritzi in a play called *The Rascal*. Two years later he made his first London appearance in *Gallows Glorious* at the Arts Theatre. Between 1934 and 1937 he continued his stage education with the Old Vic Company and at the Gate Theatre, Dublin. He played his first film part in 1935. This was in *Late Extra*, a low-budget 'quickie' of the kind then being made by the dozen in England to enable film exhibitors to comply with the Quota Act.

He played in more quota films and in doing so began to identify and acquire the special skills needed to act effectively for the camera. He also made new friends, among them Roy Kellino, a cameraman turned director, and his wife Pamela. She was the daughter of Isidore Ostrer who, with his brothers, then controlled half the British film industry, including the Gaumont-British cinemas and the Shepherd's Bush and Islington studios. He was not, however, an indulgent father. When, in 1937, Mason and the Kellinos decided to make a film of their own, using their own pooled savings and a script written by the three of them, they were unable to get it properly distributed. *I Met a Murderer* (1939) was an intelligent little crime thriller and well received by the better critics, but the Ostrers were reluctant to exhibit in their cinemas a British film that had not been made in their studios. Mason returned to the stage to repair his fortunes and was in rehearsal for the BBC at Alexandra Palace when television production was halted there in August 1939.

He had an eventful but confusing war. He was estranged from his family who disapproved of his living with Mrs Kellino, not yet divorced. His attempt to register as a conscientious objector was frustrated by a tribunal which directed him to non-combatant military service. His appeals against this ruling, however, became in the end irrelevant. After he and Pamela were married in 1941, he found that work in the film industry had been declared of national importance. As long as he worked in films his call-up would be deferred and he would remain a civilian. He had worked his way through some very bad films when, at the Islington studios of Gainsborough Pictures, he played the wicked Lord Rohan of *The Man in Grey* (1943). It was the first of a series of costume melodramas which had a phenomenal popular success. *Fanny by Gaslight* (1944), *They Were Sisters* (1944), and *The Wicked Lady* (1945, with Margaret Lockwood) followed. In 1944 he was polled by the New York *Motion Picture Herald* as

Britain's top box-office star. The following year he appeared, with Ann Todd, in *The Seventh Veil*, the film that introduced him to American audiences. *Odd Man Out* (1946, directed by (Sir) Carol Reed), an exceptionally good film made shortly after the war ended, established Mason as a fine actor as well as a star. In less than four years he had become what Hollywood then called 'a hot property'.

In post-war England the problems of managing a success of that sort were unfamiliar; and, perhaps inevitably, the solutions were decided upon by the property himself, assisted by his wife. Determined at that time to produce films as well as act in them, he proceeded to dissipate much of his potential influence as a star by writing newspaper articles and open letters denigrating the British film industry in general (lacking in glamour, third-rate) and J. Arthur (later Lord) Rank, by then its major proprietor, in particular. He made other mistakes. In deciding which of his Hollywood suitors to accept, he used his own judgement rather than his agent's. As a result he spent most of his first year in America preoccupied with an expensive lawsuit. He won the suit, but not all the costs of it. He needed work and was glad to play in two minor Hollywood films directed by Max Ophüls. It was his successful portrayal of a German field-marshal in *Rommel, Desert Fox* (1951) that re-established him as a box-office attraction, and his Brutus in the 1953 film version of *Julius Caesar* reminded the public of his qualities as an actor.

In his fifty years as a screen actor he appeared in over a hundred films. Those of his middle years were perhaps the best. His fine performance in George Cukor's version of *A Star is Born* (1954) brought him an Oscar nomination; his portrait of a middle-aged man infatuated with a teenage girl in the film of Vladimir Nabokov's *Lolita* (1962) was a triumph. He was remarkably versatile and could always make even a small part memorable. *Georgy Girl* (1966) and James Ivory's *Autobiography of a Princess* (1975) are examples.

His marriage to Pamela was dissolved in 1965, when he left Hollywood. They had a daughter, Portland, and a son, Morgan. In 1971 he married the Australian actress Clarissa Grace Kaye, daughter of Austin Knipe, racehorse training manager, of Sydney, Australia. There were no children of this marriage. The Masons settled in Corseaux/Vevey in Switzerland where they were near neighbours of Sir Charles Chaplin and his wife Oona. Corseaux was their base from which they travelled and went to work in other places. They took up bird-watching. Their favourite subjects were a family of crows which occupied the large pine on the lake side of their house. Mason died in hospital in Lausanne 27 July 1984.

[*The Times*, 28 July 1984; *Who's Who in the Theatre*, 14th edn., 1976; James Mason, *Before I Forget* (autobiography), 1981; Sheridan Morley, *Odd Man Out: James Mason*, 1989; Diana de Rosso (sister-in-law), *James Mason*, 1989; personal knowledge.]

ERIC AMBLER

*published 1990*

## MATTHEWS Alfred Edward

(1869–1960)

Actor, was born at Bridlington, Yorkshire, 22 November 1869, the son of William Matthews and his wife, Alice Mary Long. His father was one of the Matthews brothers of the original Christy Minstrels and his great-uncle was the famous clown, Thomas Matthews, who had been a pupil of Grimaldi. He was educated at Stamford, Lincolnshire. Thereafter, according to his own story (of which he had plenty), he proceeded to an office-boy's desk in London on which were carved the initials 'J.H.B'. which he was told were those of (Sir) Henry Irving whose original name was Brodribb. Inspired by this coincidence he got himself a job as a call-boy. He soon rose, via stage management and understudy, to touring actor and, in 1889, he toured South Africa with Lionel Brough. In 1893–6 he toured Australia and then returned to the west end of London in a long list of plays. In 1910 he made his first trip to New York and played Algernon Moncrieffe in *The Importance of being Earnest*. By then 'Matty' was in great demand at home and overseas, among his authors being Pinero, Galsworthy, and Barrie.

After the war one finds him taking over from such players as (Sir) Gerald du Maurier (in *Bulldog Drummond*, 1921, New York and London), Owen Nares, or Ronald Squire. Yet, at all times, like other actors in his constellation who employed initials rather than their Christian names, his star, though minor, was truefixed and constant, only waiting for the opportunity to show it had no fellow in its chosen firmament. It had to wait another twenty years. Meanwhile, however, in the twenty-five years after 1918, he was in a further thirty different plays.

In 1947, in his seventy-eighth year, Matty at last became a great star in his own right, in the line of Sir Charles Hawtrey and du Maurier—the part the Earl of Lister, the play *The Chiltern Hundreds*, the theatre the Vaudeville where he had once been call-boy. In 1949 he went to New York in the same play (renamed *Yes, M'Lord*) and then returned to make the film at Pinewood in his eightieth year. He was appointed O.B.E. in 1951, published *Matty*, his autobiography, in 1952, repeated his success as Lord Lister in a sequel to *The Chiltern Hundreds* in 1954, and went on acting in both films and plays. Aged ninety, indomitable to the last and working still, 'How do I do it?' he echoed an inquiring reporter, 'Easy! I look in the obituary column of *The Times* at breakfast and, if my name's not in it, I go off to the studio'.

Matty was a playwright's dream—the grand old man of the theatre without being remotely grand—the oldest actor acting with the youngest mind—the best-dressed member of the Garrick Club, even though he would travel by underground on a wet day in a deerstalker hat and a pyjama coat over his tweed suit and gumboots. He knew more about the technique of light comedy acting than any of his colleagues, yet, such was his spontaneity, he succeeded in giving the impression that he knew nothing at all. He was as selfish as any actor ever was but he was kindness personified. He was crochety but he had a heart of gold. He was unpredictable, easily bored, perhaps a shade close with the drinks, but he had as much charm as any man in any other walk of life and he loved beauty in women and animals and he encouraged youth.

He married first, in 1909, Caroline May, divorced wife of Richard Cave Chinn and daughter of James Blackwell. They had twin sons and a daughter. The marriage was dissolved and in 1940 he married Patricia Lilian, the divorced wife of William Robson Davies and daughter of Jeremiah O'Herlihy, solicitor.

Matthews died at Bushey Heath 25 July 1960.

[Private information; personal knowledge.]

William Douglas-Home

*published 1971*

## MATTHEWS Jessie Margaret

(1907–1981)

Actress, was born in Soho, London, 11 March 1907, the seventh of eleven surviving children of George Ernest Matthews, owner of a greengrocery stall in Berwick Street market, and his wife, Jane, daughter of Charles

Henry Townshend, a timber porter. She went to Pulteney Street School for Girls, Soho, and showed such promise as a dancer that her oldest sister, Rosie, arranged for her to be trained in classical ballet by Mme Elise Clerc. When Mme Clerc died suddenly, Rosie determinedly arranged for Jessie to train as a chorus girl with Miss Terry Freedman of Terry's Juveniles.

Jessie Matthews made her first London appearance in 1919 in *Bluebell in Fairyland* produced by (Sir) E. Seymour G. Hicks. Four years later she played in Irving Berlin's *Music Box Revue* presented by (Sir) Charles Cochran. In his book *I Had Almost Forgotten . . .* (1932) Cochran described her as 'an interesting looking child with big eyes, a funny little nose, clothes which seemed a bit too large for her, and a huge umbrella'.

At the age of sixteen she made her New York début in the chorus of *André Charlot's Revue of 1924*. Gertrude Lawrence was the leading lady in that show, and when she fell seriously ill with pneumonia in Toronto, Jessie Matthews took over her part.

She reached full star status in *The Charlot Show of 1926* when she danced in ballet numbers with Anton Dolin and in musical comedy items with Henry Lytton Jun. (Lord Alva Lytton, died 1965), son of (Sir) Henry Alfred Lytton, actor. She married Henry Lytton in 1926 but from the outset the marriage was a failure, and in 1929 it was dissolved. Meanwhile, Jessie Matthews had obtained a £25,000 contract from Cochran, and in 1927 she starred with John Robert Hale Monro ('Sonnie Hale') in *One Dam Thing After Another*, finding in him the perfect dancing partner. In the next year they appeared together in *This Year of Grace* by (Sir) Noël Coward, in which they sang Coward's romantic duet, 'A Room with a View'. The critics acclaimed her performance, which was followed by similar triumphs in Cole Porter's *Wake Up and Dream* (1929) and *Ever Green* (1930). She had now reached the peak of her theatrical career.

Sonnie Hale (died 1959), son of Robert Hale, actor, was married to Evelyn Laye, another highly successful actress. In 1930 they divorced, and Jessie Matthews received much unwelcome publicity as the woman responsible for the break-up of the marriage. Her own divorce had been finalized and in 1931 she and Hale married. In that year she made her first sound film, *Out of the Blue*, which was a failure, but her second, *There Goes the Bride* (1933), was a triumph, and led to her becoming Britain's first international film star. During the 1930s she starred in fourteen films, including *The Good Companions* (1933) opposite (Sir) John Gielgud, *Friday the Thirteenth* (1933) opposite (Sir) Ralph Richardson, and *Evergreen* (1934), all directed by Victor Saville.

During the filming of *Evergreen* Jessie Matthews had her first nervous breakdown; many, more serious, were to follow. In 1934 her first baby, a son, only lived four hours; the doctors advised the desolate mother to adopt a child, and early in 1935 she and her husband adopted a baby girl, Catherine. In 1936 there was another serious nervous breakdown. In spite of Jessie Matthews's spectacular successes she was always beset by feelings of insecurity; at the beginning of her autobiography, *Over My Shoulder* (1974), she wrote: 'All my life I had been frightened'. She was now directed by her husband in *Head Over Heels* (1937) and feared it would be a failure; but it made money. *Gangway* (1937) and *Sailing Along* (1938), however, were disappointments, and relations with Sonnie Hale were becoming more and more strained. Her only Hollywood film was *Forever and a Day* (1943).

The Hales returned to the stage in 1939 in their own musical production *I Can Take It*. Its provincial tour was a great success. It was due to open at the London Coliseum on 12 September 1939; war broke out on 3 September, and cancellation of the show meant financial disaster. In 1941 Jessie Matthews had an offer to appear on Broadway in *The Lady Comes Across*, and her husband urged her to accept. She reluctantly left him and Catherine, and set off alone for New York, but, before the show could open she was ill again and the play flopped. At the age of thirty-four her doctors predicted that her theatrical career was over. During her absence in America her husband was having an affair with Catherine's nurse, Mary Kelsey, and in 1942 he and his wife parted company; two years later they divorced.

Jessie Matthews resumed her stage career in the West End in Jerome Kern's *Wild Rose* (1942). While appearing in concerts with ENSA, she met Lieutenant (Richard) Brian Lewis, of the Queen's Royal Regiment, who was twelve years her junior; in 1945 they married. Brian Lewis was the son of Norman Percy Lewis, a schoolmaster, from West Hartlepool. Four months later Jessie Matthews had a stillborn son and her doctors warned her that another pregnancy would threaten her life. In 1948, after six years' absence, she reappeared on the London stage in *Maid to Measure*, followed in 1949 by the revue *Sauce Tartare*. She also appeared in *Pygmalion* (1950) and *Private Lives* (1954). She and Brian Lewis divorced in 1958.

She returned to films in *Tom Thumb* (1958), and demonstrated that she could still command an audience when she sang one of her well-known songs, 'Dancing on the Ceiling', in the 1960 *Night of One Hundred Stars*. By this time she had lost her sylphlike figure but not her charm. In 1963 the BBC invited her to take over the matronly role of Mrs Mary Dale in the radio serial *The Dales*. She played this part for the next six years. She also appeared frequently in television drama and returned to the stage in such plays as *The Killing of Sister George* (1971) and *Lady Windermere's Fan* (1978). In 1979 her one-woman show *Miss Jessie Matthews in Concert*, produced in Los Angeles, won the US Drama Critics award. Her last appearance was at the National Theatre, London, in *Night of One Hundred Stars* on 14 December 1980. She was appointed OBE in 1970. She died at Eastcote, Middlesex, 19 August 1981.

[*The Times*, 21 August 1981; Jessie Matthews and Muriel Burgess, *Over My Shoulder*, 1974; Michael Thornton, *Jessie Matthews*, 1974; David Shipman, *The Great Movie Stars: The Golden Years*, 1979; Jeffrey Richards, *The Age of the Dream Palace: Cinema and Society in Britain 1930–1939*, 1984.]

H. F. Oxbury

*published* 1990

## MAUGHAM William Somerset

(1874–1965)

Writer, was born in Paris, at the British Embassy, 25 January 1874, youngest of the four sons of Robert Ormond Maugham, solicitor and legal adviser to the embassy, by his wife, Edith Mary, daughter of Major Charles Snell, of the Indian Army. His grandfather, Robert Maugham, and his brother, Frederic (later Viscount) Maugham, were both eminent lawyers.

Maugham lived in France until he was ten, when his father died (his beloved mother having died two years earlier), and he was transported to the guardianship of his uncle, the Revd Henry MacDonald Maugham, vicar of Whitstable, Kent; he was educated at the King's School, Canterbury, and then at Heidelberg University, where he attended lectures for a year but did not take a degree. French was his first language, and during his later childhood he was a foreigner in his own country; he stammered, and he was unhappy both at school and in the vicarage. His escape was travel, which was to become a lifelong habit. At sixteen, on the suspicion that he had tuberculosis, he was sent for a time to Hyères on the Riviera. He read de Maupassant and became familiar with French authors. His uncle wanted him to go into the Church, but he had £150 from his father's estate, and in 1892 he enrolled as a medical student at St. Thomas's Hospital, London. He completed the course, but at the same time he continued to read omnivorously and to keep a writer's notebook. When he began to work in the wards he was 'exhilarated' by his contact with 'life in the raw', and in 1895 he was for three weeks an obstetric clerk in the slums of Lambeth, which he found 'absorbing'.

His first novel, *Liza of Lambeth*, was published in 1897; its vivid portrayal of low life gave it a mild *succès de scandale*, and Maugham, who later that year qualified MRCS, LRCP, was encouraged to abandon medicine for literature. He went to Spain, which was to become, after France, the country of his heart, and lodged in Seville. He read; he travelled; he wrote. After his return to England, he published further books without making any mark, although he attained a certain entrée into literary and social circles, where a lack of money humiliated him. In 1903 his first play, *A Man of Honour*, was performed by the Stage Society, but not until 1907, at the age of thirty-three, did he wake one morning to find himself, at last, famous. *Lady Frederick* had been mounted as a stopgap at the Court theatre, but its success was so sweeping that within a short time Maugham had four plays running simultaneously in the West End, and a sketch by (Sir) Bernard Partridge in *Punch* (24 June 1908) showed the shade of Shakespeare turning enviously from the playbills. From then onwards Maugham never looked back. His wit was sharp but rarely distressing; his plots abounded in amusing situations, his characters were usually drawn from the same class as his audiences and managed at once to satirize and delight their originals.

The theatre was never entirely to satisfy him. Although he attempted to use it as a platform for less amiable subjects, he was constrained by the exigencies of the managers and by his audiences' expectations. Yet by the mid twenties he was an acknowledged master of light, sometimes mordant comedy. He attempted serious themes with courage and assurance, but the public wanted to be amused. In 1933 he ceased writing plays altogether, but already as early as 1911 he had retired temporarily from the theatre to work on his long novel, *Of Human Bondage*. He was to correct the proofs under the admiring eyes of (Sir) Desmond MacCarthy in a small hotel at Malo, near Dunkirk; the two men were drivers in an ambulance unit for which they had volunteered at the outbreak of war in 1914. MacCarthy became one of the most vociferous of Maugham's literary advocates, but his voice was never wholly to prevail against those who regarded public success as evidence of vulgarity.

In 1915 Maugham was recruited into the Intelligence Department; his facility with languages made him a 'natural' for the work, and he was sent to Geneva where he posed with no great difficulty as a literary man. Willie Ashenden, his *alter ego* in many spy stories and novels, was born of this experience. In 1917 he was selected by Sir William Wiseman to go to Russia, where the overthrow of the Tsar threatened to lead to a Russian withdrawal from the war. He was to say later that he believed that, had he gone six months earlier, he might have averted the Bolshevik revolution and held Kerensky to the Allied cause. By the time Lenin came to power,

Maugham's health had temporarily failed, and after spending three months in a sanatorium he remained an invalid for the next two years.

The war years were also eventful in his literary and private life. In 1916 he married Gwendoline Maude Syrie Wellcome, daughter of the philanthropist Thomas John Barnardo, after being cited co-respondent in her divorce from (Sir) Henry Wellcome. Their liaison had existed for some years, but the marriage was not happy. By the time Maugham and his wife were again together for long enough to set up house, he had discovered a new interest: the East, which he first visited in the year of his marriage. Travelling in the company of a young American, Gerald Haxton, who became the companion of his middle years, he 'stepped off his pedestal', as he put it. So far as the British were concerned, Haxton was an undesirable alien; Maugham could not both live in England and retain his friendship. He went frequently on his travels, and in 1928 decided to live permanently in the south of France. His marriage had been dissolved the previous year; he and Syrie, who became a fashionable interior decorator, had one daughter, Elizabeth Mary ('Liza'), whose second husband was Lord John Hope (later Lord Glendevon).

*Of Human Bondage* was published in 1915. It was less noticed in wartime London than in New York, where Theodore Dreiser reviewed it with enthusiasm. It remains Maugham's most impressive literary work, and by the time of his death was said to have sold ten million copies. *The Moon and Sixpence* (1919), *The Painted Veil* (1925), and *Cakes and Ale* (an elegant piece of literary malice, 1930), followed and found a prompt public. Having quit the theatre, he discovered a fertile new field in the short story and was widely regarded as the supreme English exponent of both the magazine squib and the more elaborate *conte*.

At his home, the Villa Mauresque at St. Jean, Cap Ferrat, he entertained smart company with stylish generosity, although he himself ate sparsely of the lotus he offered others: he worked steadily. His prose style changed little; he prided himself on his plain speaking and lack of literary frills. He was never a modern: he neither favoured experiment nor disdained public success. His books sold hugely; one short story, *Rain* (1921), was filmed several times. No one denied his intelligence, but the more severe critics never conceded his importance. He affected indifference.

In 1940 he had to leave France in a coal boat: he was on the Nazi's wanted list. He went to America, where he lived quite modestly: although rich, he refused to be too much at his ease while England was in sore straits. In 1944 he published his last substantial novel, *The Razor's Edge*, in which he paid tribute to the ascetic mysticism he had encountered in India and of which he was more an admirer than a practitioner. He returned to France after the liberation and resumed life at the Villa Mauresque. Gerald

Haxton had died in America in 1944 and Alan Searle, a man of more reliable stamp, took his place as Maugham's private secretary.

During the twenty years which remained to him, Maugham established himself in many eyes as a cosmopolitan oracle. He had a talent for worldly moralizing, already displayed with concise elegance in *The Summing Up* (1938), and he now turned to the essay, although he continued to write short stories and historical novels. Some of the stories were filmed, with his usual success, and he himself appeared on the screen to provide introductions. He had become perhaps the most famous living English author, and claimed casually that sales of his books exceeded 64,000,000 copies; yet he was not a happy man. He was rather short, about five feet seven, and prognathous in appearance, with olive complexion and penetrating eyes. He was tortured by his stammer, and by the conviction that he was unloved. He was drawn to religion, although he affected sturdy agnosticism. He was very widely read, but claimed to be uneducated. His tongue was sharp and he could make enemies easily, yet he was capable of great courtesy, and his uncensorious scepticism brought comfort as well as diversion both to millions of readers and to private acquaintances. His conversation was urbane and he was a good listener no less than an amusing commentator. His old age was soured by public wrangles with his daughter and, in the regrettable memoir *Looking Back* (1962), with the ghost of his wife, who had died in 1955. However, he could be kind as well as caustic. He was a thoughtful correspondent and a generous private critic of unsolicited manuscripts. In 1947 he founded the Somerset Maugham Award, which gives young writers an opportunity to travel. He died in hospital in Nice 15 December 1965, and left a substantial legacy, including his books, to the King's School, Canterbury, where his ashes were interred, next to the library he had endowed.

He was appointed CH in 1954, and C.Lit. in 1961. He was a fellow of the Royal Society of Literature, a commander of the Legion of Honour, and an honorary D.Litt. of the universities of Oxford and Toulouse. On his eightieth birthday the Garrick Club gave a dinner in his honour; only Dickens, Thackeray, and Trollope had been similarly honoured.

There are many portraits of Maugham: Sir Gerald Kelly painted him about thirty times—for example, 1911, in the National Portrait Gallery; 1935, privately owned; and 1948, at the King's School, Canterbury; a bronze by (Sir) Jacob Epstein (1951, lent by the Tate Gallery) is in the National Portrait Gallery, where there is also a portrait by P. Steegman (1931). A drawing by Sir William Rothenstein is reproduced in *Contemporaries* (1937), while the best-known portrait, by Graham Sutherland (1949), is in the Tate Gallery. Others, by Marie Laurencin (1936), H. A. Freeth (1946), and Vasco Lazzolo (1953), are in private hands.

[W. Somerset Maugham, *The Summing Up*, 1938; *The Times*, 17 December 1965; Robin Maugham, *Somerset and All the Maughams*, 1966; Frederic Raphael, *Somerset Maugham and his World*, 1976; Richard B. Fisher, *Syrie Maugham*, 1979; personal knowledge.]

FREDERIC RAPHAEL

[Ted Morgan, *Maugham, a Biography*, 1980.]

*published 1981*

## MAVOR Osborne Henry

(1888–1951)

Better known as the playwright James Bridie, was born in Glasgow 3 January 1888, the eldest son of Henry Alexander Mavor, a man of many gifts who made a comfortable living as an engineer, and his wife, Janet Osborne. 'The houses in which the Mavors lived had an atmosphere of dignity and good manners and a smell of old books and ink'. So wrote O. H. Mavor in *One Way of Living* (1939), an autobiography which refuses, with charm and gaiety, to endow its subject with the importance he deserved. Educated at Glasgow Academy, he took advantage of the solid comfort in which he had grown up to spend nine or ten years at Glasgow University, ostensibly as a medical student, but more remarkably as a source of high spirits, light verse, ingenious ragging, and talkative and persistent friendships: one of his fellow students, and a friend until death, was Walter Elliot.

Having qualified in 1913 Mavor, like Elliot, joined the Royal Army Medical Corps and the war of 1914 with an enthusiasm typical of his generation. This enthusiasm somehow survived service in Flanders, was depressed in Mesopotamia, but revived in the romantic circumstances of the expedition which Major-General Dunsterville led from northern Persia to the Caspian shore of Russia. Some twenty years later, at the age of fifty-one, Mavor returned to the R.A.M.C. and a second war, and saw brief service in Norway. Although by then he had found his true vocation, it was not so exclusive as to despise a latent romanticism or reject an old-fashioned call to duty.

As a practitioner and teacher his medical career was respectable: he was a consulting physician to the Victoria Infirmary and for some time professor of medicine in the Anderson College of Glasgow. But the work for which he is known began, or had its public beginnings, in 1928, when he wrote a play called *The Sunlight Sonata* which bewildered a Glasgow audience and included in its *dramatis personae* Beelzebub, some ebullient Deadly Sins, and three starchy redeeming Graces. This was a romping prologue to the vigorous, imaginative, and wonderfully diversified *œuvre* of the next twenty years.

He wrote in all some forty plays, under the pseudonym James Bridie, and entered the great world of the theatre under the auspices of Sir Barry Jackson, who presented *The Switchback* in Birmingham in 1929 and at the Malvern Festival in 1931. *The Anatomist*, with Henry Ainley in the leading part, had a London production in the latter year, and Bridie was involved in an argument which was to becloud his reputation for the rest of his life. It was said—by James Agate the first time—and endlessly repeated, that he could not construct a last act. The accusation may not be logically maintained, for his last acts were always logical, but what may readily be admitted is that they did not always meet the expectation of critics or of an audience anticipating a conventional gesture of conclusion. The eponym of *The Anatomist* was Dr. Knox, the teacher of anatomy whose cadavers were supplied by Burke and Hare. In 1933 Bridie again found a subject for drama in his familiar medical world and wrote one of his best plays, *A Sleeping Clergyman*, in which, declaring that 'to make for righteousness is a biological necessity', he admitted his sanguine temperament and the stubborn remnant of a faith which his Calvinist forebears had bred in him. It was one of his private jokes to pretend that he kept the Calvinist belief; more certainly, an invaluable part of his heritage was his profound knowledge of the Bible.

His biblical plays—*Tobias and the Angel* (1930), *Jonah and the Whale* (1932), *Susannah and the Elders* (1937)—are the most delightful of his writings, instinct with wit, insight into character, and essential common sense; or, perhaps, uncommon understanding. They are, moreover, written with a gracious and fluent command of language, and his dialogue demonstrates to perfection how phrases may be carpentered to reveal the precise and necessary meaning of their words. He was a master of polite English, he was at home on the borderland of poetry, and he could make his Scotch characters talk as convincingly as did Sir Walter at his best.

As popular successes, *Mr. Bolfry* (1943), a brilliant and immensely comic sermon with Alastair Sim in the pulpit, and *Daphne Laureola* (1949), in which Dame Edith Evans played with entrancing virtuosity, were outstanding. A good play, *The Queen's Comedy*, was insufficiently rewarded at the Edinburgh Festival in 1950; *The Baikie Charivari* (1952), his last work, is admittedly difficult, and, unique in his *œuvre*, darkened by pessimism and anger; but Walter Elliot declared it to be Scotland's *Peer Gynt*.

Of Bridie's importance to Scotland, as well as to the Scottish theatre—which, indeed, hardly existed before his time, and has shown no great liveliness since his death—there is no doubt whatever. He was an innovator, and a creator of more than words and dramatic scenes: he created an *ambiance* of confidence, gaiety, and affection, and while he might describe his fellow man as 'a droll wee slug wi' the shifty e'e', he loved all life and welcomed all sorts and kinds of his fellow men for their comical and unexpected contributions to it. Although fundamentally serious, passionately devoted to the Citizens' Theatre which he established in Glasgow in 1943, and most patiently concerned with the improvement of young writers whom his work had inspired, Bridie never let solemnity darken his utterance or magnify his personality. He thought well of his work, but preferred to live in the relaxed and easy temper which his natural geniality prompted. Without protestation of virtue or inhibition of his fine talent for invective, he was essentially a good man, and the clarity, the fine manners, and the fun which pervade his writings were all reflections of his intrinsic charity.

Bridie himself was a man of no great physical attraction, but his appearance in maturity acquired a ponderous, craggy, and magnificent benignity. In compensation for his own plainness, he married in 1923 Rona Bremner, a girl of notable beauty, who had loved him all her life. They had two sons, one of whom, serving with the Lothians and Border Horse, was killed in France in 1944; the other, having qualified and practised in medicine, chose to exemplify the proverb *Bon chien chasse de race* by taking to the theatre and dramatic criticism.

Bridie was appointed C.B.E. in 1946 and died in Edinburgh 29 January 1951. In 1939 he received the honorary degree of LL.D. from Glasgow University where there is a bronze bust of him by Loris Rey. A watercolour self-portrait is in the possession of Mrs. Bannister; a terracotta by Benno Schotz belongs to the Arts Council, Scottish committee; an oil painting by Stanley Cursiter, showing Bridie in conversation with other Scottish authors (Edwin Muir, Neil Gunn, Eric Linklater) is in the Glasgow City Art Gallery.

[James Bridie, *Some Talk of Alexander*, 1926, and *One Way of Living*, 1939; Winifred Bannister, *James Bridie and his Theatre*, 1955; personal knowledge.]

ERIC LINKLATER

*published 1971*

## MILLAR Gertie

**(1879–1952)**

Actress, was born at Bradford 21 February 1879, of humble and obscure parentage. When still under fourteen she had an instantaneous success on her first public appearance in a Manchester pantomime, and thereafter she never looked back. Slender, tall, and remarkably graceful, Gertie made no pretence at rivalling the more massive and handsome beauties of the lyric stage. But her small and winning face sparkled with fun and her smile was enchanting and infectious. Her singing voice had a delicious squeak to it, and it was this combined with the champagne-like effect of her personality which led an Edwardian wag to bestow on her the nickname 'Bubble and Squeak'. Her histrionic ability did not range very widely beyond the sparkling (as in *Our Miss Gibbs*) and the demure (as in *The Quaker Girl*). These two musical comedies (1909–10) belong to her heyday, and both had lilting music by Lionel Monckton whom she married in 1902.

It was a halcyon time when ladies wore feather-boas and huge hats with osprey feathers, and when a dashing new game called diabolo was all the rage, and the world seemed to revolve in three-four time to the irresistible tunes of composers like Monckton and Ivan Caryll and Paul Rubens, or Leo Fall and Franz Lehar. *The Toreador* (1901) at the Gaiety (with music by Monckton and Caryll) began Gertie Millar's triumphant series, and the revival of *A Country Girl* at Daly's Theatre (the music wholly by Monckton) concluded it in the darkling autumn of 1914. She made some intermittent appearances thereafter in less successful plays and in variety. Most often her manager was the great George Edwardes; usually, although by no means always, the theatre was the Gaiety, and throughout the first half of the century she was regarded as the Gaiety Girl *par excellence*. Long afterwards ancient playgoers were still to be met who could hum her favourite ditties in *Our Miss Gibbs*: 'We never do that in Yorkshire' and 'I'm such a silly when the moon comes out'. In other of the shows she had an unfailing appeal when being sung to by the young men of the chorus in top hats, addressing her gallantly as 'Elsie from Chelsea', or 'Sweet Katie Connor—I dote upon her', or even, at the beginning of the war, as 'Sister Susie sewing shirts for soldiers'.

After Monckton's death in 1924, she married the second Earl of Dudley, a second happy marriage which lasted until his death in 1932. To the end of her life she was a keen first-nighter, and her appearance always caused a stir of acclaim in the crowd outside as well as in the foyer. In her last few years she might be supported by two walking-sticks or even be wheeled into the theatre in a chair. But she was enthusiastic for the theatre to the end of her charmed and charming life. She wrote no autobiography nor any books or articles of reminiscence.

Gertie Millar died at Chiddingfold in Surrey 25 April 1952. She had no children.

[Private information.]

ALAN DENT

*published* 1971

## MORECAMBE Eric

(1926–1984)

Actor and comedian, was born (John) Eric Bartholomew in Morecambe, Lancashire, 14 May 1926, the only child of George Bartholomew, a manual worker for the Morecambe and Heysham Corporation, and his wife, Sarah ('Sadie') Elizabeth Robinson. Educated at Euston Road Elementary School, he was prompted by his mother to leave school at thirteen and embark on the professional stage as a child act.

In 1940, as a result of winning one of the many juvenile talent contests then in vogue, Eric Bartholomew earned a place in a touring 'discovery' show, *Youth Takes a Bow*, presented by Bryan Michie under the emergent impresario Jack Hylton. Coincidentally, Ernie Wise (Ernest Wiseman) was a fellow juvenile already engaged on the show. In 1941 Sadie Bartholomew inspired the pair to form a double act (at the Empire Theatre, Liverpool), but it was to be some years before they adjusted their roles with Eric predominantly as the comedian. The war intervened and Eric was drafted as a 'Bevin Boy' in the mines; he was discharged unfit eleven months later. Upon Ernie's release from the Merchant Navy, the couple resumed their partnership in 1947 in *Lord George Sanger's Variety Circus*. Over the next five years, now billed as Morecambe (the name taken from Bartholomew's birthplace) and Wise, they gradually broke into radio and television.

The critics' response to their first television series, *Running Wild* (BBC, 1954), indicated that they had not yet discovered a winning combination. Soul-searching and experimentation filled their subsequent summer seasons and pantomimes. In 1958 they undertook a six-month variety tour of Australia. Upon their return, their act was purged of its brashness and relied more on subtlety.

They became regular guests on TV variety shows, being at their most effective on Val Parnell's *Sunday Night at the London Palladium*. They felt at home on the ATV commercial network. By this time Morecambe's burgeoning genius as a comedian was making a mark. The first period of the long-running *The Morecambe and Wise Show* ran uninterruptedly on ATV between 1961 and 1968 and undoubtedly established them as national favourities. Their writers, Sid Green and Dick Hills, stimulated by Morecambe's limitless range, were inexhaustibly inventive. The first of many distinguished awards came in 1963 when Morecambe and Wise were chosen by the Guild of TV Producers and Directors as Top Television Light Entertainment Personalities of the Year.

In 1968 Eric Morecambe suffered a major heart attack, but he recovered sufficiently to continue the outstanding run of *The Morecambe and Wise Show*, which had now moved to the BBC and was aided by its more opulent budgets and the new scriptwriter, Eddie Braben.

Meanwhile the pair had appeared many times on the *Ed Sullivan Show* in New York, and in several royal command performances. At Windsor, they were favourites at royal family Christmas parties. Their three films for the Rank Organization—*The Intelligence Men* (1964), *That Riviera Touch* (1965), and *The Magnificent Two* (1966)—made noble attempts to translate their comedy on to the large screen. In 1979 Morecambe had to undergo open-heart surgery. During his convalescing periods he turned author. *Mr Lonely*, a novel, was published in 1981. Then followed two children's books—*The Reluctant Vampire* (1982) and *The Vampire's Revenge* (1983), which were subsequently translated into several languages. *Eric Morecambe on Fishing* (his main hobby) was published posthumously.

Morecambe was a director of Luton Town Football Club from 1969, retiring in 1975 to become a vice-president. He served as president of the Lord's Taverners between 1976 and 1979. He actively supported the Variety Club's charities, the Stars Organization for Spastics, the Sport Aid Foundation, and (among others) the British Heart Foundation. In 1976 he was appointed OBE and in the same year became a freeman of the City of London. Lancaster University conferred upon him an honorary D.Litt. in 1977.

Morecambe's eyebrows arched over the upper rims of his spectacles like twin circumflexes of bewilderment and surprise; his chirpy head movements, like a sparrow's, showed him as always qui vive, while his baggy underlids hinted at the world-weariness and sadness of the clown. Apart from various running jokes, among them 'What d'you think of the show so far?' (audience: 'Rubbish!'), Morecambe did not cultivate catchphrases for the sake of them; although some of his stock comments—'There's no answer to that!', 'My buddy Ern with the short fat hairy legs', 'What do I think of it? *Not a lot . . .*'—and his habit in moments of endearment towards Wise of clapping both hands on his partner's cheeks, will evoke memories of his style.

Morecambe and Wise, like Laurel and Hardy and Hope and Crosby, gave the double act a new dimension, moulding the archetypal 'straight man and comic' into a more complex but totally believable human relationship, and shared their art of being able to involve mass audiences in an enormous sense of fun. Morecambe possessed a needle-sharp awareness of the comic potentialities of any situation, and a comedic flexibility which enabled him, more so even than past masters like Robb Wilton and Jimmy James, to rebound off any number of characters on stage and so widen the comedy impact. No comedian can achieve greatness however unless he embodies those endearing human weaknesses which are the essence of laughter. This Morecambe did in his classic roles with Wise, as the one whose unquenchable exuberance often caused embarrassment, whose performance never quite matched his self-proclaimed ability, and whose sharp wit was used to cover up his ignorance or as a Parthian shot to rescue his self-esteem. Later in life, he became more the nation's humorist, with prestigious people queuing up to be the buttress of his quips. Whatever the role, Eric Morecambe shared the talent of, for example, Will Fyfe and Gracie Fields, to inspire as much love and affection as laughter. By the time of his death he was a national institution.

In 1952 he married a dancer, Joan Dorothy, daughter of Harold Bartlett, a captain in the Royal Army Medical Corps. They had a son and a daughter of their own and they later adopted another son. Morecambe died from a heart attack 28 May 1984 in Cheltenham General Hospital, to which he had been taken after performing at the Roses Theatre, Tewkesbury.

[E. Morecambe and E. Wise, *Eric and Ernie*, 1973; Gary Morecambe (son), *Funny Man*, 1982; private information; personal knowledge.]

Dick Hills

*published 1990*

## NIVEN (James) David (Graham)

(1910–1983)

Actor and author, was born 1 March 1910 in Belgrave Mansions, London, though in his best-selling autobiographies he later followed the example of his own Hollywood studio publicists by listing the more romantic and picturesque birthplace of Kirriemuir in Scotland. He was the youngest of four children, two sons and two daughters, born to William Edward Graham Niven, a landowner, and his wife Henrietta Julia, daughter of Captain William Degacher, of the South Wales Borderers. At the outbreak of World War I, Niven's father enlisted in the Berkshire Yeomanry and was killed in action at Gallipoli on 21 August 1915, leaving a widow to bring up their children in somewhat reduced circumstances until she remarried, in 1917, (Sir) Thomas Platt (from 1922 Comyn-Platt), a businessman who contested, for the Conservative Party, Southport (1923) and Portsmouth Central (1929).

Niven neither knew his father well nor cared for his stepfather at all, his childhood being largely spent at a succession of preparatory boarding schools (from one of which, Heatherdown in Ascot, he was summarily expelled for stealing) and then at Stowe where he at last found in the pioneering headmaster J. F. Roxburgh the father figure he so lacked at home. It was at Roxburgh's urging that Niven was taken into the Royal Military College at Sandhurst in 1928, and his final school report on Niven was unusually prescient: 'Not clever, but useful to have around. He will be popular wherever he goes unless he gets into bad company which ought to be avoided because he does get on with everybody'.

It was while at Sandhurst that, in a college production of *The Speckled Band*, Niven made his first notable stage appearance, though there was as yet little indication of any desire to enter the acting profession. Instead he was dispatched from Sandhurst in 1929 into the Highland Light Infantry as a junior officer and stationed on Malta, which conspicuously lacked the social and night life to which he had now become accustomed as a young man about London. After several military pranks born of tedium had misfired, and his army future looked extremely bleak, he sent a telegram to his commanding officer in the summer of 1933 reading simply 'Request Permission Resign Commission', a request which was met with evident relief and almost indecent haste.

With no immediate job prospects in England, his mother recently deceased, and only a vague idea that he might perhaps quite like to be an actor, Niven set sail for Canada: he was just twenty-three and it seemed as good a place as any to start out on a new life. Within a matter of weeks he had travelled south to New York and found work as a whisky salesman before joining a dubious pony-racing syndicate in Atlantic City. From there he travelled on to Los Angeles and began to seek employment as an extra in minor westerns. His Hollywood fortunes distinctly improved when he formed a romantic attachment to Merle Oberon however, and by 1939 as a contract artist at the Goldwyn Studios he had made starring appearances in *The Charge of the Light Brigade* (1936), *The Prisoner of Zenda* (1937), *The Dawn Patrol* (1938), *Raffles* (1939), and *Wuthering Heights* (1939), among a dozen other and lesser films. His Hollywood image was that of the 'grin and tonic' man, a veneer actor who traded in a kind of jovial good fortune, that of the happy-go-lucky adventurer who once shared a beach house with Errol Flynn known locally as Cirrhosis-by-the-Sea on account of its constant stock of alcohol.

In truth, Niven was a considerably more serious, astute, and talented man, one whose behaviour at the declaration of World War II showed characteristic courage: abandoning a lucrative studio contract and a career which was at last successful, he was the first of the few English actors to return from California to enlist. He rejoined the army as a subaltern in the Rifle Brigade, was released to make three of his best films (*The First of the Few*, 1942, *The Way Ahead*, 1944, and *A Matter of Life and Death*, 1945), and returned to Hollywood in 1946 accompanied by his beloved first wife Primula Susan, whom he had married in 1940, and their two young sons, David and James. Primula was the daughter of Flight-Lieutenant William Hereward Charles Rollo, solicitor, grandson of the tenth Baron Rollo. Within a few weeks of the Nivens' arrival in California however, 'Primmie' was killed in a fall down a flight of cellar stairs, and although Niven was to marry again in 1948 (the Swedish model Hjördis Paulina Tersmeden, who survives him and with whom he adopted two daughters, Kristina and Fiona) a certain sadness was now discernible behind the clenched grin of the gentleman player.

Niven's post-war career as an actor was remarkably undistinguished, coinciding as it did with the collapse of the Hollywood Raj of expatriate British officers and gentlemen on screen. By 1951, however, with the publication of a first novel (*Round the Rugged Rocks*) Niven had discovered a second career as a writer, and in the 1970s he was to publish two anecdotal volumes of memoirs (*The Moon's a Balloon*, 1971, and *Bring on the Empty Horses*, 1975) which were the most successful ever written by an actor and ran into many millions of paperback reprints. Shortly before his death he also published a second novel (*Go Slowly, Come Back Quickly*, 1981) and had become a regular guest on British and American television chat shows where, as himself, he gave some of his best performances.

In 1958 Niven deservedly won an Oscar for *Separate Tables*, in which he played an army officer who invented a private life when his own proved unsatisfactory, a habit often endorsed by Niven himself in his autobiographies. His later films of note included *The Guns of Navarone* (1961), *Paper Tiger* (1974), and *Murder by Death* (1976), but during an author tour for his last novel in 1981 he was stricken by motor-neurone disease which condemned him to a lingering and painful death, one he approached with all the courage and good humour that were the hallmarks of his life. Niven died 27 July 1983 at his home in the Swiss village of Château d'Oex where he spent many of his later years skiing. He was buried there. There was a memorial service at St Martin-in-the-Fields in London attended by more than five thousand people.

[David Niven, *The Moon's a Balloon*, 1971, and *Bring on the Empty Horses*, 1975 (autobiographies); Sheridan Morley, *The Other Side of the Moon*, 1985 (biography); private information; personal knowledge.]

SHERIDAN MORLEY

*published 1990*

## NOVELLO Ivor

(1893–1951)

Actor-manager, dramatist, and composer, whose real name was David Ivor Davies, but who took the name of Ivor Novello by deed poll in 1927, was born in Cardiff 15 January 1893. He was the only son of David Davies, a rate collector for the municipality of Cardiff, and his wife, Clara Novello Davies, a well-known musician and teacher of music and singing, who won many international awards with her Welsh Ladies' Choir. Brought up in an atmosphere of music, he showed an early aptitude both as musician and singer. He was educated privately in Cardiff and Gloucester and then won a scholarship at Magdalen College School, Oxford, in the celebrated choir of which he became prominent as soloist; but after his voice broke he had no mature singing voice at all. He soon began to compose and evinced a great love for the theatre. In his early teens his first song was published. Called 'Spring of the Year' it was sung at the Royal Albert Hall with Novello as accompanist and attracted no attention whatever, but when in 1910 his song 'The Little Damozel' was sung there it scored a considerable success.

For a time Novello taught the piano in Cardiff but soon he joined his mother in London, spending all the time he could at the theatres, especially Daly's and the Gaiety, watching the musical productions of George Edwardes by which he afterwards set his standards. He would wait at stage doors for the autographs of players many of whom were later to appear under his own management. He wanted to go on the stage, but his mother disapproved and managed to prevent him from joining the chorus at Daly's. He continued to compose and Ada Crossley sang his setting of 'Oh God Our Help in Ages Past' at the Crystal Palace. Novello wrote some music for a Festival of Empire there and when this went to Canada and the United States he went with it. He spent some time in New York and there wrote and composed his first musical play, *The Fickle Jade*, which was never produced, although he used much of the music from it in subsequent successes. His mother now moved into a flat on the roof of the Strand Theatre—No. 11, Aldwych—which remained his home until he died there. Later he bought his beloved country house, 'Redroofs', at Littlewick Green, near Maidenhead.

When war broke out in 1914 Novello was twenty-one. In competition with his mother, he wrote a patriotic song, 'Keep the Homes Fires Burning', which was an immediate success when sung at a National Sunday League concert. It swept the country, made him a fortune, and rocketed him into fame. He had songs in revues and musical comedies, such as *See-Saw, Arlette*, and *Tabs*, and had his first chance to write a full score in 1916 for *Theodore and Co.* which was a big success at the Gaiety Theatre. In the meantime he had joined the Royal Naval Air Service, but he was no good as an airman and after two bad crashes was put on to clerical work at the Air Ministry. Demobilized in 1919 he again visited America. On the ship returning home he received a cable offering him, on the strength of a photograph, a part in the film *The Call of the Blood*. Almost at once this dark, handsome young man with the wonderful smile and exceptional profile became a star of the silent, as later of the talking, films. He made many, but his heart was firmly in the theatre. He had music in *Who's Hooper?* (1919), *A to Z* (1921), and other shows, and was successful with his second full-length score, *The Golden Moth*, at the Adelphi in 1921.

Novello's chance to appear on the stage came in the same year when he played a small part in *Deburau* at the Ambassadors' Theatre. The play failed, but he never looked back. Very soon crowds of admirers began to wait at the stage door for Ivor, as everybody called him, and nobody, with the possible exception of Lewis Waller in his prime, ever had such a tremendous or so devoted a following of fans. He made many more pictures and at the end of 1922 went to Hollywood for D. W. Griffith, the great film director; but he was using the films as a means to becoming an actor-manager. He achieved that ambition in 1924 when with Constance Collier he wrote *The Rat*, staged it himself at the Prince of Wales's Theatre, London, and played the lead. It was an immense success and they followed it with *Down Hill* at the Queen's Theatre in 1926. Novello also made acting successes in 1925 in revivals of *Old Heidelberg* at the Garrick Theatre and *Iris* at the Adelphi. He was now an established actor as well as dramatist. Between 1928 and his death in 1951 he wrote thirteen comedies, only four of which were not successful, and he played in the greater number of them himself. They included *The Truth Game, A Symphony in Two Flats, Fresh Fields, Proscenium, Murder in Mayfair, Full House, Comedienne*, and *We Proudly Present*. In 1936 he presented a very beautiful version of *The Happy Hypocrite* by (Sir) Max Beerbohm, dramatized by Clemence Dane, in which he played Lord George Hell.

In 1935 Novello undertook to supply the book and music for a musical play at the Theatre Royal, Drury Lane. He had not an idea when he accepted the offer, but the result was *Glamorous Night* which brought that famous theatre back into success and prestige. He wrote, devised, composed, and played in three more successes at Drury Lane: *Careless Rapture* (1936), *Crest of the Wave* (1937), and *The Dancing Years* (1939). He also played *Henry V* there (1938), composing the incidental music. He wrote and composed *Arc de Triomphe* produced at the Phoenix Theatre in 1943, but this was less successful than his other musical plays, chiefly because he did not appear in it himself. His plays, straight or musical, were always successes when he was in them.

*The Dancing Years*, brought back to the Adelphi Theatre in 1942, was the outstanding success of the war of 1939–45 and Novello's own popularity in it was undiminished after a month's absence in 1944 whilst he served a prison sentence for evading the petrol restrictions. Before the end of the war he had written and composed—and played in—*Perchance to Dream* which ran for over a thousand performances at the London Hippodrome. He followed this in 1949 with *King's Rhapsody* at the Palace Theatre which was in many ways his best work and in which he gave his best performance. Whilst it was running he wrote and composed *Gay's The Word* which proved a big success at the Saville Theatre. It was whilst playing in *King's Rhapsody* that early in the morning of 6 March 1951 he died very suddenly of thrombosis. He was unmarried.

Novello was a good and improving, although never a great, actor, and his complete understanding of the art of the theatre made him one of the notable figures of the British stage. He was a completely happy man and never happier than when working in the theatre which he loved so much. His success never turned his head or made him conceited; he took infinite pains to achieve it and was always grateful for it. He set himself a high standard and never fell below it. He was much beloved in and out of the theatre and tens of thousands of people attended his funeral, as a tribute to the man who had given them so much pleasure. As a composer he will always be remembered, for his works are in the national repertory of theatre music.

A bust of Novello by Clemence Dane stands in the Theatre Royal, Drury Lane.

[Peter Noble, *Ivor Novello*, 1951; W. Macqueen-Pope, *Ivor*, 1951; personal knowledge.]

W. MACQUEEN-POPE

*published 1971*

## O'CASEY Sean

**(1880–1964)**

Irish dramatist and author, was born in Dublin of Protestant parents 30 March 1880, the youngest of the five surviving children of Michael and Susanna Casey. His real name was John Casey, but he subsequently Gaelicized his name to Sean O'Cathasaigh and still later changed the surname to O'Casey. His father, who worked as a clerk for the Irish Church Mission, died when John was six; two brothers and a sister who were already approaching adulthood went their several ways. O'Casey with his mother and the remaining brother, who was able to provide but little financial support, lived in the poverty and squalor of tenement life.

O'Casey himself suffered from a painful eye disease which prevented any formal education; but by the age of fourteen he had taught himself to read. From then onwards he read voraciously. His inborn feeling for the splendour of language had been nourished from an early age by reading from the Bible. His bent for the theatre quickly showed itself: two authors in whose work he took special delight were, at their different levels, masters of stagecraft—Shakespeare and Dion Boucicault.

But self-education, though it may be intense and profound, is almost of necessity narrow—especially when it starts late and from illiteracy. Not for many years was O'Casey able to make use of his hard-earned culture to improve his way of life. Until he was thirty he worked as a casual labourer, often unemployed and further handicapped by poor health. Even when he did escape from drudgery, it was into the fervid atmosphere of Irish politics rather than the comparatively calm world of Irish literature. He was in turn a member of the Gaelic League, the Irish Republican Brotherhood, Jim Larkin's union, the Irish Citizen Army, and the Irish Socialist Party. But he was too independent to remain long in any movement. After 1916 he turned seriously to writing plays. Although the first three which he submitted to the Abbey Theatre were rejected, he received encouragement from Lady Gregory and W. B. Yeats. Not until he was forty-three was his first play staged; but it was quickly followed by others which made it clear that he was a writer of genius.

Genius was a word which came easily to commentators on O'Casey's command of language, once his career was fully launched. His prose had about it an amplitude and a poetic colour which set it apart from and above the drab realism which was the aim of most of his contemporaries; and while many faults of craftsmanship were laid to his charge as his career continued the special magic of his style was never, or very seldom, questioned.

This special quality was seen at its finest in his early plays about the Irish troubles produced at the Abbey Theatre, all written from his own personal experience, and in the six volumes of his magnificent autobiography (1939–54). But even in his least successful plays he showed this quality. He was still unmistakably a genius, but one who had somehow lost his way to the heights.

O'Casey's three Dublin plays established him as a great writer but destroyed him as a dramatist. While the first of them, *The Shadow of a Gunman* (1923), was packing the Abbey Theatre he was still working as a day labourer, mixing cement. After the success of his masterpiece, *Juno and the Paycock* (1924), he turned professional. But his next play *The Plough and the Stars* (1926), of which the setting was Dublin during the Easter rising of 1916 and the main characters non-combatants, gave great offence. When he was awarded the Hawthornden prize in 1926 for *Juno* he was invited to London and he determined to retreat to an exile in England which was to endure for the rest of his life.

An exile indeed it was, and continued to be. O'Casey never understood England, nor she O'Casey. Even the welcome which his Dublin plays received in London was based on a misapprehension. English audiences of the time had little patience with any dramatic dialogue which was not realistic, and they took O'Casey's lyric prose to be the authentic speech of Irish slum dwellers. Consequently when he turned later to more obvious fantasy the English public, expecting more realism, lost interest in his work.

O'Casey in his turn contributed strongly to this misunderstanding. After a perfunctory glance at the London theatre he decided that its aims were too trivial to be worth his attention. A man more worldly wise or less self-assured might have realized that London had much to teach him, both in the way of broader culture and a greater experience of stagecraft; but O'Casey, who had a theory that an artist should develop naturally along his own lines, saw no need for this. As a result, his lack of education remained always in his way.

For example, he had the idea, in itself brilliantly original and destined to be valuable in the hands of later generations, of using different styles of writing in the same play. But because he was not skilled in the various techniques he employed, such a play was foredoomed to failure. His anti-war play, *The Silver Tassie*, with its symbolic second act, was a case in point. Its rejection by the Abbey Theatre in 1928 gave rise to a public dispute between the author and Yeats. Produced in London at the Apollo (1929) it was praised by the critics for its originality, but it did not draw the public. *Within the Gates* (Royalty, 1934), written with a similar disregard of realism, was found incomprehensible by critics and public alike. It gave ample evidence of O'Casey's inability to adapt himself to his new surroundings. It was set in Hyde Park and the characters included a kind of chorus of down-and-outs. Yet there was not a hint of a London atmosphere in the whole composition. It was not surprising that this was the last of his plays to command an important production as a matter of course.

After that he had to fight a losing battle to obtain production of any kind at all, although *Red Roses for Me* was favourably received by the critics when it was produced at the Embassy in 1946. In 1938 O'Casey settled in Devon where he continued to write busily but it was as an increasingly frustrated, disappointed, and embittered man with his mind's eye always on the Ireland which had rejected, and continued to reject, him. For the Dublin International Theatre Festival of 1958 he was invited to provide a new play. But difficulties were made about its production and O'Casey withdrew the play (*The Drums of Father Ned*) and went on to withdraw all his plays from production in Dublin.

In 1927 O'Casey married Eileen Reynolds, an actress (as Eileen Carey) of Irish Roman Catholic parentage. They had two sons, the younger of whom died in 1957, and one daughter. O'Casey died in Torquay 18 September 1964.

The National Portrait Gallery has a drawing by Powys Evans.

[*The Times*, 21 September 1964; O'Casey's autobiography; David Krause, *Sean O'Casey, The Man and his Work*, 1960; Eileen O'Casey, *Sean*, 1971; private information; personal knowledge.]

W. A. Darlington

*published 1981*

## OLIVIER Laurence Kerr

(1907–1989)

*Baron Olivier*

Actor and director, was born in Dorking 22 May 1907, the second son and youngest of three children of the Revd Gerald Kerr Olivier, assistant priest at St Martin's church there, and his wife, Agnes Louise Crookenden. Educated at St Edward's School, Oxford, he showed precocious acting ability, which was recognized even by his clerically blinkered father, and made his stage début at the age of fifteen as Kate in a boys' performance of *The Taming of the Shrew* at the Shakespeare festival theatre, Stratford-upon-Avon. After leaving school, he won a scholarship to the Central School of Speech Training and Dramatic Art, founded by Elsie Fogerty, and went on to join the touring company run by Lena Ashwell and then (in 1927) the Birmingham repertory theatre, directed by (Sir) Barry Jackson.

His first years on the stage were marked by fierce ambition and energy, but no clear sense of direction. An outstandingly good-looking young actor, he was in some danger of falling into the matinée idol trap—as when, having created the role of Stanhope in the try-out of *Journey's End*, by R. C. Sherriff, he abandoned that fine play for the option of a short-lived lead in *Beau Geste* (1929). At the invitation of (Sir) Noël Coward (to whom he remained lastingly in thrall) he took the tailor's dummy role of Victor Prynne in *Private Lives* (1930–1). He also began uncertainly in Hollywood as a Ronald Colman look-alike; he was fired from the cast of *Queen Christina* in 1933 at the request of Greta Garbo.

After the failure of *Beau Geste* he went on to play five leading parts in under two years without ever achieving a decent run; an ominous experience for a young star in a hurry, though it forecast one of the greatest strengths of his maturity: the refusal ever to please the public by repeating himself. Late in his career, when he played James Tyrone in Eugene O'Neill's *Long Day's Journey into Night* (1971), there was a sense of personal horror in his portrait of a once hopeful young talent destroyed by years of profitable type-casting.

In Olivier's own view, the turning point in his career came with the 1934 production of *Queen of Scots*, by Gordon Daviot (the pseudonym of Elizabeth Mackintosh): a long forgotten play which, again, met with small success, but which marked the beginning of a group of lifelong professional friendships with, among others, George Devine, Glen Byam-Shaw, Gwen Ffrangçon-Davies, and, supremely, the show's director, (Sir) John Gielgud. Olivier the fiery egoist had discovered his need for a family, and with it his future course as a company-based classical actor. The first fruits of this discovery were bitter when—playing Romeo to Gielgud's Mercutio (1935)—he ran into opposition from the London critics, who did not like his verse speaking. The fact that he then turned a flop into a triumph by switching roles with Gielgud, did not really heal the wound.

Olivier described his duel with Gielgud as one between 'earth and air'. The two stars were, and remained, opposites. But it was not long before the public learned to value both; to relish Olivier's animal magnetism, physical daring, and power to spring surprises, as much as his conversion of speech into another form of action. He struggled to extract every ounce of dramatic meaning from the text, often driven into harsh sardonic resonance and shock inflections, and detonating isolated words. Following Gielgud (whose theatrical families kept breaking up), Olivier's other main partnership was with his friend from the Birmingham rep, (Sir) Ralph Richardson, with whom he played in two Old Vic seasons in the late 1930s—consolidating his Shakespearian position in a sequence of contrasted leading roles (Toby Belch, Henry V, Macbeth, Hamlet, Iago, and Coriolanus) before their reunion (with John P. Burrell) as directors of the postwar Old Vic company.

In the flush of his pre-war Shakespearian success, Olivier was wary of another summons from Hollywood. However, in 1939 he deigned to accept the role of Heathcliff in *Wuthering Heights*, and suffered a baptism of fire from his director, William Wyler, who criticized him unmercifully for his theatrically exaggerated style and patronizing attitude towards the art of film. Made ill by this treatment, Olivier endured it and emerged from the experience as a major star. 'Wyler', he later acknowledged, 'taught me how to act in movies; taught me respect for them; taught me how to be real'. It was another victory for naturalism; and an apprenticeship in film-making which swiftly led to mastery in the first and best of his own films: *Henry V* (1943–4), probably the first successful Shakespeare film ever made, at once for its cunning blend of picturesque artifice and point-blank realism, and for Olivier's outstanding performance, which long outlived its patriotic morale-boosting intentions.

Olivier had entered the war in 1941 with the intention of putting acting away for the duration, and qualified as a pilot in the Fleet Air Arm. An incompetent aeronaut, he destroyed five aircraft in seven weeks. He was seconded into propaganda entertainment by the Ministry of Information and saw no active service. On completing *Henry V*, he led the Old Vic company in 1944 from their bombed-out Waterloo Road house into temporary West End premises at the New theatre. The company flowered as never before. These were the years of Olivier's Richard III, Hotspur, and Lear; and the inspired double bill of *Oedipus*, and *The Critic* by R. B.

Sheridan, in which Olivier, as Puff, was whisked off, still talking, up to the flies. Coupled with Richardson's Falstaff (to Olivier's Shallow) and Peer Gynt (to which Olivier, in a supreme stroke of luxury casting, played the tiny part of the Button Moulder) these seasons formed a glorious chapter in the Old Vic's history. But neither that, nor the knighthood Olivier received in 1947, inhibited the theatre's governors (headed by Viscount Esher) from picking a moment in 1948 when Olivier was leading the troupe on a tour of Australia, to inform him that the directors' joint contract would not be renewed.

Indignantly repulsing Esher's subsequent offer to re-engage him as sole director, Olivier set up his own management at the St James's theatre for a mixed classical and modern repertory, in which he directed and co-starred with his wife, Vivien Leigh. These seasons included premières of plays by (Sir) Terence Rattigan and Christopher Fry, new work from Thornton Wilder and Tennessee Williams, and two Cleopatras from Vivien Leigh, with Olivier paying successive court to her as Shakespeare's Antony and G. B. Shaw's Caesar.

By this time, Olivier had reached the summit of his worldly ambitions. All his desires had been satisfied: as an actor, for whom audiences would queue all night, he was the undisputed monarch of the London stage; he had succeeded as a director and as a manager; unlike Gielgud and Richardson, he also had an international film career, known to a vast public who had never set foot in a theatre. He had made a fairy-tale marriage; his residence was a twelfth-century abbey including a home farm. But under the glittering public image he felt he had come to a stop; his work had again lost its sense of direction, and his private life was becoming a hostage to Vivien Leigh's increasing manic depression.

To repair the 'aching void' he made some random career changes: embarking on an unconvincing singing début in the film of *The Beggar's Opera* (1952), which at least forged an alliance with Peter Brook, with whom he again broke new Shakespearian ground in the 1955 Stratford production of *Titus Andronicus*; and directing and playing the title role in the film of Rattigan's *The Prince and the Showgirl* (1957), in which he was outshone by Marilyn Monroe. By that time he had already discovered the route to renewal in the English Stage Company's new play-writing revival at the Royal Court theatre, under his old friend George Devine. Unlike the other leading actors of his generation, Olivier took the plunge into the new wave and, to the dismay of some admirers, appeared as Archie Rice, the seedy bottom-line comedian in John Osborne's *The Entertainer* (1957), which became one of his favourite parts. He discarded his West End wardrobe with zest, swaggering on in a loud check suit, exchanging all the obligations of eminence for the free speech of the dregs of the profession.

'Don't clap too loud, lady', he leered out to the house; 'it's a very old building'. This was the time of the Suez crisis.

At the Royal Court (where he also played in Eugène Ionesco's *Rhinoceros*, 1960) he met the actress Joan Plowright, whom he married after divorcing Vivien Leigh. His attachment to the Court became crucial in 1963 when, after running the first seasons of the Chichester festival theatre, he achieved his ultimate professional goal as first director of the newly formed National Theatre, where he confirmed his alliance with the young generation by engaging Devine's protégés, John Dexter and William Gaskill, as his associate directors, and appointing the *Observer*'s campaigning critic Kenneth Tynan (formerly an arch foe) as his literary manager. Just as he transformed his stage physique from role to role, Olivier instinctively altered his public identity according to the mood of the times; and as head of the National Theatre he put off West End glamour and re-emerged in the likeness of a go-ahead bank manager, thoroughly at home in the new world of state subsidy and permanent companies. He was uniquely qualified for the job, as a natural leader who commanded the loyalty of the whole profession, and as an artist who had nothing more to prove.

There remained one unscaled Shakespearian peak, *Othello*, which he played (directed by Dexter) in 1964 in a final burst of incandescent sensuality. Otherwise, though he was a regular NT player in roles ranging from punishing leads like Edgar in August Strindberg's *The Dance of Death* (1967) to walk-on parts like the Jewish divorce lawyer in *Home and Beauty* (1969) by W. Somerset Maugham, his main energy went into creating an ensemble that could tackle any play in the world. The opening seasons were a surprise: plays by Harold Brighouse, Noël Coward, Henrik Ibsen, Georges Feydeau—works with nothing in common beyond the fact that almost every one of them brought the theatre another success and redefined the reputation of the playwright.

One criticism of the National Theatre—voiced, among others, by Olivier's former Old Vic colleague, Sir W. Tyrone Guthrie—was that the ensemble was failing to present Britain's leading actors. With the exception of Sir Michael Redgrave, no actor approaching Olivier's own rank became a member of the team; and Olivier unceremoniously sacked Redgrave and took over his role in Ibsen's *The Master Builder* (1965), mistaking the onset of Redgrave's Parkinson's disease for drunkenness. Possibly the criticism he received for importing Peter O'Toole over the heads of the regular troupe for the opening production of *Hamlet* (1963–4) made him shut his door against visiting stars. What he did achieve was a theatre that became a second home to its actors and which developed its own stars—including Colin Blakely, Derek Jacobi, Edward Petherbridge, Geraldine McEwan, and Joan Plowright.

Olivier's years at the National Theatre were wracked with troubles of which the general public knew little or nothing. His artistic associates' support for controversial work such as Frank Wedekind's *Spring Awakening* and Rolf Hochhuth's *Soldiers* brought him into collision with the governors and completely estranged him from their chairman, the first Viscount Chandos. For the first time in his career, Olivier also became plagued with stage fright and memory loss. He suffered five major illnesses—including thrombosis, cancer, and muscular dystrophy—and came through them by sheer force of will. But after appearing in Trevor Griffiths's *The Party* (1974)—delivering a twenty-minute speech as an old Glaswegian Trotskyite—his stage career was at an end. In the previous year, with mixed feelings, he handed over the directorship of the National Theatre to (Sir) Peter Hall, who led the company from the Old Vic theatre into its new South Bank premises.

In his remaining years Olivier had a busy film and television life, though (with a few exceptions, such as the roles of Dr Christian Szell in *Marathon Man*, 1976, and Loren Hardemann in *The Betsy*, 1978) his film work consisted of cameo parts which he took to support his new young family. He was more scrupulous when it came to television, and the last flowering of his talent can be seen in his performances of Lord Marchmain in the Granada adaptation of Evelyn Waugh's *Brideshead Revisited* (1981), the blind protagonist of John Mortimer's *A Voyage Round My Father* (1982), and a valedictory *King Lear* (1983). In his last decade he also published two books: *Confessions of an Actor* (1982) and *On Acting* (1986), both absorbingly informative but no guide to the man himself. As an author, as on stage, he disappeared into a role. He left behind a Dickensian gallery of characters, each one composed with the copious observation and imaginative investment of a novelist. Olivier did more to advance the art of acting than anyone since Sir Henry Irving, and just as Irving had become the English theatre's first knight, so Olivier, in 1970, became its first life peer. In 1981 he was admitted to the Order of Merit. He had honorary degrees from Tufts, Massachusetts (1946), Oxford (1957), Edinburgh (1964), London (1968), Manchester (1968), and Sussex (1978). He had numerous foreign awards and in 1979 was given an honorary Oscar.

In 1930 he married an actress, Jill Esmond (died 1990), daughter of Henry Vernon Esmond, whose original surname was Jack, actor and playwright; they had one son. The marriage was dissolved in 1940 and in the same year he married the actress Vivien Leigh (died 1967), daughter of Ernest Richard Hartley, exchange broker in Calcutta, and former wife of Herbert Leigh Holman, barrister. There were no children and the marriage was dissolved in 1961. In the same year he married the actress Joan Ann Plowright, daughter of William Ernest Plowright, editor of the local newspaper in

Brigg, Lincolnshire, and former wife of Roger Gage. They had one son and two daughters. He died 11 July 1989 at his home in Steyning, West Sussex.

[Laurence Olivier, *Confessions of an Actor*, 1982, and *On Acting*, 1986; Felix Barker, *Laurence Olivier*, 1984; Melvyn Bragg, *Laurence Olivier*, 1984; Donald Spoto, *Laurence Olivier*, 1991.]

IRVING WARDLE

*published 1996*

## ORTON John Kingsley (Joe)

### (1933–1967)

Playwright, was born in Leicester 1 January 1933, the eldest child in the family of two sons and two daughters of William Orton, gardener, and his wife, Elsie, machinist and charwoman. He was educated at Marriots Road Primary School; and after failing his eleven-plus examination took a secretarial course at Clark's College, Leicester. Bored by a series of office jobs, Orton became interested in amateur dramatics and in 1951 won a scholarship to RADA. Puckish and handsome, Orton did well enough at RADA to earn his diploma in 1953. But he did not enjoy it: 'I completely lost my confidence and my virginity. I was lost. I didn't have a very good time because I found that in the very first term that I wasn't learning anything'.

After a four-month stint at the Ipswich Repertory Company, Orton became disenchanted with acting. Too young and inadequate a performer to get major roles, he was also too ambitious and full of fun for the arid grind he discovered was the regimen of the repertory actor. Returning to London, he set his sights on a literary career. He was ill equipped for this task. The idea of writing was suggested by Kenneth Leith Halliwell (1926–67) whom Orton met at RADA and with whom he lived until his death. Halliwell was seven years Orton's senior and much better educated. He set about to transform Orton into his intellectual equal and constant companion. Orton was especially influenced by the writings of Ronald Firbank whom Halliwell also imitated. Together, between 1953 and 1962, they wrote a series of novels, none of which deserved to be published. The books included *The Silver Bucket* (1953), *The Mechanical Womb* (1955), *The Last Days of Sodom* (1955), and *The Boy Hairdresser* (1956). They lived a hermetic existence first at 161 West End Lane in West Hampstead, moving in 1959 to another bedsitter in Islington at 25 Noel Road. For a time they existed on Halliwell's small inheritance; but when that ran out they worked at odd jobs six months at a time to subsidize their writing.

By 1957 Orton had begun to write novels and plays on his own. He had no luck; but he had begun to identify in himself a great appetite for anarchy. 'Cleanse my heart, give the ability to rage correctly', prays Gombold, Orton's spokesman in *The Vision of Gombold Proval* (1961)—posthumously published as *Head to Toe* (1971). In the novel, Orton dreamed of a cauterizing verbal power which would create a 'seismic disturbance'. In his writing Orton had not found the right tone or target for his rage. But in public pranks he found another way of satisfying his hunger for vindictive triumph, and one in which the verbal and visual power of his plays were first planted. Under the pseudonym of Edna Welthorpe, he assumed a suburban attitude and wrote letters to a variety of institutions which goaded them into idiotic correspondence. (In later years, Edna Welthorpe would damn and praise Orton's plays in the letters columns of newspapers to stir up controversy.) In 1959 Orton also began to deface public library books by writing false blurbs in the jacket sleeves and pasting outrageous images on book jackets. The cut-up images were well done: concise, irreverent, and very funny. Orton admitted later that he was 'enraged that there were so many rubbishy novels and rubbishy books' in libraries. His prank was intended to shock. He and Halliwell would return the tampered books to the shelves and wait to see if they got a response. In 1962, they did. They were arrested and sent to prison for six months. Prison brought a saving detachment to Orton's writing and clarified his view of life. 'Before prison, I had been vaguely conscious of something rotten somewhere: prison crystallized this', Orton said.

In 1963, after a decade of total literary failure, Orton completed a radio play, *The Ruffian on the Stair*, which was accepted by the BBC and broadcast on 31 August 1964. Between 1964 and 1967 when he died, Joe Orton became a playwright of international reputation. His output was small but his impact was large. By 1967 the term 'Ortonesque' had worked its way into the English vocabulary, a shorthand adjective for scenes of macabre outrageousness. Orton wrote three first-class full-length plays: *Entertaining Mr. Sloane* (1963, produced in 1964), which (Sir) Terence Rattigan called the best first play he had ever seen; *Loot* (presented in 1965); and the posthumously produced *What the Butler Saw* (1967, produced in 1969). Orton wrote four one-act plays: *The Ruffian on the Stair* (1965, produced in 1966), *The Good and Faithful Servant* (1964, produced in 1967), *The Erpingham Camp* (1965, produced in 1966), and *Funeral Games* (1966, presented in 1968). Films were made of *Sloane* (1969) and *Loot* (1970), which also won the *Evening Standard* award for the best play of the year (1966). Orton wrote one original, but unproduced, film script, *Up Against It* (1967).

Orton's plays often scandalized audiences, but his wit made the outrage scintillating. He found people 'profoundly bad and irresistibly funny'. He was the first contemporary English playwright to transfer into art the clown's rambunctious sexual rapacity from the stage to the page. He aspired to corrupt an audience with pleasure. Orton's laughter bore out Nietzsche's dictum that 'he who writes in blood and aphorisms does not want to be read, he wants to be learned by heart'. Orton brought the epigram back to modern theatre to illuminate a violent world. 'It's life that defeats the Christian Church, she's always been well-equipped to deal with death' (*The Erpingham Camp*). 'All classes are criminal today. We live in an age of equality' (*Funeral Games*).

Orton searched for a way to marry terror and elation and found it in farce. In his hands, farce became a paradigm of the tumult of consciousness as well as of society. Orton fed his characters into farce's fun machine and made them bleed. He found a way of making laughter at once astonishing and serious. A voluptuary of fiasco, Orton's career ended as sensationally as it began. On 9 August 1967 he and Halliwell were found dead in their Islington flat. Halliwell, disturbed by the contrast between Orton's success and his own failure and by Orton's homosexual promiscuity, had battered in his friend's head with a hammer and taken his own life with an overdose of sleeping pills. Orton's death—laced as it was with the irony of his own fascination with the grotesque—had special public interest. No playwright in living memory had met a more gruesome end. It was a great loss to world drama. *The Times* obituary called Orton 'one of the sharpest stylists of the British new wave ... a consummate dialogue artist and a natural anarch'.

[John Lahr, *Prick Up Your Ears: The Biography of Joe Orton*, 1978; Orton's private diaries; *The Times*, 10 August 1967; private information.]

JOHN LAHR

*published 1981*

## PAYNE Ben Iden

**(1881–1976)**

Director and actor, was born at Newcastle upon Tyne 5 September 1881, the youngest in the family of two sons and two daughters of the Revd Alfred Payne, a Unitarian minister, and his wife, Sarah Glover. He was educated privately and at Manchester Grammar School. He went into the theatre, making a début in November 1899 with the company of (Sir) F. R. (Frank) Benson—regarded then as the university of the theatre—at Worcester as Diggory in *She Stoops to Conquer*. During the following spring he had a few small parts with Benson in a London season at the Lyceum. He acted in various minor tours; and while he was at Waterford, in his mid-twenties, he met somebody he would describe later as 'a tall, dark man who looked, in his coal black suit and the dim light behind the scenery, so like a priest that for a moment I thought he was one'. This personage was the poet W. B. Yeats; it appeared that the actor-director A. Granville-Barker, impressed by Payne after one short talk in an ABC teashop, had recommended the thoughtful and intelligent young man to Yeats as stage director of the Abbey Theatre, Dublin. Payne was out of key there; but presently he met the wealthy theatre-minded philanthropist, Miss A. E. F. Horniman, who was dissatisfied with events in Dublin where, a critic said, she had been 'acting as fairy godmother to the singularly ungrateful Cinderella' of the Abbey; she and Lady Gregory had been antipathetic. Liking Iden Payne, she engaged him to advise on her further theatrical activities; he told her that Manchester, civilized in the arts, should be her centre, and when he was twenty-six, wise beyond his years, he inaugurated the English repertory movement—at first, during the autumn of 1907, in an oblong ballroom known as the Midland Hotel Theatre.

Soon, at Easter 1908, the company moved to the old Gaiety Theatre, before long to be reconstructed without any concession to more flamboyant tastes: no gilt, no flock wallpaper, neither brass nor drums in the orchestra. Payne's tastes, which matched those of Miss Horniman, were for a quiet, gentle austerity that he would not lose during the rest of his long career. The first Gaiety production was *Measure for Measure*, directed by a single-minded puritan zealot, William Poel, whose work for Shakespeare, with its insistence on fluidity of action, influenced Payne all his life. The Gaiety company was remarkable; it would include, at various times, (Dame) Sybil Thorndike, (Sir) Lewis Casson, Mona Limerick, Herbert Lomas, Ada King, and the young Basil Dean. After four years of tireless, unassuming endeavour during which he encouraged a regional school of dramatists and gave to Manchester an uncommon run of major plays, he left to tour and to originate seasons elsewhere, with his first wife, the actress Mona Limerick, a much more forceful figure than the calm idealist Payne, though he did have an idealist's persistence. In the autumn of 1913 he went to America where he directed at Chicago and Philadelphia and where most of his later life would be spent.

As general producer to Charles Frohman's company in New York (1917–22), he directed a wide variety of plays; with his experience he was able to take on anything and face the frustrations of the commercial Broadway stage, but his heart was always with the intellectual drama and particularly with Shakespeare. Later he held a number of academic appointments and acted two or three times (Henry Straker in *Man and Superman* by G. B. Shaw in Newport, Rhode Island, 1932, was the last); he still thought of himself as primarily an actor. His special reputation was as visiting professor (1919–28) at the Carnegie Institute of Technology in Pittsburgh (the 'Carnegie Tech'), which had the first American university drama department.

Payne was particularly delighted when Sir Archibald Flower invited him to succeed W. Bridges-Adams as director of what was then the new Shakespeare Memorial Theatre in Stratford-upon-Avon, opened only three years before. He was there for eight years from 1935 (when he began with *Antony and Cleopatra*), a disappointing period in a theatre unkind to his methods and to his use of modified Elizabethan staging, with its penthouse, various acting areas, and 'curtain-boys'. Relinquishing his post in 1942, in 1943 he gratefully returned to the United States. He became head of drama at several American universities; his work, now largely Shakespearian, was almost entirely so from 1946. He was appointed guest professor of drama at the University of Texas; a new 500-seat theatre there was named after him in 1976, only a month before his death. One production, *Hobson's Choice* (1953) would be a wistful memory of the 'Manchester school'.

As innovator and teacher (his great gift) he was always warmly respected, though his name—for he believed modesty to be the best policy—was never as potent as it should have been in the wider world of the theatre. E. Martin Browne, the English director, who for some time in the late 1920s was his assistant at the 'Carnegie Tech', called him a professional to the bone, 'slight and smallish, very agile, with a mobile face of great charm'. He was 'quite without the grand manner that his record in the theatre would have justified'. He had many theatrical awards and was honorary LL D of the University of Alberta, Canada (1963).

Payne's first marriage in 1906, to Mary Charlotte Louise Gadney ('Mona Limerick') was dissolved in 1950. They had one son and two daughters, one of whom married (Sir) Donald Wolfit. In 1950 he married, secondly, Barbara Rankin Chiaroni who survived him. He died in Austin, Texas, 6 April 1976, at the age of ninety-four.

[Ben Iden Payne, *A Life in a Wooden O*, 1977; E. Martin Browne, with Henzie Browne, *Two in One*, 1981; Sally Beauman, *The Royal Shakespeare Company: a History of Ten Decades*, 1982; *The Times*, 8 April 1976, 9 May 1977, and 2 April 1978; personal knowledge.]

J. C. TREWIN

*published* 1986

## PINERO Sir Arthur Wing

(1855–1934)

Playwright, was born in Islington 24 May 1855, the only son of John Daniel Pinero, a solicitor with a practice in London, who belonged to a family of Portuguese Jews—the name is said originally to have been Pinheiro—which had, however, been settled in England for several generations. His mother was Lucy Daines. Of his early life little is known. He left no records and seems to have left no relations, other than a stepdaughter, who died before this account of him was written. His education appears to have been scanty and spasmodic. Part of it was received at private schools and in evening classes at the Birkbeck Institute, but the more important part was obtained from the age of ten in his father's office where, following the example of his paternal ancestors in England, he bound himself to the law. The law, however, attracted him little. His bent was towards the stage, but as an actor, not as a playwright; and the fact that he studied elocution at the institute more assiduously than he studied any other subject indicates what his intentions were about his career.

When he was nineteen Pinero was engaged as 'a general utility man' by Mr. and Mrs. R. H. Wyndham, of the Edinburgh Stock Company, and made his first appearance at the Theatre Royal, Edinburgh, on 22 June 1874. His salary was a guinea a week. His next employment, in 1875, was at the Alexandra Theatre, Liverpool, under the management of Edward Saker, and here, while acting in *Miss Gwilt* by Wilkie Collins, he was confused by that author with another actor in the cast whom Collins admired. This mistake caused Pinero to be engaged for the London production of *Miss Gwilt* in 1876, and immediately afterwards he joined the Lyceum company on tour, playing Claudius to Henry Irving's Hamlet. He remained in this company, first under Mrs. S. F. Bateman and then under Irving, for more than five years. In 1881 he went to the Haymarket Theatre to join (Sir) Squire Bancroft and his wife. In 1884 he ceased to act. Acting, in spite of his love of it, was not his work. He was competent in small parts, exact and industrious, but devoid of the spirit and vivacity of mood which actors require. A dramatic critic in Birmingham said of his King in *Hamlet* that it 'was the worst Claudius the city has ever seen'. His failure did not depress him. He knew that he was the thwarted actor who becomes a playwright, and could console himself with the heartening thought that if he was a poor Claudius, the creator of Claudius had been a poor Ghost in the same play.

It was not until 1877, when he was twenty-two, that Pinero began to write plays. A one-act play, entitled *£200 a Year*, was produced as a 'benefit' performance in aid of Francis Henry Macklin at the Globe Theatre on 6 October 1877. This small and forgotten piece, which brought him a set of shirt-studs from Macklin, was the first of a remarkably long and diversified series of works which established their author as one of the most distinguished playwrights of his era. In fifty-five years he wrote fifty-four plays of every sort, beginning with 'one-acters' and including a few adaptations from the French, a comic opera, *The Beauty Stone* (written in 1898 in collaboration with Joseph Comyns Carr and with music by Sir Arthur Sullivan), and a mime, *Monica's Blue Boy* (with music by Sir F. H. Cowen, 1918). His productivity was not more remarkable than the variety and quality of the work thus rapidly composed. All his plays were written with superb technical skill. Some critics acclaimed him as the most accomplished craftsman of the English theatre since the time of Shakespeare, and held that that master alone could match and surpass him in construction, although Sheridan and Barrie were not far behind them. In sheer suspense, the bedroom scene in *The Gay Lord Quex* may be placed alongside of the trial scene in *The Merchant of Venice*, and the screen scene in *The School for Scandal*.

It was with farces that Pinero first attracted attention; and these farces were of a far finer and more intelligent type than was commonly found in farce at that time. The English theatre, after a great period in the eighteenth century, had fallen to a state so low that in the time of Macaulay a dramatist was regarded with contempt as a poor hack hired to throw mindless words together for undemanding audiences; and it was not until T. W. Robertson began to write his domestic comedies, of which *Caste* (1867) is the best known, that it raised its head again. Pinero's sense of Robertson's services to the English theatre is shown in his charming comedy, *Trelawny of the 'Wells'* (1898), in which Robertson figures as Tom Wrench. The farces had immense vitality, a fact amply demonstrated in 1943, when *The Magistrate*, which was performed for the first time in 1885, was revived.

Pinero's mind, however, now under the influence of Ibsen, was not likely to be limited to skilfully contrived farces; and a play called *The Profligate*, with (Sir) Johnston Forbes-Robertson in the principal part, which was produced by (Sir) John Hare at the Garrick Theatre on 24 April 1889, revealed a dramatist more gravely concerned than was the author of *The Magistrate*. Its end was sorrowful: the repentant profligate committed suicide; and this was an end which the public would not tolerate. Pinero, much against his will, made the ending happy. The public was not sentimentally foolish in demanding that Renshaw should dash the cup of poison from his lips: it showed a true instinct in its estimate of Renshaw's character. But, right or wrong, the fact that a different Pinero had arrived in the theatre was now plain; and this Pinero steadily rose in stature and esteem. The first performance of *The Second Mrs. Tanqueray* at the St. James's Theatre on 27 May 1893, when Pinero was thirty-eight, established his renown beyond a shadow of doubt; and it also established the renown of an actress, Mrs. Patrick Campbell, until that night unknown. Pinero, whose eye for a player was uncommonly shrewd, found her. This play, which started the vogue of 'problem plays', extended Pinero's reputation far beyond his own country. It had faults which were acidly noted down, but it was serious and adult, and it was written with high skill and sincerity. The plays which followed it, notably *The Notorious Mrs. Ebbsmith* (1895), *The Gay Lord Quex* (1899), *Iris* (1901), *Letty* (1903), *His House in Order* (1906), and *Mid-Channel* (1909), were nearly all works of gravity; and one of them, *His House in Order*, showed his craftsmanship at its highest. Among his last plays, *The Enchanted Cottage*, produced at the Duke of York's Theatre on 1 March 1922, was a charming and most tender comedy, in which his kindliness and humanity were abundantly revealed. Thirty of the plays (from 1891 to 1930) were published in twenty-nine volumes, of which the first eleven contain introductions by Malcolm Charles Salaman.

Pinero's dialogue was sometimes stilted, and his mind did not move easily among ideas. He had none of the grace of Barrie, nor any of the wit and audacity of Mr. Bernard Shaw. But within the convention which he followed his dialogue was serviceable, and his sense of situation and his skill in contrivance enabled him to use it very effectively. He was the first English dramatist to cast plays to type: that is to say, to employ actors and actresses because they were physically and intellectually suitable to the parts which they performed. He was opposed to the fashion of his time of expecting a player to be capable of performing almost any part. His experience as 'a general utility man' had cured him of that illusion. His star set as that of Mr. Shaw rose, but it will rise again, although not, perhaps, as high as once it did.

A portrait of Pinero by Joseph Mordecai (1891) is in the National Portrait Gallery. A sketch by Phil May is reproduced in Mr. Hamilton Fyfe's book, and there is a bust in the Garrick Club. A cartoon by 'Bulbo' appeared in *Vanity Fair* 1 February 1906. His appearance was extraordinary. Except for very heavy, black eyebrows, he was almost hairless; his features were sharp, but not in the least Hebraic. All his movements were slow and deliberate, not as of a man naturally lethargic, but as of one whose mind has been well made up in advance of action. He was courteous and kind and without long resentment or any rancour, but he was ruthless in casting a play and would discard actors or actresses without the slightest compunction if he thought them unsuitable to their parts. He was not content to take the second best or to manage with what was at once available, preferring to wait until he could obtain the best. Stoical virtues seemed to be highly developed in him, for he bore his prosperity with as much fortitude as his adversity. If he felt his decline from popularity, he did not show his feeling, nor did he permit himself to become envious of those who displaced him. Shaw dislodged him from his pinnacle, but in spite of some wounding things Shaw had said, Pinero's friendship for Shaw deepened as the two men grew older.

Pinero was knighted in 1909. He died in London 23 November 1934. He married in 1883 Myra Emily Wood (an actress under the name of Myra Holme), daughter of Beaufoy A. Moore and widow of Captain John Angus Lushington Hamilton. She died in 1919, leaving, by her first husband, a daughter to whom Pinero was deeply attached.

[*The Times*, 24 November 1934; *Who's Who in the Theatre*; Clayton Hamilton, *The Social Plays of Sir Arthur Pinero*, 4 vols., 1917; Wilbur Dwight Dunkel, *Sir Arthur Pinero* (Chicago), 1941; H. Hamilton Fyfe, *Sir Arthur Pinero's Plays and Players* (written without Pinero's knowledge and inaccurate as to certain facts), 1930; personal knowledge.]

ST. JOHN ERVINE

*published 1949*

## PLAYFAIR Sir Nigel Ross

## (1874–1934)

Actor-manager, was born in London 1 July 1874, the younger son of the obstetric physician William Smoult Playfair, and nephew of Lyon Playfair, first Baron Playfair of St. Andrews, and Sir Robert Lambert Playfair. He was a second cousin of the actor Arthur Wyndham Playfair (1869–1918). His mother was Emily, daughter of James Kitson, of Elmete Hall, Yorkshire, and sister of James Kitson, first Baron Airedale. He was educated at Harrow and at University College, Oxford, where he at once found his feet in the Oxford University Dramatic Society. He was called to the bar by the Inner Temple in 1900, but soon began to take part in the amateur productions of the 'Old Stagers' and the 'Windsor Strollers'. His first appearance on the professional stage was in 1902 at the Garrick Theatre in *A Pair of Knickerbockers*. For a short time he was a member of the Benson

Repertory Company with which he toured in the West Indies and where he specialized in farcical Shakespearian parts. In 1904 at the Royalty Theatre he acted Ralph in *The Knight of the Burning Pestle*, his favourite part. He produced the play at the Kingsway Theatre in 1920. In 1907 he was at His Majesty's Theatre, and four years later was given a leading part in H. G. Granville-Barker's production of Arthur Schnitzler's *Anatol*. Thereafter he was continuously engaged, notably as Sir Benjamin Backbite in *The School for Scandal* and as Cutler Walpole in *The Doctor's Dilemma* (1913). Although by this time he had achieved a sure position by reason of his very individual gift for dry but good-humoured comedy, dry as the driest sherry and as pungent in private life as on the stage; it was not until after the war of 1914–1918 that his real lifework may be said to have begun.

In 1918, together with Arnold Bennett and Alistair Tayler, Playfair formed a syndicate of three which purchased a long lease of the Lyric Theatre, Hammersmith, a derelict playhouse in what was then little more than a slum. Although situated within a stone's throw of an important traffic centre, this theatre seemed the last place in the world where high-class entertainment could possibly succeed. But in his choice Playfair proved well justified.

For its opening performance, in February 1919, the theatre was cleverly let to (Sir) Barry Jackson, who brought from the Birmingham Repertory Theatre *Abraham Lincoln* by John Drinkwater. Contrary to expectation this play ran for over a year, thus laying the trail for that long series of Playfair's own productions which were to make the Lyric Theatre, Hammersmith, a household word. The first of these productions was the famous revival in 1920 of *The Beggar's Opera*, decorated by Claud Lovat Fraser, which ran without a break for 1,463 performances. There followed *The Way of the World* and *The Duenna* (1924), *The Rivals* (1925), *Riverside Nights* (1926), *When Crummles Played* (1927), *She Stoops to Conquer* and *The Critic* (1928), and other plays of a similar type, a blend of eighteenth-century comedy and twentieth-century satire which was perfectly adapted to the taste of the time. Besides taking parts in many of these productions, Playfair gathered round him a company of young players, musicians, and stage designers who, under the inspiration of his genial leadership, made their own reputations as well as helping to make his. It was indeed a family party, the work of which had much of the impromptu charm of a family charade—but a charade with a difference, for nothing could exceed the neat finesse which characterized all Playfair's work as a producer. He combined scholarship with a native sense of 'style' which was something new in the theatre of those days, and his essentially personal contribution was fitly recognized by the knighthood which was conferred upon him in 1928. Still at the height of his powers, he died in London after a short illness 19 August 1934, and there closed a unique if brief episode in the history of the English stage.

In 1905 Playfair married Annie Mabel, daughter of Francis Thomas Platts, district superintendent of police, Dacca: she was an actress under the name of May Martyn. She made his home a centre of welcome to artistic people, young and old. They had three sons.

There is a portrait of Playfair in the part of Tony Lumpkin by Walter Sickert in the Tate Gallery, and a drawing by George Belcher was at Singapore when Mr. Giles Playfair left his belongings there during the war of 1939–1945.

[Sir Nigel Playfair, *The Story of the Lyric Theatre Hammersmith*, 1925, and *Hammersmith Hoy*, 1930; Giles Playfair, *My Father's Son*, 1937; *The Times*, 20 August 1934; *Who's Who in the Theatre*, 1933; personal knowledge.]

GEOFFREY A. WHITWORTH

*published* 1949

## POEL William

(1852–1934)

Actor, stage-director, and author, was born in London 22 July 1852, the third son of William Pole, engineer and musician, a friend and supporter of the pre-Raphaelites, by his wife, Matilda, daughter of Henry Gauntlett, vicar of Olney, and sister of the organist and composer H. J. Gauntlett. His father's interest in the pre-Raphaelites strongly influenced the boy, who was to bring kindred ideals to bear upon the stage. He was chosen by William Holman Hunt to pose for the well-known picture in the Birmingham Art Gallery of 'The Finding of the Saviour in the Temple'. At an early age young Pole decided to become an actor, changing his name to Poel for stage purposes on the suggestion of a misprint in an early programme. He joined the company of C. J. Mathews in 1876, went to Italy with Tomaso Salvini, and in 1881 began a lifework which was to revolutionize stage-production by presenting the first quarto *Hamlet* without scenery at the St. George's Hall, himself playing Hamlet to the Ophelia of Helen Maude, afterwards Lady Tree. In the same year he became manager of the Royal Victoria Hall, Waterloo Road, afterwards known as the Old Vic, and two years later joined (Sir) F. R. Benson as his first stage-manager. In 1895 Poel founded the Elizabethan Stage Society, an outgrowth of the Shakespeare Reading Society to which he had been instructor for eight years. He presented Elizabethan and other classics in the halls of City companies, the Inns of Court, and elsewhere, in conditions approximating to those of their original performance, without scenery. The plays could thus be acted in accordance with the text, instead of being transposed and cut for scenic purposes, as had become the habit in spectacular revivals. Poel also insisted upon rapid and clear speaking of blank verse, with varied emphasis.

Altogether Poel produced seventeen of Shakespeare's plays under these conditions, notably *Romeo and Juliet*, with a Romeo (Esmé Percy) of sixteen and a Juliet (Dorothy Minto) of fourteen, the right ages according to the text; *Troilus and Cressida*, with (Dame) Edith Evans as Cressida; *Twelfth Night*, presented, as in Shakespeare's day, at the Middle Temple hall; and *The Comedy of Errors* at Gray's Inn. Among other memorable revivals of his were Marlowe's *Dr. Faustus*, the anonymous *Arden of Feversham*, Ford's *The Broken Heart*, Milton's *Samson Agonistes*, the Book of Job in dramatic form, and Jonson's *Sejanus; His Fall*. At the Playhouse, Oxford, in 1924, he gave the first performance in England of *Fratricide Punished*, a translation of what is probably an early German version of *Hamlet*. In 1901, in association with (Sir) P. Ben Greet, he arranged the first modern production of the morality-play, *Everyman*, in the Charterhouse. He himself gave a remarkable grotesque study of the character of Death. This production brought new life to the old morality, which has been constantly presented ever since in all sorts of forms the world over. In 1909 Poel took over the part of Father Keegan in Mr. Bernard Shaw's *John Bull's Other Island*, lending to it a personal inspiration and dignity.

Apart from his work as actor and producer, Poel was the author of several plays, including *Priest or Painter*, adapted from William Dean Howell's novel, *A Foregone Conclusion*, and produced at the Olympic Theatre in 1884, and *Mehalah, or The Power of Will*, adapted from the novel by Sabine Baring-Gould and produced at the Gaiety Theatre two years afterwards (1886). In 1913 was published his *Shakespeare in the Theatre*, an invaluable exposition of his views both on the plays themselves and on their production. He published from time to time many pamphlets, notably *Prominent Points in the Life and Writings of Shakespeare* (1919), arranged in four tables, which originally appeared in the *Bulletin of the John Rylands Library, Manchester*.

Towards the close of his life Poel prepared a privately printed record of his productions, with inserted photographs and notes by himself, and presented it to twenty-five of his friends. Shortly before his death at Putney 13 December 1934 he was twice offered a knighthood, but declined it. His love for the theatre was entirely selfless. His initiative, imagination, learning, and kindly but strong personality never won in his lifetime the recognition which they deserved. He married in 1894 Ella Constance, eldest daughter of the Rev. Alfred Locock, and a devoted and understanding helpmeet. Their only child died some years before her father.

A portrait of Poel in the character of Father Keegan, by Henry Tonks, was presented to him by his friends on his eightieth birthday and is now in the National Portrait Gallery.

[W. Poel, *Notes on Some of William Poel's Stage Productions* (privately printed), 1933, and *Shakespeare in the Theatre*, 1913; *The Times*, 14 December 1934; personal knowledge.]

S. R. LITTLEWOOD

*published 1949*

## POWELL Michael Latham

(1905–1990)

Film director, was born 30 September 1905 in Bekesbourne, near Canterbury, Kent, the second son and younger child of Thomas William Powell, farmer, and his wife Mabel, daughter of Frederick Corbett, of Worcester. He was educated at King's School, Canterbury, where he was a King's scholar, and at Dulwich College. After joining the National Provincial Bank in 1922, Powell entered the film business in 1925 by joining Rex Ingram, a Hollywood director who was working at a studio in Nice, and Harry Lachman, a Chicago-born painter who secured employment for Powell with British International Pictures. In 1931 Powell formed Film Engineering with Jerry Jackson, an American lawyer, to produce 'quota quickies', British films given a market by the Cinematograph Act of 1927.

After a successful contract with Gaumont-British, Powell directed a personal project set on the island of Foula in the Shetlands, *Edge of the World* (1937), produced by the American Joe Rock. The film received good reviews and a cup for the best direction of a foreign film at the Venice film festival (1938). This led to a contract with (Sir) Alexander Korda, who facilitated Powell's first collaboration with screenwriter Emeric Pressburger on *The Spy in Black* (1939), the first of twenty-one films they made together, adopting a joint title in 1943, the 'Archers'. But before their partnership was more permanently forged Powell directed *The Lion Has Wings* (1939) and co-directed Korda's Technicolor *The Thief of Baghdad* (1940).

During World War II Powell and Pressburger produced some of their finest work, including *Forty Ninth Parallel* (1941), *One of Our Aircraft Is Missing* (1941), and *The Life and Death of Colonel Blimp* (1943), a film which was criticized by (Sir) Winston Churchill and the Ministry of Information for its satirical portrayal of the military. The films were imaginative, creative, cinematic, and rather unconventional. Whereas most British films were made with an intense style of realism, Powell and Pressburger used fantastical situations, dream sequences, bold colour, and disjointed narratives. The Archers broke new ground with *A Canterbury Tale* (1944), a lyrical meditation for the postwar world which suffered from studio cuts to render it more conventional. At the time Powell's films were considered to stray beyond the critical boundaries of British films usually associated with 'quality' and realism. Nevertheless, the Rank Organization gave the Archers a firm production base and considerable freedom in the development of their projects. Powell excelled at location shooting and had a particularly poetic response to landscape. At the end of the war he directed *I Know Where I'm Going* (1945) and his favourite film, the spectacular *A Matter of Life and Death* (1946), starring David Niven as a British pilot on the verge of death. It was an aesthetic experiment involving imaginative sets and innovative film techniques to represent the pilot's hallucinations. Powell's passion for experiment, risk taking, and creative use of colour influenced many film directors.

In a spirit of resourceful creativity *Black Narcissus* (1946) reproduced south India in a studio and *The Red Shoes* (1948) was an extravagant gamble. Rank allowed the Archers to produce a high budget film about ballet at a time when the British film industry was enjoying a brief period of protection against American film imports. Its excess stretched the limits of the relationship with Rank and ended the Archers' partnership with the studio until *The Battle of the River Plate* in 1956. From 1948 to 1955 Powell worked with Alexander Korda again on *The Small Back Room* (1949) and *The Tales of Hoffman* (1953), an experimental adaptation of Jacques Offenbach's opera. Powell's last film with Pressburger was *Ill Met by Moonlight* (1956). The Archers' partnership ended after a mutual distancing and several unsuccessful attempts to raise finance for film projects.

In 1959 Powell directed the controversial *Peeping Tom*, later widely regarded as a classic but at the time considered to be sadistic cheap horror. Its reception was so bad that Powell could get no further funding for his work and had to go to Australia in 1966 to make two films: *They're a Weird Mob* (1966) and *Age of Consent* (1969), the last feature film he was to direct. In the 1970s Powell's talent was fully recognized by critics and film-makers, especially Martin Scorsese and David Thomson, who encouraged him to move to America in 1980 to teach at Dartmouth College, New Hampshire.

In 1981 he became director in residence at Francis Ford Coppola's Zoetrope Hollywood studio, where he also worked on his boastful and vengeful autobiographies, *A Life in Movies* (1986) and *Million-Dollar Movie* (1992). Powell was remarkable for his liveliness, enthusiasm, and passion for both cinema and Rudyard Kipling. His physical appearance was distinctive: he had clear blue eyes, ruddy cheeks, and a moustache, and was bald from an early age. He loved the outdoors and always shot on location when possible.

In recognition of his work Powell received a number of awards, among them fellowship of the Royal Geographic Society; honorary doctorates from the universities of East Anglia (1978) and Kent (1984), and the Royal College of Art (1987); and the British Film Institute's special award in 1978 and a fellowship in 1983.

Powell was married three times. His first marriage was to an American dancer, 1927–36 (they were married in France and stayed together for three weeks only). In 1943 he married Frances, daughter of Dr Jeremiah Reidy JP, medical practitioner and mayor of Stepney in 1917–18. They had two sons. His wife died in 1983 and in 1984 Powell married film editor Thelma Schoonmaker, daughter of Bertram Schoonmaker, a clerical worker in the Standard Oil Company. Powell died of cancer 19 February 1990 in Avening, Gloucestershire.

[Ian Christie, *Arrows of Desire*, 1985; Michael Powell, *A Life in Movies*, 1986, and *Million-Dollar Movie*, 1992; private information.]

SARAH STREET

*published 1996*

## PRESSBURGER Emeric

(1902–1988)

Author and screenwriter, was born Imre Josef Pressburger at 3 St Peter's Street, Miskolc, Hungary, 5 December 1902, the only son (he had one elder half-sister from his father's previous marriage) of Kálmán Pressburger, estate manager, and his second wife, Kätherina Wichs. He went to a boarding school in Temesvar. He then studied mathematics and engineering at the universities of Prague and Stuttgart before his father's death forced him to abandon his studies. He moved to Berlin in 1926 to work as a journalist and writer of short stories and film scripts. Ufa, the major European film studio, employed Pressburger as a contract writer and his first screen credit was for *Abschied* (1930), co-written with Erich Kästner, novelist, and directed by Robert Siodmak. Pressburger was not listed on the credits for a screen adaptation of Kästner's *Emil and the Detectives* (1931), which was signed by Billy Wilder. One Pressburger script, *Monsieur Sans-Gêne* (1935) was remade in Hollywood as *One Rainy Afternoon*. He also worked with Max Ophuls and Reinhold Schünzel.

After collaborating on many scripts in Germany (where he changed his name to Emmerich) and France, Pressburger went to Britain in 1935, on a stateless passport, to work for fellow Hungarian (Sir) Alexander Korda, of London Film Productions. In England his name became Emeric. His first British assignment was *The Challenge* in 1938, the year he met Michael Powell, his director and collaborator for the next eighteen years. Their first joint projects were *The Spy in Black* (1939), an espionage thriller filmed at Denham Studios, starring Conrad Veidt and Valerie Hobson, and *Contraband* (1940). Pressburger's most successful work was with Michael Powell as the 'Archers' production company, which they formed in 1943, with its distinctive trademark of nine arrows thrusting into a target.

During World War II Pressburger's screenplays provided excellent scope for Powell's distinctive visual style, which employed colour in an imaginary way, fantasy and unreal spectacle, complex and challenging narrative structures, and flamboyant visual and camera devices. The films involved were *Forty Ninth Parallel* (1941), *One of Our Aircraft Is Missing* (1941), *The Silver Fleet* (1943), *The Life and Death of Colonel Blimp* (1943), based on the cartoon character created by David Low, *A Canterbury Tale* (1944), and *I Know Where I'm Going* (1945). Pressburger's ability to see Britain from the point of view of a fascinated outsider suited the films' quizzical perspective on British society and history. Now regarded as a classic in a mystical tradition, *A Canterbury Tale* was misunderstood at the time of release, initiating the Archers' reputation as film-makers who were ahead of their time, and whose work was characterized by wit, fantasy, ambition, and originality. The film celebrated British heritage and freedom, two themes that were extremely important to Pressburger.

After the war Pressburger (who was naturalized in 1946) experimented with time in *A Matter of Life and Death* (1946) and with a clash of communities and values in *Black Narcissus* (1946), about a group of nuns in the Himalayas. *The Red Shoes* (1948, based on a Hans Christian Andersen story), showed how Powell's visual sense of colour could be assisted by Pressburger's ambitious screenplay. This was followed by adaptations of challenging material for *The Tales of Hoffman* (1953, adapted from a Jacques Offenbach opera at the suggestion of Sir Thomas Beecham) and *Oh Rosalinda!* (1955, based on Johann Strauss's operetta *Die Fledermaus*). These films separated the Archers from the conventional canon of British film production, often to their cost, for puzzled critics dismissed their work as pretentious, extravagant, and confusing. In 1952 Pressburger directed for the only time, the film being *Twice Upon a Time*. *The Battle of the River Plate* (1956) was chosen for the Royal film performance in 1956. After their last Archer collaboration, *Ill Met by Moonlight* (1956), Powell and Pressburger parted. Their work was beginning to lose its experimental edge and both agreed to separate as their interests began to diverge.

Pressburger wrote and produced *Miracle in Soho* (1957) and published two novels, *Killing a Mouse on Sunday* (1961), on which was based Fred Zinnemann's film *Behold a Pale Horse* (1964), and *The Glass Pearls* (1966). He worked again with Powell in 1972 when they collaborated on a film for the Children's Film Foundation, *The Boy Who Turned Yellow*, and on a novel of *The Red Shoes* (1978). Pressburger more or less retired after this, but enjoyed the critical appreciation of his work encouraged by Martin Scorsese and Francis Ford Coppola. A key event in the reappraisal of the Archers' work was the showing of a restored print of *The Life and Death of Colonel Blimp* at the National Film Theatre in 1978. Michael Powell was always keen to stress that his skill as a director was stretched to the best advantage when Pressburger had written the screenplay. There was a mutual sense of trust between them and a joint desire to explore the boundaries of word and image. A keen gastronome, Pressburger loved French food. He had a great sense of humour and his physical appearance contrasted with that of Michael Powell. Pressburger was short, wore glasses, and had a sagacious, bird-like facial expression. He was a keen supporter of Arsenal football team.

Pressburger received the British Film Institute special award (with Powell) in 1978 and fellowships from BAFTA in 1981 and the BFI in 1983. *Forty Ninth Parallel* earned an Oscar (1942) for Pressburger for best original story. In 1938 Pressburger married Agnes, daughter of Andrew Anderson, factory owner. This marriage was dissolved in 1941 and in 1947 he married Gwynneth May Zillah ('Wendy'), former wife of Abraham Jacob Greenbaum ('Jack Green'), gambler, and daughter of Edward Orme, professional soldier. They had two daughters, one of whom died as a baby in 1948. The marriage was dissolved at Reno, Nevada, in 1953 and in Britain in 1971. Pressburger died of bronchial pneumonia 5 February 1988 in Saxstead, Suffolk.

[Ian Christie, *Arrows of Desire*, 1985; Michael Powell, *A Life in Movies*, 1986, and *Million-Dollar Movie*, 1992; Kevin MacDonald, *Emeric Pressburger*, 1994; private information.]

SARAH STREET

*published* 1996

# PRIESTLEY John Boynton

## (1894–1984)

Novelist, playwright, and essayist, was born 13 September 1894 at 34 Mannheim Road, Toller Lane, Bradford, the only child of Jonathan Priestley, schoolmaster and Baptist layman, and his wife, Emma Holt, who died when John was an infant. He was brought up by a stepmother, Amy Fletcher, 'who defied tradition by being always kind, gentle, loving'. He had one stepsister. He attended Belle Vue Grammar School, Bradford, but left at sixteen by his own choice, and worked as a junior clerk at the wool firm of Helm & Co. When G. B. Shaw later praised Stalin's Russia 'because you meet no ladies and gentlemen there', Priestley retorted: 'I spent the first twenty years of my life without meeting these ladies and gentlemen'. But he made the most of Bradford's two theatres, two music-halls, flourishing arts club, and vigorous musical life, as well as the Bradford Manner, 'a mixture of grumbling, irony and dry wit'. He sported Bohemian dress, including a jacket 'in a light chrome green', enjoyed an attic study, where he produced poetry and articles, had them typed by a professional, 'a saucy, dark lass' who was 'paid in kisses, for I had no money', and got a few printed in the local Labour weekly, the *Bradford Pioneer*, and even in *London Opinion*.

Priestley later portrayed his Bradford life as idyllic, asserting 'I belong at heart to the pre-1914 North Country', but at the time he was bored by it and when war came promptly enlisted in the Duke of Wellington's Regiment. He had two long spells in the Flanders front line, was wounded twice, commissioned in the Devon Regiment in 1918, and demobilized the following March. He always refused to be unduly impressed by any event, however momentous, and put his war experiences quietly behind him, never collecting his medals and declining to write about the war, except briefly in *Margin Released* (1962). But it left its mark. Half a century later, when a young guest told him she never ate bread at meals, he snorted: 'I can see *you* never served in the trenches'.

With an ex-serviceman's grant he went to Trinity Hall, Cambridge, where he refused to be enchanted by the atmosphere, let alone to acquire what he termed 'a private income accent', but did a vast amount of reading, laying the foundation for his later *tour de force, Literature and Western Man* (1960). He obtained a second class in English (1920) and a second in division I of part ii of the history tripos (1921). He also produced there his first volume of essays, *Brief Diversions* (1922), which brought him the patronage of (Sir) J. C. Squire at the *London Mercury*, reviewing from

Robert Lynd at the *Daily News*, and a job as reader for the Bodley Head. For the rest of the decade he led the life of a London literary journalist, producing reviews, articles, and books, including two novels, workmanlike biographies of George Meredith and Thomas Love Peacock for Macmillan's English Men of Letters series, and a little volume, *The English Comic Characters* (1925), which became a particular favourite of actors. Such work gave him a living but no leisure and in 1928 (Sir) Hugh Walpole, always eager to assist new talent, collaborated with him in a novel, *Farthing Hall* (1929), so that the advance Walpole's fame commanded would give Priestley the time to write the major picaresque story he was plotting.

*The Good Companions* was begun in January 1928 and its 250,000 words finished in March 1929. Heinemann's, who had daringly printed 10,000 copies, brought it out in July and by the end of August it had sold 7,500. Thereafter it gathered pace and, to the accompaniment of the Wall Street collapse, became one of the biggest sellers of the century. By Christmas the publishers were delivering 5,000 copies a day by van to the London bookshops. Priestley, typically, did not allow his head to be turned and privately pooh-poohed the merits of his warm-hearted tale of a travelling theatrical troupe. He thought his next novel, *Angel Pavement* (1930), set in London, much better. But *The Good Companions*, besides being twice filmed (1932 and 1956), was put on the stage in 1931, where it brought out the talents of the young (Sir) John Gielgud and opened up a new career for Priestley as a dramatist.

While not a natural novelist, always having difficulty with the narrative flow, Priestley was stimulated by any kind of technical challenge and the stage offered plenty. He dismissed his first West End play, *Dangerous Corner* (1932) as 'merely an ingenious box of tricks'. But James Agate, then the leading critic, called it 'a piece of sustained ingenuity of the highest technical accomplishment' and it began a decade of theatrical success. In 1937 three Priestley plays opened within a few weeks and for several years his earnings from the theatre alone exceeded £30,000. His were not, like Shaw's, literary plays, at their best when read, but solid pieces of theatrical machinery, dependent on stagecraft and timing, offering rich opportunity for actors. Priestley never turned success into formula: all his plays are different, many of them experimental. *Eden End* (1934) evokes pre-1914 nostalgia, *Time and the Conways* (1937) deals with the theories of J. W. Dunne, *I have Been Here Before* (1937) explores the philosophy of P. D. Ouspensky, *Music at Night* (1937) examines the psychological impact of sounds, *Johnson Over Jordan* (1939) probes life after death, and *When We Are Married* (1938) is mordant Yorkshire comedy.

Priestley's desire never to repeat himself was strength and weakness. 'I am too restless', he told Agate in 1935, 'too impatient, too prolific in ideas. I am one of the hit-or-miss school of artists'. He wrote quickly—his novel *The Doomsday Men* (1938) took only nineteen days—but whatever he did had to be new and this disappointed admirers anxious to typecast him as the provider of provincial warmth. He took a close interest in new media, producing screenplays, studying pre-war TV, and writing for the BBC, including a novel, *Let the People Sing* (1939), the first instalment of which was broadcast the day war was declared. Priestley had the instincts of an actor, and indeed would act whenever opportunity offered, though his face, which he described as 'a glowering pudding', limited his range. His voice was another matter: it combined unmistakable northern values with mesmeric clarity, 'rumbling but resonant, a voice from which it is difficult to escape', he wrote. In spring 1940, with Hitler triumphant, the BBC had the inspired idea of getting Priestley to broadcast brief 'Postscripts' after the main news bulletin on Sundays at 9 p.m., starting on 5 June and running till 20 October. Throughout that historic summer, his talks, combining light-hearted pleasure in things English with sombre confidence in final victory, and delivered with exceptional skill, formed the perfect counterpoint to the sonorous defiance of (Sir) Winston Churchill's broadcasts. They made him an international figure. Indeed they excited, he believed, Churchill's jealousy and when the BBC, in its mysterious way, dropped him, he thought the prime minister responsible, though it was more probably Conservative Central Office.

Priestley never belonged to a party, but he described his father as 'the man socialists have in mind when they write about socialism' and his own ideas were usually radical. His novels, like Emile Zola's, were often journalistic in choice of subject, taking a topical theme, and such wartime stories as *Black-out in Gretley* (1942) and *Three Men in New Suits* (1945) seemed to place him on the Left. Along with the *Daily Mirror* and the Left Book Club he was credited with the size of Labour's 1945 victory and in 1950 he even made an official Labour election broadcast. He contributed regular essays on current trends to the *New Statesman*, later collected as *Thoughts in the Wilderness* (1957), *The Moments* (1966), and *Outcries and Asides* (1974). But Priestley was incapable of acting in concert with a political group, or indeed any organization which valued 'sound men' (a favourite term of disapproval). He resigned in disgust from the British committee to Unesco and from the boards of both the National Theatre and the *New Statesman*. He contributed to the latter a remarkable article in 1957 which led directly to the Campaign for Nuclear Disarmament. But at a private meeting to plan it, an objection by Denis Healey MP, 'we must be realistic', evoked a characteristic Priestley explosion: 'All my life I have heard politicians tell us to be realistic and the result of all this realism has been two world wars and the prospect of a third'. He was briefly associated with the Aldermaston marches but left the movement when it became an arena for left-wing faction. 'Commitment' was a posture he despised.

Priestley liked to think of himself as a lazy man but there were very few days in his long life when he did not write something, usually in the morning. His output was prodigious in size and variety. In the 1940s he wrote two of his most striking plays, *An Inspector Calls* (1947) and *The Linden Tree* (1948); his post-war novels included *Lost Empires* (1965) and his own favourite, *The Image Men* (2 vols., 1968 and 1969), a sustained attack on the phenomenon he called Admass. He travelled constantly, and both painted (in gouache) and wrote about what he saw. *English Journey* (1934), recording light and shade during the Slump, was constantly revived and imitated, and became a classic; there is fine descriptive writing in his autobiographical works, *Midnight on the Desert* (1937) and *Rain upon Godshill* (1939), while *Trumpets over the Sea* (1968) records an American tour with the London Symphony Orchestra. In 1969–72 he produced a historical trilogy dealing with the period 1815–1910: *The Prince of Pleasure*, *The Edwardians*, and *Victoria's Heyday*. Above all, there were scores of essays, long and short, relaxed and serious. He always wrote clear, unaffected, pure English, but it is his essays which best display his literary skills.

Priestley never claimed genius, another word he despised, merely 'a hell of a lot of talent'. He fought a lifelong battle with the critical establishment: 'I was outside the fashionable literary movement even before I began'. He believed himself to be undervalued after 1945, having been overvalued before it, and often pointed out that his plays were more highly regarded abroad than in Britain. In fact from the 1970s onward they were revived with increasing frequency and success. His work brought substantial material rewards. While making a decisive shot at croquet (a game he relished), he once startled a guest by listing to him the formidable aggregate sums he had paid in income tax and surtax. In 1933 he bought Billingham Manor and estate, where a roof-top study gave him a panoramic view over the Isle of Wight; after the war he moved to an ample Regency house near Stratford-upon-Avon. There, in its splendid library, its bookshelves hiding a bar where he mixed formidable martinis, he would receive a constant stream of guests and interviewers, or switch on monumental gusts of stereophonic music and, when he thought no one was watching, conduct it. He turned down a knighthood and two offers of a peerage but accepted the OM in 1977 and a clutch of honorary degrees, 'as a chance to dress up'. He was never the 'Jolly Jack' of his popular image; rather, a shrewd, thoughtful, subtle, and sceptical seer, a great craftsman who put a good deal into life, and a discriminating hedonist who got a lot out of it. In old age he became a little deaf and forgetful but stayed fit and industrious almost to the end, pleased to have got excellent value from his annuities.

In 1919 Priestley married Emily ('Pat'), daughter of Eli Tempest, insurance agent. She died in 1925 after a long distressing illness, leaving him with two daughters. In 1926 he married Mary ('Jane'), the former wife of Dominic Bevan Wyndham Lewis, author, and daughter of David Holland, marine surveyor, of Cardiff. She already had a daughter, who was brought up in the Priestley household, and she and Priestley had a son and two daughters. The marriage ended in 1952 and, after a contested divorce which left him with an abiding dislike of lawyers, especially judges, in 1952 he married the archaeologist Jacquetta Hawkes, daughter of Sir Frederick Gowland Hopkins, biochemist, and former wife of Professor (Charles Francis) Christopher Hawkes, archaeologist, by whom she had one son. Priestley died at his home, Kissing Tree House, Alveston, 14 August 1984.

[John Braine, *J. B. Priestley*, 1978; Susan Cooper, *J. B. Priestley*, 1970; private information; personal knowledge.]

PAUL JOHNSON

*published 1990*

## QUAYLE Sir (John) Anthony

**(1913–1989)**

Actor and stage director, was born 7 September 1913 at 2 Delamere Road, Ainsdale, Southport, Lancashire, the only child of Arthur Quayle, solicitor, and his wife, Esther Kate Overton. The Quayle family had Manx roots. During a rather lonely youth Anthony's interest in the theatre was encouraged by his lively and imaginative mother. He was educated at Rugby and the Royal Academy of Dramatic Art, where he stayed only a year. His first appearance on the professional stage, unpaid, was in *The Ghost Train* at the Q theatre while on holiday from RADA. He began his career in earnest playing both Richard Cœur de Lion and Will Scarlett in *Robin Hood* at the same theatre in 1931.

The following year, after touring as feed to a music-hall comic, he found his feet in classical theatre and met two men whose influence was to be an important factor in his career, (Sir) Tyrone Guthrie and (Sir) John Gielgud. By 1939 he had appeared in many supporting roles, with Old Vic seasons in 1932 and 1937–8, had appeared in New York, and had played Laertes in the famous Guthrie production of *Hamlet* at Elsinore. Strongly drawn to the classics and especially to Shakespeare, he took over the lead from Laurence (later Baron) Olivier in *Henry V* during an Old Vic tour of Europe and Egypt just before World War II. Though not yet at the top of his profession, he was known and liked by many who were.

He spent the war in the Royal Artillery, reaching the rank of major. Characteristically, he gave up an administrative job in Gibraltar, learned to parachute, and joined Albanian partisans behind German lines. He later wrote two slight novels suggested by his wartime experiences.

After the war he returned to the stage and as Enobarbus in *Antony and Cleopatra* (1946) was a great success in the first of the many supporting roles he was to make his own. He also turned to directing, and in 1946 his *Crime and Punishment*, starring John Gielgud, was considered outstanding.

In 1948, through Guthrie, he joined the Shakespeare memorial theatre in Stratford-upon-Avon as actor and stage director. He was soon promoted to run the whole memorial theatre. In eight years he transformed it from an unfashionable provincial theatre to a world-famous centre of classical drama. Because of his many contacts, he was able to attract illustrious players and directors to Stratford, as well as encourage such major new talents as Richard Burton and (Sir) Peter Hall. He took companies on tours of Australasia in 1949 and 1953 and tried, although without success, to secure the kind of London shop window for the company which was later obtained by the Royal Shakespeare Company. With his 'Cycle of the Histories' for the Festival of Britain in 1951 he foreshadowed the later practice of staging Shakespeare's historical plays in chronological order. Among his own parts during these strenuous years were Henry VIII, Falstaff, and Othello. His work was not entirely confined to Stratford, but his enthusiastic leadership and hard work at the memorial theatre, proudly unsubsidized, put it on the map. He paved the way for the subsequent achievements of Peter Hall, Trevor Nunn, and the Royal Shakespeare Company.

In 1956 he resigned from Stratford and returned to mainstream theatre. For over twenty more years he continued to act and direct in the West End, having a steady if unspectacular career, occasionally taking the lead, as in *Tamburlaine* in 1956, but more often in highly praised supporting parts. He also appeared in over thirty films, most of them British, again in strong supporting roles. His portrayal of stiff-upper-lip Englishmen was much admired in films, especially in *The Battle of the River Plate* (1956), *The Guns of Navarone* (1961), and *Lawrence of Arabia* (1962). The first of his many television appearances was in 1961.

In 1978, at sixty-five, his career took a different course and he toured with the Prospect Theatre Company, playing leading roles in *The Rivals* and *King Lear*. The company closed, however, when its Arts Council subsidy was withdrawn. Several years later, in 1983, he formed his own Compass Theatre, which bravely stumped the country without subsidy, dedicated to bringing major plays to people who could otherwise never see them.

Quayle had a big physique, a vigorous personality, and a steadfast—even romantic—devotion to great plays and classical traditions. Despite his fine technique he had neither the personality nor the face for a great actor. As he grew older his face became more rugged but there was something about his amiable blue eyes which suggested a warm and pleasant person and deprived his acting of some of its emotional impact. However, as a man of great courage and integrity he was a natural leader and a major influence on the theatre in Britain.

He was appointed CBE in 1952 and knighted in 1985. He had honorary D.Litt. degrees from Hull (1987) and St Andrews (1989). He was guest professor of drama at the University of Tennessee in 1974, and was nominated for an Oscar as best supporting player for his performance as Cardinal Wolsey in the 1969 film about Anne Boleyn, *Anne of the Thousand Days*.

In 1935 he married Hermione (died 1983), actress daughter of actor Nicholas James Hannen, but the marriage was dissolved in 1943. In 1947 he married another actress, Dorothy Wardell, divorced wife of Robert Douglas Finlayson and daughter of another actress, Dorothy Dickson, and Carl Hyson, of independent means. They had a son and two daughters. He was still touring until two months before his death from cancer at his Chelsea home, 20 October 1989.

[*Daily Telegraph*, *The Times*, and *Independent*, 21 October 1989; Anthony Quayle, *A Time to Speak* (autobiography), 1990.]

RACHAEL LOW

*published 1996*

## RAMBERT Dame Marie

**(1888–1982)**

Ballet director and teacher, was born Cyvia Myriam Ramberg 20 February 1888 in Warsaw, Poland, the youngest of the three children, all daughters, of Yakov Ramberg, a bookseller of Jewish descent whose father's surname was Rambam, and his wife, Yevguenia Alapina. For a time she called herself Myriam Ramberg, but when she came to London she assumed the name by which she was thereafter to be known, Marie Rambert. She was educated at the Gymnasium in Warsaw, and in 1905 was sent to Paris with the intention of studying medicine. Instead she began to associate with the artistic world, attracting the attention of Raymond Duncan, brother of Isadora, with whose free style of dancing she first identified. Between 1909 and 1912 she worked in Geneva under Emile Jaques-Dalcroze, whose influence was central to her artistic development.

Towards the end of 1912 she was engaged by Serge Diaghilev to give classes in Dalcroze eurhythmics to the dancers of his Ballets Russes and more especially to assist Nijinsky in the difficult task of choreographing *Le Sacre du Printemps*. Shortly after that ballet's riotous première she accompanied the company on its visit to South America. From her association with the Diaghilev Ballet she received a lasting legacy: a profound interest in classical dance. Her engagement was not renewed when the company returned to Europe, and she went back to Paris, moving to London on the outbreak of war in 1914. There she met the playwright Ashley Dukes (died 1959), whom she married on 7 March 1918, and by whom she had two daughters. Dukes was the son of the Revd Edwin Joshua Dukes, Independent minister. Rambert became a British subject by this marriage. After the war she became an assiduous pupil of the celebrated ballet teacher, Enrico Cecchetti, and was soon teaching ballet on her own account, gathering around her, as time went by, students of exceptional promise, among them (Sir) Frederick Ashton, Harold Turner, and Pearl Argyle.

Such talented young dancers needed stage experience to fulfil themselves, and in the later 1920s Rambert began to supply this, first with the ballet, *A Tragedy of Fashion* (1926), which she persuaded Ashton to choreograph: it was his first ballet, and can now be seen as a historic landmark, from which a national ballet tradition was to spring. In the years that followed her students continued to make occasional appearances under the name of the 'Marie Rambert Dancers'. When Diaghilev died in 1929, there was a sudden dearth of ballet in London. In 1931, to fill the void, Rambert formed the Ballet Club with the object of forming a permanent ballet company with a theatre of its own. She even had a theatre—the minuscule Mercury Theatre near Notting Hill Gate, purchased by her and her husband out of their savings. It was to be the home of their ballet until 1939, and for many years housed their remarkable collection of historic ballet lithographs (now in the Theatre Museum).

Rambert possessed a unique gift for discovering and nurturing young choreographers, and Ashton, Antony Tudor, and Andrée Howard were all greatly in her debt for the cultural enrichment that she brought them. Under her inspired direction, Ballet Rambert (renamed thus in 1934) became part of the fabric of the growing English ballet tradition, although it was to fall to (Dame) Ninette de Valois' Vic-Wells Ballet to be chosen as the national company. Owing to the tiny dimensions of the Mercury Theatre, Ballet Rambert operated as 'chamber ballet', but the absence of spectacle was compensated for by exquisite taste and attention to detail. During World War II the company became larger and outgrew the Mercury. But it never lost its strong interpretative quality, and in 1946 Rambert herself staged a production of *Giselle* that was remarkable for its dramatic content.

Towards the end of her active life Rambert guided the steps of another budding choreographer, Norman Morrice, who succeeded her as director in 1966 and launched Ballet Rambert on a new course with greater emphasis on modern dance. Rambert's support of this bold move was an indication of her extraordinarily active and receptive mind. She enjoyed a long retirement and lived on to 12 June 1982, when she died at her London home in Campden Hill Gardens.

Considered as one of the architects of British ballet, she was appointed CBE in 1953 and DBE in 1962. In 1957 she became a chevalier of the Legion of Honour; she received the Royal Academy of Dancing's Queen Elizabeth II Coronation award in 1956. The University of Sussex awarded her an honorary D.Litt. in 1964.

She had inexhaustible energy (she could turn cartwheels until she was seventy), an infectious sense of fun, and a very retentive memory (displayed in reciting poetry by the page). Above all she gave inspiration to others, without which British ballet would today be much poorer.

[Mary Clarke, *Dancers of Mercury*, 1962; Marie Rambert, *Quicksilver*, 1972 (autobiography); Richard Buckle, *Nijinsky*, 1971, and *Diaghilev*, 1979; Clement Crisp and others (ed.), *Ballet Rambert: 50 Years and On*, 1981; Mary Clarke, obituary in *Dancing Times*, July 1982.]

IVOR GUEST

*published 1990*

## RATTIGAN Sir Terence Mervyn

(1911–1977)

Playwright, was born in Cornwall Gardens, Kensington, 10 June 1911, the second of two children, both sons, born to (William) Frank (Arthur) Rattigan and his wife, Vera Houston. His father, Frank, was the son of Sir

William Rattigan, at one time chief justice of the Punjab and, later, MP for North-East Lanark. Frank's career was less distinguished than his father's had been. He resigned from the Diplomatic Service in 1922 after a disagreement with the foreign secretary, the Marquess Curzon of Kedleston, over the best approach to the Chanak crisis. (Frank, who was assistant high commissioner at Constantinople, favoured intervention on behalf of Greece.) Thereafter the finances of the family were never soundly based.

Vera was seventeen when she married. She outlived her husband who, by all accounts, had a lifelong attachment to 'fluffy blondes' (his second son's expression) which may have steered that impressionable boy, not only into the arms of his mother but also, in true Freudian style, down less conventional emotional paths in later life. One of his mother's Houston relatives had, in 1863, given a public lecture, later published (Arthur Houston, 'The English Drama. Its Past History and Probable Future' in *The Afternoon Lectures on English Literature*, 1863), in which may be read the following prophetic passage: 'The highest type of dramatic composition is that which supplies us with studies of character, skilfully worked out, in a plot not deficient in probability, and by means of incidents not wanting in interest'. No truer definition of the future products of his relative, as yet unborn, is ever likely to be penned.

In 1920 Rattigan went to Sandroyd, a preparatory school near Cobham in Surrey. For one summer holiday his mother took a cottage, in which the bookshelves held nothing but plays, from a drama critic, Hugh Griffiths. Rattigan read them all and, as he said in later years, that holiday determined his career. In 1925 he won a scholarship to Harrow, thus relieving his now hard-up father from the onus of financing him. He wrote a one-act play in French, which the French master marked two out of ten, conceding that the 'theatre sense was first class'. He also wrote an article, in the *Harrovian*, on modern drama, in which he discussed 'the ceaseless conflict between Entertainment and Instruction'. Broadly speaking, the position he adopted in that article foreshadowed the stance he took, forty years on, in his battle with the New Guard drama critics, during which, in his own words, 'I had no chance with anything. They didn't give me reasons for it. They just said, "It must be bad"'.

At Harrow he played cricket for the school and took the Bourchier history prize. In 1930, having won a minor scholarship to Trinity College, he went up to Oxford. By now he was a fair-haired, charming youth, with one foot on the playing-fields, the other firmly planted in the Oxford University Dramatic Society. His father, whose ambition was that he should be a diplomat, sent him to France in his first long vacation. Rattigan came home with the idea for his first successful play already in his mind.

In 1932 he and a friend, Philip Heimann, collaborated in the writing of *First Episode*, produced in 1933 at the Q Theatre and transferred to the Comedy in 1934. This play, though adolescent in conception and, indeed, in plot—the scene was set in Oxford—earned mild praise from the reviewers (not excluding James Agate, of the *Sunday Times*). At once, the fledgling dramatist left Oxford with his father's grudging blessing and a small allowance from the same source.

In November 1936 the play he had conceived in France, *French Without Tears*, came on at the Criterion. From curtain-fall until the day of his death, forty-one years later, in the same month, Rattigan was famous and his name a household word. Unhappily, the path Rattigan trod, as an outstanding British dramatist, was not invariably strewn with roses. None the less, for more than twenty years in London and New York, his touch was golden. Audiences felt not only confidence but also fulfilment in his company.

*French Without Tears*, his greatest comedy success (in spite of Agate's strong aversion to it) was succeeded by another triumph. With *Flare Path* (1942), based on his RAF experience, he proved himself to be a good all-rounder, capable of writing with uncanny skill on any theme that took his fancy. He reverted to light comedy, in 1943, with *While the Sun Shines*; then—his war service concluded—he again took up more serious themes—*The Winslow Boy* (1946), *The Browning Version* (1948), *The Deep Blue Sea* (1952), and *Separate Tables* (1954). His screen-plays, too, were equally successful. Many of them were produced by Anatole de Grunwald and directed by Anthony Asquith, with both of whom he worked in total harmony.

In later life the quality of Rattigan's plays fell somewhat short of what it had been at its zenith. It was never less than adequate, however, and did not merit the hostile criticism it received. His obituary in *The Times* (1 December 1977) states: 'Rattigan's opponents, at an hour of theatrical rebellion, took every chance to belittle a probing storyteller'. Kenneth Tynan called him 'the Formosa of the British Theatre', asserting that he had betrayed the revolution (the New Wave) by staying with the Old Guard. None the less, although the argument around which this sad controversy raged was sterile from the start, it needled Rattigan beyond endurance and—unwisely—to the point of fighting back, thus provoking the New Wave with his constant references to his middle-class 'Aunt Edna'—a fictitious figure he invented—whose tastes, so he said, deserved as much attention as the avant-garde.

Rattigan was a homosexual and never married. He received a knighthood in 1971, having been appointed CBE in 1958. He came to England from Bermuda, for his last play *Cause Célèbre* (1977), aware that he was dying. '*Cause Célèbre*', wrote Bernard Levin, in the *Sunday Times*, 'betrays no sign of failing powers'. Its author died, back in Bermuda, 30 November 1977. *The Times* described him as an 'enduring influence in the English theatre'. Sir Harold Hobson, in the *Sunday Times*, wrote that 'he had the greatest natural talent for the stage of any man in this century'.

In a memoir for the *Sunday Telegraph* William Douglas-Home said: 'Consider *Separate Tables*. Here, most notably, in all the goings-on concerning an unhappy army officer, the many gifts bestowed on Rattigan by providence are on parade, his humour, his integrity—above all, his compassion. There is not one character who does not speak true. There is not one sentiment expressed which is not grounded in humanity, not one line that, in any way, diminishes the dignity of man. And, as for the compassion, that most Christian of all Christian virtues, it is there in such full measure that no member of the audience, unless his heart be made of stone, will go into the street at curtain-fall, without a lift in spirit and a fuller understanding of mankind as his companion. That is Rattigan's achievement and his triumph. That, so long as theatres exist and players strut their hour upon the stage and speak the dialogue he wrote for them, is his eternal monument.'

[Michael Darlow and Gillian Hodson, *Terence Rattigan. The Man and his Work*, 1979; personal knowledge.]

William Douglas-Home

*published 1986*

## REDGRAVE Sir Michael Scudamore

(1908–1985)

Actor, was born 20 March 1908 in theatrical lodgings at St Michael's Hill, Bristol, the only child of George Ellsworthy ('Roy') Redgrave, actor, a specialist in melodrama, and his second wife, Daisy (known later in the theatre as Margaret), actress, daughter of Fortunatus Augustin Scudamore, dramatist. Sixteen months after his birth his mother took him for a short time to Australia where his father was acting. Three years later his parents were divorced. In 1922 his mother, who looked after him, married J. P. Anderson, who had formerly been employed by the Ceylon and Eastern Agency in Ceylon. A half-sister, Peggy, was born.

Michael Redgrave went to Clifton College where he became a competent schoolboy player in male and female parts. His Macbeth, at seventeen, made his mother, who had been opposed to this, think twice about him becoming a professional actor. In 1927 he went to Magdalene College, Cambridge, where he undertook much undergraduate acting and wrote for and edited university magazines. He obtained second classes in both the German section of the medieval and modern languages tripos (part i, 1928) and the English tripos (part i, 1930); in 1931 he gained a third class in part ii of the English tripos. He then went to Cranleigh School, Surrey, as modern languages master. Here, in effect, he was an actor-manager, doing six productions and playing, among other parts, Samson Agonistes, Hamlet, and Lear; moreover he was given work in the semi-professional Guildford repertory company, which was glad to have a recruit so accomplished and personable: he was six feet three and strikingly handsome. Confidently he resigned from Cranleigh and got an audition from Lilian Baylis of the Old Vic, who offered him a contract at three pounds a week. Before deciding, he had an interview with William Armstrong, director of Liverpool Playhouse, who persuaded him to go there; between 1934 and 1936 he had a wide variety of parts in the most sympathetic circumstances.

More important to him, he fell in love with Rachel Kempson when they acted together in John van Druten's *The Flowers of the Forest*; two years his junior, she was the daughter of Eric William Edward Kempson, headmaster of the Royal Naval College at Dartmouth. They were married in the college chapel during the spring of 1935 and for another year remained at Liverpool. It was then that (Sir) Tyrone Guthrie, becoming one of the principal directors of his time, invited them for a season at the Old Vic where in September 1936 they opened as Ferdinand of Navarre and the Princess of France in *Love's Labour's Lost*. In 1936–7 Redgrave was Horner in *The Country Wife* (with the American actress, Ruth Gordon) and, to his delight, Orlando in *As You Like It* to the Rosalind of (Dame) Edith Evans, forty-eight then but, with her unerring sense of comedy, ready for the adventure. At once they were attracted to each other, an association they sustained during the Old Vic run and a transference for three months to what was then the New Theatre. Before then Redgrave had another rich experience, Laertes to Laurence (later Lord) Olivier's vigorous Hamlet. A daughter was born to Rachel in January 1937 and they named her Vanessa. They later had a son Corin (born 1939) and another daughter Lynn (born 1943). All became well known on the stage.

Even after so brief a time in London, it was clear that Redgrave would be an important player; recognizing this, (Sir) John Gielgud gave him several parts (including Tusenbach in *Three Sisters*) in a season at the Queen's Theatre (1937–8). Work came easily. When he played, surprisingly, Aguecheek during a West End *Twelfth Night* in 1938 the drama critic James

Agate called him 'a giddy, witty maypole'. At the Westminster in 1939 he was the first Harry Monchensey in *The Family Reunion* by T. S. Eliot, and he had also, inevitably but reluctantly, gone into films: (Sir) Alfred Hitchcock cast him in *The Lady Vanishes* (1939). With the outbreak of war he had to abandon an Old Vic opportunity; instead, during 1940, he was acting and singing Macheath in *The Beggar's Opera* at the Haymarket; later, at a small Kensington theatre and in the West End, he appeared most sensitively as the idealistic recluse of Robert Ardrey's *Thunder Rock*.

His call-up papers reached him in June 1941 in the middle of a film and he found himself, as an ordinary seaman, training in devastated Plymouth. Discharged after a year for medical reasons, he returned to the stage in a sequence of plays, some as successful as Turgenev's *A Month in the Country* (he was Rakitin in 1943) and an American melodrama, *Uncle Harry* (1944), in which he acted with exciting nervous power. Curiously in 1947 he appeared to be out of key in an elaborate production of *Macbeth*. Another good spell was coming: first, the relentless tragedy of Strindberg's *The Father* (1948–9), then a long season with the Old Vic company at the New (its final period before going back to Waterloo Road). Redgrave ended with Hamlet (1950), a performance which lacked only the final quality of excitement: as a disciple of Konstantin Stanislavsky he was apt to concentrate upon a close dissection of the text. Thence he went to Stratford-upon-Avon for a pair of remarkable performances, an intellectually searching Richard II (1951) in which he did not disguise the man's sexual ambiguity, and a Hotspur, grandly direct, with a precise Northumbrian accent. That summer he also played Prospero and the *Henry V* Chorus. In 1952, at the St James's, he was admirable in Clifford Odets's American drama, *Winter Journey*, though at the time there were awkward differences of opinion with a fellow actor. A good company man, Redgrave never hesitated to speak his mind. Meanwhile he gave an excellent performance in the film *The Browning Version* (1951).

During another Stratford year (1953) he had the unnerving trinity of Shylock, Lear, and the Antony of *Antony and Cleopatra*. As the triumvir at sunset Redgrave reached his Shakespearian height—(Dame) Peggy Ashcroft was Cleopatra—and the play had a London season at the Princes. Films, such as *The Dam Busters* (1954), continued to occupy much of his time. He returned in 1958 to Stratford—his last appearance there—and again, at fifty, acted as Hamlet, a performance mature and deeply considered. His final major work in the theatre was at the Chichester Festival of 1962 (as Uncle Vanya) and at the opening of the National Theatre in 1963, in the Old Vic, when he was an authoritative Claudius to the Hamlet of Peter O'Toole. The next year (1964) he was Solness in *The Master Builder*.

At the opening of the Yvonne Arnaud Theatre, Guildford, in May 1965 he returned to *A Month in the Country* which also had a West End showing. He had become a prodigiously popular film star in such productions as *Kipps* (1941) in which he played the title part, *The Way to the Stars* (1945), *The Importance of Being Earnest* (1952), and *The Quiet American* (1957); one of his last roles was General Wilson in *Oh What a Lovely War* in 1969. Illness was developing: he had Parkinson's disease and he kept to readings, on various international tours, during the ebb of his career. He made his last appearance in Simon Gray's *Close of Play* (National, 1979), a practically silent part during which he sat most of the night in a wheelchair. He died 21 March 1985 in a nursing home at Denham, Buckinghamshire.

Redgrave's publications include *The Actor's Ways and Means* (1953) and *Mask or Face* (1958), and a version of *The Aspern Papers* by Henry James, in which he acted, as 'H. J'., at the Queen's in 1959. He published in 1983 an autobiography, *In My Mind's Eye*. He was made a Commander of the Order of Dannebrog (1955) and a D.Litt. of Bristol in 1966. He was appointed CBE in 1952 and knighted in 1959.

[Rachel Kempson, *A Family and its Fortunes*, 1986; personal knowledge.]

J. C. Trewin

*published 1990*

## RICHARDSON Sir Ralph David

**(1902–1983)**

Actor, was born 19 December 1902, the third son and third and youngest child of Arthur Richardson, art master at Cheltenham Ladies' College, and his wife, Lydia Susie, daughter of John Russell, a captain in the merchant navy. When Richardson was four years old, his mother left his father and took him to live with her at Shoreham, Sussex, in a makeshift bungalow constructed out of two old railway carriages. Their allowance from her husband (with whom the two older boys remained) was two pounds and ten shillings a week, and on his own admission Richardson grew up as a 'mother's boy', educated by her at home and at the Xaverian College in Brighton, a seminary for those who intended to be priests from which he soon ran away.

His education thereafter was erratic, and by 1917 he was working as an office boy for the Liverpool and Victoria Insurance Company in Brighton. Two years later, when his grandmother died leaving him £500 in her will, he resigned immediately from the office and enrolled at the Brighton College of Art. Once there, he rapidly discovered that he had no gift for painting; instead, he briefly considered a career in journalism but then, inspired by a touring production of *Hamlet* which had come to Brighton with Sir F. B. (Frank) Benson in the title role, decided that his future lay in the theatre.

He joined a local semi-professional company run by Frank Growcott, who charged him ten shillings a week to learn about acting with the understanding that, once he had learned how to do it, Growcott would in turn pay him the same amount to appear in his company. Richardson seldom saw the colour of Growcott's money but he did make his first stage appearances at Brighton having already created some memorable off-stage sound effects ('I first burst on to the English stage as a bombshell'). He then auditioned successfully for Charles Doran's touring players, with whom he stayed for five seasons while rising through the ranks to such roles as Cassio in *Othello* and Mark Antony in *Julius Caesar*.

In 1924 Richardson married the seventeen-year-old student actress Muriel Bathia Hewitt, daughter of Alfred James Hewitt, a clerk in the Telegraph & Cable Company. They were to have no children. The following year the pair joined the Birmingham Repertory Company, and Richardson made his first London appearance for the Greek Play Society on 10 July 1926 as the Stranger in *Oedipus at Colonus*.

He spent the next four years largely in small West End roles, notably in two plays by Eden Phillpotts (*Yellow Sands* and *The Farmer's Wife*), and at the Royal Court where he spent much of 1928 in H. K. Ayliff's company, which also included a young Laurence (later Lord) Olivier. After touring South Africa in 1929, already aware that his young wife had contracted sleepy sickness (encephalitis lethargica), Richardson returned in 1930 to join the Old Vic Company where he met (Sir) John Gielgud for the first time. Of the three great actor knights of the mid-century (Richardson, Olivier, Gielgud), Richardson was the eldest and the least predictable, the one who looked most like a respectable bank manager possessed of magical powers, and the one who had the most trouble with Shakespeare: the critic James Agate said that his 1932 Iago 'could not hurt a fly' and Richardson soon turned with what seemed a kind of relief to the modern dress of G. B. Shaw, W. Somerset Maugham, and James Bridie before starting in 1934 (with *Eden End*) an alliance with J. B. Priestley which was to lead to some of his best and most characteristic work.

A year later he was on Broadway for the first time, playing Mercutio in *Romeo and Juliet* for Katharine Cornell's company, and in 1936 he returned to London for a long-running thriller, *The Amazing Dr Clitterhouse*, in which he was supported by the actress Meriel Forbes whom he married in

1944, two years after the death of his first wife in 1942. She was the daughter of Frank Forbes-Robertson, actor-manager, and grandniece of Sir Johnston Forbes-Robertson.

By now, a theory had developed in the theatre that Richardson was at his best playing 'ordinary little men', though as one critic later noted, anyone who believed that could seldom have met many ordinary little men. Those played by Richardson always had an added touch of magic, of something strange, though Agate was still not won over. When Richardson returned to the Old Vic in 1938 to play Othello in a production by (Sir) W. Tyrone Guthrie, for which Olivier had elected to play Iago homosexually, much to his partner's horror, Agate simply noted 'the truth is that Nature, which has showered upon this actor the kindly gifts of the comedian, has unkindly refused him any tragic facilities whatever . . . He cannot blaze'.

Richardson returned to Priestley and triumph (*Johnson over Jordan*, 1939) and then, when the war came, rose to the rank of lieutenant-commander in the Royal Naval Volunteer Reserve where he was affectionately known as 'pranger Richardson' on account of the large number of planes which seemed to fall to pieces under his control.

It was in 1944, when he was released to form a directorate of the Old Vic with Olivier and John Burrell, that Richardson reached the height of his considerable form: over four great seasons at the New Theatre with Olivier, Dame A. Sybil Thorndike, and Margaret Leighton, he played not only the definitive Falstaff and Peer Gynt of the century but also the title role in Priestley's *An Inspector Calls*, Cyrano de Bergerac, Face in *The Alchemist*, Bluntschli in *Arms and the Man*, and John of Gaunt in *Richard II*, which he unusually also directed.

When the triumvirate was summarily sacked in 1947 by the Old Vic governors who were uneasy about the Olivier and Richardson stardom in what was supposed to be a company of equals, Sir Ralph (it was also the year of his knighthood) returned to the life of a freelance actor, enjoying many more triumphs—as well as another Shakespearian defeat at Stratford-upon-Avon in the title role of *Macbeth* (1952).

The 1960s were highlighted by *Six Characters in Search of an Author* (1963), where in Pirandello he found an ethereal author to satisfy his own other-worldliness, and then in 1969 by a courageous move away from the classics and into the avant-garde as Dr Rance in *What the Butler Saw* by Joe Orton. A year later he was with Gielgud at the Royal Court in David Storey's *Home*, starting a late-life partnership which took them on to Harold Pinter's *No Man's Land* (1975) in the West End and on Broadway, as well as to countless television interviews in which they appeared as two uniquely distinguished but increasingly eccentric brokers' men.

Richardson first joined the National Theatre in 1975, shortly after Olivier left it, as John Gabriel Borkman in the play of that name, and it was there under Sir Peter Hall's administration that he was to do the best of his late work, which culminated a few months before his death in a haunting and characteristic final appearance as Don Alberto in Eduardo de Filippo's *Inner Voices*.

Deeply attached to his second wife, their only child Charles, and a racing motor cycle on which he would speed across Hampstead Heath, Richardson achieved theatrical greatness by turning the ordinary into the extraordinary: on stage as off, he managed to be both unapproachable and instantly accessible, leaving like Priestley's Inspector the impression behind him that perhaps he had not really been there at all, or that if he had, it was only on his way to or from somewhere distinctly unworldly.

He turned somewhat uncertainly to the cinema in the 1930s, at the start of a long contract with (Sir) Alexander Korda, which led to such successes as *Things to Come* (1936), *The Four Feathers* (1939), *The Citadel* (1939), *The Fallen Idol* (1948), *An Outcast of the Islands* (1952), and *Richard III* (1955), before he went on to *Long Day's Journey Into Night* (1962), and *A Doll's House* (1973). It was with one of his very last screen roles, however, as the Supreme Being in the 1980 *Time Bandits*, that he achieved the perfect mix of the godly and the homespun that had always been at the heart of his acting.

Richardson left an estate valued at just over a million pounds, and the memory of a great and mysterious theatrical wizard. At the National Theatre, and at his suggestion, a rocket is fired from the roof to denote first nights. It is known as Ralph's Rocket. Richardson was awarded an honorary D.Litt. by Oxford (1969) and the Norwegian Order of St Olaf (1950). He died 10 October 1983 in London.

[Harold Hobson, *Ralph Richardson*, 1958; Garry O'Connor, *Ralph Richardson*, 1982; Kenneth Tynan, *Show People*, 1980; personal knowledge.]

Sheridan Morley

*published 1990*

## ROBERTSON Sir Johnston Forbes-

(1853–1937)

Actor, was born in Crutched Friars, London, 16 January 1853, the eldest child and eldest of the six sons of John Forbes-Robertson, by his wife,

Frances, daughter of John Cott, of London. The father was a Scot who came from Aberdeen and won some success in London as an art critic and journalist: environment gave the son a single-minded ambition to become a famous painter. He was educated at Charterhouse, then still a London school, and was sent for a great part of his holidays for over six years to Rouen. On leaving school he qualified in 1870, at the age of seventeen, for a studentship at the Royal Academy Schools, and at the end of three years' hard work had shown so much promise that his future as a painter seemed assured. Instead, he turned for his profession to the stage, where he was later joined by two of his brothers and one of his sisters.

By his own account Forbes-Robertson never liked acting, and considered himself temperamentally unfitted for it; but a desire to relieve his not very prosperous family of the expense of his upkeep made him take an unexpected opportunity. He had appeared in an amateur production, and the ascetic beauty of his face—he had sat to D. G. Rossetti, Ford Madox Brown, and other artists—and the resonance of his deep voice led to an offer from W. G. Wills in March 1874 of a part in his play *Mary Stuart*, then running at the Princess's Theatre, at a salary of £4 a week. The characteristic quality of Forbes-Robertson's playing was always to be beauty rather than intellectual or emotional strength, and this may fairly be ascribed to his idea of himself as essentially a painter.

In April 1874 Forbes-Robertson appeared with Ellen Terry in Charles Reade's *The Wandering Heir*, and after a tour with her he played a round of parts in Manchester under C. A. Calvert. By the end of the year, no longer quite a novice, he was back in London, playing with Samuel Phelps at the Gaiety Theatre. Forbes-Robertson afterwards paid affectionate tribute to Phelps as his master, and painted the portrait of Phelps as Wolsey in the Garrick Club collection. Perhaps he owed it as much to Phelps's teaching as to his own natural graces that he surely and speedily made a name. Engagement followed engagement until in September 1876 he made his first notable personal success as Geoffrey Wynyard in (Sir) W. S. Gilbert's *Dan'l Druce, Blacksmith*. From that time onwards his name appears constantly in stage records, now with the Bancrofts, now with Wilson Barrett and Madame Modjeska, now with (Sir) Henry Irving, and now with (Sir) John Hare; and the list of his parts is as remarkable for its variety as for its growing importance.

Forbes-Robertson made the first of many appearances in the United States of America in October 1885 as Orlando with Mary Anderson in New York; and after a long tour there he appeared with her in London at the Lyceum Theatre in September 1887 as Leontes in a famous production of *The Winter's Tale*, for which he designed the dresses. He was by now recognized as one of the leading London actors, and for eight more years he continued in constant demand until in 1895 he decided to go into management for himself. Here again, as at the beginning of his stage career, he was taking an opportunity rather than realizing an ambition.

Forbes-Robertson's first season, at the Lyceum with Mrs. Patrick Campbell as his leading lady, was only a moderate success; it reflected a high-minded devotion to the cause of art rather than an ability to gauge the taste of playgoers. Indeed, his venture did not begin to ride on an even keel until, at the same theatre and with much misgiving, he presented himself as Hamlet in September 1897. This was not only the greatest artistic success of his career; it also established his fortunes. His Hamlet was acclaimed as the greatest of his time—some boldly said of any time. Thenceforward playgoers would always be eager to see him in the part, and even in his farewell season, when he was sixty years of age and the fire of youth had burnt itself out, the dignity and the poetic beauty of his interpretation were not to be forgotten.

During the next decade Forbes-Robertson continued to enjoy high artistic prestige and a modest prosperity. His choice of plays reflected his own taste, which sometimes ran far ahead of that of the public. For instance, he gave an early hearing, in days when the name of Mr. Bernard Shaw was still unpopular, to *The Devil's Disciple* (1900) and *Caesar and Cleopatra* (U.S.A., 1906). Success, when it came his way, was won with productions of the calibre of *The Light That Failed* (1903), a dramatization of Rudyard Kipling's sombre novel. He seemed not to be in search of easy success in less distinguished plays, although once, in *Mice and Men* (1902), which ran for nearly a year, he achieved it. The most important event in his life during this time was the engagement for a tour in the autumn of 1900 of a young American actress, May Gertrude, daughter of Thomas Dermot, of Rockland, Maine; her stage name was Gertrude Elliot, and she was sister of a more famous actress, Maxine Elliott. In December of the same year he married her, and she remained his leading lady until his retirement, and his devoted companion until his death. They had four daughters, the second of whom, Jean, followed her parents on to the stage and achieved distinction.

Then in 1908 there came to Forbes-Robertson that stroke of material good fortune for which every great actor must hope but which might easily have been denied to one of his fastidious spirit; he found a play which combined strong popular appeal with a chief part exactly suited to his personality. Jerome K. Jerome's *The Passing of the Third Floor Back* has little artistic merit, but the part of the Christ-like 'Stranger' who puts to shame the petty human failings of his fellow guests in a boarding-house brought out the sweetness and goodness that formed the basis of Forbes-Robertson's character. The appeal of play and actor to religious sentiment was irresistible. People for whom the theatre had normally no message flocked to see the piece in both England and America.

When at last this tide of fortune had spent itself, Forbes-Robertson found himself able and ready to retire from the stage. During his farewell London season, in June 1913, he was knighted by King George V. His last professional appearance was given at Harvard University in April 1916 as Hamlet. After more than twenty years of contented retirement he died at his home at St. Margaret's Bay, near Dover, 6 November 1937. In 1925 he published his autobiography *A Player Under Three Reigns.* He received honorary degrees from the universities of Columbia (1915) and Aberdeen (1931), being the first actor of any nationality upon whom an American degree was conferred.

A portrait of Forbes-Robertson by Alfred Collins (1885) is in the possession of Lady Forbes-Robertson; another portrait by Meredith Frampton is at the Shakespeare Memorial Theatre, Stratford on Avon; and a drawing of him as Hamlet was made by J. P. Gülich (1897). A cartoon by 'Spy' appeared in *Vanity Fair* 2 May 1895.

[*The Times*, 8 November 1937; Sir J. Forbes-Robertson, *A Player under Three Reigns*, 1925; *Who's Who in the Theatre*, 1936; personal knowledge.]

W. A. DARLINGTON

*published 1949*

## ROBEY Sir George Edward

(1869–1954)

Comedian, whose original name was George Edward Wade, was the elder son of George Wade, civil engineer, and his wife, Elizabeth Mary Keene. He was born at 334 Kennington Road, London, 20 September 1869. Since his father's profession involved moving from one constructional task to another, Robey spent his boyhood and youth in a variety of addresses and at several schools. The family moved at various times from London to Hoylake, back to London, and then to Germany, where his father was engaged on tramway work. At the age of eleven, Robey was at an academy in Dresden, where he learned to speak excellent German and did well in classics. He then moved to Leipzig University where he studied science for a year and a half and was wounded in a duel which might have proved fatal to both parties.

When his father's contract was concluded the Wades returned to England and Robey found a post in his father's profession, beginning on the clerical side in connection with tramway work in Birmingham. His recreations were football, painting, and music: he soon developed a talent for singing, was a favourite amateur performer at concerts, with voice and mandolin, and then discovered his capacity as a comedian. He returned to his family at Brixton Hill in London and there he continued his amateur appearances with increasing success: soon he found that he could earn small but welcome fees. Since there was some domestic dismay that he should be earning money in this way, he took the stage-name of Roby, later Robey. This was the name of a builder's business in Birmingham, and it appealed, for stage purposes, as simple, robust, and easily pronounced. He adopted it later by deed poll.

His first success came by co-operation with a hypnotist, 'Professor' Kennedy, who staged a popular act at the Royal Aquarium in Westminster. This hall had largely abandoned the display of fish and was exploiting a variety entertainment. Young Robey's miming of a hypnotized singer was so effective that he attracted professional and managerial notice and was engaged to make his first music hall appearance at the Oxford in June 1891 at the age of twenty one. He was billed only as 'an extra', but his popularity was immediate and his name was soon exhibited on the posters and proved an attraction. He rapidly established not only a name but an aspect, the aspect by which the public knew and richly enjoyed his turns for much of the rest of his long life. Part of the aspect was conventional: the 'red-nosed comedian' was a fact as well as a phrase and so, accepting the tradition, he applied the scarlet. But to this he added strongly blackened eyebrows and he chose, as a contrast to the bibulous colour-scheme, a long black frock-coat and top-hat. (Later this was abandoned and a squashed bowler took its place.) This almost funereal solemnity was countered by the total absence of any collar and by the carrying of a masher's cane. So the total effect was that of a debauched piety and of a respectability at once tattered, raffish, and gay, half Bardolph, half Stiggins, wholly Robey.

His career in 'the halls' was one of great assiduity—often he played several 'houses' a night—and of continuously mounting esteem. He possessed the qualities essential to capturing the huge and often restless audience of the old 'palaces of variety': quenchless vitality and an immense power of attack. He was billed later on as 'The Prime Minister of Mirth', but prime ministers are the dominant figures of democracies, ruling by persuasion. Robey could more accurately have been called the dictator of laughter, so firmly did he grip and subdue his audiences. The immediate assault upon the centre of the stage, the beetling brows, the abrupt and shattering defiance of any unruly laughter, the swift plunge into song and patter, the absolute sureness of command—these were the signs and proofs of sovereign power.

There were occasional alterations from the customary Robey uniform. He ransacked history for a series of famous or infamous characters; and in pantomime, where he was a constant favourite, he usually played the dame, bonneted and bridling, at once grotesque and genial, creating out of a termagant's tantrums a fountain of hilarity. The leading dramatic critics made a point of seeing Robey when they could and he evoked notices from the most distinguished pens. C. E. Montague wrote of Robey's work in his *Dramatic Values* (1911) that, while the range of characterization was small, 'the study is diabolically intimate, and the execution edged and finished like a cut jewel. . . . You may call the topics outworn and trivial, the mere words insignificant, the humour metallic, rasping, or worse, but the art, within its limits, is not to be surpassed in its gleaming, elliptical terseness, the volumes it speaks in some instants, its suddenness, fire, and zest'.

When the 'single turn' began to go out of fashion, Robey appeared frequently as the comedian of large-scale revues. One of his most notable appearances in this kind of revue was during the war of 1914–18. With Alfred Lester and Violet Loraine he made *The Bing Boys are Here* at the Alhambra one of the greatest of war-time consolations for men on leave. Its most popular number was the straight duet, 'If you were the only girl in the world . . .', which he sang with Violet Loraine.

He left revue for operetta in 1932 when he played Menelaus in (Sir) A. P. Herbert's version of Offenbach's *La Belle Hélène* with Max Reinhardt as producer and (Sir) C. B. Cochran as manager. The weak husband was an odd part for Robey, to whose comedy truculence was natural. In such a situation he had to tone down the vigour of his usual bravura comicality and he accepted the discipline so well that James Agate described his performance as 'a miracle of accommodation like that of a trombone-player obliging with a pianissimo'.

In 1935 came a Shakespearian interlude. Robey was persuaded to play Falstaff in a revival of *Henry IV, Part I* at His Majesty's Theatre. He took this risk with natural trepidation and, although on the first night he had not completely mastered his lines, he triumphantly mastered his audience, including the critics. It was agreed that the man from the music-halls could play the classic character as well as the classic buffoon, with communicable relish of Shakespeare's wit and with a well-controlled ability to make the most of the fat knight's ebullience and humiliations. When a colour film of *Henry V* was produced by (Sir) Laurence Olivier nine years later, the death-scene of Falstaff, only described in the text, was inserted pictorially, with Robey briefly appearing as the knight in his last moments.

At all times, and especially during two wars, his services to charity were ungrudging: he was at the head of an always generous profession and he led the appropriate response to all calls on its good will. Honours were now coming to the theatre and he had been offered a knighthood after the first war, but he modestly thought that this was too much for a comedian and in 1919 accepted a C.B.E. instead. Knighthood did come to him in the late evening of his life, in 1954.

Robey's recreations, when beyond the years of field-sports, were the collection of stamps, china, and porcelain, painting, and the making of violins. Thus he relieved the leisure moments of a long and industrious as well as an illustrious life, during which he won a full meed of friendships far and wide as well as of honours from the State. An athletic youth, prudent living, and great natural vigour sustained him to his ripe maturity, and great knowledge of the comedian's craft promoted him at length from the broader to the finer drollery. That he could hold his own in a Shakespearian company of many talents showed the measure of his art and his adaptability. But it was as Robey of the abbreviated bowler-hat and the suit of solemn black, rubicund and raffish, that his contemporaries would most gratefully remember a radiant and uproarious presence.

His first marriage, in 1898, to a musical-comedy actress, Ethel, daughter of Thomas Haydon, of Melbourne, was dissolved in 1938; his second wife, whom he married in that year, was Blanche, daughter of F. R. Littler, an active member of a family highly placed in theatrical management. By his first marriage he had a son, Edward George Robey, who practised at the bar and in 1954 became a metropolitan magistrate, and a daughter, Eileen Robey, a portrait painter. Robey died at Saltdean, Sussex, 29 November 1954. Drawings of himself are at the National Portrait Gallery.

[George Robey, *My Life Up Till Now*, 1908, and *Looking Back on Life*, 1933; A. E. Wilson, *Prime Minister of Mirth*, 1956; private information; personal knowledge.]

Ivor Brown

*published 1971*

## ROBSON Dame Flora

**(1902–1984)**

Actress, was born in South Shields 28 March 1902, the third of four daughters and the sixth of seven children of David Mather Robson, marine surveyor, and his wife, Eliza, whom he married when second engineer to her father, John McKenzie, a sea captain. The family left their native Scotland, first for Tyneside and later Palmer's Green, London, where Flora was taught singing and elocution to further a talent for speaking poetry when sitting on her father's knee. At her first public appearance, aged six, she recited 'Little Orphan Annie'. In 1919 she left Palmer's Green High School.

Unlike her sisters, she was not good looking and, at five feet eight and a half, was tall for a budding actress. Nevertheless her father sent her to Sir Herbert Beerbohm Tree's (later the Royal) Academy of Dramatic Art. In 1921 she was disappointed to win only the bronze medal. Her first professional engagement was in *Will Shakespeare* at the Shaftesbury Theatre (1921). Advised to acquire more experience, she joined the company at Bristol run by (Sir) P. B. Ben Greet. In 1923, at the Oxford Playhouse, she worked with a younger set of actors including (Sir) John Gielgud and (Sir) Tyrone Guthrie, who invited her to his family home in county Monaghan—'a magic and memorable time for both'. Unable to earn her living as an actress, she became welfare officer of the Welgar Shredded Wheat Company at Welwyn Garden City, where her parents now lived. In 1929 Guthrie, the producer at the Festival Theatre, Cambridge, brought her back to acting in Pirandello's *Six Characters in Search of an Author*, with F. Robert Donat as leading man. Her appearance as the stepdaughter was an apparition of innocent corruption voluptuously embodied in an Aeschylean Fury. She and Guthrie became engaged.

However, in 1931 Guthrie married his cousin, Judith. This coincided with his production of *The Anatomist* by James Bridie at the Westminster Theatre, London, in which Flora Robson, playing an Edinburgh prostitute, had only one scene. Her success in the play, as at Cambridge, was overwhelming. The haunting quality of her voice, singing 'My Bonnie Wee Lamb', was remembered long after the play was over.

She conquered the West End, progressing through *Dangerous Corner* (1932, by J. B. Priestley) and *All God's Chillun's Got Wings* (1933, by Eugene O'Neill), with Paul Robeson, to the Old Vic where, again under Guthrie, in 1933 she played in several productions, including *Macbeth* (as Lady Macbeth), *Measure for Measure* (as Isabella), *Love for Love* (as Mrs Foresight), and *The Cherry Orchard* (as Varya). She had reached the peak of her achievement, although she herself thought the play *Autumn*, at St Martin's in 1937 (James Agate, called it 'Robsonsholm'), was her greatest success.

It was her nature to be immensely happy or unhappy; love could turn to hate and reverse at a moment's notice. She longed so much for Guthrie's children that she lost him; Robert Donat had children of his own; Paul Robeson she loved most but she deeply respected his wife and confided her fear to Bridie that her career would be 'a line of tortured spinsters'.

Bridie wrote *Mary Read* (a female pirate) for her and Donat. (Sir) Alexander Korda presented the play in 1934 but hopes of romantic fulfilment through a film version were dashed when he failed to renew her contract. In 1938 she left for America but did not achieve film stardom. She stayed in America during the early years of World War II but returned to England in 1944, when she reappeared at the Lyric, Hammersmith, as Thérèse Raquin in *Guilty*.

But she had missed the wartime Council for the Encouragement of Music and the Arts and ENSA tours which led to reopening the Old Vic and the formation of national companies to which she should have belonged. Her poetry readings remained faultless; but plays like *Black Chiffon* (1949) were pot-boilers and often her passion was diluted into sentimentality. She was appointed CBE in 1952 and DBE in 1960. She was awarded honorary degrees by London (1971), Oxford (1974), Durham, and Wales.

She rejoiced at earning money to support her many relatives, friends, and causes. In her last performance in 1975, as Miss Prism in *The Importance of Being Earnest* by Oscar Wilde, she was reborn. A role, usually considered as farcically eccentric, was transformed into a sweet Innocent of high comedy. She died 7 July 1984 at Brighton. She was unmarried.

[Kenneth Barrow, *Flora*, 1981; Janet Dunbar, *Flora Robson*, 1960; personal knowledge.]

Marius Goring

*published 1990*

## RUTHERFORD Dame Margaret

(1892–1972)

Actress, was born in Balham 11 May 1892, the only child of William Rutherford, a traveller in silks in India, and his wife, Florence Nicholson. William Rutherford had been born a Benn, the brother of Sir Joshua Benn, but decided to change his name to Rutherford, as being more suitable for a writer. Margaret Rutherford was taken to India as a baby, but was returned to England, to live with an aunt, Bessie Nicholson, when her mother died when the child was three. The father died shortly afterwards. Margaret Rutherford was educated at Wimbledon High School and Raven's Croft School in Seaford. She qualified as a licentiate of the Royal Academy of

Music and became a music teacher, doing nothing to further her wish to act professionally until, at the age of thirty-three, she inherited a small income when her aunt died. A letter of introduction from John Drinkwater enabled her to join the Old Vic Company as a student in 1925, the year in which (Dame) Edith Evans played the leading parts there, but this led to no further work in the theatre, and she returned to teaching at Wimbledon, where she spent two more years before being engaged to understudy at the Lyric, Hammersmith, by (Sir) Nigel Playfair.

From Hammersmith she went to Croydon, Epsom, and Oxford, playing in weekly repertory, and at Oxford she made the acquaintance of (Sir) Tyrone Guthrie, who immediately recognized her unique personality and talent. He directed her soon afterwards at His Majesty's in London (where in 1935 she played for him in an ill-fated but star-studded drama called *Hervey House*, with Fay Compton, Gertrude Lawrence, and Nicholas Hannen) and later in *Short Story*, a comedy by Robert Morley. On this occasion she won a spirited battle against the redoubtable (Dame) Marie Tempest, who was attempting to thwart her by distracting the attention of the audience during their scenes together, but finally capitulated good humouredly when she found her rival had the courage to stand up to her. In 1938, under the direction of (Sir) John Gielgud, she achieved a big personal success as a comic aunt, betting secretly on horses with the butler, in an Irish comedy, *Spring Meeting*. But the director had considerable difficulty in persuading her to undertake the part, since she saw little humour in the play when it was first given her to read. 'Don't you think that as we are living in such gloomy times', she wrote, 'that people want to laugh?'

Her seriousness was, of course, an invaluable asset in her solemn acting of farce. With an unfailing instinct for execution and timing, there was always a hint of sadness, as in many of the greatest comedians, behind the comicality of her performances.

In 1939 (a year before she somewhat improbably created the part of Mrs Danvers, the baleful housekeeper in (Dame) Daphne du Maurier's *Rebecca*) she appeared as Miss Prism in John Gielgud's production of *The Importance of Being Earnest* for some special matinées. For the run of the play which followed she accepted the offer to repeat her performance, but only on condition that she might also understudy Edith Evans—an unheard of stipulation for an important actress. When, some years later, the production was taken to America, Edith Evans did not wish to go and Margaret Rutherford was asked to replace her, which she did with notable success. But even then she begged to be allowed to wear similar costumes to those that Edith Evans had worn in London, and despite her own markedly different personality, she played the part on exactly similar lines, though without appearing to imitate Edith Evans, whose work she so greatly admired.

Her successes in films did not perhaps give her very great satisfaction, though she was always touchingly appreciative of praise and popularity. As the spiritualist Madame Arcati in *Blithe Spirit* (1941) by (Sir) Noël Coward—another of her great successes in the theatre—she suffered great agonies in fearing to make mock of a cult which she knew to be taken very seriously by its devotees, and at the end of the long run she suffered a nervous breakdown as a result.

Not long before Margaret Rutherford's death, her friends were approached by a lady journalist who was endeavouring to help her complete her autobiography, for which she had already accepted an advance fee. Dame Margaret had been incapacitated by illness, and neither she herself, nor her husband, J. B. Stringer Davis, an actor whom she had married in 1945, were able to complete the assignment, and the ghost-writer was at a loss how to gain the further material which she needed and was trying to fill the gaps with tributes from some of her friends and colleagues. But it appeared that in the course of detailed researches, a certain amount of information had come to light about Margaret Rutherford's earlier life involving an unhappy family background and recurrences of mental disturbance which would be pointless and painful to bring to light, and the book was finally cobbled together as well as possible under these unhappy circumstances.

Margaret Rutherford was a most modest and dedicated actress. She adored her husband, was infinitely kind, unassuming, and intensely professional, but increasingly disturbed. She insisted on continuing to fulfil commitments after she was already seriously ill, and failed to complete a film, from which she retired, after some humiliation at the hands of the impatient director, with the greatest dignity. And her last appearance at the Haymarket with Sir Ralph Richardson in *The Rivals*, an engagement which she was finally obliged to give up after a few weeks, was a most poignant struggle against her obviously failing powers.

Though never slender, or good-looking, she had extraordinary grace and charm. Light on her feet, she moved with grace and distinction, taking the stage with confidence and apparent ease. She wore costume to perfection, and her phrasing and diction, whether in William Congreve, R. B. Sheridan, or Oscar Wilde, were equally impeccable. On the night she left the cast of *The School for Scandal* (1962), in which she was a memorable Mrs Candour, she gave a party on the stage after the performance, and there is a last happy memory of her dancing joyously up and down the stage hand in hand with the stage carpenter.

Among the awards she won was an Oscar for best supporting actress for the film *The VIPs* in 1964. She was appointed OBE in 1961 and DBE in 1967. She died at Chalfont and Gerrard's Cross Hospital 22 May 1972.

[*Margaret Rutherford*, an autobiography as told to Gwen Robyns, 1972; Eric Keown, *Margaret Rutherford*, 1956; personal knowledge.]

John Gielgud

*published 1986*

## SELLERS Richard Henry ('Peter') (1925–1980)

Comedian, was born in Portsmouth 8 September 1925, the only child of William Sellers, a pianist of modest ability, and his wife, Agnes ('Peg') Marks, who was one of the Ray Sisters entertainers, and the great-granddaughter of Daniel Mendoza, the pugilist. Although his mother was Jewish, he was primarily educated at St. Aloysius College in Hornsey Lane, Highgate, a Roman Catholic school run by the Brothers of Our Lady of Mercy. He left school at fourteen and entered the theatre world, doing most backstage jobs. He then developed a desire to play drums in a dance band. At this he became very proficient and, but for his ability at mimicry, might well have stayed a jazz drummer.

Called up into the RAF during the war despite his mother's desperate efforts to have him disqualified on medical grounds, he finally ended up in its Entertainment Section in India, Ceylon, and Burma with Ralph Reader's Gang Show. Within a short time of leaving the Services in 1947, such was his confidence and his ability as an impressionist, that he duped a BBC producer, Roy Speer, by using the voice of Kenneth Horne. The producer was duly impressed, and gave him a small part in a comedy show.

In a short space of time he had appeared in the following series: 'Petticoat Lane', 'Ray's a Laugh', 'Variety Bandbox', 'Workers' Playtime', 'Third Division' (the first comedy show to come on the erudite Third Programme), finally reaching the highest acclaim in the revolutionary *The Goon Show*, which began in 1951 and ran for nine years. During this period he also appeared in Variety, including the Royal Command Performance. There were a few second-rate films: *Penny Points to Paradise* (1951), *Orders are Orders* (1954), *John and Julie* (1955), and *The Smallest Show on Earth* (1957). Then came a strangely original short film written and directed by Spike Milligan, entitled *The Running Jumping Standing Still Film* (1957–8), which won numerous awards because of its innovatory ideas. Sellers's big commercial break came with *The Ladykillers* (1955), but he received world acclaim for his outstanding performance in *I'm All Right Jack* (1959).

There followed a series of quality films, some successful and some not, including *The Millionairess* (1960), where he played opposite Sophia Loren, and *Waltz of the Toreadors* (1962), and one produced and directed by himself, *Mr. Topaze* (1961). He soared to new heights in his multi-character *Dr. Strangelove*. He did some black comedy films, one being *What's New Pussycat?* (1965), with Peter O'Toole and Woody Allen. But the watershed in his career was his portrayal of Inspector Clouseau, in *The Pink Panther* (1963). There followed a period of indifference, and it would appear at one time that his career might have come to a conclusion. However, there followed *The Return of the Pink Panther* (1974) and *The Pink Panther Strikes Again* (1976), which renovated his career and made him a millionaire.

To summarize him, one would say that he had one of the most glittering comic talents of our age, but what few people knew was that he never reached or was allowed to perform the levels of comedy that he delighted in most: the nonsense school. To his dying day he said his happiest days were performing in the Goon Shows. He made a desperate attempt to recreate *The Goon Show* atmosphere by making the film *The Fiendish Plot of Dr. Fu Manchu* (1980), which he co-wrote. But the fact that he never was a writer, or ever would be, and the collaboration with Americans, who had no like sense of humour, made the film a failure. However, most extraordinarily, he gave his finest performance in his last but one film, *Being There* (1979). This showed his incredible ability to recreate a character, in which Peter Sellers himself seemed to be totally excluded. His last wry contribution to comedy was having Glen Miller's 'In the Mood' played at his cremation.

Sellers was appointed CBE in 1966. He won many awards: Best Actor for 1959 (British Film Academy award); the Golden Gate award, 1959; the San Sebastian film award for the best British actor, 1962; Best Actor award, Tehran Film Festival, 1973; and the *Evening News* best actor of the year award, 1975.

Sellers suffered from a heart condition for his last fifteen years which made life difficult for him and had a debilitating effect on his personality. None of his marriages lasted long. His first one, in 1951, to Anne Howe produced two children, Michael and Sarah, but was terminated in 1964. In the same year, after a whirlwind romance, he married the starlet, Britt Ekland. There was one daughter of this marriage, Victoria, but the marriage was dissolved in 1969. In 1970 he married Miranda, daughter of Richard St. John Quarry and Lady Mancroft; the marriage was dissolved in 1974; there were no children. His last marriage, in 1977, to Lynne Frederick, also underwent emotional undulations, and all the signs point to a marriage that had failed; they had no children.

Sellers died in the Middlesex Hospital, London, 24 July 1980. Among the many who attended a later service of thanksgiving in London were Spike Milligan, Harry Secombe, and Michael Bentine, his former colleagues on *The Goon Show*.

[Peter Evans, *The Mask Behind the Mask, a Life of Peter Sellers*, 1968 and 1969; Alexander Walker, *Peter Sellers*, 1981; Michael Sellers with Sarah and Victoria Sellers, *P.S. I Love You*, 1981; personal knowledge.]

SPIKE MILLIGAN

*published 1986*

## SHAW George Bernard

**(1856–1950)**

Playwright, was born 26 July 1856 at 3 Upper Synge Street, later renamed and renumbered 33 Synge Street, Dublin. His grandfather, Bernard Shaw, was 'a combination of solicitor, notary public, and stockbroker that prevailed at that time' in Dublin, who was ruined when his partner decamped with £50,000 of his money, together with large sums belonging to their clients. The shock was too much for him, and he collapsed and died, leaving his widow almost destitute. George Bernard Shaw's father, George Carr Shaw, was the eighth of her fifteen children, and was twelve at the time. He grew up to be a genial, ineffective man with a sardonic sense of humour and a keen appreciation of anticlimax: gifts which he transmitted to his son. He had no capacity to cope with the general traffic of existence. Through the influence of his kinsman, Sir Robert Shaw, the founder of the Royal Bank of Ireland, popularly known as Shaw's Bank, he was appointed to a sinecure in the Dublin Law Courts, which he held until it was abolished in 1850. He received a pension of £60 a year, which was immediately compounded for a lump sum and invested in a corn-mill in Dublin about which he knew nothing. His partner, a cloth merchant named Clibborn, was equally ignorant, with the result that the firm, Clibborn and Shaw, never flourished; nevertheless it maintained George Carr Shaw, although not Clibborn, until his death. He was still short of thirty-eight when he met Lucinda Elizabeth Gurly, a wilful young woman of twenty-one, who had a cold unloving heart, a ferocious chin, and no sense of humour whatsoever. She was the daughter of Walter Bagnall

Gurly, an impoverished and unscrupulous country gentleman with an estate in county Carlow which was deeply embogged in debt, but she had been brought up by her aunt, Ellen Whitcroft, a hunchback with a pretty face and a severely puritanical temper. She sought refuge from her in marriage. It is improbable that George Carr Shaw married her: it seems certain that, although she bore him no love, it was she who married him. He was her senior by seventeen years, a feckless and unimpressive man with a squint, and a vice of which she was unaware. He was, he protested, 'a lifelong and bigoted teetotaller', a statement which he believed to be true because he tippled in secret and was morbidly ashamed of his habit when he was sober.

They rented a house in a lower-middle-class street in Dublin, and here were born two daughters and then George Bernard Shaw. It was loveless and genteelly poor: a place of 'downstarts', as Shaw was to call it. 'The adult who has been poor as a child', he once remarked, 'will never get the chill of poverty out of his bones'. This house was ruled by a disillusioned young woman of iron will who had no talent for domesticity, and was married to a drunkard whom she despised; a 'throughother' house, as the Irish say, where the meals were erratic and ill-cooked, and the children were brought up in an untidy kitchen by slatternly servants. Yet its gentility was overpowering. Catching him in conversation with the child of a retail ironmonger, Shaw's father rebuked him severely. The fact that the ironmonger was a richer and more efficient man than the corn miller merely aggravated his offence. It was subversive of all civilized society that a person who probably sold nails by the pennyworth across a counter should be better off than a descendant of Macduff, the thane of Fife, who slew Macbeth, and of Oliver Cromwell by way of his daughter Bridget and General Fleetwood, and was himself a wholesale merchant and second cousin to a baronet alive at that moment in Dublin.

His father's tippling seems not to have been noticed by the boy until he was past the age when it would have been observed by less remarkable infants. One evening George Carr Shaw took his son for a walk along a bank of a Dublin canal. Feeling jocular, he threatened to throw the boy into the water and, in a clumsy pretence at doing so, nearly did. This incident opened the boy's eyes, and he said to his mother, on his return, 'Mamma, I think Papa is drunk!', and was astounded to hear her reply, 'Ah, when is he anything else?' In later life he wrote to (Dame) Ellen Terry: 'I have never believed in anything since: then the scoffer began. . . .' When he was accused of dishonouring his father by exposing his weakness, he retorted on his accusers with unaccustomed bitterness that neither his mother, his sisters, nor he himself had ever thought intoxication funny.

It was his father's tippling which turned Dublin into a desert for him and made a naturally romantic-minded lad with a vivid imagination a shy and nervous Ishmael. The father when drunk was impatient of contradiction. He lost his temper easily and was accustomed in his anger to smash anything breakable. Because he was excluded therefore from family parties, his wife and children were excluded too.

The characteristics of this singular household were, however, not totally disadvantageous. If the meals were casual, if the children were neglected by their mother and avoided their father, they were compelled to develop their own characters. And if there was no love or ordinary affection in the nearly graceless house, yet there was music in abundance. It was the music in the house, and the pictures in the National Gallery of Ireland, and the books in his father's attic, which saved Shaw from despair. His mother, who had a mezzo-soprano voice of unusual purity, had become acquainted with a lame musician in the next street. This was George John Vandaleur Lee who was the leader of an orchestra in Dublin and taught voice production by an unorthodox system which Shaw's mother reverentially named 'The Method'. In association with Lee, she filled her house with musicians, vocal and instrumental, and her son listened to them so well that he was able to boast that before he was fifteen he 'could sing and whistle from end to end leading works by Handel, Haydn, Mozart, Beethoven, Rossini, Bellini, Donizetti, and Verdi'.

Shaw's formal education, after some elementary instruction from a governess, and a grounding in Latin by his uncle, the Rev. William George Carroll, was, he declared in later life, entirely useless. In 1867 he entered the Wesley Connexional School (later Wesley College) where he was 'generally near or at the bottom of the class', and seemed to his masters to be an incorrigible dunce and 'a source of idleness in others, distracting them from their studies by interminable comic stories'. Despite these reports, he claimed with justice to be more cultured and widely read than any other person, teacher or pupil, in the school. Apart from his knowledge of music, he haunted the National Gallery of Ireland so persistently that he 'knew enough of a considerable number of painters to recognize their work at sight'. His reading ranged from the Bible and Bunyan to William Robertson's *History of Scotland*, Walter Scott, and Dickens.

His entrance to Wesley School had been preceded by a change greatly for the better in the economic circumstances of the Shaws. About the year 1866, Lee proposed that he and they should share a larger house in a more select street, and they removed to 1 Hatch Street. He also bought Torca Cottage, high on a hill at Dalkey, above Killiney Bay, and in full view of the Dublin and Wicklow mountains, where they lived during the summer months. It was here that Shaw first became aware of natural beauty, and the memory of happy days at Dalkey never faded.

After a few years of this felicity, Lee suddenly decided to remove to London; and the Shaws were faced with economic disaster, despite the fact that the father, sobered by a fit, had ceased to be a drunkard. Shaw's mother solved this problem abruptly and drastically. She broke up her home and virtually deserted her husband and son. Since her hopes of obtaining employment as a teacher of music, as well as the prospects of her elder daughter as a singer, depended upon Lee, she and the two girls would follow him to London. Her husband, tied to his mill, would remain in Ireland, and so would 'Sonny', who had now ended his formal education and had in 1871 become a junior clerk in the estate agency of two brothers, Charles Uniacke and Thomas Courtney Townshend, at a salary of eighteen shillings a month. A few months later, in 1872, his mother, with her daughters, departed from Dublin, to which she never returned. Except once, when he visited her in London, her husband never saw her again. If she wrote to her son, or showed the slightest interest in a boy who was now at the most difficult period of adolescence, no record of her letters or interest survives. Shaw's life with his father in dreary lodgings seems to have been largely one of isolation so complete that he was ignorant of elementary knowledge of social intercourse in the class from which he had sprung, and had to read a work entitled *Manners and Tone of Good Society, or Solecisms to be Avoided*. It was characteristic of him that he studied this work in the British Museum, and that his gratitude for its help forbade him to show any snobbery about acknowledging his debt to it.

His career in the estate office was spectacularly successful, despite his habit of training the premium apprentices to sing opera. The Townshends' cashier departed in haste, taking with him some of the rents which he had collected for his employers. Shaw, then sixteen, was appointed temporarily to his post, and filled it with such skill that he was confirmed in it; and within a year of entering the office his salary had risen to £48 a year. While he was in this employment he made his first appearance in print. In 1871 he had sent a letter to the *Vaudeville Magazine* which enraged the editor because he had to pay excess postage on it. The letter was not published. Four years later, in April 1875, he went to a revival meeting, conducted in Dublin by Dwight L. Moody and Ira D. Sankey, and was so repelled by what he saw that he wrote to *Public Opinion* to rebuke 'those members of the aristocracy' who participated in the services, which were suitable only for 'the rough' and 'the outcast of the streets'. Those who were redeemed became so 'highly objectionable' that 'their unconverted friends' longed for their relapse from grace! This letter, which appeared over the signature 'S', caused him to be regarded by his acquaintances as an atheist, although there is nothing in it to justify such a conclusion, nor, indeed, was Shaw at any time in his life an atheist or even an agnostic. It was a remarkable letter for a young man, not yet twenty, to have written, and it contained the germ of his creed. He was still saying when he was ninety substantially what he had written when he was nineteen. He had then no thought of authorship in his head. His ambition, so far as he had one, was to become a painter: a profession for which he had no talent whatsoever. He had, however, without perceiving the fact, qualified himself for criticism: the knowledge of pictures and music and drama which he gained in Dublin was to prove invaluable in London. But his mind was vague about his future, except in one respect: he knew that he did not intend to remain a clerk, despite the brightness of his prospects.

In 1876 Shaw's younger sister, who had suffered from consumption for several years, died at Ventnor, Isle of Wight. Her death brought her brother to a swift and definite decision. Dublin had become repulsive to him. He would join his mother and elder sister, now a popular singer, in London. He had already given a month's notice to the Townshends, who had offered him a higher salary to remain. Shaw now left Ireland, to which he did not return for twenty-nine years (and then only to please his wife). In a cul-de-sac, 13 Victoria (later Netherton) Grove, off the Fulham Road, began nine years of deep discouragement, amounting to desolation, which would have broken the spirit of a less resolute and courageous man.

His account of this period, which appeared in the 1905 edition of *The Irrational Knot*, exposed him to profound disapproval as a selfish son, who, 'callous as Comus to moral babble', lived on his aged parents when he should have striven manfully to keep himself. This myth does not survive examination. He took an impish delight in upsetting routine-minded people who like poor boys who rise to riches to be models of kindly consideration for all with whom they come in contact. He may have admired the genius who will not be dissuaded from his intention, no matter what suffering he may cause, but he did not behave like one. He had earned his livelihood at a time when other boys of his social class were at public schools and universities; he arrived in London when there was a deep trade depression and employment was not easy to obtain; in 1881 he was sick of the smallpox; nevertheless for about three of the nine years he engaged in several occupations; nor was he idling when he was out of employment, but was applying himself with great industry to writing novels. Moreover, his share, amounting to more than £1,000, of a bequest left by his maternal great-grandfather, to which he became entitled in 1877, far more than covered the cost of the very poor entertainment which his mother gave him. The whole of the bequest, about £4,000, with the consent of her children, was spent by their mother, as it became legally available, on the maintenance of her ramshackle home. Shaw, who was exceptionally generous to his relatives and had the rare habit of being continuously grateful for any kindness he ever received, lived in the utmost discomfort with his mother until he married. For the greater part of the time he provided the means which kept her ill-managed house together; and he rewarded her well for the little she did for him, allowing her £400 a year at a time when that was a substantial sum, and buying the leases of the houses in which she lived.

Between the years 1878 and 1883, he wrote five novels: *Immaturity*, the best of the five, *The Irrational Knot, Love Among the Artists, Cashel Byron's Profession*, and *An Unsocial Socialist*, all of which were at that time refused by publishers in England and America. *Immaturity* was not published until fifty years after it was written. Shaw had little talent for narrative, and these novels, although they are interesting enough to read, are important only as scenarios for the plays he was eventually to write. He was economical: he did not waste his material. The end of *Love Among the Artists* is almost identical with the end of *Candida*; and some of the characters in the novels are sketches for characters in the plays. It is a singular fact that the thought of becoming a dramatist did not occur to him during these years, although it must have been plain to him that his efforts to make a living as a novelist were hopeless. His intellectual growth, however, was remarkable, and he was making important friendships which were to last until they were ended by death. He heard Henry George lecturing in London on the taxation of land values, and at once became a convert to land nationalization; but, soon afterwards, as a result of reading Karl Marx's *Das Kapital* in a French translation, he abandoned George's limited Socialism for the belief that all forms of capital should be nationalized.

The most important of Shaw's achievements at this time was his conquest of himself. Sensitive and shy and very nervous, he perceived that he could not hope to become effective unless he hardened his skin; and so, with astonishing persistence, he forced himself to speak on platforms, in public parks, and at street-corners, until he turned himself into one of the most effective orators and debaters in Great Britain. Few public speakers had so much power over an audience as Shaw, who could make it rock with laughter at one moment, and silence it at the next with a remark that went to the root of his matter. The shy young man, whose knees were almost knocking together as he addressed derisive or indifferent labourers in Victoria Park, held himself so tenaciously to his self-appointed task that Shaw who in 1884 could scarcely open his lips in public was, in 1888 with great confidence and assurance, addressing the British Association on economics for an hour. His industry was, he maintained, due to his superfluity of nervous energy caused by his conversion, when he was twenty-five, to vegetarian diet, but it was strengthened far more by the invincible will which refused to let him acknowledge defeat. His fertility and invention were as great as his application. From 1885, when he was twenty-nine, until 1926, when he was seventy, his record of great and diversified employment, which included the writing of thirty-six plays, most of them major works, as well as a vast amount of journalism and public service, was unsurpassed and not easily equalled.

Yet it was not until 1892 that he turned his thoughts to the theatre, and even then the impulse was not his, but a friend's. Oscar Wilde once stupidly remarked that Shaw had no enemies, but that his friends disliked him. In fact, like any man of distinctive character, Shaw had many enemies, some of whom were deeply embittered, and had numerous friends who were devoted to him. A man who could include among his close and faithful friends such diverse men and women as Beatrice Webb, William Morris, Annie Besant, Edward Carpenter, Ellen Terry, Mrs. Patrick Campbell, Harley Granville-Barker, T. E. Lawrence, Gilbert Murray, and Sir Barry Jackson, must have had unusual qualities of charm and personality.

Among the first of his friends were Sidney Webb and William Archer who were not only very dissimilar from each other, but from Shaw himself. Webb was born a bureaucrat and planner, with one uncontrollable passion, for statistical surveys. Shaw joined the newly founded Fabian Society in 1884 and Webb followed in 1885, and they soon became its most powerful members. This society's influence not only on the Labour Party, but on all political parties in Great Britain, was out of all proportion to the size of its membership, and it was a main factor in preserving British Labour from domination by Marxist beliefs. Its effect on local government was profound. Archer, who was a dramatist as well as a dramatic critic, was a man of such integrity and generous character that he could tell an author to his face how bad his play was without hurting his feelings. It was he who discovered Shaw studying *Das Kapital* and the score of *Tristan and Isolde* in the reading-room of the British Museum, and found the tall, red-headed young man—Shaw was over six feet in height—so much to his taste that he became his devoted friend for the rest of his life, although his conception of drama was so different from Shaw's that he once publicly appealed to him to abandon the theatre since he had no talent for writing plays. He was to recant that opinion handsomely. In 1885 Archer performed two great services. He persuaded the editor of the *Pall Mall Gazette* to employ Shaw as a reviewer of books at two guineas a thousand words, a task which Shaw performed until 1888, and he suggested that they should collaborate in writing a play. Archer could construct a plot, but was unable to write speakable dialogue: Shaw could write reams of fluent dialogue, but, he modestly asserted, could not construct plots. In this respect he underestimated himself. Archer supplied Shaw with his plot, and was dismayed to hear that it had been used up in two acts. The script revealed that Archer's work, except for the setting of the first act, had been entirely ignored, and that Shaw, now rampantly socialistic, had produced a singular comedy about slum landlords. Archer dissociated himself from the piece, and Shaw, feeling that he had failed as a dramatist, put his two acts away, and turned to other work. Archer, in no wise wounded by this abortive effort at collaboration, in refusing the post of art critic on the *World*, insisted that it should be given to Shaw, who held it from 1886 to 1889.

The years of poverty had ended, and the years of plenty now began. T. P. O'Connor founded a London evening paper, the *Star*, and Shaw, following failure as a leader-writer because he would propagand Socialism in Liberal columns, was appointed music critic at two guineas a week: a position he held from 1888 to 1890. Under the pen-name of Corno di Bassetto, he not only wrote the liveliest musical criticism then published, but innovated a custom, not yet fully adopted, of writing in excellent and understandable prose. There was none of the technical jargon which passed for profundity in Shaw's articles, which remain as readable after more than sixty years as they were on the day they were written. They have been collected under the title of *London Music in 1888–89* (1937). In 1889 *Fabian Essays in Socialism* was published, edited by Shaw, who contributed 'The Economic Basis of Socialism' and the text of his address to the British Association, 'The Transition to Social Democracy'. It immediately had an influential effect on current politics. In 1890 he retired from the *Star* and joined the *World* as its music critic at a salary of £5 a week. In the following year he published *The Quintessence of Ibsenism*.

Ibsen's effect on the world theatre was far greater than the popularity of his plays; and it was to be found not only in the work of advanced dramatists, such as Shaw was to become, but also in the work of conventional authors. A young Dutchman, J. T. Grein, in 1891 founded the Independent Theatre, the forerunner of the Stage Society, for the production of unusual and probably unprofitable plays. The first piece to be performed was Ibsen's *Ghosts*, which was received by an outburst of violent denunciation such as could have been displayed only by men with guilty consciences. *Ghosts*, however, seemed to deprive the Independent Theatre of its vitality, for Grein had no play with which to open his season in 1892. Shaw suggested that he should be announced as the author of the next piece, and, raking out the play he had abandoned, he hurriedly added a third act to it, gave it 'the far-fetched mock-scriptural title of *Widowers' Houses*', and had it performed at the Royalty Theatre, 9 December 1892. It was received with a howl which, although not so vulpine as that excited by

Ibsen's tragedy, was sufficiently fierce. The play is ramshackle, and creates the impression of having been written while its author was descending from the plinth in Trafalgar Square and striding at great speed to a portable platform in Victoria Park. But it revealed the quality of its author, already renowned in a limited circle for the vigour of his criticism, and was the pioneer of a long series of exceptionally diversified plays, written with great rapidity, which had the utmost difficulty in obtaining performance in regular theatres, but most of which were eventually to be performed with great success all over the civilized world. It was followed, in 1893, by *The Philanderer*, which is Shaw's worst play, apart from pieces written in his extreme old age, and has seldom been performed. *Mrs. Warren's Profession* came next, and was banned, until 1925, by the lord chamberlain because of a faint suggestion of incest in its theme. The piece proved that Shaw could, if he chose, write a 'well-made play'; a fact which was confirmed by the three succeeding plays, *Arms and the Man*, *Candida*, and *You Never Can Tell*. None of these plays, except the first, received public performance until some time later; and *Arms and the Man* (Avenue Theatre, 1894) lasted only a few weeks, taking about £20 at each performance.

It appeared, therefore, that Shaw was destined to failure as a dramatist no less than as a novelist; and, in 1895, he seemed to accept this as irrevocable, for he consented to become dramatic critic of the *Saturday Review*, which was then edited by J. T. (Frank) Harris. Shaw held the post for more than three years, at a salary of £6 a week, and enormously increased his prestige. In 1897 an American actor, Richard Mansfield, who had produced *Arms and the Man* in the United States in 1894, made a considerable success in New York of Shaw's next play, *The Devil's Disciple*. The royalties exceeded £2,000. Fortune now began to favour Shaw. Sir Henry Irving accepted a long one-act play, *The Man of Destiny*, and Cyril Maude accepted *You Never Can Tell*. It was during this period that Shaw and Ellen Terry conducted the brilliant correspondence which was eventually published in 1931. His luck did not, however, last long. Within a fortnight, in April 1897, disaster fell upon him: Irving refused to produce *The Man of Destiny*, and *You Never Can Tell* was withdrawn during its rehearsals because of the total inability of several members of the cast, two of whom threw up their parts, to perceive any point in the play. This blow might have discouraged some tough men for ever, but Shaw met misfortune with gay courage. He used it as a stimulant to write more plays. Nothing seemed able to daunt him from his purpose to capture the theatre, although he now realized that he had not only to attract an audience, but also to create actors. The single sign of discouragement detectable in his correspondence is to be found in a letter to Ellen Terry, who had deeply disappointed him by disliking *Captain Brassbound's Con-*

*version*. He had written the part of Lady Cecily Waynflete for her, but she could not see herself in it: a singular defect in an actress of genius, as was plain to those who saw her in the part many years afterwards, when her powers were waning.

From 1897 until 1903 Shaw participated in municipal government as a vestryman and later borough councillor of St. Pancras, London, an experience which resulted in the publication of his small book, *The Common Sense of Municipal Trading* (1904). In 1898, as a result of overwork, he had a physical collapse, caused primarily through an injury to his foot. He had met, while staying with the Webbs, a wealthy Anglo-Irishwoman, Charlotte Frances, daughter of Horace Payne-Townshend, an Irish barrister, and Mary Susannah Kirby, an Englishwoman. On hearing of his illness, Miss Payne-Townshend went to nurse him in his mother's house, 29 Fitzroy Square, and was so horrified by the discomfort in which he was living that she proposed to remove him to a house in the country; but he, fearing that her generous impulse might bring scandal upon her, insisted that they should marry, which they did, 1 June 1898, in the register office of the Strand district. The bridegroom was not quite forty-two, and the bride his junior by six months. Their life together was entirely felicitous.

While Shaw was recovering from his illness, but still on crutches, *Caesar and Cleopatra* was completed, in 1899, and was produced in Newcastle upon Tyne with Mrs. Patrick Campbell as Cleopatra. From then onward, scarcely a year passed without the completion of a play. In 1901–3, his most brilliant comedy, *Man and Superman*, was written, but it was not until 1904, when he was forty-eight, that he began to gain authority in the west-end theatre, although he had for a number of years been recognized as a distinguished dramatist in the United States. In the autumn of that year, the famous seasons of plays, conducted by John E. Vedrenne, a business man, and Harley Granville-Barker, an actor and producer of genius, began at the Royal Court Theatre, Sloane Square, London. The first of Shaw's plays to be performed was his latest piece, *John Bull's Other Island*, which attracted many members of the Cabinet and was seen by King Edward VII in 1905. *Man and Superman* followed, and was also produced in New York by Robert Loraine where it was an instantaneous success and earned large sums for its author and producer. In November 1905 the first performance was given at the Court of *Major Barbara*, a play about armaments and the Salvation Army, in which a character called Cusins was plainly modelled on Professor Gilbert Murray. In 1906 *The Doctor's Dilemma*, with Sir Almroth Wright as the source of one of the characters, was produced, but in 1907 the productions at the Court ceased. There followed *Getting Married* (Haymarket Theatre, 1908), *The Shewing-Up of Blanco Posnet* (which was banned in Great Britain but produced at the Abbey Theatre, Dublin,

1909), *Misalliance* (Duke of York's Theatre, 1910), and *Fanny's First Play* (Little Theatre, 1911). This was written for Miss Lillah McCarthy (subsequently Lady Keeble) who had taken the leading part in several of Shaw's plays, and was performed 624 times.

It was in 1908 that Shaw's brilliant essay, *The Sanity of Art*, in which he made an overwhelming reply to Max Nordau's curious work, *Degeneration*, was published. Nordau had sought to prove that the rebel-artist was a decadent. In 1909 Shaw gave evidence before the joint select committee on dramatic censorship, but was less effective than he might have been because he used shock-tactics when he should have been indulgent to the weakness of other people's flesh. His meaning when he described himself as 'an immoral author' was plain enough to those who understood in what sense the word 'immoral' was used—that is, 'non-customary'—but the effect of the description on the general public was deplorable. His account of the proceedings is given in his preface to *The Shewing-Up of Blanco Posnet*. Shaw published his own plays, accompanied by prefaces, 'in a simple desire to give my customers good value for their money by eking out a pennorth of play with a pound of preface'. The prefaces were collected and published in a separate volume in 1934, as the plays had been in 1931.

In 1913 a charming play, *Androcles and the Lion*, was produced by Granville-Barker at the St. James's Theatre. In the following year, Sir Herbert Tree produced *Pygmalion* at His Majesty's Theatre with Mrs. Patrick Campbell as the flower-girl; Tree himself played the professor. It was surprisingly popular having regard to the fact that its main theme was concerned with phonetics, a subject which had occupied Shaw's mind from his young manhood, and was almost the last thought in his head, as his will amply demonstrated. Yet he had no gift for languages. A minor element in the play's success was the flower-girl's remark, 'not bloody likely', which put the word 'bloody' almost into polite usage. The play had already been produced in Berlin in 1913.

The outbreak of war, however, cancelled all Shaw's popularity, and brought him great odium even among some of his friends. In November 1914 he published *Common Sense about the War* as a supplement to the *New Statesman* which he had helped to found in 1913. The general effect of the article, especially in the United States, was adverse to Great Britain, although its argument in some respect was identical with that used in a very popular work, *Ordeal by Battle*, by F. S. Oliver. The Germans were quick to exploit it, causing Shaw greater uneasiness than did his ostracism, although that was distressing enough, for there was a period when his arrival in a public place was a signal for those already there to leave it. But he was received into favour again after the end of the war, especially when it was observed how popular *Arms and the Man*, revived in London in 1919 by Robert Loraine, was with soldiers and ex-servicemen. In 1920 *Heartbreak House*, which had occupied him from 1913 until 1916, was performed for the first time in New York. It did not reach England until 1921. This impressive, Lear-like play, which contains his profoundest thoughts and many passages of sombre beauty, was considered by Shaw to be his best play, 'worth fifty *Candidas*', although this belief is challenged by many critics who give the premier place in his work to *Saint Joan*. His attitude to *Heartbreak House* was singularly reticent and reverential: he discussed it with reluctance and less often than any other play he wrote. It was followed by *Back to Methuselah*, 'a metabiological pentateuch', which received its first performance in New York (1922) and was first performed in England in 1923 at the Birmingham Repertory Theatre under the management of Sir Barry Jackson. This is a long, unequal, and difficult work, five plays rather than five acts, given on successive nights. It turns on Shaw's belief that the term of life is too short for us to profit by our experience, and that man must, therefore, will himself into greater longevity. It begins in Eden, passes through the first half of the twentieth century and ends 'as far as thought can reach', when everybody is all but immortal, no one dying except by accident or from discouragement. It is hard to understand why life should be wilfully extended when extended life is made by Shaw to seem so repulsive and dismal. But the play ends with a fine philosophic speech and a suggestion that time will not end except, perhaps, in an eternity of felicity when man, all passion spent, will live in a whirlpool of pure thought.

In 1923 Shaw translated a play by his Austrian translator, Siegfried Trebitsch, under the title of *Jitta's Atonement*, which Trebitsch had intended to be a tragedy: Shaw made a comedy of it. His major work in this year was *Saint Joan*, produced in New York in 1923, and in London (New Theatre) in 1924, with (Dame) Sybil Thorndike in the title-role. The play was an immense success in both cities, despite its length which was increased by a long and unnecessary epilogue in which, however, there are beautiful passages. The natural end of the play is the sixth scene, but Shaw was never able to convince himself that the audience brought any knowledge into the theatre or that any person who saw *Saint Joan* without the epilogue would realize that the Maid had been canonized.

Shaw was now beyond question the most famous living dramatist in the world. The single country which remained indifferent to his work was France, a country for which he himself, while he was still a music critic and unknown as a dramatist, had felt no affection. Its reputation as the citadel of the arts, he maintained, was spurious. Everywhere else, however, his works were frequently performed, and the dramatist who, until he was forty, could not obtain a regular public performance for any of his plays, was now in process of becoming the wealthiest author in history. He had always declined public honours, whether from the community or from universities, but he accepted the Nobel prize for 1925. (The money, more than £7,000, was used to establish the Anglo-Swedish Literary Foundation for the translation of Swedish literature into English, and it had issued four volumes of Strindberg's plays by 1939.) Shaw now resumed political writing. In 1928 he published *The Intelligent Woman's Guide to Socialism and Capitalism*, which had a wide sale, and in 1944 *Everybody's Political What's What?*. A remarkably popular short work, *The Adventures of the Black Girl in Her Search for God*, finely illustrated by Mr. John Farleigh, was written in South Africa and published in 1932.

Shaw was now an old man, and his work, although it was still astonishingly vigorous and vivacious, showed unmistakable signs of his age. He became increasingly careless about form. The best of his work in this period, however, was full of wisdom and the beauty of mind often displayed by old men who keep their wits about them. *The Apple Cart* was unexpectedly popular, chiefly because of its avowal of anti-democratic doctrine and its acclamation of an able monarch. It was produced in Warsaw in June 1929, and was given in England in August at the first of the Malvern Festivals inaugurated by Sir Barry Jackson. *Too True to be Good* (Malvern, 1932) had a character, Private Meek, who was manifestly derived from T. E. Lawrence, for whom Shaw had great personal liking; *Geneva* (Malvern, 1938) included portraits of Mussolini and Hitler; in *In Good King Charles's Golden Days* (Malvern, 1939), Isaac Newton and George Fox are brilliantly portrayed. But Shaw's great work virtually ended with *Saint Joan*, which bears to him the same relationship that *The Tempest* bears to Shakespeare. The advent of the talking film, however, and in particular Gabriel Pascal's production of *Pygmalion*, followed by *Major Barbara* and *Caesar and Cleopatra*, brought Shaw new fame, and, incidentally, fortune.

Much of Shaw's time was spent in extensive travel to please his wife whose delight was in journeys abroad. His health, which was less robust than, in his advocacy of vegetable diet, he was accustomed to maintain, broke down seriously in 1938, when he suffered from pernicious anaemia; nor was the distress of his illness lessened by the fact that the injections by which it was eventually cured involved a violation of his beliefs about diet. His recovery was darkened by the decline in his wife's health. Her illness was long and painful and she died in 1943. There were no children of the marriage. In 1946 when Shaw reached his ninetieth year he was made an honorary freeman of Dublin and the first honorary freeman of the metropolitan borough of St. Pancras, London.

The rest of Shaw's life was quiet and solitary. The loss of his wife was more profoundly felt than he had ever imagined any loss could be: for he prided himself on a stoical fortitude in all loss and misfortune. All his friends who were his contemporaries, with a single exception, Edward R. Pease, first secretary of the Fabian Society, were dead. He had outlived his time. Music was still a comfort to him, and he kept his wireless set almost continuously in operation; but reading, which had been his chief resource, no longer satisfied him: his mind could not concentrate as it had been accustomed to do, nor could he remember anything as well as he once had. Yet his spirit was unbroken, although his body was frail, and he was unwilling to acknowledge decline. He fell frequently, but then he had always fallen, even as a young man. There were trees to be lopped and pruned in his garden at Ayot St. Lawrence where he had lived since 1906, and he would lop and prune them, although he had gardeners to do the work. In September 1950, while trimming his trees, he fell and fractured his thigh. He was removed to hospital where he remained until 4 October when his wish to return home was granted. The will to live was ebbing, and he wished to die where he had lived so long with Charlotte. On 2 November 1950 he died. The whole world paid tribute to him. In America the lights of Broadway were lowered; the Indian Government, under Pandit Nehru who had visited him the year before, adjourned a Cabinet meeting; and *The Times* gave him a first leader. There was a universal feeling of loss. His body was cremated, as his wife's had been, and their ashes were mingled and scattered in the garden of their house at Ayot which was left to the National Trust.

When Shaw's will was published, his fortune was found to be more than £300,000, the greater part of which was devoured by the State. The residue, after some bequests had been made, was left on trust to institute and finance inquiries for a 'Proposed British Alphabet' of at least forty letters. Subject to other directions regarding the alphabet, the ultimate residue was to be given in equal shares to the National Gallery of Ireland, the British Museum, and the Royal Academy of Dramatic Art. The bequests to the first two are significant of Shaw's unending gratitude for kindness or benefit received. In the National Gallery of Ireland he had learnt to understand pictures, and in the British Museum, when he was almost desperately poor, he had found the facilities for reading and study that he needed.

Shaw's general belief about life had its foundation in a religious faith; for Shaw was essentially a religious-minded man. But in religion, as in all else, he was heterodox—a heathen mystic, as G. K. Chesterton called him. His faith, so far as it can be put in a few words, was in creative evolution, based on Bergson, whose attraction to Roman Catholicism at the end of his life would have surprised Shaw had he known of it. The Life Force, an arid expression for Shaw's idea of God, is an imperfect spirit seeking to become perfect, using the method of trial and error, and scrapping its instruments when they are worn out or prove intractable. A cardinal point in his doctrine is that human beings, if they do not assist the Life Force to find perfection, may be scrapped as the mammoth beasts and other creatures now extinct have been. But the belief, although it was firmly held, was never adequately worked out and did not attain to the position of a philosophy. It may be found most simply expressed in *The Shewing-Up of Blanco Posnet*. His Socialism was no more than a desire for an orderly community. Poverty and ignorance and ill health were untidy conditions and must, therefore, be abolished. But no man was less democratic than Shaw, whose admiration was given largely to dictatorial people. He was essentially aristocratic and individualistic in temper. His purpose was to provoke thought, and he provoked it for more than half a century.

Of the many portraits and busts of Shaw, the house at Ayot has a portrait by Augustus John, a bust in bronze by Rodin, and a bronze statuette by Troubetzkoy, whose bust of Shaw is in the Tate Gallery. Another portrait by Augustus John entitled 'The Sleeping Philosopher' is in the possession of Queen Elizabeth the Queen Mother. There is a portrait by Feliks Topolski, at Glasgow City Art Gallery. The National Gallery of Ireland has a portrait by John Collier and a life-size statue by Troubetzkoy. A bust by Epstein is in the National Portrait Gallery; busts by Rodin belong to the Royal Academy of Dramatic Art and the Municipal Gallery of Modern Art, Dublin; one by Strobl in the custody of the London County Council was bequeathed by Shaw to the future Shakespeare memorial national theatre.

[G. B. Shaw, prefaces to *The Irrational Knot*, 1905, *Immaturity*, 1930, and *London Music in 1888–89*, 1937; G. B. Shaw, *Sixteen Self Sketches*, 1949; Archibald Henderson, *Bernard Shaw: Playboy and Prophet*, 1911; Frank Harris, *Bernard Shaw*, with a postscript by Bernard Shaw, 1931; Hesketh Pearson, *Bernard Shaw*, 1942, followed by a *Postscript* by the same author, 1951; Blanche Patch, *Thirty Years with G.B.S.*, 1951; R. F. Rattray, *Bernard Shaw, a Chronicle*, 1951; St. John Ervine, *Bernard Shaw, His Life, Work and Friends*, 1956; private information; personal knowledge.]

St. John Ervine

*published 1959*

# SIM Alastair George Bell

**(1900–1976)**

Actor and director, was born 9 October 1900 at Lothian Road, Edinburgh, the youngest in the family of two sons and two daughters of Alexander Sim, tailor and clothier, and his wife, Isabella McIntyre. He was educated at the James Gillespie School at Edinburgh which he left at the age of fourteen, taking successive jobs as a delivery boy, a clerk with Gieves the outfitters, and, later, a post in the borough assessor's office. He had ideas, at this time, of becoming an analytical chemist and was studying at Edinburgh University, leaving it to join the Officers' Training Corps. The war ended before he had any opportunity of putting his military training to the test.

His first connection with the stage was from 1925 to 1930 when he was Fulton lecturer in elocution at New College, Edinburgh, a post which he obtained as a result of his work in the Edinburgh Provincial Training Centre. While holding this post he had established his own School of Drama and Speech Training. It was here that he first met Naomi Merlith, daughter of Hugh Plaskitt, solicitor. She was herself a promising actress, who gained a scholarship at RADA. They were married in 1932 and she was able to help him, professionally and enthusiastically, throughout his subsequent career. They had one daughter.

At the comparatively late age of thirty he played his first part on the professional stage, doubling the roles of messenger and sentry in the production of *Othello* (1930) in which Paul Robeson and (Dame) Peggy Ashcroft played the principal parts. This was followed by two years at the Old Vic. He was then out of action for a year with a slipped disc which was put right by an osteopath, and in the mid-thirties his face and personality became increasingly familiar to audiences in a series of film comedies and comedy-thrillers; the Inspector Hornleigh series, Edgar Wallace's *The Squeaker* (1937), *Alf's Button Afloat* (1938), and *Wedding Group* (1936), in which Sim played the Scottish minister and his wife the maid-of-all-work.

A return to the stage and to more serious work was signalled by the last of the pre-war Malvern drama festivals where he took one of the leading parts in *What Say They?* (1940) by James Bridie (O. H. Mavor). It was the beginning of a valuable, though not always peaceful, association as Bridie wrote and Sim both acted in and directed plays of the calibre of

*Mr. Bolfry* (1943), *Dr Angelus* (1947), *The Forrigan Reel* (1945), and *Mr Gillie* (1950).

It was in *Mr Bolfry* that he introduced one of his best-remembered directorial touches. The play dealt with a confrontation between a Scots minister and the Devil. As written by Bridie (who, said James Agate, could never construct a satisfactory third act) the Devil turned out to be an escaped lunatic. Sim reacted strongly against the feebleness of this. He insisted 'the Devil must be the Devil'. The difficulty was how to get him off the stage at the end of the play and back where he belonged. Sim's solution was a *coup de théâtre*. The Devil, off stage at that point, had left his umbrella propped in a corner. The door opened. No one appeared. The umbrella picked itself up and walked slowly out by the far door.

The death of Bridie in 1951 put an end to this fruitful association and in some ways Sim never achieved the same magical alchemy which results when the separate talents of author, actor, and director are fused into a single whole. He gave many notable performances on stage and screen. On the screen he played in *Scrooge* (1951) and (fondest memory for many) *The Happiest Days of Your Life* (1950) with (Dame) Margaret Rutherford. On the stage there were William Golding's *The Brass Butterfly* (1958), annual appearances as the sardonic old Etonian, Captain Hook, and towards the end of his career two notable successes at the Chichester Festival, both of which came subsequently to the West End, *The Magistrate* (1969) and *Dandy Dick* (1973) by Sir A. W. Pinero.

In 1948 Sim achieved a remarkable feat, being elected rector of Edinburgh University by a majority greater than that achieved by any of the prime ministers and field marshals who had preceded him. His address ('the only one of eight that I have actually been able to hear', said Bridie) was delivered to that most critical of audiences, with all his professional skill. As one reads it one can hear it being spoken, in the inimitable Sim manner; the clipped words, the sardonic intonation, the crocodile smile. His own character appears in every line: 'I admit that even to this day I enjoy being called an artiste, and if anyone likes to qualify it with some such adjective as "great", "incomparable", "superb", then you can rely on me to finish the ritual by reacting with becoming modesty. But I shall know it is all nonsense'.

He was as devastating at the pricking of pomposity in others as in himself.

He was made an honorary LL D of Edinburgh University in 1951 on his retirement as rector, appointed CBE in 1953, and refused the knighthood offered to him by Edward Heath on the grounds that it would be ridiculous to be addressed as Sir Alastair. He died in London 19 August 1976. There is a portrait of him by Edward Seago in the Garrick Club of which he was a long and enthusiastic member and from which he regularly threatened to resign.

[Private information; personal knowledge.]

MICHAEL GILBERT

*published 1986*

## SYNGE John Millington

(1871–1909)

Irish dramatist, born at Newtown Little, near Rathfarnham (a suburban village adjoining Dublin), on 16 April 1871 was youngest child (in a family of one daughter and four sons) of John Hatch Synge, barrister-at-law, by his wife Kathleen, daughter of the Rev. Robert Traill, D.D. (d. 1847), of Schull, county Cork, translator of Josephus.

His father dying when he was a year old, his mother moved nearer Dublin to Orwell Park, Rathgar, which was his home until 1890, when he removed with his mother and brother to 31 Crosthwaite Park, Kingstown, which was his family home until shortly before his death.

After attending private schools, first in Dublin and then at Bray, he studied with a tutor between the ages of fourteen and seventeen. The main interest of his boyhood was an intimate study of nature. 'He knew the note and plumage of every bird, and when and where they were to be found'. In youth he joined the Dublin Naturalists Field Club, and later took up music, becoming a proficient player of the piano, the flute, and the violin. His summer vacations were spent at Annamoe, co. Wicklow, among the strange people of the glens.

On 18 June 1888 he entered Trinity College, Dublin, as a pensioner, his college tutor being Dr. Traill (later provost). He passed his little go in Michaelmas term, 1890 (3rd class), obtained prizes in Hebrew and in Irish in Trinity term, 1892, and graduated B.A. with a second class in the pass-examination in December 1892. His name went off the college books six months later (3 June 1893).

While at Trinity he studied music at the Royal Irish Academy of Music, where he obtained a scholarship in harmony and counterpoint in 1891. On leaving college he thought of music as a profession, and went to Germany to study that art and to learn the German language. He first visited Coblentz, and (in the spring of 1894) Würzburg. Before the end of 1894 he altered his plans, and, deciding to devote himself to literary work, settled by way of preparation as a student in Paris in January 1895. For the next few years his time was generally divided between France and Ireland, but in 1896 he stayed in Italy long enough to learn Italian. He had a natural gift for languages, and during these years he read much. From 1897 he wrote much tentative work, both prose and verse, in French and English, and contemplated writing a critical study of Racine and a translation from the Italian (either the 'Little Flowers', or the 'Companions of St. Francis of Assisi'). In May 1898 he first visited the Aran Islands.

In 1899, when he was living at the Hôtel Corneille (Rue Corneille), near the Odéon theatre, in Paris, Synge was introduced to Mr. W. B. Yeats, one of the founders and the chief inspiration of the Irish Literary Movement. Mr. Yeats suggested that Synge should give up writing criticism either in French or English and go again to the Aran Islands off Galway, or some other primitive place, to study and write about a way of life not yet expressed in literature. But for this meeting it is likely that Synge would never have discovered a form in which he could express himself; his mind would have continued to brood without vitality upon questions of literary criticism. As a result of this meeting, Synge went again to the Aran Islands (September 1899); the visit was repeated in the autumns of 1900, 1901, and 1902. He lived among the islanders as one of themselves, and was much loved by them; his natural genius for companionship made him always a welcome guest. He took with him his fiddle, his conjuring tricks, his camera and penny whistle, and feared that 'they would get tired of him, if he brought them nothing new'.

During his second stay he began a book on the Aran Islands, which was slowly completed in France, Ireland, and London, and published in April 1907, with illustrations by Mr. Jack B. Yeats.

Meanwhile he wrote two plays, 'The Shadow of the Glen' and the 'Riders to the Sea', both founded on stories heard in Aran, and both finished, but for slight changes, by the winter of 1902–3. 'The Shadow of the Glen' was performed at the Molesworth Hall, Dublin, on 8 Oct. 1903. 'Riders to the Sea' was performed at the same place on 25 Feb. 1904. They were published in a single volume in May 1905. 'Riders to the Sea' is the deepest and the tenderest of his plays. 'The Shadow of the Glen' is the first example of the kind of tragically hearted farce which is Synge's main contribution to the theatre. Of two other tragic farces of the same period, 'The Tinker's Wedding' (the first drama conceived by him), was begun in 1902, but not finished till 1906, and only published late in 1907; the more beautiful and moving 'The Well of the Saints' was written in 1903–4. 'The Tinker's Wedding', the only play by Synge not publicly acted in Ireland, was produced after his death at His Majesty's Theatre, by the Afternoon Theatre, on 11 Nov. 1909.

In the winter of 1902–3 Synge lived for a few months in London (4 Handel Street, W.C.). Afterwards he gave up his lodging in Paris (90 Rue d'Assas), and thenceforth passed much time either in or near Dublin, or in the wilds of Wicklow and Kerry, the Blasket Islands, and the lonely places by Dingle Bay. There he found the material for the occasional papers 'In Wicklow' and 'In West Kerry', published partly, from time to time, in the 'Manchester Guardian' and the 'Shanachie', and reprinted in the fourth volume of the 'Works'. From 3 June till 2 July 1905 he made a tour with Mr. Jack B. Yeats through the congested districts of Connemara. Some descriptions of the journey, with illustrations by Mr. Jack B. Yeats, were contributed to the 'Manchester Guardian'. Twelve of the papers are reprinted in the fourth volume of the 'Works'.

The Abbey Theatre was opened in Dublin 27 Dec. 1904, and Synge became one of its three literary advisers, helping to direct its destinies until his death. There on 4 Feb. 1905 was first performed 'The Well of the Saints' (published in December following). There, too, was first acted (26 Jan. 1907) 'The Playboy of the Western World', written in 1905–6. This piece excited the uproar and confusion with which the new thing is usually received, but was subsequently greeted with tumultuous applause both in Dublin and by the most cultured audience in England.

During his last years Synge lived almost wholly in Ireland, mostly in Dublin. His health, never very robust, was beginning to trouble him. His last months of life, 1908–9, were spent in writing and rewriting the unfinished three-act play 'Deirdre of the Sorrows', which was posthumously published at Miss Yeats's Cuala Press, on 5 July 1910, and was acted at the Abbey Theatre on 13 Jan. 1910. He also worked at translations from Villon and Petrarch, wrote some of the strange ironical poems, so like the man speaking, which were published by the Cuala Press just after his death, and finished the study 'Under Ether', published in the fourth volume of the 'Works'. He died unmarried at a private nursing home in Dublin on 24 March 1909. He was buried in a family tomb at the protestant Mount Jerome general graveyard at Harold's Cross, Dublin. His 'Poems and Translations'—the poems written at odd times between 1891 and 1908, but most of them towards the end of his life—was published on 5 June 1909 by the Cuala Press.

Synge stood about five feet eight or nine inches high. He was neither weakly nor robustly made. He was dark (not black-haired), with heavy moustache, and small goatee on lower lip, otherwise clean-shaven. His hair was worn rather long; his face was pale, drawn, seamed, and old-looking. The eyes were at once smoky and kindling; the mouth had a great play of humour on it. His voice was very guttural and quick, and lively with a strange vitality. His manner was generally reserved, grave, courteous; he talked little; but had a bright malice of fun always ready. He gave little in conversation; for much of his talk, though often wise with the criticism seen in his prefaces, was only a reflection of things he had seen, and of phrases, striking and full of colour, overheard by him at sea or on shore; but there was a charm about him which all felt.

He brought into Irish literature the gifts of detachment from topic and a wild vitality of tragedy. The ironical laughter of his comedy is always most mocking when it covers a tragic intention. He died when his powers were only beginning to show themselves. As revelations of himself, his poems and one or two of the sketches are his best works; as ironic visions of himself, 'The Playboy', 'The Shadow of the Glen', and 'The Tinker's Wedding' are his best; but in 'The Well of the Saints', in 'Riders to the Sea', in the book on Aran, in the heart-breaking lyric about the birds, and in the play of Deirdre, he touches with a rare sensitiveness on something elemental. Like all men of genius he awakened animosity in those anxious to preserve old standards or fearful of setting up new ones.

Among the most important portraits (other than photographs) are: 1. An oil painting by Mr. J. B. Yeats, R.H.A., now in the Municipal Gallery in Dublin. 2. A drawing by Mr. J. B. Yeats, R.H.A. (the best likeness), reproduced in the 'Samhain' for December 1904. 3. A drawing by Mr. J. B. Yeats, R.H.A., 'Synge at Rehearsal', reproduced as a frontispiece to 'The Playboy of the Western World', and to the 'Works', vol. ii. 4. A drawing by Mr. James Paterson (the frontispiece to the 'Works', vol. iv.).

'The Works of John M. Synge' (4 vols. 1910), with four portraits (two from photographs), contain all the published books and plays, and all the miscellaneous papers which his literary executors thought worthy of inclusion. Much unpublished material remains in their hands, and a few papers contributed to the 'Speaker' during 1904–5 and to the 'Manchester Guardian' during 1905–6–7–8, and an early article in 'L'Européen' (Paris, 15 March 1902) on 'La Vieille Littérature Irlandaise', have not been reprinted.

[Personal memories; private sources; Mr. W. B. Yeats's *Collected Works*, viii. 173; Contemp. Rev., April 1911, p. 470; art. by Mr. Jack B. Yeats in *New York Sun*, July 1909; *Manchester Guardian*, 25 March 1909; *J. M. Synge: a Critical Study*, by P. P. Howe, 1912; notes kindly supplied from M. Maurice Bourgeois's forthcoming study of the man and his writings; information from Mr. J. L. Hammond.]

JOHN MASEFIELD

*published 1912*

# TERRY Dame (Alice) Ellen

(1847–1928)

Actress, was born in Smithford Street, Coventry, 27 February 1847, the third daughter and third of the eleven children of Benjamin Terry, actor, by his wife, Sarah Ballard, actress, daughter of a Scottish minister at Portsmouth. Benjamin Terry's father was H. B. Terry, an innkeeper at Portsmouth. Three of Ellen Terry's sisters, Kate, Marion, and Florence, and a brother, Fred, also went on the stage. Ellen's first appearance on the stage was as the boy Mamillius in Charles Kean's production of *The Winter's Tale* at the Princess's Theatre, London, 28 April 1856. With Kean she also acted Puck in *A Midsummer-Night's Dream* (1856), Arthur in *King John* (1858), and Fleance in *Macbeth* (1859), besides a fairy in a pantomime and many other parts.

Ellen Terry's childhood was full of work, and in 1862 she went to the Theatre Royal, Bristol, to the company of J. H. Chute, for whom she appeared as Titania at the opening of the Theatre Royal, Bath, in March 1863. Her dress for that part was designed by the architect Edward William Godwin, whose acquaintance she first made at Bristol. In the spring of 1863 she joined the company of John Baldwin Buckstone at the Haymarket Theatre. Her parts there included Hero, Desdemona, Nerissa, Lady Touchwood in *The Belle's Stratagem*, Flora in *The Duke's Motto*, Julia in *The Rivals*, and Mary Meredith in *Our American Cousin* by Tom Taylor, in which Edward Askew Sothern was giving his celebrated performance of Lord Dundreary. But Ellen Terry regarded her season at the Haymarket as a lost opportunity. She was restless and not happy, and the theatre had come to seem to her less interesting than the studio. Tom Taylor had introduced her to the painter George Frederic Watts, who was enchanted with her beauty; and on 20 February 1864 she was married to him at St. Barnabas church, Kensington. Watts was then nearly forty-seven years old. He and his circle treated his wife like a child—not without some provocation from her playful high spirits. Against her will a separation was arranged in June 1865. She went back to the stage, and in October 1867 joined Alfred Sydney Wigan at the New Queen's Theatre, Long Acre, to play Mrs. Mildmay in Tom Taylor's *Still Waters Run Deep* and other parts, among them Katharine in *Katharine and Petruchio* (Garrick's version of *The Taming of the Shrew*), in which, in December 1867, she acted for the first time with (Sir) Henry Irving. She was still neither happy nor successful on the stage, and in 1868 she left it and set up house in Hertfordshire with her friend Godwin. The theatre saw her no more for six years, during which time she gave birth to her daughter Edith Craig, and her son Edward Gordon Craig.

Anxiety for her children's future induced Ellen Terry to accept an offer from Charles Reade. On 28 February 1874 she took up the part of Philippa in Reade's *The Wandering Heir* at the New Queen's Theatre, and in the summer toured with Reade, from whom she learned much of the art of acting. On 17 April 1875, at the age of twenty-eight, she reached the turning-point of her career, when she appeared as Portia in the production of *The Merchant of Venice* at the old Prince of Wales's Theatre staged by (Sir) Squire Bancroft and his wife. The play ran for only three weeks, but Ellen Terry, in looks and in acting, was the high point of beauty in a beautiful production. Her personal success led to further work with the Bancrofts.

In November 1876 Ellen Terry went for eighteen months to the Court Theatre, where (Sir) John Hare gave her her second great opportunity, namely the part of Olivia in the adaptation by W. G. Wills of Goldsmith's *Vicar of Wakefield* (28 March 1878). In that part, which remained in her repertory until 1900, she proved her power of reducing her audience to tears. Godwin and she had parted company, but not friendship, in 1875; and on 21 November 1877 (Watts having divorced her in that year) she married Charles Clavering Wardell, who acted under the name of Charles Kelly. In 1881 they were judicially separated.

In 1878 Henry Irving, having become sole lessee of the Lyceum Theatre, engaged Ellen Terry to play Ophelia in his forthcoming production of *Hamlet*, and she appeared in that part on the opening night of his management (30 December). Thus began an association which lasted unimpaired until 1896 and unbroken until 1902. Up till 1896 Ellen Terry played the leading female parts in all Irving's productions. The list (excluding revivals and single performances for charity) is as follows: 1878, Ophelia. 1879, Pauline in *The Lady of Lyons*; Ruth in *Eugene Aram*; Henrietta Maria in *Charles I*; Portia. 1880, Iolanthe in a play of that name by Wills. 1881, Camma in *The Cup*; Letitia Hardy in *The Belle's Stratagem*; Desdemona. 1882, Juliet; Beatrice. 1883, Jeannette in *The Lyons Mail*; Clementine in *Robert Macaire*. 1884, Viola. 1885, Olivia in *Olivia*; Marguerite in *Faust*. 1886, Peggy in James Kenney's farce *Raising the Wind*. 1887, Ellaline in *The Amber Heart*. 1888, Lady Macbeth. 1889, Catherine Duval in *The Dead Heart*. 1890, Lucy Ashton in *Ravenswood* by H. C. Merivale. 1891, Nance Oldfield in the play of that name by Charles Reade. 1892, Queen Katharine in *King Henry VIII*; Cordelia. 1893, Rosamund in *Becket*. 1894, Guinevere in *King Arthur* by Joseph Comyns Carr. 1896, Imogen. 1897, Catharine in *Madame Sans-Gêne*. 1898, Catherine in *Peter the Great* by Laurence Irving; Sylvia Wynford in *The Medicine Man* by Robert Hichens and H. D. Traill. 1899, Clarice in *Robespierre*, an adaptation by Laurence Irving from the French. 1901,

Volumnia. She took part in Irving's eight American tours between 1883 and 1901. In the summer of 1902 she was acting at the Lyceum only twice a week, in matinées of *Charles I* and *The Merchant of Venice*. Her last appearance at that theatre was as Portia, 19 July 1902. She decided not to go to America with Irving to act a part in *Dante*; and in the autumn of that year, neither at her suggestion nor by her desire, they finally parted.

Egoist though he was, Irving had too much sense to stint his theatre of the genius of Ellen Terry at her best. Certain plays he chose rather for her sake than for his own. And Ellen Terry made the most of her chances. In face, dress, and movement she was so beautiful, her voice was so thrilling, her personal charm so inextinguishable, and, above all, her vitality so exuberant that these qualities won much of the credit due to histrionic power dependent upon nothing but her intelligence, sympathy, and hard work. As Lucy Ashton she showed that she could conquer her besetting temptation to restlessness. In Madame Sans-Gêne and Volumnia, parts out of line with her personality, she showed her accomplishment and power of impersonation. When her natural attractions (which she had perfectly at command) chimed with her skill, she was a great actress. There was nothing insipid about her. In the young women of Shakespeare, Desdemona or Ophelia, she found character; as Lady Macbeth she was an exquisite woman aflame with ambitious imagination; in Queen Katharine her majesty proved her patience to be no weakness. But she was at her best when her sense of fun and her high spirits could join forces with her strength, her intensity, and her grace. Her Beatrice, surpassing even her Portia, was as near perfection as acting can go. With every sign of complete spontaneity, it was a work of precisely calculated art.

In April 1902, while Irving was acting *Faust* with Cissie Loftus as Marguerite, Ellen Terry went to Stratford-upon-Avon in order to play Queen Katharine with (Sir) Frank Benson's company. In June she appeared with great success at His Majesty's Theatre as Mrs. Page in *The Merry Wives of Windsor* produced by (Sir) Herbert Beerbohm Tree. In 1903 she ventured into management. The theatre was the Imperial, in Westminster; and there in April she produced *The Vikings*, an English version by William Archer of Ibsen's *The Vikings at Helgeland*, herself taking the part of Hiordis. The staging was by Gordon Craig, and was the first example of his art on a large scale. It won golden opinions, but the cost was very heavy and the public rather shy. The play was soon withdrawn. The same ill-success attended her production, also staged by Gordon Craig, of *Much Ado about Nothing*; and in June she closed the theatre. In July 1903 at a charity performance at Drury Lane Theatre Ellen Terry played Portia and acted for the last time in her life with Henry Irving. The next two years saw her well established in modern prose drama. She showed her own faith in it by producing Christopher St. John's (Miss Christabel Marshall's) version of *The Good Hope* by Hermann Heijermans, in which for the first time she played the part of an old woman. On 5 April 1905 she created the part of Alice Grey in (Sir) J. M. Barrie's *Alice Sit-by-the-Fire* at the Duke of York's Theatre; and on 20 March 1906 at the Court Theatre she played Lady Cecily Waynflete in G. Bernard Shaw's *Captain Brassbound's Conversion*.

That month saw the fiftieth anniversary of Ellen Terry's first appearance on the stage; and the occasion was taken to pay public tribute to her. On 12 June a 'jubilee' matinée was held at Drury Lane, in the course of which she played Beatrice in the first act of *Much Ado about Nothing*, with scenery designed by her son and with twenty-two other members of her family in the cast. Foreigners as well as English people joined in the expression of admiration and affection; and nearly £10,000 was subscribed as a gift to her. In September 1906 at His Majesty's Theatre she played Hermione in *The Winter's Tale*. In the early part of 1907 she took *Captain Brassbound's Conversion* and *The Good Hope* on tour in the United States; and on 22 March of that year she was married at Pittsburg, Pennsylvania, to James Usselmann, a young American acting in her company under the name of James Carew, with whom she lived until 1910.

Failure of memory now made it difficult for Ellen Terry to take up new parts; but she appeared not infrequently in special performances. On 19 December 1908 at His Majesty's Theatre she created the part of a sweet old lady, Aunt Imogen, in Walford Graham Robertson's *Pinkie and the Fairies*; in 1917 and 1918 she acted the trial scene from *The Merchant of Venice* and scenes from *The Merry Wives of Windsor* at the Coliseum, and on 12 April 1919 at the Lyric Theatre she took the part of the Nurse in Doris Keane's production of *Romeo and Juliet*. Her last appearance on the stage was at the Lyric Theatre, Hammersmith, in Walter de la Mare's *Crossings* on 19 November 1925. Meanwhile in 1922 and 1923 she had taken part in four productions for the cinematograph. But she had found a wider outlet for her genius.

In 1903 Ellen Terry had composed, with the help of Christopher St. John, and delivered a lecture on 'The Letters in Shakespeare's Plays'. A few years later, with the same assistance, she composed two lectures on Shakespeare's heroines and one on the children in Shakespeare. That she had a talent for verbal expression, and much to say by that means, is proved by her memoirs and by her published letters to Bernard Shaw; and these lectures, with illustrations recited by the lecturer, proved her to be a fine critic and provided a delightful entertainment. In 1910–1911 she delivered the lectures on tour in America; in 1911 and 1912 she gave them in England, and in May 1914 she began a tour of Australia and the United States which lasted until the spring of 1915.

Ellen Terry's eyesight had long been troubling her and sometimes causing her acute pain; and in February 1915 she underwent an operation for cataract in New York. From 1921 onwards her health was failing, and her too lavish generosity had much reduced her means. She seldom went into public, but she was not forgotten. In 1922 the university of St. Andrews conferred upon her the honorary degree of LL.D.; and at the New Year, 1925, she was created G.B.E. She died 21 July 1928 at her house at Small Hythe, Tenterden, Kent. Her ashes were placed in a casket on the wall of St. Paul's church, Covent Garden. Her house at Small Hythe was bought by public subscription and converted into an Ellen Terry museum.

Portraits of Ellen Terry are very many, the most important being as follows. In the Tate Gallery hangs a well-known oil-painting by J. S. Sargent, of Ellen Terry as Lady Macbeth. In the National Portrait Gallery are a profile head of her at the age of seventeen by G. F. Watts, and an oil-sketch in black and white of her as Lady Macbeth coming out to meet Duncan, made by J. S. Sargent for reproduction in the *Souvenir* of her jubilee. The Watts Gallery at Compton, Surrey, possesses Watts's portrait of Ellen Terry as Ophelia. Lord Somers owns 'Ellen Terry and her Sister' (Kate), by Watts, and Mr. Kerrison Preston the portrait by Watts entitled 'Choosing'. Mr. W. Graham Robertson retains in his collection his pastel head of Ellen Terry, which Irving used to call 'Ellen in Heaven', his large oil-portrait, and a portrait which he painted in 1923. Miss Edith Craig owns an oil portrait painted in 1926 by Clare Atwood; and in the Memorial Museum at Small Hythe there is a replica in oils by W. Graham Robertson of his pastel head, besides many other portraits. At His Majesty's Theatre Ellen Terry is seen as Mistress Page, with Madge Kendal as Mrs. Ford and Tree as Falstaff, in a picture by the Hon. John Collier.

[*The Times*, 22 July 1928; *Ellen Terry's Memoirs*, with notes and additional chapters by E. Craig and C. St. John, 1933; Ellen Terry, *Four Lectures on Shakespeare*, edited by C. St. John, 1932; *Ellen Terry and Bernard Shaw, A Correspondence*, edited by C. St. John, 1931; Edward Gordon Craig, *Ellen Terry and her Secret Self*, 1931; Walford Graham Robertson, *Time Was*, 1931; Bram Stoker, *Personal Reminiscences of Henry Irving*, 2 vols., 1906; Austin Brereton, *Life of Henry Irving*, 2 vols., 1908; *Souvenir Programme, Ellen Terry Jubilee Commemoration*, 1906.]

H. H. Child

*published 1937*

## TERRY-THOMAS (1911–1990)

Actor and comedian, was born 14 July 1911 at his parents' home in Finchley, London, as Thomas Terry Hoar Stevens, the third child and third son in the family of four sons and one daughter of (Ernest) Frederick Stevens, managing director of a produce merchant's business, and his wife Ellen Elizabeth, daughter of Joseph Hoar, horse-dealer, of London. He was educated at Ardingly College, Sussex. During World War II he served in the Royal Corps of Signals (1941–6) and with ENSA (the Entertainments National Service Association).

Thomas began his career as a clerk at Smithfield market, but his interest in amateur theatricals led him to work as a film extra. He took the stage name of Terry-Thomas, which he hyphenated to match the gap in his front teeth. His props were a diamond-encrusted cigarette holder, monocle, raffish waistcoat, and red carnation. Six feet in height, handsome in appearance, with a neat moustache and a natural upper-class accent, Terry-Thomas personified the Englishman as an amiable bounder. With his drawling accent, he commonly used phrases such as 'rotter' and a leering 'jolly good show'. Once established, the character changed little from film to film. He toured with ENSA during World War II and, when demobilized, turned to cabaret work. In 1946 he found success with Sid Field in the West End hit, *Piccadilly Hayride*. He soon became popular on radio, with his own personal caddish humour, on *To Town with Terry* (1948–9) and *Top of the Town* (1951–2). He also presented his own television series—*Strictly T-T* (1949–56) and *How Do You View?* (1951–2).

The Boulting brothers brought his natural comic talents to universal acclaim when they cast him, with Ian Carmichael, Dennis Price, and Richard (later Baron) Attenborough, in their film *Private's Progress* (1956), in which he uttered the words 'You're an absolute shower' in his best upper-crust voice, words which were to become a catch-phrase. This led to a succession of memorable films, which included *Brothers in Law* (1957), *Carlton-Brown of the FO* (1958), *Lucky Jim* (1958), *I'm All Right, Jack* (1960), and *School for Scoundrels* (1960). In the early 1960s Terry-Thomas went to Hollywood, where he had to coarsen his already not very subtle persona, and he made several films, including *How to Murder Your Wife* (1964, his favourite film, in which he acted with Jack Lemmon), *Those Magnificent Men in Their Flying Machines* (1965), and *Monte Carlo or Bust* (1969). He was also a frequent performer on American television, appearing with Danny Kaye, Judy Garland, Andy Williams, and others. A return to the BBC in 1968, with a series called *The Old Campaigner*, had only a modest impact. In the late 1970s he discovered that he was suffering from Parkinson's disease, which put an end to his career.

In 1938 Terry-Thomas married a dancer, Ida Florence (died 1983), the divorced wife of Ernest Stern and daughter of Philip Patlansky, hotel proprietor. There were no children of the marriage. After a divorce in 1962 he married in 1963 Belinda, daughter of Geoffrey Percy Cunningham, a lieutenant-colonel in the Royal Artillery. They had two sons.

A millionaire at the height of his fame, after his premature retirement he and his wife went to live in a villa on Ibiza, where he had built up land and property holdings. However, his illness caused him to spend £40,000 a year on medical bills and he had to return to Britain. Following a succession of house moves, he was discovered in the late 1980s living in reduced circumstances in a church charity flat in Barnes, south-west London, furnished by the Actors' Benevolent Fund. Friends in show business staged a benefit concert for him at London's Drury Lane theatre in April 1989. The money that it raised enabled him to live in comfort at Busbridge Hall Nursing Home in Godalming, Surrey. He died there of pneumonia 8 January 1990. At his funeral service, the organist played the theme tune to one of his favourite films, *Those Magnificent Men in Their Flying Machines*.

[Terry-Thomas, *Filling the Gap* (autobiography), 1959; Terry-Thomas and Terry Daum, *Terry-Thomas Tells Tales* (autobiography), 1990; *A Tribute to Terry-Thomas*, a documentary made by the Serendipity Film Company and screened by ITV in May 1990.]

RICHARD HOPE-HAWKINS
C. S. NICHOLLS

*published* 1996

## THORNDIKE Dame (Agnes) Sybil

(1882–1976)

Actress, was born 24 October 1882 at Gainsborough in Lincolnshire, the elder daughter and eldest of the four children of the Revd Arthur John Webster Thorndike and his wife, Agnes MacDonald, daughter of John Bowers, shipping merchant. The other children—Russell, Eileen, and Frank—all went into the theatre for some time as, later, did all four of Sybil Thorndike's own children and many of her grandchildren. When she was two her father was appointed a minor canon of Rochester Cathedral and the family moved to Kent where they stayed throughout the rest of her childhood.

Sybil Thorndike made her parlour début at the age of four and within three years was regularly performing, for family and cathedral friends in Rochester, a melodrama called 'The Dentist's Cure' and subtitled 'Saw Their Silly Heads Off' (after *Sweeney Todd*), which she and Russell had written and produced—the beginnings, perhaps, of a fascination with Grand Guignol which was to lead to her celebrated seasons at the Little Theatre in the 1920s.

Around the time of her tenth birthday, her father was offered the living of the nearby St. Margaret's parish and the family moved from Minor Canon Row (immortalized by Charles Dickens in *Edwin Drood*) to more spacious vicarage quarters. By now there was little doubt that Sybil Thorndike would be going into public performance of one kind or another, although it might well have been musical rather than dramatic since her mother was an excellent pianist. Educated at Rochester High School, she also made weekly visits to London for lessons at the Guildhall, which were coupled with occasional visits to Her Majesty's when (Sir) Herbert Beerbohm Tree was performing Mark Antony.

On 13 May 1899 Sybil Thorndike gave a recital of Bach, Schumann, and Chopin at the Corn Exchange in Rochester. Very soon afterwards however, she began to feel pain in her right wrist which made it impossible to span an octave; piano cramp was diagnosed, and although she persevered for a while with the dogged tenacity which was already a hallmark of her personality, it was soon clear that she would be in need of another career.

She auditioned for (Sir) P. B. Ben Greet who agreed that she should join his company on 24 August 1904 as they set off to tour America; in the preceding weeks she was to walk on with the company during a summer season at Cambridge where she made her professional début in the grounds of Downing College on 14 June, as Palmis in *The Palace of Truth*.

The following two years were spent largely with Greet in America, touring the length and breadth of the country in often rough conditions, playing a clutch of lesser roles (including Lucianus, nephew to the king, in the play scene of *Hamlet* and Ceres in the masque of *The Tempest*) as well as frequently stepping into the breach for more important actresses afflicted by the rigours of primitive touring schedules and appalling transport. Thus by 1907 Sybil Thorndike had played 112 parts in all for Greet on the road, ranging from Viola, Helena, Gertrude, and Rosalind to Ophelia, Nerissa, 'Noises Off' and (in Kansas City, 1905) Everyman. It was a baptism of fire, but on those American tours Sybil Thorndike, still in her twenties, learnt the elements of her trade, of which the most important remained sheer survival.

On her final return to London in 1907 she landed a Sunday-night job with the Play Actors' Society as an American girl in a farce called *The Marquis*; G. B. Shaw was present for the play's sole performance and next morning asked her if she would be willing to understudy Ellen O'Malley in a revival of *Candida* for the company of Miss A. E. F. Horniman. They were to play a split week in Belfast, the first three evenings being taken up with Shaw's *Widowers' Houses* in which Sybil Thorndike noticed, playing Trench, 'a young man called Lewis Casson'. Lewis Thomas Casson, who was knighted in 1945, was born in Birkenhead 26 October 1875, the son of Major Thomas Casson, of Festiniog and Port Madoc.

That one Belfast week in the spring of 1908 was to condition the remaining seventy years of Sybil Thorndike's public and private life; it established an alliance with Shaw (who in 1923 was to write *St. Joan* for her) and with Casson whom she married the Christmas after that first meeting. They had two sons and two daughters and celebrated their diamond wedding anniversary in 1968 by which time she was over eighty and he over ninety. He died the following year.

At the time of her wedding Sybil Thorndike was a permanent member of Miss Horniman's pioneering repertory company at the Gaiety, Manchester; the following year she joined the Charles Frohman company at the Duke of York's in London, before returning briefly to America to tour and appear on Broadway as Emily Chapman in *Smith* by W. Somerset Maugham. Then, in June 1912, she returned to the Gaiety, Manchester, to play Beatrice in *Hindle Wakes* by W. Stanley Houghton, a major play of the 'northern' school of semi-documentary dramas. Until the outbreak of World War I she remained a leading player for Miss Horniman's company in Manchester and on their occasional London visits with productions of which Lewis Casson was, increasingly, the director.

Three children were born to Sybil Thorndike during short breaks from repertory work at the Gaiety; when war was declared Lewis Casson at once joined the army and his wife moved the rest of the family down to London where she had been offered a season at the Old Vic by Lilian Baylis. In the event she was to stay at the Vic for four years playing Rosalind, Lady Macbeth, Portia, Beatrice, Imogen, Ophelia, the Fool in *King Lear* (male actors being hard to come by in wartime), Kate Hardcastle, Lydia Languish, and Lady Teazle among a vast range of other and sometimes lesser roles: 'Miss Thorndike will be a great actress', wrote a *Sunday Times* critic, 'so long as she learns to keep her hands beneath her shoulders'. But those wartime seasons at the Vic, some of them played during the earliest air raids, forged and fired and confirmed for London audiences the talent that was soon to hallmark her St. Joan.

But first came the Greek plays: she played Hecuba in the translation by G. Gilbert Murray of Euripides' *The Trojan Women* for a series of special matinées at the Vic in October 1919; by March 1920 she was at the Holborn Empire (though again for matinées only) as Hecuba and Medea, performances to which she would also add Candida for good measure. Then came a two-year run at the Little Theatre in a series of Grand Guignol melodramas which was something of a family concern: Sybil Thorndike and her brother Russell co-starred with Casson (who also directed) in plays like *The Hand of Death, The Kill*, and *Fear* in which they were gainfully employed terrifying theatre-goers, never more so than in *The Old Women* where Sybil Thorndike had her eyes gouged out by the knitting needles of the crazed fellow inmates of an asylum.

But as the vogue for horror drew to a close, the Cassons themselves set up in management of the New Theatre, with (Sir) Bronson Albery and Lady Wyndham; they opened with *The Cenci* in 1922, and at one of its matinées Sybil Thorndike was seen again by Bernard Shaw. *St. Joan*, which he then wrote for her, opened at the New Theatre in March 1924, and marked the early but unchallenged climax of her career. It ran initially for 244 performances, and was to be revived at regular intervals at home and abroad until Sybil Thorndike's final performance of the role in March 1941. Throughout the late 1920s and 1930s she also did a great deal of other classical and modern work, often under her husband's direction, ranging from Jane Clegg in the play of that name to Emilia in *Othello* in 1930, playing with Paul Robeson, to Miss Moffat in *The Corn is Green* (1938) by Emlyn Williams. In 1931 she was appointed DBE, the sixth actress to be so honoured.

As World War II started the Cassons toured the Welsh mining villages and towns, bringing *Macbeth, Medea*, and *Candida* to audiences who had often never seen them before. In 1944 Sybil Thorndike joined the legendary (Lord) Olivier–(Sir) Ralph Richardson Old Vic season at the New, playing, among many other roles, Margaret to Olivier's Richard III and Aase to Richardson's Peer Gynt as well as the Nurse in *Uncle Vanya* and, in 1946, Jocasta in *Oedipus Rex*.

Then began a gentle post-war decline; the great years of Shaw and the Greeks and Miss Horniman all belonged to a lost pre-war world. Sybil Thorndike was already in her early sixties and, though still indefatigable, having now to spend her time in minor West End comedies or guest-starring in films. The 1950s brought her considerable successes (*Waters of the Moon, A Day by the Sea*) in London but it was on long and gruelling tours of Australia and South Africa only that the Cassons were now to be seen in their more classical work.

But in 1962, when Olivier was forming at Chichester the company he would take with him to open the National Theatre at the Old Vic, both Cassons were in his *Uncle Vanya* again, Sybil Thorndike now playing the old nurse Marina. From that, as if to prove her now septuagenarian versatility and vitality, she went into a short-lived musical of *Vanity Fair* (1962). The stage roles now were fewer and further between, and in 1966 the Cassons made their farewell appearance in London with a revival of *Arsenic and Old Lace*. Then came the opening of the Thorndike Theatre in Leatherhead where she was to make her final appearance in October 1969, six months after the death of her husband. In 1970 she was made a Companion of Honour; she also had several honorary degrees, including an Oxford D.Litt. (1966). After two heart attacks within four days, Sybil Thorndike died at her flat in Swan Court, Chelsea, 9 June 1976.

[J. C. Trewin, *Sybil Thorndike*, 1955; Russell Thorndike, *Sybil Thorndike*, 1950; Sheridan Morley, *Sybil Thorndike*, 1977; E. Sprigge, *Sybil Thorndike Casson*, 1971; John Casson, *Lewis and Sybil*, 1972; personal knowledge.]

Sheridan Morley

*published 1986*

## TILLEY Vesta

(1864–1952)

Male impersonator, whose real name was Matilda Alice Powles, was born in Worcester 13 May 1864, the second child of the family of thirteen of William Henry Powles and his wife, Matilda Broughton. Her father was a painter on chinaware and also a clever entertainer and musician, playing the violin and piccolo. He found this more lucrative than his painting and became manager of a variety hall in Gloucester, to which city the family moved. He took the name of Harry Ball. Father and daughter were devoted to each other and when she was three years old little Matilda showed remarkable talent. Her father took her to the hall with him each evening and on returning home she would re-enact all that she had seen. He arranged a medley of songs which she sang to friends and when he was given a benefit in Gloucester Matilda made her début at the ripe age of three and a half. She first wore boy's clothes on the stage at Birmingham when she was five and that determined her future. Touring with her father, she appeared all over the country and came to London in 1878. She was a great success and appeared at three or four music-halls each evening, billed as 'The Great Little Tilley'. Since audiences were puzzled whether she was a boy or a girl she eventually adopted the name of Vesta Tilley. As she grew up she represented the perfect pattern of the well-dressed man of the period. Her clothes, hats, gloves, shirts, everything she wore, were of superlative cut and quality.

She became a celebrated principal boy in provincial pantomimes and twice appeared at Drury Lane: in *Sindbad* in 1882 in a part specially written for her and in 1890 as principal boy in *Beauty and the Beast*. She also appeared in musical comedy, straight plays, and burlesque, and was as successful in the United States as in her own country. Her real fame was achieved on the music-halls which were then at the very peak of their popularity. Popularly known as 'the London Idol', in the eyes of her faithful public she could do no wrong. She never descended to vulgarity; no breath of scandal ever touched her; and she was a perfectionist in everything she undertook. This tiny woman with the trim figure, the piquant face, and the clear voice and diction and the most immaculate male clothing, had a succession of splendid songs and sang them in a manner all her own. Among them were 'Following in Father's Footsteps', 'Burlington Bertie', 'The Piccadilly Johnny with the little glass eye', 'The Midnight Son', 'Angels without wings', 'Oh! you Girls', 'The Tablet of Fame', 'For the sake of the dear little Girls', 'Daughters', and 'Sweetheart May'. She represented not only smart young men-about-town, but also judges, clergymen, and boys in Eton suits. Some of her biggest successes were sung in military uniform. She championed the soldier when most music-hall songs glorified the sailor. One such song, 'Jolly Good Luck to the Girl who Loves a Soldier', caused a boom in recruiting; another big hit was 'The Army of To-day's all right'. During the war of 1914–18 her soldier songs 'London in France', 'Six Days' Leave', and 'A Bit of a Blighty One' were a great aid to morale.

On 5 June 1920 she retired and said farewell from the stage of the London Coliseum. It was an occasion of great enthusiasm and very considerable emotion. The immense auditorium was packed from ceiling to floor. And as Vesta Tilley stood, in khaki uniform and half buried in bouquets, bowing to the wonderful ovation, (Dame) Ellen Terry made a charming speech and presented her with a set of handsomely bound volumes containing the signatures of nearly two million of her admirers.

In 1890 Vesta Tilley married (Sir) Walter de Frece (died 1935), a music-hall magnate who later entered politics and was a member of Parliament from 1920 to 1931. It was an ideally happy marriage. She greatly helped him in his political career and did much quiet unobtrusive work for charity. They had no children. She died in London 16 September 1952.

[Lady de Frece, *Recollections of Vesta Tilley*, 1934; private information; personal knowledge.]

W. MACQUEEN-POPE

*published* 1971

## TRAVERS Benjamin

(1886–1980)

Dramatist, was born 12 November 1886 in Hendon, Middlesex, the elder son and the second of the three children of Walter Francis Travers, clerk and later merchant, of London, and his wife, Margaret Travers Burges. He was a great-grandson of Benjamin Travers, pioneer in eye surgery and serjeant-surgeon to Queen Victoria. Always called Ben by his family and friends, he was educated at the Abbey School, Beckenham, and Charterhouse, where his first form master in the lower school was Leonard Huxley, father of Aldous and (Sir) Julian. He was an unusually small boy for his age. 'And that was a terrible handicap to me', he later recalled, adding 'I was a complete failure at school'. The only thing he enjoyed there was cricket, having become an enthusiast for the sport when he saw England's legendary batsman W. G. Grace make a century.

On leaving Charterhouse, in 1904, his parents sent him to Dresden for a few months to learn German. The performances of Sarah Bernhardt and Lucien Guitry which he saw there gave him a taste for the theatre, so that on his return he informed his parents that he wished to become an actor. This request was promptly vetoed, and instead he was put into the family business, Messrs Joseph Travers and Sons Ltd., one of the oldest wholesale grocery firms in the City dating from 1666. He found the work of 'tea-clearing' which he was set to do uncongenial, and after six months he was transferred to the Malayan branch in Singapore. Here the local manager took an instant dislike to him with the result that he was then consigned to the branch in Malacca where he had practically no work to do but was able to find a complete set of plays of Sir A. W. Pinero in the local library. This further stimulated his interest in the theatre, since he found them an excellent guide to the technique of stagecraft. In 1908 his mother died, and as his sister Mabel was already married and his younger brother Frank was still at school, he felt he should return home to keep his father company.

This he did, but at the same time he unwillingly went back to the family business in the City, which he found as distasteful as before. However he endured it until 1911 when a literary friend introduced him to the *avant-garde* publisher John Lane of the Bodley Head. He spent the next three years in Lane's office and Lane took him with him on business visits to the United States and Canada.

In 1914 Travers joined the Royal Naval Air Service, in which he served throughout the war, much of the time as a flying instructor, in the rank of flight lieutenant and later as a major when the RNAS was amalgamated with the Royal Flying Corps. For his wartime exploits, which ended with a brief spell of duty in Russia during the allied intervention, he was awarded the Air Force Cross (1920).

During the war he had got married, and his wife had an income of £1,000 a year, a useful sum in those days, which was a help when he returned to civilian life and decided to become a writer, settling with her in Somerset. He began as a novelist, returning as an author to the Bodley Head, where Lane published his first novel *The Dippers* (1922). He then turned the novel into a farce and sent it to the actor-manager Sir Charles Hawtrey who produced it, after a try-out in the provinces, at the Criterion Theatre in August 1922 with Cyril Maude in the lead. It had a fair success, running for 173 performances. *The Dippers* was followed by another novel, *A Cuckoo in the Nest* (1925), which he also dramatized after the reviewers praised its humour. Then Travers had a stroke of luck. Tom Walls, ex-policeman, actor-manager, and future Derby winner, needed a new play to succeed his current success *It Pays to Advertise* at the Aldwych. In the result he produced *A Cuckoo in the Nest* there in July 1925, with Yvonne Arnaud, Mary Brough, Ralph Lynn, J. Robertson Hare, and himself in the principal parts. It was an immediate success and notched up 376 performances.

During the next seven years Travers wrote eight more farces for the Aldwych: *Rookery Nook* (1926), *Thark* (1927), *Plunder* (1928), *A Cup of Kindness* (1929), *A Night Like This* (1930), *Turkey Time* (1931), *Dirty Work* (1932), and *A Bit of a Test* (1933). Between 1926 and 1932 the Aldwych box office grossed £1,500,000 in receipts, while the aggregate number of performances of the nine farces totalled nearly 2,700.

Travers continued to write plays, but with one exception he never repeated the success of the Aldwych farces. His later most successful pre-World War II play was *Banana Ridge* (1938). The scene was laid in Malaya, and the author himself played the part of a Chinese servant, whose colloquial Malay, which Travers remembered from his Malacca days, was most convincing. However, he was disappointed by the failure of his only serious play, *Chastity My Brother* (1936), based on the life of St. Paul, which suffered when the author's anonymous identity became known. During

World War II he was commissioned in RAF intelligence, becoming a squadron leader and being attached to the Ministry of Information as air adviser on censorship. He wrote several more plays, and also some film scripts and short stories. Then, in 1951, his wife died of cancer. Grief-stricken, he lost most of his old zest for writing, and spent more and more time in travelling and staying with friends in Malaya.

Then the removal of the lord chamberlain's censorship of the theatre in 1968 encouraged Travers to write a comedy extolling the joys of sex, which was in some ways his greatest theatrical triumph. This was *The Bed Before Yesterday* which was produced at the Lyric in 1975 with Joan Plowright in the lead. Its public acclaim owed much to the fact that the author treated the subject with urbanity and sophistication, never, as he put it, 'dragging in dirt for dirt's sake'.

He also wrote two autobiographies, *Vale of Laughter* (1957) and *A-sitting on a Gate* (1978), and a volume of cricket reminiscences *94 Declared* (1981) published posthumously.

Travers was a most amusing companion, full of fun, and greatly loved in the theatre and in the Garrick Club, with his eager eye for a pretty woman and a similar ear for a good story. His hobby was watching cricket and he used to visit Australia regularly to do so. He was vice-president of the Somerset County Cricket Club and belonged to the MCC. He was also an entertaining after-dinner speaker and in 1946 served as prime warden of the Fishmongers' Company, an office which gave full scope to his characteristic wit. In 1976, when he was in his ninetieth year, he was appointed CBE, a somewhat belated honour for the country's greatest living master of theatrical farce. In the same year he received the *Evening Standard* special award for services to the theatre.

In 1916 he married (Dorothy Ethel) Violet, daughter of Daniel Burton William Mouncey, a captain in the Leicester Regiment. They had two sons and a daughter. Ben Travers died in London 18 December 1980. Shortly before his death he told an interviewer that he would like his last words, engraved on his tombstone, to be 'This is where the real fun starts'.

His portrait, painted for the Garrick Club by his friend and fellow member Edward Halliday, hangs in the club.

[Ben Travers, *Vale of Laughter*, 1957, and *A-sitting on a Gate*, 1978 (autobiographies); *The Times*, 9 December 1980; J. W. Lambert, 'Ben Travers', *Listener*, 31 December 1981; personal knowledge.]

H. Montgomery Hyde

*published 1986*

## TREE Sir Herbert Beerbohm

(1852–1917)

Actor-manager, the second son of Julius Ewald Beerbohm (a London grain merchant of mixed German, Dutch, and Lithuanian extraction who had become naturalized as a British subject) by his wife, Constantia Draper, was born in London 17 December 1852. He was educated in England and at Schnepfenthal College, Thuringia, and was engaged for some time in his father's business. He was, however, already a member of several amateur dramatic clubs, and known privately as a clever mimic of popular actors. As an amateur he made several public appearances under the stage name of Beerbohm Tree in 1876, 1877, and 1878, notably at the Globe Theatre (February 1878) in the part of Grimaldi in *The Life of an Actress*. His success on this occasion resulted in the offer of a professional engagement for a short tour, at the conclusion of which he was engaged by Henry Neville to play at the Olympic Theatre. From July to December 1878 he appeared at that theatre in several plays, and in the following year was definitely committed to a professional career, appearing in a succession of parts at several London theatres. From the first he was noticeable for his ingenuity in the playing of parts inclining towards eccentricity and giving scope for elaborate invention. He was also recognized as a cosmopolitan, and his first great success was in the part of the old Marquis de Pontsablé in *Madame Favart*, in which he toured towards the end of 1879. This brought him into prominence, and on his return to London in April 1880 he appeared at the Prince of Wales's Theatre with Geneviève Ward, as Prince Maleotti in *Forget-me-not*. Between July 1880 and April 1887, when he first entered into management on his own account, Tree appeared in over fifty plays, rounding a reputation for extraordinary versatility. His repertoire included Sir Anthony Absolute, Sir Benjamin Backbite, and Joseph Surface, Malvolio, Prince Borowsky in *The Glass of Fashion* by Sydney Grundy, the Rev. Robert Spalding in *The Private Secretary*, Paolo Macari in *Called Back*, Mr. Poskett in (Sir) A. W. Pinero's *The Magistrate*, Baron Hartfeld in *Jim the Penman*, and Fagin in *Oliver Twist*. His most conspicuous successes during this period were in *The Glass of Fashion* (8 September 1883) and *The Private Secretary* (29 March 1884), the latter play owing a great deal to his invention.

On 20 April 1887 Tree became his own manager, and had the good fortune to begin with a popular success, appearing as Paul Demetrius in the Russian revolutionary play, *The Red Lamp*, by W. Outram Tristram. It was the kind of part in which he excelled, Paul Demetrius being a 'character' in the popular sense of the word. Tree might here indulge to the full an impishness which was the secret of his personal charm and of his success as a comedian. The play was so successful that in September of the same year he was able to take the Haymarket Theatre as lessee and manager, and there, with occasional absences, he remained until the opening of Her Majesty's Theatre in April 1897. During the ten years of his management he produced, and acted in, over thirty plays, appearing as Iago (7 March 1888), Falstaff (13 September 1888), Beau Austin in the play of that name by W. E. Henley and R. L. Stevenson (3 November 1890), the Duke of Guisbery in *The Dancing Girl* (15 January 1891), *Hamlet* (8 September 1891), the grandfather in Maeterlinck's *The Intruder* (27 January 1892), Lord Illingworth in Oscar Wilde's *A Woman of No Importance* (19 April 1893), Dr. Stockman in Ibsen's *An Enemy of the People* (14 June 1895), and Falstaff in *Henry IV, Part I* (8 May 1896). These productions are mentioned either as popular successes in the kind of part in which Tree personally excelled, or as bringing him definitely into relation with contemporary developments of the drama. His production of plays by Ibsen, Wilde, and Maeterlinck indicates an interest in the more important dramatic movements of the time not invariably shown by contemporary actor-managers, while the productions of Shakespeare were a preparation for the impressive exploits of his closing period. The number and variety of the plays from which these few examples are taken are a further proof of Tree's versatility and ardour in experiment. The seasons at the Haymarket were broken by journeys to America in January 1895 and November 1896, and by occasional visits to the provinces.

Her Majesty's Theatre, Tree's final theatrical home and the appropriate monument of his theatrical genius, was opened on 28 April 1897. Henceforth, with occasional diversions, all was to be done in the high Roman fashion. Shakespeare shared a noble stage with Tolstoi; and, if the author were not of the classic rank, Tree himself would appear, for the most part in illustrious disguise as the Duc de Richelieu, Mephistopheles, or Beethoven, in plays that endeavoured, if in vain, to do dramatic justice to their protagonists. The following is a selection from the list of parts in which he appeared at Her Majesty's: the Duc de Richelieu in *The Silver Key* (10 July 1897), Petruchio in *Katharine and Petruchio* (1 November 1897), Mark Antony in *Julius Caesar* (22 January 1898), D'Artagnan in *The Three Musketeers* (3 November 1898), King John (20 September 1899), Bottom (10 January 1900), Herod (31 October 1900), Malvolio (5 February 1901), Ulysses (1 February 1902), Falstaff in *The Merry Wives of Windsor* (10 June 1902), Prince Dmitri Nehludoff in *Resurrection* (17 February 1903), King Richard II (10 September 1903), Benedick in *Much Ado About Nothing* (24 January 1905), Fagin in *Oliver Twist* (10 July 1905), Colonel Newcome in a play of that name (29 May 1906), Nero (25 June 1906), Mark Antony in *Antony and Cleopatra* (27 December 1906), Shylock (4 April 1908), Mephistopheles (5 September 1908), Sir Peter Teazle (7 April 1909), Ludwig von Beethoven in *Beethoven* (26 November 1909), Cardinal Wolsey in *King Henry VIII* (1 September 1910), Macbeth (5 September 1911), and Count Frithiof in *The War God* (8 November 1911).

During the closing period of Tree's activities the natural comedian was obscured by his serious ambition to rank as a great tragedian and a producer in the grand manner. There were interludes of condescension towards fashionable romantic drama. There was one notable essay in modernism in the production of G. B. Shaw's *Pygmalion* in 1914. But the impression which he finally left on the public mind was the result of his later productions of Shakespeare and of his attempt to revive poetic drama (*Herod*, 1900; *Ulysses*, 1902; *Nero*, 1906) under the influence of Stephen Phillips. The exuberant vitality which in Tree's earlier work had found a natural outlet in a fanciful elaboration of characters like Paul Demetrius in *The Red Lamp*, or the Rev. Robert Spalding in *The Private Secretary*, demanded in later life an ampler and more dignified expression. He fell in love with magnificence, and it was a magnificence that ran to big designs packed with extravagant detail. His stage arrangements, as in the forum scene in *Julius Caesar* or in the costly pageant of *Henry VIII*, were, like his personal performances, too elaborate and too full of invention and ingenuity to serve the purpose of tragedy, for which they lacked the necessary simplicity.

It was natural for a producer with an increasing passion for emphatic splendour to fall under the spell of Stephen Phillips, who was greeted by many serious critics of the time as the founder of a modern poetic drama. It was even more natural that he should take to its extravagant limit a method of producing Shakespeare which insisted on a sumptuous illustration of the author's lines, as close and as detailed as the arts of the scene painter and stage carpenter could compass. Tree lived to see a reaction in the art of production, which swung violently back from the method of illustrative realism to the method of suggestive decoration, and he had to encounter a good deal of hostility from younger men. But, in estimating his achievement, it must be remembered that the movement which he led to such clamant extremes began as a protest against the tawdriness and indifference of an earlier generation of producers, and that he did succeed in keeping an open house for Shakespeare in London by striking the popular imagination with splendid spectacle mounted with convincing enthusiasm and ability. The climax was his celebrated performance of Mark Antony in the forum scene, where all the complicated gestures and ingenious pantomime of his craft were displayed at leisure. In 1905 Tree began a series of Shakespeare festivals, repeated annually and culminating in 1910–1911 with an entire season during which only plays by Shakespeare were performed. His last professional adventure was a visit to Los Angeles in 1915 in fulfilment of a contract with a film company. He was in America for the greater part of 1915 and 1916. He returned to England in 1917 and died quite suddenly in London on 2 July of that year.

Tree's devotion to his profession and natural generosity of disposition prompted him to take a leading part in all that concerned its dignity and well-being. In 1904 he founded the Academy of Dramatic Art, and on the death of Sir Henry Irving he was elected president of the Theatrical Managers' Association. He was a trustee and vice-president of the Actors' Benevolent Fund and president of the Actors' Association. He was knighted by King Edward in 1909, having in 1907 received the order of the Crown from the German Emperor, and the order of the Crown of Italy from the King of Italy.

Tree was the author of several books, in which an enthusiastic personality may be seen at issue with an unpractised pen: *Some Interesting Fallacies of the Modern Stage* (1893), *An Essay on the Imaginative Faculty* (1893), *Thoughts and After-Thoughts* (1913), *Nothing Matters* (1917). He also wrote a one-act play entitled *Six-and-Eightpence*, produced in 1884. In 1882 he married Maud, daughter of William Holt, by whom he had three daughters.

There is a pencil-drawing of Tree by the Duchess of Rutland, executed in 1891, and a charcoal-drawing by J. S. Sargent.

[*The Times*, 3 July 1917; Max Beerbohm, *Herbert Beerbohm Tree*, 1920.]

J. L. PALMER

*published 1927*

## TYNAN Kenneth Peacock

**(1927–1980)**

Theatre critic, was born 2 April 1927 in Birmingham, the only son (a daughter had previously died in infancy) of Sir Peter Peacock, merchant and former mayor of Warrington, and Letitia Rose Tynan, a union kept quite separate from Peacock's accepted household and family in Lancashire. Tynan never met his much older half-brothers and half-sisters. From King Edward's School, Birmingham, he won a demyship to Magdalen

College, Oxford, where he obtained a second class in English in 1948. At Oxford he embarked upon a systematic campaign to outshine or outrage all contemporaries as undergraduate journalist, actor, impresario, party-giver, and (despite a stammer) debater. If you were going to be a show-off in the midst of colonels, fighter pilots, and other heroes back from the war, he said later, you had to be a professional show-off. At the same time he was amassing enough serious and enthusiastic consideration of the theatre to provide him with his first book, *He that Plays the King* (1950), and a wider reputation.

After a spell as a repertory theatre director he seized the chance to become a professional theatre critic. Invited by (Sir) Alec Guinness to take the part of the Player King in Guinness's luckless production of *Hamlet* for the Festival of Britain, Tynan became the target of especially scornful remarks from the *Evening Standard*'s reviewer (Sir) A. Beverley Baxter. He replied with a letter to the editor so droll that according to legend he was immediately hired in Baxter's place. In fact some weeks elapsed, and he had in any case been writing about the theatre in the *Spectator*, but no doubt his flair for attracting attention played its part. With the *Evening Standard* (1952–3) and to a lesser extent with the *Daily Sketch* (1953–4) Tynan established himself as a funny and scathing writer on the theatre, if still one who wanted from it heroics and illusions. It was only after he was invited to join the *Observer* in 1954 that he started to apply to drama the political convictions which he was in the process of acquiring, with characteristic intemperance, about this time. 'I doubt that I could love anyone who did not wish to see it', he affirmed in a review of John Osborne's *Look Back in Anger* inspired as much by the play's tirades against respectability and authority as by its theatrical virtues. He went on to embrace socialism, nuclear disarmament, and the didactic drama of Bertolt Brecht.

His new-found beliefs did not prevent him from remaining a socializer as well as a socialist. He had married in 1951 Elaine, daughter of Samuel M. Brimberg, office equipment manufacturer, of New York. As Elaine Dundy she published two sparkling novels of the decade, *The Dud Avocado* (1958) in which a barely-disguised Kenneth Tynan appears, and *The Old Man and Me* (1964). Their Mayfair flat became a salon for celebrities passing through London, particularly from the United States. Tynan was fascinated by the outsize stars of Hollywood and Broadway. It was inevitable that he would be lured to America himself, as theatre critic of the *New Yorker*, though without severing his *Observer* connection. In the end he stayed only two years before returning to London in 1960.

Tynan was never averse to trying his hand in some production capacity as an adjunct to his criticism. He was story editor for Ealing Films in its last years (1955–7); produced two television programmes for ATV on the Stanislavskian method (1958) and dissent in America (1960), and edited the arts magazine *Tempo* for ABC Television (England) (1961–2). In 1963 came the invitation which was to tempt him away from his critic's seat altogether. Sir Laurence (later Lord) Olivier asked him to be literary manager of the National Theatre which was finally being set up in the temporary home of the Old Vic Theatre. Tynan threw himself into the task with energy and confidence. He disinterred forgotten classics, edited texts, and directly inspired such new works as Tom Stoppard's *Rosencrantz and Guildenstern are Dead* and Peter Shaffer's *Black Comedy*. These first seasons are generally regarded as having given the National's repertoire its stamp, but among the hits were one or two misfires, including a Brecht, which Tynan's critics could cite when in 1968 he clashed with the governors of the theatre over his determination to introduce *Soldiers*, by the German dramatist Rolf Hochhuth. The play alleged *inter alia* that Sir Winston Churchill had ordered the death of the wartime Polish leader General Sikorski. As a former colleague of Churchill's, the National's chairman Viscount Chandos was adamant that the production should not go ahead. Tynan responded by mounting the play himself in the commercial theatre and the following year resigned his post, though he remained a consultant until 1973.

There followed the exploit which prompts the most mixed feelings among Tynan's friends and admirers, the revue *Oh! Calcutta!* which he devised and produced first in New York, in 1969, and then in London. He had embraced the sexual 'liberation' of the era with the same enthusiasm he brought to its political concomitant, listing his recreations in *Who's Who* as sex and eating and in 1965 earning himself a footnote in the annals as the first Briton to say the word 'fuck' on television. *Oh! Calcutta!*'s mix of rather attractive nudity and distinctly seedy humour might have been designed to shock the bourgeoisie; ironically (if inevitably) it was a commercial success everywhere, and made Tynan well off.

He also ventured into film production with the 1971 version of *Macbeth* directed by Roman Polanski, but as the seventies wore on journalism reclaimed his energies, sadly beginning to dwindle as his health deteriorated. Mainly for American magazines he wrote a series of lengthy reflective profiles of actors and entertainers which, published in book form as *Show People* (1979), confirm Tynan's talent as a writer, his ability to conjure up time and place, people and performances, whether he is defining the extraordinary allure of Louise Brooks or conveying exactly what it was like to experience (Sir) Donald Wolfit and Frederick Valk (two of his heroes) in a barnstorming wartime production of *Othello*. He became FRSL in 1956.

He also published two collections of theatre reviews but disappointingly few original books. A long-planned memoir of his Oxford days materialized only in the form of his contribution to the television series *One Pair of Eyes* in 1968. Towards the end of his life he was planning an autobiography, but it was not to be realized. To lessen the ravages of the emphysema from which he suffered he was now living in Santa Monica, California. He died there 26 July 1980.

His first marriage had ended in divorce in 1964. There was one daughter. In 1967 Tynan married Kathleen, daughter of Matthew Halton, journalist and writer, herself a novelist and screenwriter; they had a son and daughter. Tynan was tall, slender, always elegant. In youth his habit of baring his teeth as he strove to overcome the stammer, coupled with flaring nostrils and a rather skull-like head, gave him the look of a startled rocking-horse. He matured into a relaxed and attractive human being, full of unexpected subsidiary enthusiasms (cricket, word games, bullfighting). His conversation, as Tom Stoppard put it, always had the jingle of loose change about it. When he died it was apparent that he had inspired quite exceptional affection in many who knew him. Whatever his enduring influence on the theatre may prove to be, he brought excitement, authority, and glamour to the business of writing about it.

[Godfrey Smith in *Sunday Times* (magazine section), 25 August 1963; Laurence Olivier, *Confessions of an Actor*, 1982; personal knowledge.]

PHILIP PURSER

*published 1986*

## VANBRUGH Dame Irene

(1872–1949)

Actress, whose original name was Irene Barnes, was born at Exeter 2 December 1872, the fourth and youngest daughter of the Rev. Reginald Henry Barnes, prebendary of Exeter Cathedral and vicar of Heavitree, by his wife, Frances Mary Emily, daughter of William Nation, barrister. The Nations were an old Exeter family, members of which had given great support to the theatre and had helped in the discovery of Edmund Kean. Irene was the fifth child in a family of six, Violet Vanbrugh being the eldest. The stage-name of Vanbrugh was first adopted by Violet at the suggestion of (Dame) Ellen Terry who remained throughout her life an invaluable friend. Violet's successful entry upon a stage career under

J. L. Toole in 1886 set Irene an example rare in those days among strictly brought-up daughters of professional men.

Irene was educated at Exeter High School and by prolonged trips to the continent with her father, and at a school near Earl's Court, recommended by Ellen Terry, when the family removed to London. Like Violet, Irene had a spell of training under Sarah Thorne at the Theatre Royal, Margate, where she made her first stage appearance in August 1888, as Phoebe in *As You Like It*. On Boxing Day of the same year she made her London début, on the recommendation of Lewis Carroll, as the White Queen and Jack of Hearts in a revival of *Alice in Wonderland* at the Globe Theatre in Newcastle Street, Strand. She then again followed Violet's lead by joining Toole's company. She played a big round of parts in already popular plays like *Dot* and *Uncle Dick's Darling*. With Toole she toured Australia in 1890. On her return, still with Toole, she made her first original creations as Thea Tesman in the first play by (Sir) James Barrie, his burlesque, *Ibsen's Ghost* (1891), and as Bell Golightly in his *Walker, London* (1892). She then joined (Sir) Herbert Tree at the Haymarket Theatre as Lettice in *The Tempter* (1893) by H. A. Jones. In the following year she passed to the St. James's Theatre and played a number of secondary parts under the management of (Sir) George Alexander, afterwards joining the company of her brother-in-law, Arthur Bourchier, at the Royalty Theatre and on an American visit. On her return, at the Court Theatre (1898) she created the part of Rose in *Trelawny of the 'Wells'* by (Sir) Arthur Pinero, and, during the same season, of Stella in Robert Marshall's *His Excellency the Governor*.

Then came Irene Vanbrugh's first great triumph, her Sophy Fullgarney in the production by (Sir) John Hare at the Globe Theatre of Pinero's *The Gay Lord Quex* (1899). As with many of her creations, Irene Vanbrugh's intelligence, sympathy, and alertness avoided extravagance in a subtle expression of class-contrast. This gave the character an intensity of appeal which was at the time something quite new. Her Letty in Pinero's play of that name at the Duke of York's Theatre (1903) was a less memorable success. It was at the St. James's Theatre as Nina Jesson in Pinero's *His House in Order* (1906)—a delicately temperamental study of the second wife of a pompous member of Parliament—that Irene Vanbrugh touched the heights once more. She also scored notably as Marise in *The Thief*, adapted from Henry Bernstein, at the St. James's Theatre (1907). Her Zoe Blundell, too, in Pinero's *Mid-Channel* at the same theatre (1909) was specially worthy of remembrance. She gave another poignant performance in the title-part of Mr. Somerset Maugham's play *Grace*, at the Duke of York's Theatre (1910). She created many other attractive characters of a quite different order, such as Lady Mary Lasenby in Barrie's *The Admirable Crichton* at the Duke of York's Theatre (1902), Kate, in his one-act play *The*

*Twelve-Pound Look* at the Hippodrome (1911), and Rosalind in his one-act play of that name also produced at the Duke of York's Theatre (1912). In this she was commanded to appear before the King at Queen Alexandra's birthday-party at Sandringham. Norah Marsh in Mr. Maugham's *The Land of Promise* at the Duke of York's Theatre (1914) was an achievement of high merit; but its deserved success suffered from the outbreak of war. She was more fortunate with her Olivia in A. A. Milne's *Mr. Pim Passes By* at the New Theatre (1920). Even so, she never excelled her early Pinero creations.

One of her latest and most appreciated successes was in Mr. Norman Ginsbury's *Viceroy Sarah* in which she succeeded (Dame) Edith Evans as the Duchess of Marlborough for the run at the Whitehall Theatre (1935). She appeared three times in plays by G. B. Shaw, the last being as Catherine of Braganza in *In Good King Charles's Golden Days* when it was produced at the Malvern Festival (1939) and afterwards presented in London at the New Theatre (1940) only to be stopped by the war. During the Battle of Britain she carried out a characteristic piece of war work by giving, with Violet Vanbrugh and (Sir) Donald Wolfit, extracts from *The Merry Wives of Windsor* at the Strand Theatre during lunch-time.

Irene Vanbrugh, who was appointed D.B.E. in 1941, celebrated her golden jubilee at a testimonial matinée in His Majesty's Theatre, 20 June 1938. At this she appeared in an act from *The Gay Lord Quex* and one from A. A. Milne's *Belinda* in which she had been seen at the New Theatre in 1918, and also in the title-part of Barrie's *Rosalind*. The performance was attended by Queen Elizabeth and realized over £2,000 which was divided between the Elizabeth Garrett Anderson Hospital and the Theatrical Ladies' Guild. Irene Vanbrugh was constant in her promotion of every theatrical good cause. She was a particularly keen supporter of the Royal Academy of Dramatic Art, both because her brother, Sir Kenneth Barnes, was its first principal and because she was deeply conscious of its value to the art and welfare of the theatre. Notable among her performances for charities was her appearance as Lady Gay Spanker in an 'all-star' revival at the St. James's Theatre of her father-in-law's famous comedy, *London Assurance* (1913), given in aid of King George's Pension Fund for Actors and Actresses. In 1919, to avert selling the (Royal) Academy of Dramatic Art theatre, then partly completed, she had the old film *Masks and Faces* remade with a star-cast, as well as Shaw, Pinero, Barrie, and Sir Squire Bancroft sitting round at a council meeting.

Although Irene Vanbrugh allowed nothing to deter her main interest from the living theatre, which she loved and in the future of which she believed with her whole heart, she found time from 1933 to appear in a number of films, including *Head of the Family, Catherine the Great, The Way of Youth, Escape Me Never, Wings of the Morning*, and *Knight Without Armour*.

Towards the close of her life she wrote a delightful autobiography entitled *To Tell My Story* (1948). It contains some characteristically well-informed character-sketches of the dramatists, actors, actresses, and others with whom it was her lot to work; letters from Pinero, Barrie, Shaw, and others; and vivid glimpses of life in America, Australia, and other parts of the world visited during her tours. In her writings, and otherwise, she gave the impression of having enjoyed a career of manifold opportunity and fulfilment.

Irene Vanbrugh married in 1901 Dion Boucicault the younger, who became her manager (1915) and with whom she acted until his death in 1929. There were no children. She died in London after a short illness 30 November 1949.

Among the portraits of Irene Vanbrugh may be numbered a painting of her as Rose Trelawny by Sir William Rothenstein, in the possession of Mr. George Spiegleberg; as herself by Solomon J. Solomon, the property of Sir Colin Anderson; as Lady Mary Lasenby in Act I of *The Admirable Crichton* by Charles Buchel, which was the property of Sir Kenneth Barnes, and in Act II, by the same, at the Royal Academy of Dramatic Art; as herself by (Sir) Oswald Birley, in the possession of the Melbourne Art Gallery; as Rosalind in Barrie's *Rosalind* by Sir John Lavery, the property of Mr. Michael Barnes; at her jubilee martinée by Ursula Bradley, at the Royal Academy of Dramatic Art; and as herself by Joseph Oppenheimer, the property of the artist.

[Dame Irene Vanbrugh, *To Tell My Story*, 1948; private information; personal knowledge.]

S. R. Littlewood

*published* 1959

## VANBRUGH Violet

(1867–1942)

Actress, whose original name was Violet Augusta Mary Barnes, was born at Exeter 11 June 1867, the eldest sister of Irene Vanbrugh. After schooling in Exeter, France, and Germany, Violet determined to go on the stage at a time when this was by no means usual with girls of her education and social standing, and when there were no dramatic schools outside the theatre itself. Remembering the advice of General Gordon a friend of the family, to allow his children to follow their bent, her father permitted her to make the attempt. With fifty pounds to spend and a nurse as companion she journeyed to London and after three months succeeded in interesting (Dame) Ellen Terry, on whose recommendation J. L. Toole gave her her first engagement: at Toole's Theatre in February 1886 she walked on in fantastic male costume as one of the crowd in the burlesque, *Faust and Loose*. From there she went to the Criterion Theatre and had her first speaking part in London as Ellen in *The Little Pilgrim*. She then joined Sarah Thorne's repertory company at the Theatre Royal, Margate, where she had an invaluable training, learning a new part every week. In the autumn of the same year she rejoined Toole, playing Lady Anne in *The Butler* both on tour and afterwards in London. Among other parts in which she appeared with Toole were May Fielding in *Dot* and Kitty Maitland in *The Don*. She then returned to Margate and gained valuable experience in a variety of parts. After returning to London in 1888, she joined W. H. and (Dame) Madge Kendal whom she accompanied on their first two American tours, having the supreme benefit of Madge Kendal's advice and example. Violet Vanbrugh played Baronne de Préfont in *The Ironmaster*, Lady Ingram in *A Scrap of Paper*, and other leading parts which fell to her quite unexpectedly when she was called upon to replace Olga Brandon, who at the last moment was unable to go.

After two years in America, Violet Vanbrugh returned to London, intending to take the rest of which she felt in need. Shortly after, an extraordinary and unexpected piece of good luck came, when (Sir) Henry Irving, with whom she had then a slight acquaintance, stopped a hansom-cab in which she was driving and offered her there and then the part of Ann Boleyn in his production of *King Henry VIII* at the Lyceum Theatre. In this she duly appeared (5 January 1892) at the same time understudying Ellen Terry as Cordelia in *King Lear* and as Rosamund in *Becket*.

In the following year Violet Vanbrugh was engaged by Augustin Daly, the American manager, to join his company at Daly's Theatre, headed by Ada Rehan, whom she understudied. Among the parts she played at Daly's in 1893–4 were Lady Sneerwell in *The School for Scandal*, Alithea in *The Country Girl*, and Olivia in *Twelfth Night*. In 1894 she married Arthur Bourchier, who had been a member of Daly's company. She joined him, taking the title-part in *The Chili Widow*, when he went into management at the Royalty Theatre, afterwards appearing as Stella in *The Queen's Proctor*—a version of *Divorçons*. With Bourchier she went to America, and on her return (1898) created the part of Lady Beauvedere in *The Ambassador* with (Sir) George Alexander at the St. James's Theatre. She took the leading part in a succession of plays, most of them by contemporary authors, and many of them produced by Bourchier during his lease of the Garrick Theatre. In 1906 at Stratford on Avon she played Lady Macbeth to her husband's Macbeth, the play being revived the same year at the Garrick Theatre. At Stratford also in 1910 she played Beatrice in *Much Ado About Nothing*. Both she and Arthur Bourchier were then engaged by Sir Herbert Tree at His Majesty's Theatre, where, in September of that year, she made a great success as Queen Katherine in *King Henry VIII*. In the following year she appeared in Tree's revival of *The Merry Wives of Windsor* as Mistress Ford to Ellen Terry's Mistress Page. At His Majesty's again in 1915 she played Queen Katherine in an 'all-star' revival of *King Henry VIII*, given in aid of King George's Pension Fund for Actors and Actresses.

From then onward she played many other parts, but Mistress Ford and Queen Katherine remained the characters for which she was chiefly remembered. She reappeared as Mistress Ford at the Hippodrome, Manchester, in 1934, with her sister Irene as Mistress Page, and again in a notable performance at the Ring Theatre, Blackfriars, in March 1937. In June following both sisters took the same parts in a revival at the open-air theatre in Regent's Park. In the same year her golden jubilee as an actress was celebrated with a luncheon in her honour. She appeared in one or two films towards the close of her life, including the film-version of *Pygmalion* by G. B. Shaw in 1938; but she allowed nothing to interfere with her devotion to the living theatre. She endowed every part she took with an appealing dignity and charm. As a pioneer, alike of her family and her generation, in taking up the stage as a calling for serious-minded well brought-up girls, and as one who never forfeited her pride in high ideals on or off the stage, Violet Vanbrugh deserved all the honours which came to her. She wrote a delightful book of reminiscences with, for title, the family motto, *Dare To Be Wise* (1925), in which is to be found much valuable advice to young actresses.

Violet Vanbrugh divorced her husband in 1917. Her daughter, Prudence, has done excellent work on the stage. Violet Vanbrugh died in London 11 November 1942.

There is a portrait of Violet Vanbrugh by Charles Buchel at the Stratford on Avon Memorial Theatre, showing her as Lady Macbeth, and one of her as Katherine of Aragon by the same painter at the Royal Academy of Dramatic Art. The Vanbrugh Theatre, the new private theatre of the Royal Academy of Dramatic Art, was opened in 1954 in commemoration of both sisters.

[Violet Vanbrugh, *Dare To Be Wise*, 1925; *The Times*, 12 November, 1942; *Who's Who in the Theatre*; private information; personal knowledge.]

S. R. Littlewood

*published* 1959

# WALL Max

(1908–1990)

Comic entertainer and actor, was born Maxwell George Lorimer 12 March 1908 at 37 Glenshaw Mansions, Brixton Road, Brixton, London, the second of the three children, all sons, of John Gillespie Lorimer, music-hall artiste, formerly of Forres, Scotland, and his wife Maud Clara, dancer and singer, the daughter of William and Maud Mitchison of Newcastle upon Tyne, both music-hall entertainers. He had sporadic schooling of a disjointed kind, being brought up in the music-hall theatre by his parents, who were known as Jack Lorimer and Stella Stahl. He was first taken on stage, in a kilt, at the age of two. Later he changed his name to Max Wall by deed poll.

After the break up of his parents' marriage and the death of his father, Max Wall began his long show-business career. At the age of fourteen he made his stage début in *Mother Goose* (1922), and, much encouraged by his stepfather, Harry Wallace—from whom he took his stage surname—he soon became a fully fledged professional entertainer, concentrating on eccentric dance routines and funny walks. He made his first London appearance in 1925 at the London Lyceum in *The London Revue*. Thereafter he appeared in several musical comedies and revues, including (Sir) C. B. Cochran's *One Dam Thing After Another* (1927), and he appeared in the 1930 and 1950 Royal Variety performances. He now established himself as a prominent music-hall artiste, variously billed as 'the boy with the obedient feet' or 'Max Wall and his independent legs'. He served in the Royal Air Force from 1941 to 1943, when he was invalided out on account of 'anxiety neurosis', and returned to the musical stage.

With his inventive patter, he also enjoyed radio success, notably in *Hoopla!* (1944), *Our Shed* (in which he popularized the character of Humphrey, 1946), and *Petticoat Lane* (1949). He next had a major success as Hines in the musical *The Pajama Game* (1955), and soon starred in his first television series, *The Max Wall Show* (1956). He had also perfected his role as Professor Wallofski, a weird spidery figure of a musical clown, clad in black tights, straggling wig, a short dishevelled jacket, and monstrously huge boots. His idols were the clown Grock and Groucho Marx.

By now the old variety theatre was in decline, and, with domestic problems also taking some toll, Max Wall had a lean period, during which he mainly played dates in northern clubland. In 1966 his mordant style found fresh opportunites on the legitimate stage, first as Père Ubu in Ian Cuthbertson's adaptation of *Ubu Roi* (1966), and then, *inter alia*, in Arnold

Wesker's *The Old Ones* (1972), as Archie Rice in John Osborne's *The Entertainer* (1974), and in Samuel Beckett's *Krapp's Last Tape* (1975) and *Waiting for Godot* (1980). He also appeared, in 1973, in *Cockie!*, a musical version of C. B. Cochran's life, and the *International Herald Tribune* said he was 'quite simply, the funniest comedian in the world'. He acted in several films, for instance as Flintwich in *Little Dorrit* (1987).

In 1974 he first produced what was to become a famous one-man show with songs, *Aspects of Max Wall*. In his later years he became something of a cult entertainer and in 1975 published his autobiography, *The Fool on the Hill*. He was a fluent mime, hilarious and eccentric dancer, competent musician, and acidic stand-up comedian. His stage persona had an air of melancholy, even of cynicism, and his countenance was clown-like, with glaring eyes, a prominent nose, and leering mouth.

Following an unstable upbringing, he married, in 1942, Marion Ethel ('Pola') Pollachek, dancer, the divorced wife of Thomas Patrick Charles and daughter of Alexander Pollachek, mechanical engineer, who ran a sponge rubber business in Islington. They had four sons and one daughter. The marriage was dissolved, with colourful attendant publicity, in 1956, and Wall became estranged from his family. In the same year he married a beauty queen, Jennifer Chimes, of north Staffordshire, daughter of John William Schumacher, master plumber. That marriage was dissolved in 1969, and he had a third, and extremely brief marriage, to Christine Clements, in 1970, which was dissolved in 1972.

Max Wall rarely sought the camaraderie of show business in his later years, and, despite considerable wealth, lived almost as a recluse in a bedsitting room in south London. He died in the Westminster Hospital, London, 22 May 1990, having fractured his skull in a fall outside a London restaurant.

[Max Wall, *The Fool on the Hill* (autobiography), 1975; *The Times*, *Guardian*, and *Independent*, 23 May 1990; Theatre Museum, London; private information.]

Eric Midwinter

*published 1996*

## WALLER Lewis

**(1860–1915)**

Actor-manager, whose real name was William Waller Lewis, was born at Bilbao, Spain, 3 November 1860. He was the eldest son of William James

Lewis, civil engineer, by his wife, Carlotta, second daughter of Thomas A. Vyse, of the Howard-Vyse family. He was educated at King's College School, London, and in Germany. Intended for a commercial career, he was employed for five years in his uncle's office in the City. As an amateur he acted for several years with dramatic societies, but subsequently he made up his mind to become a professional actor, and was fortunate enough to be engaged by John Lawrence Toole for Toole's Theatre, where he first appeared on 26 March 1883 in a revival of *Uncle Dick's Darling*. For the next twelve months he played in Toole's repertory, and then left in order to tour the provinces. He appeared at the Lyceum Theatre with Madame Modjeska on 30 March 1885 in *Adrienne Lecouvreur*, and then went on tour until the end of 1886. He made his first substantial success in London at the Strand Theatre on 7 February 1887 in *Jack in the Box* by G. R. Sims and Clement W. Scott. Subsequently he fulfilled engagements as leading juvenile with Kate Vaughan at the Opera Comique, with Mrs. Brown-Potter at the Gaiety Theatre, with (Sir) John Hare and William Hunter Kendal at the St. James's, with Rutland Barrington at the same theatre, and with Wilson Barrett at the Princess's.

On the opening of the Garrick Theatre by John Hare on 24 April 1889, Waller played as Hugh Murray in (Sir) A. W. Pinero's play *The Profligate*, and again in November of that year as Cavaradossi in an adaptation of *La Tosca*. After fulfilling engagements at various other theatres, he appeared in January 1893 in G. S. Ogilvie's *Hypatia* at the Haymarket Theatre under the management of (Sir) Herbert Beerbohm Tree, and later in the same year in a series of Ibsen's plays at the Opera Comique. In the autumn of 1893 Waller undertook theatrical management for the first time, in conjunction with H. H. Morell (Mackenzie), son of Sir Morell Mackenzie, the physician, when he went on tour in Oscar Wilde's *A Woman of No Importance*.

At the Haymarket Theatre on 3 January 1895 Waller began his career as a London theatrical manager, producing, in conjunction with H. H. Morell, Oscar Wilde's comedy *An Ideal Husband*. In the same year he joined forces for a short time with (Sir) Charles Wyndham at the Criterion Theatre. At the Haymarket in May 1896 he gave a brilliant interpretation of the part of Hotspur in *Henry IV, Part I*. In April 1897 he was engaged by Tree for the opening of Her Majesty's Theatre; and between that date and September 1900 he appeared there in many parts, the most notable of which were Laertes in *Hamlet*, Philip Faulconbridge in *King John*, and Brutus in *Julius Caesar*. On the conclusion of his engagement with Tree, Waller resumed management on his own account. In conjunction with William Mollison he entered into the management of the Lyceum Theatre, where he revived Henry Hamilton's adaptation of *The Three Musketeers* on

3 November 1900. During a vacation from Her Majesty's Theatre in 1898 Waller had made a notable appearance in this play in the part of D'Artagnan. In December 1900 he achieved what was possibly his finest impersonation, namely that of the King in *Henry V*.

At the Shakespeare Theatre, Liverpool, 6 October 1902, Waller appeared for the first time in the title-rôle of *Monsieur Beaucaire* by E. G. Sutherland and Booth Tarkington. On 25 October he produced the play at the Comedy Theatre; it was performed 430 times in succession, and he revived it on many subsequent occasions. On 3 November 1903 Waller opened in this play at the Imperial Theatre, which he continued to manage until May 1906. He then removed to the Lyric Theatre, where he remained, with varying success, until July 1910. He made several notable productions during his period of management, especially *Miss Elizabeth's Prisoner*, *Brigadier Gerard*, *Robin Hood*, *A White Man*, and *The Fires of Fate*. He also revived *Othello* and *Romeo and Juliet*, but these ventures were unsuccessful. In September 1911 Waller visited the United States for the first time, and in October achieved success in a production in New York of *The Garden of Allah*. In May 1913 he went to Australia, where he remained for twelve months, and on his return to England reappeared on the London stage. In June 1915 he appeared at Wyndham's Theatre as John Leighton in *Gamblers All* by May Martindale, and while appearing in this play at Nottingham in the following October caught a chill and died there of double pneumonia on 1 November. He was buried in Kensal Green cemetery.

Waller was an actor of great individuality. His pleasing voice and fine presence fascinated popular audiences. No actor of his time could compare with him in such parts as D'Artagnan, Hotspur, or Henry V. But his acting appealed less to the intellect than to the eye and ear. His energy was remarkable, and during his thirty-two years' career he played nearly two hundred parts on the London stage without missing a performance. He was a great favourite with King Edward VII.

Waller married in 1883 Florence (died 1912), eldest daughter of Horatio Brandon, solicitor. First as Florence West, and subsequently under her married name, she was for many years a popular actress. Waller was survived by a son and a daughter, both of whom appeared on the stage.

A painting of Waller as 'Beaucaire', by the Hon. John Collier, was exhibited at the Royal Academy in 1903.

[*The Times*, *Daily Telegraph*, *Standard*, 4 November 1915; Clement W. Scott, *The Drama of Yesterday and To-Day*, 1899; *Who's Who in the Theatre*; private information; personal knowledge.]

John Parker

*published* 1927

## WARNER Jack

(1895–1981)

Actor, was born Horace John Waters, 24 October 1895 in Bromley, London, the third child and second of four sons among the children of Edward William Waters, master fulling maker and undertaker's warehouseman, and his wife, Maud Mary Best. His two sisters Elsie and Doris Waters became the successful radio and variety comedians 'Gert and Daisy' in the 1930s and 1940s. He was educated at the Coopers' Company School, Mile End Road, and studied automobile engineering for one year at the Northampton Institute, now part of the City University, London. Warner was essentially a practical man, more at home with pistons and people than with books, and left to work in the garage of a firm of undertakers in Balham. In August 1913 he went to work as a mechanic in Paris where unusually for a boy of his background he acquired a working knowledge of French which stood him in good stead throughout his life socially and as an entertainer. An imitation of Maurice Chevalier, in some ways his Parisian opposite number, became a standard part of his repertoire.

During the war he served in France as a driver with the Royal Flying Corps (later the RAF), being awarded the meritorious service medal in 1918. He returned to England and the motor trade in 1919, graduating from hearses to occasional car racing at Brooklands. He was over thirty before he became a professional entertainer, having progressed from choirboy and wartime concert party performer through the Sutton Amateur Dramatic Club to cabaret work, and making his West End début in 1935 in the two-man act of Warner and Darnell. He changed his name to Warner at this point because he did not wish to appear to be resting on the reputation of his sisters. In December 1939 with BBC radio's *Garrison Theatre* he made the transition from cabaret singer to cockney comedian. He epitomized the patient, good hearted, cheeky 'Tommy' of World War I, reborn in 1939 and transferred from the music hall to the broadcasting studio, and later matured into the reliable London bobby as PC Dixon of Dock Green in television. During the war he was a regular performer in radio and stage variety shows. In 1942 he made his first film, *Dummy Talks*.

The Jack Warner father figure emerged in his fourth film, *Holiday Camp* (1947). He played Mr Huggett, with Kathleen Harrison as his wife; they were typical, if romanticized, cockney parents, coping with adversity, often in the shape of their own children. The Huggetts featured in three more films and in a radio show from 1953 to 1962, an everyday story of urban folk. Warner's acting talent and ambitions were limited but although he never aspired to play Hamlet he did hope occasionally to break away from his stereotyped roles. He succeeded in this with more serious films such as *The Captive Heart* (1946), *It Always Rains on Sunday* (1947), and *Against the Wind* (1947). In *The Final Test* (1953) he played a professional cricketer in his last great outing, exchanging his senior NCO role with that of a figure modelled on Sir J. B. (Jack) Hobbs. But after a comparatively small part in *The Blue Lamp* (1949), as a fatherly London policeman shot by a young criminal, Jack Warner was enrolled as the regular screen parental police officer, PC Dixon, in a television series created by E. H. ('Ted', later Lord) Willis that ran from July 1955 until 1976. He was a reassuring traditional officer of the law adapting his pre-war standards and wisdom to the different world of the 1960s. The series altered its style as English society changed. PC Dixon became a less cosy sergeant, but the advent of a harsher view of police life in *Z Cars* brought an end to *Dixon of Dock Green* in 1976.

The series brought Jack Warner fame and financial security, which he enjoyed with Muriel Winifred ('Mollie'), a company secretary whom he married in 1933. She was the daughter of Roberts Peters, of independent means. The Warners had no children. Warner carried on with some stage work until 1980 and died in the Royal Masonic Hospital, Ravenscourt Park, London, 24 May 1981.

Jack Warner was a tall, handsome man who possessed the solid virtues which he portrayed throughout his career. He had no formal training as an actor and performed rather than acted in a style that was ideal for radio, film, and television but was not suited to theatrical work. The character that he developed, a dependable soldier, family man, and policeman, growing from cockney irreverence to maturity, will be interesting for social historians as a picture of the working-class hero of the first half of the twentieth century, romanticized but not unreal. He was appointed OBE in 1965 and was made an honorary D.Litt. by City University in 1975. In 1972 he became a freeman of the City of London.

[Jack Warner, *Jack Of All Trades*, 1975 (autobiography).]

D. J. WENDEN

*published* 1990

## WILLIAMS (George) Emlyn

(1905–1987)

Actor and dramatist, was born 26 November 1905 at Pen-y-Ffordd, Mostyn, Clwyd (then Flintshire), the eldest of the three surviving sons (two older children, a boy and a girl, died in infancy) of Richard Williams, an ex-navy stoker become greengrocer, of Ffynnongroyw, Clwyd, and his wife Mary, a former maidservant, daughter of Job Williams, collier, of Treuddyn, Mold. He was educated at Holywell County School and St Julien, Switzerland, before winning an open scholarship to Christ Church, Oxford. At Holywell County School he had met Miss Sarah Cooke, the senior mistress, on whose character and personality he drew for much of Miss Moffett in *The Corn Is Green*. She encouraged him, fostered his gift for languages, paid for his stay in Switzerland, entered him for the Oxford scholarship, gave him much financial support, and remained a lifelong friend. At Oxford he did little work, spending his time acting with the Oxford University Dramatic Society and writing plays. In 1926 he suffered a nervous breakdown before his final examinations, mainly due to an emotional friendship with a fellow undergraduate (his autobiography is frank about his bisexuality). He sat his finals in 1927, when he was already a professional actor, and took a second class in modern languages. Williams was stage-struck, captivated by a glamorous popular theatre in which, through hard work and professional commitment, he became a dominant figure. Though he acquired great sophistication he remained, essentially, the daringly optimistic, emotional, and single-minded romantic who had worked his way up from humble beginnings.

When an undergraduate his one-act play, *Vigil* (1925) and a full-length drama, *Full Moon* (1927), were performed at the Playhouse theatre, Oxford. In London, after impressing with *Glamour* (1928) and *A Murder Has Been Arranged* (1930), he had his first commercial success with *The Late Christopher Bean* (1933), an adaptation of Sidney Howard's English version of Fauchois' *Prenez Garde à la Peinture*. *Night Must Fall* (1935) ran for over 400 performances; *The Corn Is Green* (1938) was very popular in both London and New York. His numerous plays include *The Druid's Rest* (1944), a Welsh comedy in which the young Richard Burton made his début, *The Wind of Heaven* (1945), and *Someone Waiting* (1953). He wrote features for radio and one play, *Pepper and Sand* (1947), and two plays for television, *A Blue Movie* (1968) being the better known. His film-scripts include *The Citadel* (1938), in collaboration, and *The Last Days of Dolwyn* (1949).

His professional acting career began in 1927, at the Savoy, with a small part in *And So To Bed* by J. B. Fagan. His first success was as Angelo in Edgar Wallace's *On the Spot* (1930). In a long West End career he often starred in his own plays: he was a hit as Dan in *Night Must Fall* and an even greater one as Morgan Evans in *The Corn Is Green*. In 1937 he appeared in Shakespeare at the Old Vic. He was Sir Robert Morton in (Sir) Terence Rattigan's *The Winslow Boy* (1946). At Stratford in 1956 he played Angelo, Shylock, and Iago. In 1955 he was Hjalmar Ekdal in *The Wild Duck*; he was Sir Thomas More in the New York production of *A Man for All Seasons* (1962). His films included *The Last Days of Dolwyn* (1949), *Ivanhoe* (1952), *The Deep Blue Sea* (1955), *The L-Shaped Room* (1962), and *David Copperfield* (1969).

In 1951 he began his acclaimed readings from Charles Dickens, performing all over the world until he was well over eighty. From 1955 he performed a second one-man show, as Dylan Thomas in *A Boy Growing Up*. A third, based on the writings of H. H. Munro ('Saki'), began at the Apollo in 1977.

In 1961 he published the best-selling *George: an Early Autobiography*; its sequel, *Emlyn*, followed in 1973. His interest in the psychology of murderers led to *Beyond Belief* (1967), on the 'Moors murderers', and to *Dr. Crippen's Diary* (1987).

Given the high intellectual promise of Williams's beginnings his career is disappointing. He was a fine popular actor with lucid diction and a 'mesmeric' stage presence. But, though he had a success in *The Wild Duck* and as a 'superbly dangerous' Iago, his classical roles generally received mixed reviews. He was a determinedly commercial dramatist, with little interest in the avant-garde or in exploring social or political issues. His subjects were the psychology of murder and the supernatural, the conflict between innocence and experience, and the relationship between Wales and the outside world. But, too often, his desire for immediate effect led to melodrama, sentimentality, or theatrical cleverness. His portrayal of Welsh people tended to stereotype; claims that, in his Welsh plays, he perfected a rich poetic language reminiscent of J. M. Synge are overstated. However, with such plays as *A Murder Has Been Arranged*, *Night Must Fall*, and *Someone Waiting* he contributed to the psychological thriller; his portrayal of ordinary people, particularly the rural Welsh, widened the narrow social range of West End 'drawing-room' plays. Above all, his fine command of the dramatist's craft made him a highly successful entertainer. His was the age of the well-made, middle-brow drama and the abrupt changes in British theatre during the 1950s, the advent of Samuel Beckett and John Osborne, effectively ended his writing for the stage. *Night Must Fall* and *The Corn Is Green* are occasionally revived and remain staple fare for amateurs, but he is now better remembered for his brilliantly accurate impersonation of Dickens the public reader.

His greatest literary achievement is *George*, a moving and detailed recreation of his childhood and adolescence in north Wales and an important study of a 'scholarship boy' in the 1920s. *George* is one of this century's finest autobiographies.

Williams's family was poor and Welsh-speaking. He remained proud of his roots and retained his Welsh. His upbringing made him careful with money; he died a wealthy man. He was an FRSL, received an honorary LL.D. at the University College of North Wales, Bangor, in 1949, and was appointed CBE in 1962. During his early career he lived with a fellow-actor, Bill Cronin-Wilson, who died in 1934. In 1935 he married Mary Marjorie ('Molly') (died 1970), formerly an actress, who was divorced from the barrister, Cecil Caradoc ('Jack') Carus-Wilson. They had two sons. Mary's father was Theodore Walter O'Shann, chartered accountant.

Emlyn Williams died 25 September 1987, of cancer, at his London home, 123 Doverhouse Street, SW3.

[Emlyn Williams, *George* (autobiography), 1961, and *Emlyn*, 1973; Richard Findlater (K. B. F. Bain), *Emlyn Williams*, 1956; Don Dale-Jones, *Emlyn Williams*, 1979; James Harding, *Emlyn Williams, a Life*, 1993; *The Times*, 26 September 1987; information from John Atterbury.]

JAMES A. DAVIES

*published 1996*

## WILLIAMS Kenneth Charles

**(1926–1988)**

Actor and comedian, was born 22 February 1926 at Bingfield Street, off the Caledonian Road, London, the younger child and only son of Charles George Williams, manager of a hairdressing salon in Marchmont Street, King's Cross, London, and his wife, Louisa Alexandra Morgan, who assisted in the hairdresser's. He had theatrical aspirations from an early age, although his father, a Methodist, had a hatred of loose morals and effeminacy and thought the theatre epitomized both. The young Kenneth Williams, on the other hand, found acting 'instinctive, involuntary and authentic', attributes which marked his theatrical career in later years. He received his formal education at Lyulph Stanley School, Mornington

Crescent, and from 1940 studied at the Bolt Court School of Lithography in Fleet Street, where he trained as a draughtsman.

Called up for national service in the army in 1944, he served as a sapper in the cartography section of the Royal Engineers and later as a poster designer and actor in CSE (Combined Services Entertainment), when stationed in Singapore. There, in company with such aspiring actors, playwrights, and directors as Stanley Baxter, Peter Nichols, and John Schlesinger, his theatrical aspirations hardened and developed, and he toured army bases in the Far East in the revue *At Your Service*.

He was demobilized in 1947 and by 1948 had become an established actor in various repertory companies, playing many different roles. By the early 1950s he had established his versatility. He made his début in films in a small part in the 1952 production of *Trent's Last Case*. In the same year he made his first television appearance in *The Wonderful Visit*, by H. G. Wells, in which he played the Angel. This was followed by more repertory. In 1954 he played the Dauphin in G. B. Shaw's *St Joan*, which led to his becoming the ubiquitous 'funny voice' man in the BBC radio success, *Hancock's Half Hour*.

In the theatre success followed success with Orson Welles's production of *Moby Dick* (1955), *Hotel Paradiso* (1956) with (Sir) Alec Guinness, *Share My Lettuce* (1957), *Pieces of Eight* (1959), and *One Over the Eight* (1957). Then, most importantly, with (Dame) Maggie Smith, to whom he was devoted, he acted in Peter Schaffer's *The Private Ear* and *The Public Eye* (double bill, 1962), followed by *Gentle Jack* (1963) with Dame Edith Evans, and *Loot* (1965) by Joe Orton, with whom Kenneth Williams developed a warm friendship. Later came *Captain Brassbound's Conversion* (1971), with Ingrid Bergman. His one flop was the 1956 production of Sandy Wilson's musical *The Buccaneer*, about a boys' magazine, in which Williams played the editor.

In 1958 he appeared in his first Carry On film, *Carry on Sergeant*, subsequently becoming a regular and playing in twenty-four Carry On films, all of them low farces. On radio he went from *Hancock's Half Hour* to *Beyond Our Ken* in 1958, and later to *Round the Horne* in 1965, where his brilliant characterizations contributed considerably to the show's success. In 1968 he became the star of the radio quiz *Just a Minute*, a game in which the panellists are asked to talk on a given topic 'without repetition, deviation, or hesitation'. Williams duly astonished chairman, cast, and listeners with his knowledge, erudition, humour, grasp of language, and simulated outrage when told he had deviated. One could hardly imagine him hesitating.

Williams, camp, slim, and dapper, was an amazingly versatile performer, able to switch from the vulgarities of the Carry On films and the louche characters of *Round the Horne* to more serious roles in plays by Jean Anouilh, Shakespeare, and Shaw. In addition he could be a sparkling raconteur, as he showed in the 1966–7 television series *International Cabaret*, where his long monologues happily punctuated the mundane procession of jugglers and acrobats. He was also a capable chat show guest, always ready with a new anecdote, and on more than one occasion successfully deputized for Terry Wogan as chat show host.

The public persona of a loud, brash, verbose vulgarian was very different from his private life, which was solitary, fastidious, and intellectual. He never married. His attitude to sex was ambivalent, for while he accepted his homosexual tendencies he found it difficult to consummate sexual relationships with either men or women. His writings included the books *Acid Drops* (theatrical anecdotes, 1980), *Back Drops* (personal anecdotes, 1983), and his autobiography *Just Williams* (1985). His diaries were published posthumously in 1993.

In the last entry in his diary, 14 April 1988, he complained of 'immense' exhaustion, pains in the back, and stomach trouble. He had never been physically robust, had a history of health problems, and it is likely he died as a result of accidentally taking an overdose of painkillers. Williams died in his sleep at his home in Marlborough House, Osnaburgh Street, London, 15 April 1988.

[Kenneth Williams, *Just Williams, an Autobiography*, 1985; Russell Davies (ed.), *The Kenneth Williams Diaries*, 1993, and *The Kenneth Williams Letters*, 1994; personal knowledge.]

Barry Took

*published 1996*

## WOLFIT Sir Donald

(1902–1968)

Actor-manager, was born 20 April 1902 in New Balderton, near Newark, the fourth of the five children of William Pearce Woolfitt, brewer's clerk, and his wife, Emma Tomlinson. He was educated at Magnus School, Newark. From an early age he wanted passionately to be an actor; after a very short, frustrating burst of schoolmastering, which he disliked almost as much as being at school, in 1920 he managed to join Charles Doran's touring company. From his eighteenth year he had a complete grounding in the plays of Shakespeare and the touring theatre of the time, from the humblest role as assistant stage manager. It proved invaluable. He played walking-on parts and some of the smallest parts in the great plays. He left Doran to play the small part of Armand St. Just in the autumn tour of *The Scarlet Pimpernel* with Fred Terry. He had cherished an ambition to appear with this management since he first attended a performance at Nottingham in his early teens, and after several unsuccessful interviews with Terry he achieved it in 1923. The Terrys represented the theatre of which he had dreamed; the splendour of the sets and costumes, the assurance and the style of the actors would be remembered and reproduced when Wolfit himself was to appear as Sir Percy.

Matheson Lang gave Wolfit his first chance to appear in London in *The Wandering Jew* in 1924; nearly thirty years later he recreated the leading part under his own management. After several more years out of London, he was engaged to play good parts at the Old Vic in 1929–30: Touchstone, Cassius, and the King in *Hamlet*. But the season was an unhappy one for him: he never succeeded in disguising his disapproval of actors he did not like personally and in this company he always felt he was on the outside. He was not asked to stay on for another season. In 1930–5 he appeared in plays in the West End and on tour, including for Sir Barry Jackson a tour of Canada in 1931–2, nearly always in good parts in a great variety of plays, among them *She Stoops to Conquer, The Barretts of Wimpole Street*, and new plays. His longest run, over fourteen months, was in the highly successful *Richard of Bordeaux* in which he played Thomas Mowbray to (Sir) John Gielgud's Richard; during this he was able to plan his first managerial venture, the Newark drama week, in his home town in 1934.

Wolfit's two seasons at Stratford in 1936 and 1937 brought him much critical acclaim. It was the first time he had been really stretched as an actor, playing good leading parts, and it made him even more determined to save enough money to go into management to tour the plays of Shakespeare. This he managed to do in 1937, and a nine-week tour followed the end of the Stratford season, with many of the actors who had been with him in the company. He added Shylock and Macbeth to Hamlet and Malvolio which he had already played, and at the end of the tour he was less than £100 out of pocket, which encouraged him enough to plan another for 1938. In January of that year he first appeared as Volpone—one of the parts which suited him best and which he relished playing. For the autumn tour he engaged Rosalinde Fuller as his leading lady, and added *Othello, Much Ado about Nothing*, and *Romeo and Juliet*, playing all the plays 'in repertoire' so as to mix in the comedy with the dramatic fare. It was during these early seasons that the younger members of his company grew to recognize the effect the parts he was playing had on his backstage personality; full of laughter for Benedick and Touchstone, jokes were in order during the on-stage dances; but they must be a great deal more careful when *Othello* was played, and *Macbeth* night would see them scuttling out of the way of the wrath to come.

During the summer of 1939 Wolfit took a small permanent company to Dublin, and then asked various 'star' names, who were also friends, to go over for special weeks. After the great success of these plays, several in costume but no Shakespeare, he was again planning his autumn tour when war was declared, and although his leading lady, Rosalinde Fuller, was in America, and only after three separate attempts finally reached England, the tour opened in Brighton. On all sides he was told that Shakespeare in wartime, in the blackout, would spell disaster; he approached every theatre in London, until finally his first West End season opened at the Kingsway in 1940. Although fairly short and not a financial success, it did lead to his season of 'Scenes from Shakespeare' being done at the Strand during the lunch hour. It was during this run that all his scenery and costumes, which were in store, were bombed and completely destroyed. He had also joined the Home Guard at Frensham in early 1940 and managed to combine both activities. By 1941, against all the odds, he had formed a company and was on tour again, and for the first time many people who had never dreamt of going to the theatre, especially Shakespeare, were going and finding it exciting. In this year he added a very good Richard III, and returned to the Strand for the winter and spring. Now came his first attempt at King Lear, not yet exactly as he wanted it, but ever since his first season at Stratford (when he played Kent) he was determined to make it his own, and later in his career he called it 'the brightest jewel in my crown'. His season at the Scala theatre in 1944 brought high praise from the critics, not his habitual supporters, and especially from James Agate for his Lear, but it was forced to close prematurely as the 'doodlebug' attacks on London emptied the theatres. Undaunted, he returned to touring, which included a tour to Cairo and Alexandria, for ENSA, where they celebrated VE day.

Immediately after the war Wolfit embarked on his usual tour of the British Isles, and a season at the Winter Garden in London. His life as actor-manager covered more than twenty-five years. Now his leading lady was always Rosalind Iden. He was disappointed that there was no immediate reward for his war service 'Shakespeare for the masses'. He took a highly successful company to Canada in 1947, and followed it with a visit to New York. His postwar career was largely spent touring until, in 1951, he was invited by (Sir) Tyrone Guthrie to appear at the Old Vic in four spectacular leading parts. He opened the autumn season with Marlowe's *Tamburlaine the Great*, directed by Guthrie. It was a tremendous success, and the critics heaped his performance with praise. Sadly from all points of view this state of affairs did not last. During the four weeks he became impossible to act with, resorting to every tiresome trick on-stage, and even sending notes on their performances to his colleagues. After the Old Vic they paid a visit to Stratford, and here it was found necessary to send for Guthrie, unknown to Wolfit, for him to see what had happened to his production. He was appalled to see the travesty of what had been a magnificent *tour de force*, and spoke forcefully to his leading man. Soon after, Wolfit claimed breach of contract by the governors, and never returned to the Old Vic.

In 1953, coronation year, he presented an excellent series of classical plays at the King's, Hammersmith, with an unusually strong supporting cast; exceptionally well reviewed were his performances as Oedipus. He finished the year with a splendid Captain Hook in *Peter Pan*. For the next year he did little until he found a play, *The Strong are Lonely*, which suited him, and in 1955 was to be his last major production as actor-manager, in London. The last ten years of his life he really enjoyed away from the theatre and allowed himself, at last, to rest a little, without the urge to drive himself and all those round him, ever more on tour. His last appearance on the stage was as Mr Barrett in *Robert and Elizabeth*, with song, when he took over from (Sir) John Clements in 1966–7.

Wolfit never really enjoyed filming, although he gave some excellent performances towards the end of his career, notably in *Room at the Top*, *Becket*, and just before he died as Dr Fagan in *Decline and Fall*.

He was thrice married: first in 1928 to Chris Frances Castor; they had a daughter, Margaret Wolfit, the actress; secondly, in 1934 to Susan Katherine Anthony; they had a son and a daughter; finally in 1948 and for the rest of his life, to his leading lady of long standing, Rosalind Iden, daughter of Ben Iden Payne.

Wolfit was appointed CBE in 1950 and knighted in 1957, the only actor then living to have been twice honoured. He died in London 17 February 1968.

A portrait by Stanhope Forbes is privately owned; another, by Michael Noakes, hangs in the offices of the Royal General Theatrical Fund.

[Donald Wolfit, *First Interval*, 1954; Ronald Harwood, *Sir Donald Wolfit*, 1971.]

Brian McIrvine

*published 1981*

## WOOD Matilda Alice Victoria

(1870–1922)

Music-hall comedian, professionally known as Marie Lloyd, was born at 36 Plumber Street, Hoxton, 12 February 1870, the eldest of the eleven children of John Wood, artificial flower-maker, by his wife, Matilda Mary Caroline Archer. In childhood she formed a troupe of little girls, the Fairy Bell Minstrels, who sang and acted in schoolrooms and mission halls. At the age of fourteen she appeared on the stage of the Grecian music-hall, which was attached to the Eagle public-house in the City Road; her salary was fifteen shillings a week and her stage name Bella Delmare, which she soon changed to Marie Lloyd. Before she was sixteen she was performing in the West end of London, and in 1886 she was earning £100 a week.

In 1891, 1892, and 1893 Marie Lloyd was engaged by Sir Augustus Henry Glossop Harris for his pantomimes at Drury Lane Theatre; she also appeared in a few other pantomimes in suburban and provincial theatres. But her real bent was for the music-halls, which during her career were developing into imposing theatres of variety. Her songs were all written and composed for her by others; but she moulded them as she pleased by means of look, gesture, and tone of voice, making most of them openly and joyfully improper; yet, attractive as she was with her golden hair and blue eyes, she kept her performance free from any personal display or invitation, and appealed to the women as much as to the men. Her power lay in her cheery vitality, her thorough knowledge of vulgar English—and especially Cockney—manners and humour, and her highly cultivated skill in swift and significant expression, which won praise from judges so good as Ellen Terry and Sarah Bernhardt. Tours in Australia, South Africa, and the United States of America showed that her very English humour could be enjoyed outside England.

Marie Lloyd's work fell into three periods. In the first she was girlish, almost childish, as when she made her first great hit with the song 'The boy I love sits up in the gallery'. Next came a long series of songs which she sang as a grown woman dressed in, and beyond, the height of fashion, such as 'Oh, Mr. Porter', 'Everything in the garden's lovely', and 'When you wink the other eye'. Last came certain studies of shabby and broken-down women, in which she mingled sadness and humour, and showed considerable skill in the impersonation of character.

Over the music-hall public Marie Lloyd held undisputed dominion. Some of the affection for her was due to her notorious generosity. She lavished both money and care on the poor and the unhappy; and in 1907 in a music-hall strike on behalf of the minor performers, she came out on strike with the rest and took her turn as picket. Overwork and domestic trouble hastened her end. She was taken ill on the stage of the Alhambra (the audience loudly applauding what they took for a very realistic piece of acting) and died at her home at Golders Green 7 October 1922, aged fifty-two.

Marie Lloyd married three times: first, in 1887 Percy Charles Courtenay, general dealer, by whom she had her only child, a daughter; secondly, in 1906 Alexander (Alec) Hurley, comedian; and thirdly, in 1914 Bernard Dillon, jockey.

[*The Times*, 3 and 6 October 1913, 23 February 1914, 16 July 1920, and 9 October 1922; Naomi Jacob, *Our Marie*, 1936.]

H. H. Child

*published 1937*